The Battle of
NORMANDY
1944

ROBIN NEILLANDS

D1369033

CASSELL

Cassell Military Paperbacks

Cassell
Wellington House, 125 Strand
London WC2R 0BB

First published 2002; reprinted 2003
This Cassell Military Paperbacks edition 2003

British Library Cataloguing-in-Publication Data
A catalogue record for this book is available from the British Library

ISBN 0-304-36563-7

Cartography and drawings by Terry Brown

Printed and bound in Great Britain by
Cox & Wyman Ltd., Reading, Berks.

This one is for Colin Ward, a friend of mine and once of
Z Troop, 45 Commando, Royal Marines

Halcyon Days

*'Battles are usually fought, not as they ought to be fought, but as
they can be fought; and while the literary man is laying down the law at his
desk as to how many troops should be moved here, and what rivers
should be crossed there and where the cavalry should be brought up and when
the flank should have been turned, the wretched man who has
to do the work finds the matter settled for him by pestilence, a want of shoes,
empty stomachs, heavy rains, hot suns and a thousand other stern
warriors who never show on paper.'*

CHARLES KINGSLEY, 1855

CONTENTS

LIST OF MAPS AND ILLUSTRATIONS

PHOTOGRAPHS

Troops aboard a Landing Craft Assault

The Mulberry Harbour at Arromanches

Unloading ammunition from DUKWs

General Dwight D. Eisenhower

General Montgomery and Lieutenant Generals Bradley and Dempsey

General Montgomery and his Second Army commanders

Troops advancing into a smokescreen

Rifle action in the bocage

A piped march to battle

An ammunition lorry blows up in the field

German casualties of battle

Sherman tanks at the ready

A wounded German sniper

A German machine-gunner killed at his post

British 3-inch mortars in action

The Royal Artillery in battle

General Omar Bradley and Major General Gale

A destroyed Mark IV Panzer tank

An RAF airfield in Normandy

Sherman tanks on the move

ACKNOWLEDGEMENTS

A great many Allied veterans have helped me with this book, sending in their tapes or letters, agreeing to be interviewed, offering support. Many of these are veterans I met while writing the previous D-Day book with Major Roderick de Normann, while others were contacted via the Normandy Veterans Association in Britain or through local papers in Britain, the United States and Canada.

I would also like to record my thanks to the archives at the Imperial War Museum and National Army Museum in London, the Public Records Office at Kew and numerous museums in Normandy, including the US Airborne Museum at Ste-Mère-Église, the Battle of Normandy Museum at Bayeux, the Musée de la Débarquement at Arromanches, the Sixth Airborne Museum at Pegasus Bridge, the Fort Garry Museum, Winnipeg and George Milne of the Museum of the Regiments, Calgary, Alberta. Thanks are also due to the Canadian and American Legion and the Royal British Legion for helping my search for veterans while the London Library were indefatigable in hunting down out-of-print books.

One of the great pleasures of writing military history is the people you meet. So far at least – and I have been doing this for some twenty years – they have been unfailingly kind and helpful, always willing to share information and less than scathing in the correction of my mistakes; no one could wish for better or more professional colleagues. For reading the text in draft, pointing out my errors and suggesting improvements which I have not hesitated to adopt, my thanks go to Major General Julian Thompson, CB OBE, to Major General Ken Perkins, CB MBE DFC, to Sydney Jary, MC, for his support and permission to quote from his excellent memoir *Platoon Commander*, my American friend Dr Steve Weiss of the Department of War Studies at King's College, London, Nigel Hannaford of the *Calgary Herald* and Jeanne Simpson of *Legion Magazine*, Ottawa, to Group Captain Peter Bird and Dr Tom Buchanan of Oxford University.

My thanks also go to John Coleby and to two good and long-standing American friends, Jack Capell, late of the 4th US Infantry Division and Bob Sales of the 29th US Infantry Division. Thanks also to Terry Brown of 42 Commando, Royal Marines, for the maps, to my colleague at the University of Reading, Gerry Paxton, for his encouragement and advice, to Professor Michael Biddiss, also of the University of Reading for his helpful suggestions on the text, and an old friend from 45 Commando, Colin Ward, for his help in interviewing veterans and his support in good times and bad in recent years. My thanks also to Dr Helmut Schnatz and Dr Remedio Graf von Thun for their generous help with my various problems on the German side in Normandy.

My thanks also go – in particular – to all the Allied veterans of the Normandy campaign who sent in their accounts and allowed me to question them closely about details of the various battles. I have attempted to put in as many relevant accounts as possible but it has not been possible to include them all – although all were useful not least as a check on the rest. My thanks for help, therefore, go to:

H. G. Alcock, 1/7th Middx, 51st Highland Division; James Anderson, RASC; Charles Bedford, 1st Bn the Manchester Regiment; Frank Andrews, 6th Airborne Division; Jack Andrews; Jim Barrance, 1st Bn Manchester Regiment; Bill Berry, 110th LAA Regiment, 43rd Division; Jim Bond, ML 194, Royal Navy; David Bonnell, 27th Armoured Regiment, First Canadian Army; Eric Brown MC, 73 Anti-Tank Regiment, Royal Artillery; John Butler, 6th Airborne Division; Mrs Ishbel Burgoyne; Margaret Cantwell, for her help in Canada; Jack Capell, 4th US Infantry Division; Harper Coleman, 4th US Infantry Division.

To Ralph Conte, 416th Bomb Group, Ninth USAAF; Ronald Cook, The North Shore Regiment, Canada; Donald Cheney, 617 Squadron RAF, for his help in finding Canadian veterans; L. A. Cornwall, 10th Bn Durham Light Infantry; John Travers Cosgrove, Royal Engineers, 53rd Division; D. Cowlan, Royal Navy; Ernie Cox of the 141st Regiment, RAC; A. R. (Bert) Coulter, Intelligence Corps; Dr Charles Crawford, No. 24 Field Transfusion Unit; Dixie Dean, 13th Bn, the Parachute Regiment; Les Dinning, 7th Armoured Division; Mrs I. G. Dunkley, on behalf of her husband Richard, 12th Bn the Devonshire Regiment; R. W. Dunning, 4th Canadian Field Artillery; John Frost of New Barnet; Major R. J. D. Gardner, Normandy Veterans Association; G.

Greenough, 144 Wing, RCAF; Kelvin Grant, Nova Scotia Highlanders, 9th Canadian Infantry Brigade.

To Frank Grigg, 4/5th Bn the Duke of Cornwall's Light Infantry; Fred Goatcher, HQ Squadron, 7th Armoured Division; Brian Guy, 246 Co. Royal Engineers; Neal Hamilton of the 4th Field Regiment, Royal Canadian Artillery; Eddie Hannach, Normandy Veterans Association; Richard Harris, 1st Bn the Suffolk Regiment; Jeffrey Haward MM, 7th Bn the Middlesex Regiment; A. L. Hayman, 7th Bn Somerset Light Infantry; Richard Heather, 2nd Bn the Hertfordshire Regiment and his President George Church MM; Douglas Heathfield Robinson, Patrick Hennessey, 13th/18th Hussars; R. D. Hilton, Essex Regiment; Jack Hodgson, RAMC, 2nd Bn the Lincolnshire Regiment. Bill Hodkinson, 4th RHA; Ian Isley, NVA, Chirk; James Holder Vale, Fox Troop, 92 LAA Regiment, Royal Artillery.

To Jesse Jackson, Ninth USAAF; Bill James, 53rd Welsh Division Association; Dr J. A. M. M. Janssen, Royal Netherlands Air Force; Clive E. Kemp, 71st Field Co., Royal Engineers; Tony King, Royal Inniskilling Dragoon Guards; Don Levers, Victoria, BC, on behalf of his father in the Royal Winnipeg Rifles; Eric Mattocks, Normandy Veterans Association, Somerset and his Veteran colleagues Bill Berry, Vic Jones, John Sharp and Harold Skipper; R. Kent, the Cameronians; Alan King, 4th CLY; Lawrence Jones, 'C' Company, the Calgary Highlanders; Doug Kay, the Normandy Veterans Association, West Sussex.

To Ron Lathan, Normandy Veterans Association, Canterbury; Ron Ludgater, the Rifle Brigade; Eric Lummis, 1st Bn the Suffolk Regiment; Joseph MacClatchey, Royal Ulster Rifles, 6th Airborne Division; Alan McQuillan of the Normandy Veterans Association, Cirencester; Bob McWherter, Ninth USAAF; Warrant Officer J. F C. May, No. 295 Squadron, 38 Group, RAF; Ms Carolyn Mayfield, on behalf of her father Dee Mitchell 386BG, USAAF; Norman Mitchell, 'C' Squadron, 53rd Recce Regiment for the memoir of his colleague Joe Abbot, 53rd Recce Regiment.

To Ted Morris, 225 Parachute Field Ambulance, 6th Airborne Division; Ron Moyse, NVA, Cornwall; Wilf Newman, 49th Recce Regiment; Colleen O'Brian, Halifax, Nova Scotia; Roy Page, Nova Scotia, Canada; Doug Peterson, 15th Scottish Recce Regiment; Reginald Plumb, 84 AA Regiment; Bill Powell, the Calgary Highlanders; Colonel Red Reeder, 12th Infantry Regiment, 4th US Infantry Division USA; Cyril Rees, 9 RTR; Norman Richardson, Royal Canadian

Artillery; Tom Ridley, 233 Field Co., Royal Engineers; Reg Rolfe, 41 (Royal Marine) Commando; Frank Rosier of the 2nd Bn the Gloucestershire Regiment; J. H. L Royle, DAAG, 1 Corps; J. F. Rutter, for his account of the Great Storm on Omaha beach.

To Greg Saffiere RAMC; Bob Sales, 116th Infantry Regiment, US 29th Infantry Division; Bryan Samain, 45 (Royal Marine) Commando; Zane Schlemmer, US 82nd Airborne Division; Harry J. Secretan, 2nd Bn KRRC; John Sharp 2nd Bn the Middlesex Regiment; Vic Seymour, Normandy Veterans Association, Folkestone; Harry Shaw, Normandy Veterans Association, Antwerp; Peter Shepherd, 25th Field Regiment, Royal Artillery; Mrs David Smith, on behalf of her husband David, of the Black Watch and No. 6 Commando; Harold Skipper, 10th Survey Regiment RA; Reg Spittle, 2nd Northamptonshire Yeomanry; Bill Starkey, Royal Marines, 650 Flotilla; Howard Fred Smith, 2nd Warwicks; Neil Stewart of Victoria BC, Canada, for permission to refer to his excellent book *Steel My Soldiers' Hearts.*

To Tom Stokes of the 181 Field Regiment, Royal Artillery; Bill Thompson 9 RTR; Mrs Elsie Thompson, 9 RTR – *Qui s'y Frotte Association*; Mr W. J. Turner for help in contacting veterans in Australia; Les Wager of the Queen's Own Rifles of Canada; Duke Warren of Comox, BC Canada and 66 Squadron RAF; L. A. Watson, 15th Scottish Recce Regiment; T. B. Whitehouse, DUKWs; Lt Col Philip Whitman, 94th US Infantry Division; Albert Williams, Normandy Veterans Association, Wiltshire; E. O. Wills of the 12th Bn Kings Royal Rifle Corps; Anthony Windrum, Royal Signals, 6th Airborne Division; Jack Woods, 9 RTR.

These men saw hard times. Their stories deserve to be remembered.

ABOUT THIS BOOK

*'If there is one thing worse than fighting a war with Allies
it is fighting a war without them.'*

WINSTON S. CHURCHILL

This is a book about the largest battle that ever took place in Western Europe, the three-month struggle from D plus 1 – June 7,1944 – to September 1, 1944 ... the Battle of Normandy. During that time more than 2,000,000 soldiers, American, British, Canadian, French, German and Polish, struggled for mastery in Normandy, the Allied effort backed by the strategic and tactical air forces, the bombardment warships of the Royal Navy and the US Fleet, and a supply and logistical system unmatched in military history. The prime aim of this book is to provide an account of that mighty struggle aimed squarely at the general public in the United States, Britain and Canada.

In the course of researching and writing it, however, another aim has arisen. This book also attempts to analyse the Normandy battle, to reduce its complexities to a digestible amount and, in particular, address some of the myths that have grown up about the conduct and outcome of this campaign since the end of the Second World War. In order to do so it draws heavily on the experiences of the Allied soldiers who fought in that campaign.

All wars attract myths; these can range from the fantastical – the 'Angels of Mons' in 1914, for example – to orchestrated attempts to destroy the reputations of the commanding generals of the Great War or portray Air Marshal Sir Arthur Harris and the aircrews of RAF Bomber Command as war criminals in the Second World War. I have tackled the last two sets of myths – for myths they surely are – in previous books and in the process discovered my own niche in the field of military history – as a myth-buster.

I have to point out that when it comes to examining a myth, from the professional point of view I do not care if it is true or not; either would suit my professional purposes equally well and it is essential to maintain some distance, if only in the interests of objectivity. On a personal level, it is pleasant to record that I have so far found the various allegations made against my country's former commanders totally lacking in truth – or easily destroyed by putting the situation in context. To do that takes a great deal of time and could probably not be done at all without the help of a great many people, notably – even preferably – those with some experience of war at the sharp end.

This book draws on official histories, on the published memoirs of the participants from Commanding General to Second Lieutenant, on divisional accounts and regimental histories. However, these official accounts are illustrated wherever possible by the private accounts of the Normandy veterans themselves, accounts which reveal just how difficult and bitter this battle could be; Sydney Jary and Les Wager's accounts of infantry fighting illustrate the problems created by the German superiority in automatic weapons far more clearly than any dry account from an official history.

In an on-going attempt to avoid bias, national sources have been used to describe national accounts; American accounts have been used for American exploits, British accounts for the Second Army battles, Canadian accounts for the actions of Canadian units and so on. The overall aim has been to produce a balanced, factual and readable account of the entire Normandy campaign.

That at least was the original aim and that part of the aim has not changed. This book is still, I hope, balanced, factual and readable and covers the entire campaign from D plus 1, June 7, to September 1 when General Eisenhower took command of the field armies in France and the 'invasion phase', fought under General Montgomery, was finally over.

I also hope that this account is fair to the commanders and – above all – fair to the troops on the ground in 1944 who had to do the fighting – and far too often the dying. Fairness is always necessary in military history but it seems particularly important in the case of the Battle of Normandy, for over the last sixty years or so the events of this campaign have become steadily submerged in myth. As a British historian, I hope it is myth for – put simply – the myth of Normandy is this:

'The strategy developed, and plan prepared for Operation Overlord by the Allied Ground Force Commander, the British General Sir Bernard Law Montgomery, was flawed in concept and failed to work in practice. Eventually, frustrated by the failure of Montgomery's strategy and the caution and timidity of the British and Canadian troops, American forces under Generals Eisenhower, Bradley and Patton seized the initiative, revised the plan, broke out in the west, drove back the German forces in disarray, to win the Normandy battle – and then the war.

'All this they would have done much sooner if the British and Canadians had not sat in their trenches drinking tea – American historians never fail to mention tea – while the US forces did all the fighting. The outcome of the Normandy battle – so goes the allegation – would have been far more conclusive if the aforesaid British and Canadians had not again been "timid" and "cautious" and "slow" at Falaise, thereby allowing the German Army to escape across the Seine.'

That is the myth, and a pervasive one. One purpose of this book is to discover how much truth there is in this myth ... or, indeed, whether there is any truth in it at all. It is not my intention to write a 'revisionist' history, still less to switch these painful accusations from the British and Canadians to the Americans; nothing is gained by such chauvinism.

Apart from having the greatest respect for the American front-line soldier of the Second World War, many of whom I know personally, I have attempted (see above) to insulate myself from any retaliatory temptations by using US accounts for US actions – and so with the actions of other nations. I have attempted to discover not simply what happened but why it happened; this search for a reason often reveals that some much-criticised action is simply common sense and my personal belief, reached before writing a word of this book, is that the forces engaged in Normandy – American, British, Canadian, Polish – yes, and German, all did their very best in very difficult circumstances. Even so, the myth continues to flourish.

The 'myth' of Normandy is therefore the 'back story' of this book; the story that began during the battle, the one that has increasingly taken over from any stark, factual account in the decades since and done considerable damage to the reputations of competent commanders and brave men. Reading the histories and memoirs of the battle in Normandy – and I have done little else for the past three years – one comes away with the impression that the fighting among the Allied generals, in the field and at SHAEF, during and after the battle, was waged with greater ferocity than the battle itself.

In the process much of the necessary balance that should inform a historical account has gone out the window and needs to be retrieved. Examining this 'back story', or myth, underpins much of this book, for in the course of researching and writing it became evident that no objective picture of the Normandy campaign as a whole, or many of the battles of that campaign, is now possible without first clearing away the accusations made about the way the battle was fought, tactically as well as strategically, and distributing praise and blame with an even hand.

The weight of these accusations, of incompetence, slowness and timidity, rests mainly on the British Second Army and in particular on the British soldiers, and I have therefore been at some pains to feature these British soldiers in this book so that readers – American as well as British – may judge for themselves what sort of men they were. Accusations as to the grit and competence of the British Army flourish in many US accounts and the belief laid out above – let us not call it a myth until we have examined the campaign in detail – is perpetuated at the present time and into the future by the US media, notably by a series of films which are gradually air-brushing the British out of Allied history – and even out of their own. That process too should be considered.

This process had been going on for decades and began even as the war ended with *Burma Victory,* a motion picture in which US paratroopers won the war against the Japanese in the Far East. More recently the movie *U-571* had the US Navy capturing a naval Enigma machine from a U-boat – a feat actually performed by the crew of HMS *Petard,* two British sailors dying in the attempt when the U-boat sank under them.

Every nation is fully entitled to sing the praises of its own heroes and claim the credit for its own victories. Although there was some adverse comment from British veterans and the British press that the Stephen Spielberg film *Saving Private Ryan,* covering events on and after the landing on Omaha, did not feature or refer to the British and Canadian landings elsewhere on the Normandy coast, this particular complaint seems unfair. No British historian can complain that *Saving Private Ryan* did not feature British soldiers since there were few Britons on Omaha beach on June 6, other than among the landing craft crews.

After all, no Americans appear in British films like *The Dam Busters* or *The Cruel Sea,* two movies that restrict their accounts, quite correctly, to the British, Canadian and Australian contribution. Although *The Dam Busters* does record the participation on the dams raid of Joe McCarthy, an American member of No. 617 Squadron – and rightly so – *The Dam Busters* and *The Cruel Sea* record the exploits of the British and their Commonwealth allies. One still wonders if these two British films have ever been widely shown in the United States?

It appears that while our two nations stand shoulder-to-shoulder in times of trouble, the Americans do tend to hog the limelight when the histories come to be written and the movies get to be made. It is also regrettable, for example, that in *Saving Private Ryan,* the *only* reference to the British and Canadian participation in the Normandy landings, thirty seconds shoe-horned into 162 minutes of screen time, is a conversation between two American officers, one commenting that nothing much was happening as, 'Monty had yet to take Caen' and the other replying, 'That man's over-rated'. One wonders what script consultant was responsible for that remark.

Talking to British veterans – a dwindling number – it is clear that this steady erosion of their war from the public conscience, even in Britain, is causing them anger and distress. More and more of the general public, in Britain as well as in the USA – the people to whom this book is addressed – are clearly unaware that the British and Canadians fought in Normandy *at all*; on the visits made to Normandy for this book it was noticeable that while crowds and coaches were plentiful in the car park at the US Cemetery at Colleville–St Laurent above Omaha – the cemetery featured in the movie on what must surely soon be called the Private Ryan Coast – the British cemetery in Bayeux and the Canadian and Polish cemeteries on the road to Falaise were deserted.

If this erosion of British history continues, where will it end? And if British history continues to be borrowed, altered and distorted, and the process seems unstoppable, what will be left from Britain's long and glorious history in arms that has not been filched, denigrated and exploited by somebody else?

Nor is this erosion only coming from the film makers. Visiting New Mexico recently I noticed that the local newspaper, *The New Mexican,* was announcing a lecture by a professor from the University of New Mexico, 'on how the United States cracked the Enigma code'. A letter to the paper produced an apology and an assurance that the professor was well aware that the Enigma code was cracked by the British – with due thanks to the Poles – at Bletchley Park in England, long before the United States entered the war at the end of 1941. It is not clear that *The New Mexican* ever carried a correction of their original statement for the benefit of the public.

More recently, a book on the Great War – engagingly entitled *The Myth of the Great War* – by the Professor of English Literature at Loyola University in

New Orleans claims that the Great War was won by the American Expeditionary Force, that the British Army was routed at Mons and that, to quote John Hughes-Wilson's wonderful review in the *RUSI Journal*, 'the two decisive battles of the First World War, at Belleau Wood and the Meuse–Argonne, saw the AEF force the German Army back single-handed while the ineffectual British and French commanders looked on with a mixture of jealousy and admiration'.

Belleau Wood and the Meuse–Argonne were hard-fought battles but, my American friends, let us not get carried away here; US participation in the First World War was brief. Besides, to return to the question, where will it all end? If this sort of thing continues it cannot be too long before some American academic reveals how the US contingent played a decisive part in beating the French at the battle of Agincourt in 1415 while the 'cautious' and 'timid' British archers looked on in watchful admiration.

Military historians are also somewhat eager to denigrate the British. In his well-regarded book *Decision in Normandy*, Carlo d'Este devotes an entire chapter, Chapter 16 – *The Price of Caution* – to a highly critical appraisal of the British Second Army in Normandy. Then, on page 297, Mr d'Este adds an explanatory footnote: 'This is not to suggest that the US forces had no problems of their own.' This brief comment is quite true, as we shall see, but twenty-eight pages criticising the British Army in great detail and at every level is not balanced by a one-line footnote. A balanced account has to do better than that. The Second Army certainly made mistakes in Normandy but – as this book will reveal – so did all the other armies. To state or even imply that only the British Second Army was in trouble in Normandy is offensive to the veterans and a travesty of the facts.

It would be perfectly easy to write a critical account of any of the armies in Normandy. A full examination of the evidence reveals that all the Allied armies – and the German armies – had problems during that campaign; to put the Second Army's performance in perspective you have to put it in context. That can only be done by considering the performance of the other armies – as well as the varied strength and quality of the opposition they were facing. That takes time but the result is revealing.

It is also noticeable how some historians will seek to denigrate the British even to the point of being remarkably petty-minded. Take, for an example of this particular trend, two accusations in Norman Gelb's *Ike and Monty:*

Generals at War. On page 285 alone, after mentioning that Monty 'seemed driven to giving gratuitous offence', Mr Gelb cites two attempts by Monty to denigrate Eisenhower, one 'discourteous' and the other 'impertinent' – at least according to Mr Gelb.

Gelb first relates how, when Ike arrived in London in January 1944, Monty was discourteous in not being on hand to greet him, having left to review troops in Scotland. The second 'offence' came a week later when, according to Mr Gelb, Montgomery deliberately took over Ike's car parking space at Norfolk House. As readers will appreciate, this is serious stuff in the context of the Second World War but let us just think about those two accusations for a moment.

Ike arrived in London on the late evening of January 15 – not, as Mr Gelb claims, on January 13 – Ike says in his memoirs[1], that he 'reached England on the evening of the second day'. Ike had left the USA on January 13 and arrived in London via Washington, Gander, Iceland and – London being fogbound – Prestwick in Scotland. At Prestwick he took a train for London and by the time he arrived in the British capital Ike had been travelling for two days.

We are not talking Concorde here. Ike had been travelling for the best part of two days in a cold, noisy, draughty, World War Two transport aircraft and then on a slow, cold, wartime British train. By the time Ike reached London that night what Ike needed was a stiff drink, a hot bath and his bed. What he did *not* need was the sight of General Montgomery with an armful of clipboards and a mouthful of questions, demanding urgent answers to important problems. Mr Gelb admits that Ike did not actually hold a conference of his commanders for another week – until January 22 – the interim being spent on meeting the King, Winston Churchill and various other dignitaries – and recovering from his journey. Did Ike really want – or need – to see Monty on the night he arrived?

As for the car parking incident – surely not a major concern for high commanders during a World War – this took place at that first Allied commanders' meeting on January 22. Mr Gelb mentions that Ike had a driver, the beguiling Miss Kay Summersby, but fails to appreciate that generals in the British Army also have drivers. Monty's driver would have dropped Monty at the front door of Norfolk House and then been directed by the Military Police to the car park; if anyone is to blame for this car parking 'impertinence' it has to be Monty's driver.

To whinge about *a parking space* when the generals are about to plan the invasion of Normandy is ludicrous, but when it comes to disparaging Montgomery – and the British – any accusation, however feeble, will apparently serve. I am sure my American friends and readers will appreciate how offensive to British veterans this sort of thing can be – and yet it continues.

This chauvinistic bias does great harm. It does harm to historical truth and harm to the mutual respect that one Allied nation should have for another – especially when their young men have shared the traumas of war and died in great numbers fighting a common foe. It gives me no pleasure to point this out but it certainly needs pointing out.

One final point. There is no wish on my part to turn this sort of history round and eliminate the American soldier from his due and fair share of the credit for the victory in Normandy – and award all the credit to the British and Canadians. I have the greatest respect for all the soldiers of the Second World War, not least the American soldiers and disparaging another nation's brave young men is not what I do.

This is an attempt to be even-handed about the Normandy campaign, to balance up the accounts and explore the popular myths. In the process I asked the many people who read this book in draft – including my American advisor and most friendly critic, Steve Weiss, once of the US infantry and now of the Department of War Studies at King's College, London – to check my facts and query my opinions, but to come down very hard indeed if they thought I had been unjust or unfair to anyone. How far I have succeeded in that task the readers can judge for themselves.

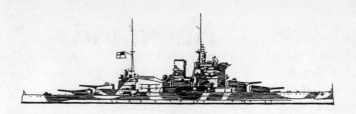

1 D-DAY JUNE 6, 1944

It had always been difficult to imagine D plus.

NORMAN SCARFE 3rd Infantry Division, Second Army

Nightfall on D-Day, June 6, 1944, brought little rest to the Allied soldiers in the Normandy beachhead. The surging tide came in again, bringing with it a number of wrecked landing craft, much débris and a quantity of bodies. From overhead came the constant drone of aircraft, either the heavy bombers of RAF Bomber Command heading for targets in France or Germany or, less frequently, the irregular beat of German aero-engines as enemy aircraft cruised above the beachhead, dropping the occasional mine or bomb. Meanwhile the build-up ashore continued.

Allied transports continued to disgorge men into the smaller landing craft, reinforcements heading for the depleted units ashore. Further out, beyond the irregular line of anchored transports, warships of the Royal and US Navies, cruisers, battleships and monitors, stood out in periodic bursts of red and yellow flame as their guns responded to appeals for support from the troops on shore. So the night wore on, until midnight came. Then D-Day – 6 June, 1944 – was over. The Allied armies had their long-awaited foothold on the enemy coast of France and the battle for Normandy was about to begin.

Ralph Conte, a bombardier-navigator with the US Ninth Air Force, records the Normandy beachhead on the evening of D-Day:[1]

Our Bomb Group, flying A-20 attack bombers, flew two missions that day, the second at 2000hrs. Weather was a factor, low cloud causing flying at under 2000ft; we normally would not take off in such weather but this day was

Normandy

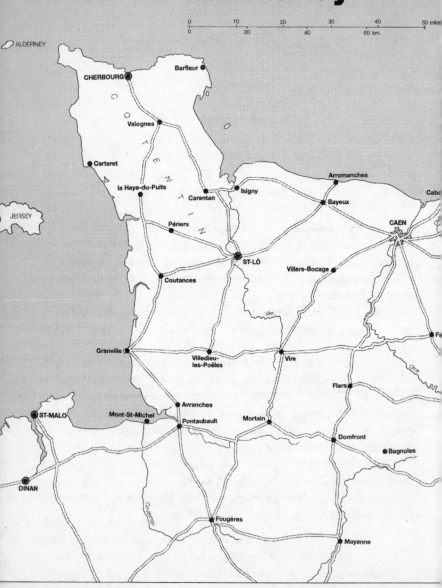

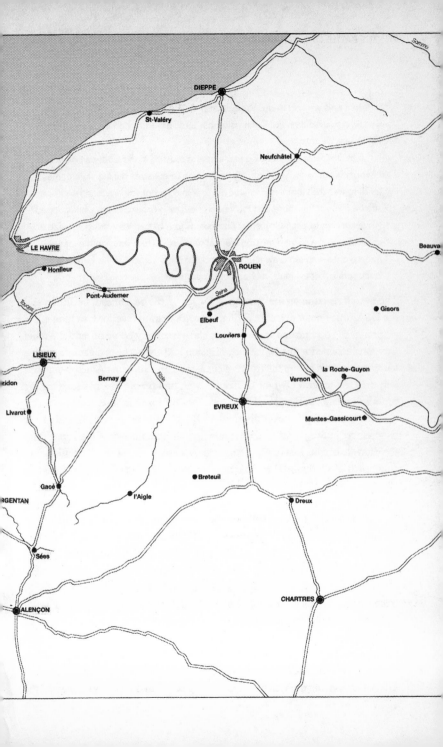

different and we had to go. We bombed at 1700ft with no fighter cover and we did not need it on the first mission but small-arms fire and tracer was reaching up we were so low.

A multitude of ocean-going vessels were massed in the Channel, all heading towards Normandy. This sight was awesome to our eyes but the sight of the landing beaches that evening was another thing what with men and equipment strewn all over the shore and the vessels bouncing around in the white-capped waves, trying to get their men or cargoes ashore before they faced capsize or crashes. On the second mission we met anti-aircraft fire, causing the loss of three planes with ten crew members and although the rest of the Group got back safely that evening, all had flak damage.

The overall reaction on the evening of D-Day, in the beachhead, in Britain and the USA, was one of joy, even exhilaration. Operation Overlord, so long in the planning, so complicated in execution, had apparently come off and the relief was considerable for this Normandy invasion had always been a gamble. Such a gamble that even before the troops went ashore, the Supreme Allied Commander, the US General Dwight D. Eisenhower, had prepared a message for the press and public, accepting all the blame for Overlord's failure.

This message was never distributed. By 2359hrs on June 6, Allied forces were ashore at five points on a fifty-mile front around the bay of the Seine, from the Ranville heights east of Ouistreham to the eastern side of the Cotentin peninsula north of Carentan. From those hard-won toe-holds strong patrols were already moving inland, 'pegging-out claims', in the words of their Ground Force Commander, the man directly responsible for the landing, the British general, Bernard Law Montgomery. His troops – American, British, Canadian – were now probing the enemy defences and preparing to hold the ground they had gained against those German counter-attacks that must soon come in.

Beyond the beaches, on the sandy bluffs and in the shell-torn coastal towns, the Allied tank crews and infantry settled down for the night, digging their slit trenches and foxholes, brewing a hot drink, grabbing a mouthful of food, sending back the wounded, burying their dead, the night broken by a thousand small and vicious fire fights. During that night their spirits fell somewhat. For the past six months every thought and effort had been devoted to the task of getting ashore; little thought or time had been devoted to what might happen after that. The realisation that the violent day they had just endured was only the start of the battle came as the soldiers waited in the dark, the exhilaration – the adrenaline rush of action – slowly wearing off.

Further inland, beyond the German defensive positions, the minefields, rifle-pits and pillboxes of the Atlantic Wall, thousands of British and American air-borne troopers, scattered across the Norman countryside on the previous night by high winds, were still seeking their units. So, slowly, as the night of D-Day changed into the grey dawn of D plus 1, the Allied units in Normandy began to get their second wind – and the myths that would eventually surround the Battle of Normandy began to accumulate.

H. John Butler, now of British Columbia, Canada, then a private in the 7th (Greenjackets) Battalion of the Parachute Regiment gives an example of the myths surrounding the taking and holding of the Caen canal and Orne river bridges at Bénouville at midnight on June 5–6. As all the world knows, these bridges were taken by a company of the Oxfordshire and Buckinghamshire Light Infantry led by Major John Howard, after landing by glider in a *coup de main*. John Butler gives another slant on this well-known story:[2]

I was 19 years and 5 days old on D-Day and serving in 9 Platoon, 'D' Company, 7 Para, a unit commanded by Lt Colonel Geoffrey Pine-Coffin, MC. The Company was the assault company, charged to reach the Caen canal and the Orne and attempt a river and canal crossing if the bridges had been blown. My platoon jumped from a Stirling bomber and about 40 people made it to the battalion DZ near Ranville on the east bank of the Orne, from where we set off for the bridges, myself in the lead as scout.

At the bridges the first thing I saw was a very young and very dead German, with both legs blown off below the knee, obviously from a grenade. This was the first dead person I had ever seen and the sight pulled me up; others dashed past me and I quickly joined them. On the far – west – side of the canal it seemed pretty quiet except for exploding ammunition in a burning half-track near the Bénouville *Mairie*. Here I joined up with the others of my platoon and we were sent on patrol.

At dawn we ran into a Jerry patrol, larger than ours. After a bit of a fight we were forced back into our battalion perimeter around the bridges, where we joined the other defenders. When it got relatively quiet, I was able to get down to the canal and drop my pants to bandage a flesh wound in my thigh. Having done that, I felt nauseous and in need of a drink so I went to the canal bridge in search of one. While I was there, a barge came into view from the direction of Caen, apparently armed with a 20mm cannon and a machine-gun. An officer appeared and ordered six of us to deal with it but just as we were about to sally down the bank there was a loud 'bang' from the opposite bank, a large piece flew off the superstructure of the barge and it beat a hasty retreat. I found out later that there was a German anti-tank gun mounted by the east side of the bridge and one of Major Howard's *coup de main* party had used it.

By the now-famous Pegasus Bridge café I then saw a White scout car and a Bren gun carrier opposite with a sergeant and a section of Royal Engineers, and it was these sappers, not the Commandos, who were the first seaborne troops to get through to us – this was about noon on June 6. They had kept clear of the road and followed a tramway parallel to the canal without incident. Their task was to survey the canal for a Bailey bridge if, as expected, the existing bridge had gone.

The Gondrée café was being used as our Aid Post. I asked the medic if he had anything to drink and he told me to knock on the inner door and ask the occupants. The door was opened by a little man, M. Gondrée, badly in need of a shave. He kissed me on the cheek and when I asked for a drink, went inside and was back in a couple of minutes with an armload of muddy champagne bottles. He poured out two glasses and we toasted each other and he was going to pour some more when he said, 'You don't want a glass, do you?' – in perfect English, and gave me the bottle. Just then one of the medics said he could hear the bagpipes.

The first thing I saw when I went back outside was a couple of Sherman tanks at the T-junction up the road by the *Mairie*. Then the pipes grew louder and round the corner came Lord Lovat with a piper at one side and another soldier, I presume his bodyguard, on the other. He looked neither to right or left but marched on down to the bridge as if he was strolling on his Highland estate. The only weapon he had in his hand was his swagger cane and he was starting across the bridge like that when the clang of a sniper's bullet made him realise that discretion was the better part of valour and he and his party scampered across. If he chatted with the *coup de main* party it was out of my sight.

The story of Lovat and Howard shaking hands at the bridge on D-Day is pure fiction. When Brigadier Lovat led his men down to the bridge he did not stop or talk to anyone. Nor was he wearing a white roll-necked sweater and carrying a hunting rifle, as shown in the Darryl Zanuck movie *The Longest Day*. He was correctly dressed in battledress, with collar and tie, and walked out of my sight in this manner. Neither was there any back-slapping or any gathering of Airborne and Commandos at the western end of the bridge, as is depicted on the 50th Anniversary stamp for example. The bridge and its approaches were under sniper and mortar fire and had there been any lingering there would have been heavy casualties. Indeed, I never saw a red beret on D-Day; we stuck to our steel helmets.

Heavy sniping and shelling commenced as the Commandos dashed across the bridge in batches, covered by smoke from smoke grenades. I was then told to go with the rest to the south of Bénouville, to reinforce 'A' Company, and this we did, joining the defence and having a busy time until about 2100hrs, when the sky was filled with tugs and gliders and they came swooping down, first to our rear and then to our front. This broke up a heavy attack that had been forming and after the Oxfordshire and Bucks had cleared our front from their gliders, things eased up a bit until the seaborne infantry from the Warwickshire Regiment arrived and took over. I made my way back to the bridge and met up again with my platoon and we were able to cross to the east side of the bridge for a rest; after 21 hours of battling, nothing was more welcome.

These are not the reminiscences of an old man. I kept a diary of my 40 days in Normandy and I could have written up D-Day much more graphically, but at the time I never gave a thought to the historical significance of the battle. That is what happened at the bridge as I saw it happen, *at the time*. The first seaborne troops there were sappers, not Commandos; Howard and Lovat did not meet on the bridge; Lovat was not in a white sweater and carrying a rifle; the bridge defenders when the Commandos arrived in the early afternoon, were from 7 Para, not the Ox and Bucks, there were no tanks around in the night. I was there and that is the truth ... but the myth is different.

The popular version has the *coup de main* party of the Ox and Bucks, under Major John Howard, gallantly seize the bridges and gallantly hold them until relieved from the sea by the Commandos and then still holding on until finally relieved by seaborne infantry. What happened to the 7th Bn of the Parachute Regiment? We don't rate a mention.

Stephen Ambrose's book on Pegasus Bridge, though it gives 7 Para more credit than most, still perpetuates the myth that Major Howard's party was being *reinforced* by 7 Para. In fact, we *relieved* Howard's party and they went into reserve. In accordance with 6th Airborne Div. orders and as the senior officer, Lt Colonel Pine-Coffin took command at the bridge from Major Howard and placed Howard's force in reserve, east of the bridge. The time this took place is disputed; Major Howard says around 0230hrs and 0300hrs on June 6 and our unit diary says 0130hrs – which is the time given on the Pegasus Bridge plaque – and Colonel Pine-Coffin says he took over from Howard at the bridge at 0210hrs but, whatever the time, 7 Para took over the defence of the bridges that night, just after midnight D-Day and we held them as ordered for the rest of the day. The truth is that Howard's D-Day exploit, while important, lasted about two and a half hours – maximum.

There is also some tale of German tanks blundering about Howard's position in the night; it is very odd indeed that none of us in 7 Para saw these 'tanks' – and blundering in the dark is something that German tanks simply did not do. I read the account by a Sergeant Wagger who claimed to have knocked out a Panzer Mark IV near the bridge – I was closer to it and can tell you that this 'tank' was a half-track and had no gun. 7 Para saw little action during the night, but at first light probing attacks began around the perimeter, mostly by infantry but accompanied by some armour in the south.

These attacks were driven off but about mid-morning an infantry attack, accompanied by a Mark IV tank, broke through Bénouville into the village square where the Regimental Aid Post (RAP) had been established, machine-gunned and killed all the wounded, including those lying on stretchers and the unarmed Quaker medical orderlies. Our padre, the Reverend Parry, though a man of the cloth, took up a Sten gun to fight and was cut down trying to defend the wounded. Deeds like this have also been submerged in the Pegasus Bridge myth. Yes, Howard's men took Pegasus Bridge, but 7 Para held it.

As a final point, on who did what at Pegasus Bridge that day, can I quote the casualty figures? Howard's party lost two men killed, one in the moment of landing, and eight or ten wounded. 7th Parachute Battalion lost 68 men killed that day and had many more wounded. I tend to think of our dead as *The Forgotten Heroes of the Lost Battalion* and surely they deserve better? But soon we will all be gone and forgotten, heroes and cowards alike.

So, even here, around one famous incident on the first day of a three-month-long campaign, the myths accumulate. Awarding credit where credit is due is always a difficult task but then nothing about Operation Overlord, the Allied invasion of German-occupied France, is easy. Dr Charles Crawford went ashore on D-Day with a blood transfusion unit and provides an account of the beaches that evening and of his work in the next twenty-four hours:[3]

I was with No. 24 Field Transfusion Unit, or FTU, aged 24, and had just qualified when I was called up. 24 FTU must have been one of the smallest D-Day units and consisted of one Medical Officer – me – two orderlies, a driver, a 3-ton truck and 200 bottles of blood. Our job was to work with Field Surgical Units, dealing with casualties that had been so severely injured that they would never have made it back to hospital level; we worked in front of the guns and were treating people within say, 20 minutes of their being hit. These are the short notes from my diary:

'Sailed about 0730hrs (on D-Day), in LCI – Landing Craft Infantry – sighted the French coast about 1900 hrs. Several areas of burning houses and HMS *Warspite* shooting inland with her 15-inch guns. First attempt at landing 1930hrs, then two more attempts after two German Me-109s had dropped bombs on the beach. Watched people in the next craft going in out of their depth and drowning. Then my turn came, gangway almost too steep to walk on and into the water. Shockingly cold and well over my waist. Leslie Brooks up to his chin. Got ashore, skirting a bloody great bombhole and found a Redcap (Military Police) to direct us to the marshalling area. Came across a dead British sergeant and six dead Jerries. Realised for the first time there was a war on at Lion-sur-Mer.

'Went on till someone said, "I wouldn't go on if I were you". Jerry still had beach under fire. Went into potato patch and began to dig my first slit trench. Bloody cold and wet still, found some straw and bedded down and slept in spite of the noise. Up at 0130hrs – June 7. Lion all ablaze to eradicate snipers, started work at 0330hrs in an orchard. Casualties in three marquees but later overflowed out into the rain".

'Smell of flesh and blood. One casualty came in with hole in chest the size of a pencil; he looked very sick and when turned over my hand went into huge exit hole in his back. Worked until 1800hrs here, then sent off to work in another field, carried on until 0600hrs. Very glad of slit trench to sleep in. Carried on like that for four days until we got our clothes off and things gradually got organised.'

The Allies were ashore, the British and Canadians against stiff resistance eased by their specialised armour, the Americans without great difficulty at Utah but in the face of determined opposition from the German 352nd Division at Omaha where the D-Day casualties in just one of the 29th Infantry Division's regiments are recounted by one survivor, Robert Slaughter:[4]

> The 1st Battalion, 116th Infantry, landed on Dog Green sector of Omaha. Company 'A' lost 91 men killed and almost as many wounded – there are 200 men in an infantry company and less than 20 men from 'A' got across that beach. 'B' Company lost almost all its officers and almost as many men as 'A'. My Company, 'D' Company lost 39 men killed and 32 wounded. On D-Day 'D' Company lost the Company Commander, 5 officers, the First Sergeant and 10 other non-commissioned officers killed and 10 other non-coms wounded. In all the 116th Regiment lost 800 men on D-Day, about a third of the men of the regiment that went ashore that day.

The fighting men, in close contact with the events ashore, large and small, had plenty to keep them occupied on D-Day but the Supreme Commander of the Allied Expeditionary Force, Dwight D. Eisenhower, better known to his troops and the general public as Ike, and the Land Forces Commander for the invasion phase, Bernard Law Montgomery – better known as Monty – could do nothing for the moment but wait.

In the months since taking up their appointments in January 1944 and with ample assistance from their naval and air force colleagues, their staffs and various subordinates, these two generals had drawn up the final plan for Operation Overlord. In the long term, the success or failure of Overlord depended on their experience and judgement but for the moment they could only read the messages coming in from the various beachheads and try to evaluate how things were going. Few military operations go exactly to plan and not all the plans laid for D-Day had worked out in detail but as far as they could tell, on the night of D-Day – and with the possible exception of the American landing on the beach codenamed Omaha – matters were going reasonably well.

This book covers the events in Normandy *after* D-Day but battles do not come in neat packages, tightly sealed at both ends, even with the benefits of hindsight. What happened from D plus 1, the point at which this story opens, was affected by the events of D-Day itself, and what happened during the later Normandy battles related to plans that had been laid down long before the first soldier stepped ashore. This being so, it would be as well to take a brief overview of what happened on that momentous day, what the main unit tasks were and then see how much of the original D-Day plan had actually come off – and how much remained to do before the plans for D plus 1 and afterwards could be put in train. This overview is given from the eastern end of the invasion area, north of the city of Caen.

The task of the British and Canadian units of the British Second Army on D-Day was to land in the eastern half of the invasion area, press inland and occupy a bridgehead at the eastern end of the invasion coast which would include the vital heights east of the river Orne, a ridge running from Ranville to Troarn and the city of Caen, six miles inland. Taking and holding the Ranville heights – or Bois de Bavant ridge – as the main defence line for the eastern end of the bridgehead together with the vital bridges over the Orne and Caen canal was the particular task of the British 6th Airborne Division and how that was managed has been described in part by the account given above.

The ground force plan for Overlord had been drawn up by Montgomery – and approved by Eisenhower and the Combined Chiefs-of-Staff – and in that plan the city of Caen was to be taken – *or effectively masked* – on D-Day by the British 3rd Infantry Division of General Dempsey's Second Army, coming ashore at Sword beach just west of Ouistreham at the mouth of the Caen canal. On their right flank came the 3rd Canadian Division, also of Second Army, landing on Juno beach by the small port of Courseulles and tasked to take the airfield at Carpiquet and the Caen to Bayeux road west of Caen and six miles inland. Then came the British 50th Infantry Division, landing on Gold beach around Arromanches and Le Hamel and charged with taking the city of Bayeux, seven miles inland.

Apart from any particular objectives, the overall task of *every* division landing that day – American, British, Canadian – was to take ground, gaining space for more troops, tanks and supplies and to absorb any German counter-attacks. The British and Canadian forces were also to seize open ground suitable for the development of airstrips – a particular requirement of the Allied Tactical Air Forces and the Deputy Allied Supreme Commander, Air Marshal Sir Arthur Tedder; these areas lay south of Caen and around the existing airfield at Carpiquet. That apart, the British and Canadian forces had to link up their various beachheads and join them with those of the US divisions landing further west at Omaha and Utah to form one continuous Allied bridgehead. This Allied meeting was to take place on the coast at Port-en-Bessin, which lay in the British sector and would be taken on D-Day by No. 47 (Royal Marine) Commando.

The Commandos were to meet V Corps of General Omar Bradley's First Army after two US divisions, the 1st and 29th Infantry Divisions had landed on Omaha beach. V Corps would move inland, also *pegging out claims* in the Bessin country south of Omaha, link up with the British to the west of Arromanches and with US airborne forces landing in the Cotentin – the Cherbourg peninsula – and with the US VII Corps landing at Utah beach. The prime task of VII Corps was to take the port of Cherbourg, which the VII Corps orders required *as quickly as possible*[5] but they were tasked to link up with their airborne forces of the US 82nd and 101st Airborne Divisions landing in the Cotentin and with men of V Corps coming west from Omaha.

Trying to establish the precise D-day objectives for the US assault divisions is not easy for the orders are complicated. For example, at one time the US forces had been tasked to take Carentan and Isigny on D-Day but, says the US Official History, 'detailed planning showed this to be unduly optimistic', and the capture of these two places was therefore to take place 'as soon as the tactical situation permits.' This order was then changed yet again to make Isigny a D-Day objective for the US 29th Division but not, apparently, for V Corps, of which the 29th Division formed part ... at least until June 3, when the commander of V Corps, General Gerow, told his subordinate commanders that the 115th Infantry Regiment, the follow-up 29th Infantry unit landing on Omaha, should get to Isigny on D-Day *if at all possible*'.[6] Such hesitation and uncertainty is understandable. No one could tell what would actually happen on the day – only that it would not happen as planned. Indeed, in his appreciation – or commander's estimate – of the D-Day battle, issued on May 7, 1944, General Montgomery had already stated:

> This represents the Commander-in-Chief's intentions, as far as they can be formulated at this stage. Whether operations will develop on these lines must, of course, depend on our own and the enemy situation, which cannot be accurately predicted at this moment.

This point is all too true and would remain true for the entire Battle of

Normandy and is a point that readers should note carefully. There is a widely held view that a commander's intentions, once issued, are written in stone and that any shortfall in the plan, either in its management or execution, is a clear sign of failure. This is a misconception; military plans, however carefully laid out and explained are, at best, declarations of intent; the enemy has not been consulted and will have something to say on how they work out in practice.

That 'no plan survives the first contact with the enemy' is a well-known military dictum but some firm guidelines are still needed by the field commanders, partly to provide them with some framework for their actions in the form of objectives, but mainly to let the logistical planners estimate the demands that will be made upon them for supplies and reinforcements. With this framework they can have the resources available to meet these demands as the battle develops. As far as historians are concerned, establishing what the various declared pre-D-Day objectives were is essential in view of what happened later – and in view of the disputes that arose subsequently and continue to flourish to this day.

At this point we must turn to the plan prepared by Montgomery in the spring of 1944, a plan accepted by the Allied Supreme Commander, General Eisenhower, and explained to the Allied commanders in two presentations given by Montgomery at St Paul's School in West London in April and May. At these meetings Montgomery declared what he intended to do – or would at least attempt to do. The point at issue here is the strategic plan for the conduct of the Battle of Normandy *after the landing;* there has never been any dispute about the landing operation on D-Day. This did not go entirely to plan either but then no one expected that it would; in the event it worked well enough to permit the troops to stay ashore, and that was considered a success.

The plan for the post-D-Day phase would be subject to change as the battle developed but the outcome of the battle as a whole would largely depend on what the field commander, General Montgomery, intended to do, and how far he succeeded in doing it. This plan provides the crux of the argument about the Battle of Normandy and therefore the core theme of this book, so it should be clearly understood now.

Montgomery's plan for Overlord required[7] 'the British Second and Canadian First Armies to assault west of the river Orne and to develop operations to the south and south-east, in order to secure airfield sites and to protect the eastern flank of US First Army while the latter is capturing Cherbourg. In subsequent operations the Second Army will pivot on its left (Caen) and offer a strong front against enemy movements towards the lodgement areas from the east'.

It is worth reading that twice, to establish these tasks clearly. However, one of the major arguments about those 'subsequent operations' concerns the plan for the eventual breakout *after* the capture of Cherbourg. Those arguments should never have arisen for Montgomery explained his plan for the breakout at the final St Paul's briefing on May 15. Having covered the points mentioned above, he stated that the British and Canadians would 'contain the maximum enemy forces facing the eastern flank of the bridgehead (i.e. around Caen) while the US forces "once through the difficult *bocage* country" would thrust rapidly towards Rennes, seal off the Brittany peninsula, and wheel round towards Paris and the Seine, *pivoting on the right flank of the British Second Army*.'(author's italics)

In short, the Allied breakout, when it came, would come on the western – or American – flank. That point was laid out in the original plan, three weeks before D-Day. This plan seems quite clear and why this decision – this plan – has been so frequently questioned by historians is hard to understand. General Omar Bradley, commander of the US First Army in Normandy, was certainly in no doubt about the plan, stating in his memoirs that 'the British and Canadian armies were to decoy the enemy reserves on to their front on the extreme eastern edge of the Allied beachhead. Thus, while Monty taunted the enemy at Caen, we were to make our break on the long roundabout road towards Paris.'[8] If the two Allied commanders in Normandy were clear about this plan at the time, it is hard to see why historians are still arguing about it sixty years later. Bradley also appreciated the need to hold firm on the eastern flank and take no risks there, 'for it is towards Caen that the enemy reserves would race once the alarm was sounded'.

The main danger in the east came from the powerful German Fifteenth Army, currently deployed north of the Seine and kept there by the Allied deception plan, Operation Fortitude. Fortitude had convinced many German commanders that the actual Allied invasion would come in the Pas de Calais and that any landing elsewhere, as in Normandy, was only a feint. Therefore, one major task of the British Second Army and the Canadian First Army – when the latter took the field – was to guard against and if necessary fend off, any thrust west into Normandy by the German Fifteenth Army.

Montgomery's orders continued: 'The US First Army is to capture Cherbourg and to develop operations southward towards St-Lô in conformity with the advance of Second British Army. After the area, Cherbourg, Caumont–Vire–Avranches have been captured, the Army will be directed southwards with the object of capturing Rennes and then establishing our flank on the Loire and capturing Quiberon Bay'.

A study of the map on page 137 will be useful at this point. It reveals that the bulk of the land due for capture initially lay in the US First Army zone and this predominance would continue. When the Avranches to Vire line had been established, the Cotentin – or Cherbourg – peninsula cleared and the port of Cherbourg taken, the US Third Army, under General George Patton, would enter the fray, clear Brittany, seize the ports of St Nazaire, Nantes and Brest and cover the advance of the US First Army which, said Monty, 'is directed N.E. with a view to operations towards Paris'.

As we shall see, not all of this happened in detail. However, the *strategic* plan for the Battle of Normandy was for the British to hold on in the east and keep that flank secure while the Americans seized the vital western ports, built up their forces there and then broke out to the east. That *strategic* plan did not change and that was the plan that eventually won the Battle of Normandy.

It is clear from these orders that Bradley's US forces were *always* tasked to make the breakout – a view reinforced by the fact that the Americans alone had the strength to make the breakout when the time came. The British and Canadian forces were committing their last reserves of manpower in Normandy in June 1944; any build-up of forces thereafter must come from the USA. This accounts for the positioning of US forces in the west, close to the Atlantic ports where reinforcements from the USA could come ashore. So let the first two points be established; the eventual Allied breakout from the Normandy bridgehead would be made by the Americans in the west – and that had *always* been the plan.

This point is still disputed. Some accounts allege that Montgomery intended to break out in the east, south of Caen, hinge on Falaise and then press east across the Seine. From this arises the main myth, that the British and Canadian failure to do so eventually obliged the Americans to take over the direction of the Normandy campaign – and break out in the west. This notion can be dismissed, partly by the facts given in the previous paragraphs, partly by reference to the map. If the British broke out and headed east, as the myth makers claim they should have done, we would have had the curious spectacle of the larger US forces trailing along in the British–Canadian wake from the west or trying to dodge round their Allies to the south; neither of these courses seems credible.

The second point of dispute was on where the Allied line should pivot. Here again, Montgomery supplies the answer. The Allied line, initially facing south and west, should pivot to the north and east on Caen; Caen would, in military parlance, be the *hinge* of the campaign and hinges, by definition, do not move. That said, there are few absolutes in military affairs and there can be little doubt that Montgomery would have preferred to push south and make his eastern front hinge at Falaise since this would have given his forces more room and freed the beaches from shell fire – and given Tedder those airfields beyond Caen. As we shall see, for various reasons, this did not happen and the eventual Allied hinge came further west.

The last point of dispute is on what the British and Canadians would be doing while the US armies built up their forces for the breakout. Here again the strategic plan provides the answer. Apart from holding the eastern flank and protecting the US First Army advances in the west, they were to advance south and southeast of the Orne, with the aim of securing airfield sites on the Caen–Falaise plain. As we shall see, this did not happen either; no airfield sites were obtained *south* of Caen until the Germans were in full retreat from Normandy at the end of August. It is arguable that this did not matter very much; the Allied tactical air forces managed to operate successfully from bases in the UK or the many Allied airfields that were soon built in the bridgehead area. It did, however, provide useful ammunition for Montgomery's enemies, at the time and since.

The final point concerns the timings, *when* all this was going to happen. The answer is again found in the strategic plan, which states that the Allied armies would have driven the Germans back to the Seine on or about D plus 90, say September 1. Various intermediate targets – phase lines – were introduced into the plan but these were largely, as stated above, for administrative reasons, to give the logistical planners some time frame. Indeed, when Lt Colonel C. P. Dawnay, Monty's military assistant, was helping his chief prepare for the first presentation of plans on April 7, 1944, eight weeks before D-Day, he asked Montgomery where the phase lines should be drawn between D-Day and D plus 90?

Monty replied, 'Well, it doesn't matter, Kit – draw them where you like'.

'Shall I draw them equally, Sir?', asked Dawnay.

' Yes, that'll do', replied Montgomery.[9]

Montgomery knew that whatever was intended two months before the landing would be altered the minute the troops went ashore. Even so, two other points need explaining. The first is that changes in plan in the course of the battle were only to be expected – *and hardly matter if the overall aim of the campaign is kept broadly on track.* The second point is that these changes would not have mattered, or provided so much ammunition to his enemies, if Montgomery had not insisted later that no changes were made to the plan and that matters after D-Day went *exactly* as he always intended. This is a point we shall discuss later, but for the moment we must return to the beginning of 1944.

Eisenhower set up his headquarters – SHAEF (Supreme Headquarters, Allied Expeditionary Force) – at Bushey, north-west of London, while Montgomery established his HQ at his old alma mater, St Paul's School in Hammersmith, West London. An outline plan – the Initial Joint Plan – was submitted by Montgomery, for Eisenhower's approval on February 1. After this was approved the detailed planning went on apace and the process culminated in a first presentation of plans – Exercise Thunderclap – on April 7.

Once the overall objectives have been set, military plans are prepared in detail from the 'bottom-up', from the lower echelons, for the very sensible reason that – within broad limits – the person responsible for executing a plan should have a major say in preparing it. Monty did not create a detailed, day-by-day plan, which he then imposed on the army commanders; nor did he insist on detailed compliance from his navy and air force colleagues. His chief concern was with the allocation of tasks, objectives and resources towards accomplishing the strategic aim. These tasks having been allocated to the various armies, the army commanders '*with their associated Naval and Air Force authorities, produced detailed plans of action*'.[10]

After Thunderclap, the whole Overlord project was examined yet again, some adjustments were made and the three joint Allied Commanders-in-Chief – Montgomery, Ramsey and Leigh-Mallory, representing the Allied Army, Navy and Air Forces – presented their plans to the Supreme Commander, General Eisenhower, to Prime Minister Churchill, General Smuts of South Africa, HM King George VI and the British Chiefs-of-Staff on May 15, three weeks before the actual invasion. This presentation was broadly in line with that given on April 7 and there is no reason to suppose that anyone was left in any doubt about the strategic plan or its viability. Indeed, in his opening address, General

Eisenhower stated: 'I consider it to be the duty of anyone who sees a flaw in the plan not to hesitate to say so.'

Monty, who had prepared this plan, decreed that the assault would be made on a frontage of two armies, with General Omar Bradley's US First Army on the west and the General Sir Miles Dempsey's British Second Army in the east. Tactical air support would be crucial and the First Army would be supported by the US Ninth Air Force, the Second Army by the RAF, Second Tactical Air Force (2nd TAF) – though in practice both air forces supported either army when the need arose.

Montgomery's command would consist initially of his own 21st Army Group, then composed of the British Second Army under General Sir Miles Dempsey, the leading elements of the Canadian First Army under Lieutenant General Crerar – which would be activated later – and General Omar Bradley's US First Army – again with General George Patton's US Third Army landing later. During the *invasion phase* – a rather loose term without a definite end – the overall land force commander would be General Montgomery.

The point to note at this stage is the one about the *invasion phase*. Once the Allied armies were ashore, some of the assault units, notably the airborne and commando units, would be withdrawn for use elsewhere and replaced with 'heavy' infantry more suitably equipped for a continuous land offensive. In practice, as we shall see, it proved impossible to withdraw these troops, and the airborne divisions, British and American, and the two commando brigades, stayed in Normandy for much of the campaign.

In the original plan, when enough Allied divisions had gone ashore, General Eisenhower, in addition to his role as Supreme Commander, would take command of the land forces. Montgomery would then revert to command of 21st Army Group – which would contain the British Second and Canadian First Army – and Bradley would take command of a new formation, 12th US Army Group, which would consist of the US First Army, under General Hodges, and George Patton's Third Army.

Now comes the first point of variance. The post-D-Day tasks were spelt out by Montgomery at his presentation on April 7 and repeated on May 15, and this must be the reliable version. However, in his memoirs[11] Montgomery states: 'Once ashore and firmly established my plan was to *threaten* to break out of the initial bridgehead in the eastern flank – that is in the Caen sector; I intended by means of this threat to draw the main enemy reserves on to this sector, to fight them there and keep them there, using the British and Canadian armies for this purpose.'

The object of this threat, he continues, was to draw the main German forces, especially his armoured forces, on to the British and Canadian front, and keep them there, grinding down his forces and sucking in his reserves. This is *not* what Montgomery proposed at the presentation in April, but rather an account of what happened later, on the ground in Normandy. In the event this hardly mattered; having got the Germans committed around Caen, Montgomery's intention, as stated on May 15, that the US armies should break out of the bridgehead in the west, *pivoting on Caen*, was still a viable proposition. The armies would hinge somewhere and it should be as far east as possible, in order to present the widest possible front to the enemy and drive him back.

Having taken Cherbourg and St-Lô, the US armies would advance into Brittany, clear the ports there and swing east, moving north of the Loire and so up to the Seine by Paris. This part of the plan was based on two factors, the need for supply ports and a wish to destroy the enemy forces confronting the Allied armies in Normandy. Much of their destruction would be accomplished by the Allied tactical air forces and one task of the British and Canadian armies was to take ground for airstrips south of Caen so that the tactical air forces could bring their full weight to bear on the ground offensive without the need for the petrol-consuming cross-Channel flight. The Normandy campaign plan was therefore quite simple; a right-flanking attack with the British and Canadians holding the enemy in the east, protecting the American flank, while more US troops arrived, and providing the pivot for the eventual breakout.

On D-Day itself the main point worth noting is that only the two British divisions were tasked to take cities well behind the beaches – the 3rd Infantry Division to take Caen, eight miles inland, the 50th Division to take Bayeux, seven miles inland. Apart from the airfield at Carpiquet, which the 3rd Canadian Division were responsible for, the other Allied landing forces were – as already stated – mainly tasked to get ashore and get inland as far as possible before the Germans counter-attacked. Most of this was accomplished, on D-Day or soon after it, but the failure of Second Army to take Caen on D-Day – 'Monty's failure', as it is usually called – was to haunt the campaign and blight Montgomery's reputation thereafter.

2 CAEN AND THE ALLIED COMMAND JUNE 7

As soon as we land, this business becomes primarily a business of
build-up. For you can nearly always force an invasion, but you
can't always make it stick.

GENERAL OMAR BRADLEY *A Soldier's Story*

With the strategic plan and the initial objectives for Overlord clarified, let us see
what actually happened on D-Day, for events in the first twenty-four hours had
a bearing on what came later. The landings, airborne and seaborne, had been
badly disrupted by the weather, which in Normandy would remain generally
foul for the rest of the summer, but by the morning of June 7 – D plus 1 – the
troops ashore, if failing to achieve the planned advance anywhere but at Bayeux,
had taken positions which would be crucial to future developments in the beachhead. They had not, however, taken the town of Caen or the airfield at Carpiquet,
two of the stated tasks for D-Day.

The British 6th Airborne Division had seized the bridges over the Caen canal
and the Orne at Bénouville at midnight on June 5–6 and on the morning of D-
Day, with the help of Lovat's 1st Commando Brigade[1] seized the vital Ranville
heights which were to form the left or eastern flank of the bridgehead. The paratroopers of 6th Airborne and the commandos of Lovat's brigade were by the
afternoon of D-Day preparing to resist a strong attack supported by the tanks
of 21 Panzer that could be heard rumbling about before their lines.

On the western flank of the bridgehead, in the Cotentin peninsula, the paratroopers of the US 82nd and 101st Airborne Divisions, though more scattered
than the British airborne units, had now taken the town of Ste-Mère-Église,

linked up with the US 4th Infantry Division coming ashore on Utah and were now on the move, north towards Montebourg and Cherbourg, south into the flooded marshes around the town of Carentan. Although their losses had been heavy, more from bad luck and high winds than enemy action, all the airborne divisions were getting stronger by the hour as more men trickled in.

The seaborne landings present a more varied picture. These had been made at half-tide on the flood and since the tides in the bay of the Seine come in from the Atlantic, the American assault divisions, the 4th on Utah and the 1st and 29th Infantry Divisions on Omaha, had landed first. All the landings had been disrupted by the high seas and surf on the beaches. The Utah landings, by troops of Major General Lawton Collins's VII Corps had gone well against light opposition apart from some long-range shellfire. The 4th Division troops landed some distance south of the correct beach but any confusion that might have arisen was quickly stamped on by the Assistant Commander of the 4th Infantry Division, Brigadier General Theodore Roosevelt Jr, son of the former US President, Theodore – Teddy – Roosevelt.

Although fifty-seven years old and by no means fit, General Roosevelt landed with the first wave, summed up the situation and declaring, 'We'll start the war right here', ordered the first troops to advance inland and the supporting waves to come in behind them. On Utah, therefore, matters on D-Day largely went according to plan and the 4th Infantry Division – three regiments – or Regimental Combat Teams (RCT), each composed of three battalions plus artillery, tanks and engineers, the equivalent of a British brigade group, had linked up with the parachute units by mid-morning on D-Day and were pushing inland against light but stiffening resistance.

Fifteen miles away, on the north shore of the bay of the Seine, it was another story. The landings on Omaha by the US V Corps were little short of a disaster. The assault troops here came from the RCT of the 116th Infantry Regiment of the 29th Infantry Division, and the 16th RCT of the 1st Infantry Division, both of General Gerow's V Corps. These units were pinned down on the beach for most of the morning, taking heavy casualties, unable to move forward in the face of drenching fire from artillery, machine-guns and riflemen on the bluffs overlooking the beach. This fire came from the well-entrenched, well-equipped and resolute German 352nd Infantry Division, which was carrying out an anti-invasion exercise along the Omaha beach when the Americans came ashore.

Helped by a thin but formidable array of prepared defences, the 352nd took a heavy toll of the US infantry. It was not until mid-afternoon that some of the 1st and 29th Infantry were able to penetrate these defences and lead their comrades inland. The two divisions took over 3,000 casualties along the three-mile strip of sand called Omaha but by nightfall they were off the beach and clinging to an area roughly three miles long and about a mile deep. It is arguable that American casualties on Omaha might have been fewer and their advance deeper if the US infantry had enjoyed more tank support and the help of the specialised armour employed by the British and Canadian divisions to the east. The US divisions had DD amphibious tanks but they were launched too far offshore and most of them foundered before reaching the beach.

Just along the coast from Omaha, the first of the two British infantry divisions to go ashore that morning, the 50th (Northumbrian) Division of the British Second Army, landed on Gold beach, between Arromanches and La Rivière, at around 0700hrs. They too met heavy opposition on the beach but fortunately the British infantry enjoyed close support from armoured units. Some of this was provided by DD (Duplex Drive) tanks – though most of the tanks landing on Gold were actually put directly ashore from landing craft. The British landings were also helped by the specialised armour of General Sir Percy Hobart's 79th Armoured Division – generally known as 'The Funnies' – a variety of tanks adapted for special tasks.

This specialised armour, 'Petard' tanks to blast pillboxes, 'Crocodile' flamethrowing tanks, 'Crabs' flail tanks to beat a path through minefields and 'Fascine' tanks carrying baulks of timber to bridge gaps, together with bridging tanks, provided the British infantry with the wherewithal to get off the beach quickly, through the small towns and beach villas which, then as now, occupy this stretch of the Calvados coast. On Gold this specialised armour and the assault infantry was supported by the tanks of the Nottinghamshire Yeomanry and the 4/7th Dragoon Guards as well as by ground attack fighters and fighter-bombers of the RAF's Second Tactical Air Force (2nd TAF). As a result, the 50th Division made the best advance of any Allied unit on D-Day and by nightfall was seven miles inland and about to capture the city of Bayeux.

Landing with this division was No. 47 (Royal Marine) Commando. This small unit had the task of advancing inland and then moving ten miles west, behind the enemy lines, to take the fishing port of Port-en-Bessin, the meeting place of the British and American armies. No. 47 Commando suffered severe losses of men and equipment even before getting ashore but by midnight on D-Day it had re-equipped with captured enemy weapons and was to take Port-en-Bessin at dawn on June 7.

Three miles to the east of Gold lay Juno beach. This beach straddled the oyster port of Courseulles at the mouth of the river Seulles and the resort town of St-Aubin-sur-Mer, a strip of coast defended by the German 716th Infantry Division. Juno was assaulted at 0745hrs by troops of the 3rd (Canadian) Infantry Division, the advance formation of General Crerar's Canadian First Army, which had yet to form; 3rd Canadian Division was currently in Second Army. As at Gold, this part of the Normandy coast is lined with small resorts and holiday villas and the Canadians were involved in street fighting from the moment they waded ashore.

This led to a certain amount of delay, not least in the town of Bernières where, according to the Canadian Official History, 'the 9th Canadian Infantry Brigade, complete with bicycles was waiting, crowded in the streets'. The divisional commander, Major General R. F. Kellner, went ashore soon after noon to sort matters out, and by mid-afternoon the 9th Brigade were on the move towards their D-Day objective, the airfield at Carpiquet and the Caen–Bayeux road.

Neither of these objectives were taken on D-Day and by the day's end the Canadians had yet to link up with the 3rd (British) Infantry Division on their left. The gaps between the British and Canadian landing beaches here were to be closed with flanking advances made by two commando units, 48 (Royal Marine) Commando moving east from St-Aubin, 41 (Royal Marine) Commando moving west from Lion-sur-Mer. Both these units were heavily engaged on landing and could not close the gaps until late on June 7.

The last of the assaulting infantry divisions was the British 3rd Infantry Division, commanded by Major General T. G. Rennie, a unit in Lieutenant General J. T. Crocker's I Corps, which went ashore on Sword beach between Lion-sur-Mer and the entrance to the Caen canal at Ouistreham. This division had a number of tasks and its three infantry brigades were supported by a quantity of armour and No. 4 Commando from Lovat's 1st Commando Brigade which was tasked with taking the town of Ouistreham at the mouth of the Caen canal. The other units of the 1st Commando Brigade marched across country to reinforce the men of 6th Airborne at the Bénouville bridges and the Ranville heights. With No. 4 Commando engaged at Ouistreham, Rennie's three infantry brigades were free to take their sector of the Normandy beachhead and then push south, up the river Orne and the Caen canal, to complete their second task, the capture of Caen, a city of some 50,000 people some six miles from the coast.

Their path would also be opposed by the German 716th Infantry Division which held a number of strongpoints on the road to Caen, of which two, codenamed Hillman and Morris, situated on rising ground, just south of Colleville and Queen Red beach on Sword, were to prove formidable obstacles to any rapid advance by British forces towards the city. The Morris and Hillman positions had depth and were arguably the most formidable defensive positions on the entire Normandy coast. The remains of Hillman, which survive to this day – a combination of sunken bunkers built of reinforced concrete and steel machinegun cupolas, the whole covering an area of several city blocks – are reminiscent of the fortifications surrounding Verdun in the Great War – with the addition in 1944 of a thick belt of mines.

These Hillman and Morris fortifications – and others named Daimler and Rover, also barring the road to Caen – were manned by men of the 716th Division. They in turn were supported by units of the only German armoured division close to the Normandy coast on D-Day, 21 Panzer. This combination, 716th Division and 21 Panzer Division and the Hillman–Morris strongpoints, was enough to stop 3rd Infantry Division taking Caen on D-Day. This failure can be attributed to the strength of the German defences north of the city. Eric Lummis of the 1st Bn The Suffolk Regiment, the unit tasked with taking Hillman, explains what they were up against[2] and rejects any suggestion that his battalion was not well-handled:

> Carlo d' Este, an American historian, states in a letter to me that Hillman was the most formidable obstacle on the Second Army front and his book *Decision in Normandy* gives proper recognition to the strength of Hillman.
>
> If Hillman was such an obstacle as to hold up the division's drive on Caen, more effort should have been directed to clearing it. Hillman was an extensive and formidable area of trenches, shelters, pillboxes and a map issued in April 1944 showed Hillman as having two 105mm and two 75mm guns. Yet arrange-

ments for dealing with this obvious strongpoint were relatively minor compared with other positions.

It was not listed for pre-D-Day bombing or naval bombardment. Six B-17s were allotted to drop a total of 228 one-hundred pound bombs an hour before D-Day compared with the 800 tons dropped on the Merville battery in May and the 340 tons dropped on Merville on the day. In the event, not a single bomb was dropped on Hillman because of heavy cloud cover and inadequate equipment for bombing blind. No flail tanks were allotted to deal with the minefield known to exist around the position.

The most significant reason for the failure (to take Caen) was almost certainly the decision by the commander of 185 Brigade to change his plans and delay the advance of two of his battalions by several hours. In all of this any delay in capturing Hillman can be seen to be irrelevant. Nevertheless, the charge in Chester Wilmot's book, *The Struggle for Europe*, that insufficient use was made of the resources available to the Commanding Officer of 1 Suffolk needs to be considered.

Wilmot's idea of more resources consisted of throwing more troops against the position and incurring much heavier casualties. It is easy to point out that to expect one rifle company to capture a position the size and strength of Hillman, moving through a single gap in a minefield and through two wire fences under fire from machine-guns a few yards away, in cupolas impervious to any available weapons, was demanding more than was reasonable, particularly as the planned bombardment from air and sea had never materialised. There was very little scope for extending the approach, though one or two extra gaps might have made a difference. Full use of resources available to the CO was made; additional resources initially depended on the planners. It is a tribute to those involved that day that the position was taken with so little resources and so few casualties.

Richard Harris, aged eighteen, was one of the private soldiers in the Suffolk Regiment at Hillman:[3]

I suppose we were a pretty unlikely lot to fling against Hitler's much vaunted Atlantic Wall. On June 6 we were green, both from inexperience and sea sickness; most of us were under twenty. Our Primary and Corps training had lasted 16 weeks when we were sent to the Young Soldiers battalion and then drafted to the Suffolks.

But Hillman. We left our positions at Colleville just off the beach and formed up for the attack and I was relieved to learn that the defenders of Morris had given up at around 1300hrs and 67 Germans came out with their hands up. The other objective, Hillman, was on rising ground, half a mile above Morris and had not been badly damaged by the naval bombardment. It also had a network of underground defences which had not been revealed by aerial photos and would be a tough nut to crack but confident after their initial success at Morris, the companies of the battalion mounted their attack on the outer defences which were protected by mines and wire.

These we breached but the inner defences remained and a second attack had to be mounted, this one supported by tanks of the Staffordshire Yeomanry; while this was going on the Luftwaffe made its only appearance, four Junkers 88 which were promptly pounced on by a swarm of Spitfires and all were destroyed.

Our joy was short-lived for we were then told to prepare for a counter-attack by German tanks advancing north from Caen. Even though Harry and I dug a slit trench we felt somewhat inadequately equipped to tackle panzers, with only a rifle apiece. Fortunately the tanks were engaged by our anti-tank gunners astride the Périers ridge; eleven were knocked out but a number by-passed the ridge and managed to reach the sea at Lion-sur-Mer, between our division and the Canadians.

By 2000hrs the attack on Hillman had been successful but not until some nasty business had taken place in the basement with some Germans intent on winning the Iron Cross. Fifty prisoners were taken and our casualties, happily, had been light. On the morning of D plus 1, the Colonel of the 736 Coast Defence Regiment, Oberst von Krug, emerged to surrender with 70 or so remaining officers and men. So ended this day and I was surprised to find myself alive and intact; many were not.

This account reveals that the road to Caen was still being contested on the evening of June 6, twelve hours after the landing, from a strong position less than a mile from Sword beach; that fact, plus the other factors listed, help to explain why the 3rd Infantry Division did not take Caen that day.

By nightfall the British had secured the left flank of the Allied landing area east of Bénouville and advanced some four miles up the Orne and the Caen canal towards the city but since the failure to take Caen on D-Day was to become another of the major issues dominating the Normandy campaign, it would also be as well to discuss Caen's place in the plan laid down for June 6. In Second Army's outline plan, issued on February 21, 1944, Caen was clearly a D-Day objective. The Second Army plan states 'The capture and retention of Caen is vital to the Army plan.' This intention is confirmed when the final Army plan for D-Day – Order No. 1, was issued on April 21. 'I Corps will capture Caen'.

Then matters grow cloudy. The orders issued by I Corps do indeed restate that the capture of Caen is vital to the Army plan and confirm that 'the task of 3 British Division is to capture Caen and secure a bridgehead over the river Orne at that place', which could hardly be more definite. However, the detailed order goes on to state that, '3 Brit Inf Div should, by the evening of D-Day, have captured *or effectively masked* (author's italics) Caen, and be disposed in depth with brigade locations firmly established, north-east of Bénouville in support of 6th Airborne Division ... having taken over the Bénouville–Ranville crossing ... and north-west of Caen, tied up with the left forward brigade locality of 3 Cdn Inf Div'.

So far so good, but the order goes on: 'Should the enemy forestall us at Caen and the defences prove to be strongly organised, thus causing us to fail to capture it on D-Day, further direct frontal assaults which may prove costly will not be undertaken without reference to I Corps. In such an event, 3 Brit Inf Div will contain the enemy in Caen and retain the bulk of its forces disposed for mobile operations outside the covering position. Caen will be subjected to heavy air bombardment to limit its usefulness to the enemy and make its retention a costly business.'

This is, in fact, what actually happened and it is interesting that this counter-proposal was made well before 3rd Infantry Division went ashore. It therefore appears that the major unit most directly concerned with the capture of Caen on D-Day – Lieutenant-General Crocker's I Corps – already had an alternative strategy in place to that of the Allied Commanders, Eisenhower and Montgomery, *but only should the defences prove too strong* (author's italics). This again seems sensible – *no plan survives the first contact with the enemy etc*. It is only necessary to add that however hard it might be to take Caen on D-Day, it would be much harder to take later in the campaign, once the advantage of surprise had been lost.

Montgomery, the Allied Land Forces Commander, had clearly hoped to seize Caen on D-Day, but in retrospect this aim seems ambitious. For a single infantry division, even with tank and naval support, even with paratroops and commandos protecting its flank across the Orne, even with the advantage of surprise, to get ashore and seize a bridgehead on a heavily defended coast, then advance off the beach and cover six miles over enemy-held territory and take a city of 50,000 people, all in twenty-four hours, seems a formidable undertaking, so much so that one wonders if Montgomery's intention was serious or, as with most orders, simply a declaration of intent.

There are, in addition, two military considerations. First, a commander does not order his troops to take an objective and then add 'but if you don't, no matter, just to threaten it will do'. Military orders stress the aim firmly – '3rd Infantry Div. *will* take Caen, – without any sign of doubt. Besides, Caen was an important objective, a road and rail junction and sooner or later it had to be taken. To complete the task of barring the eastern flank of the invasion area against any threat from the east – from Fifteenth Army across the Seine – Second Army really needed to get south as far as Falaise. Like Caen, Falaise was a road hub which the Allies needed to take and the Germans had to hold. However, these points only became critical if Fifteenth Army moved.

In the event Operation Fortitude succeeded in keeping the Fifteenth Army north of the Seine until the battle in Normandy was almost over – though infantry divisions were sent across the river to Seventh Army as required. Therefore, since the Germans were most anxious to defend Caen, the commitment of their forces to its retention would weaken their forces elsewhere and would eventually ease the passage of the US armies breaking out in the west. Even so, the issue of Caen was to bedevil relationships between Montgomery and SHAEF throughout the battle and we will return to this subject frequently in this book.

That nineteenth century guru of military affairs, Karl von Clausewitz, has stated that military matters are 'simple, but not easy' and any 'failure' to achieve all the tasks set in an initial plan should not be a surprise. No one with any experience of battle, and especially of battle against the German Army, seriously expected that the D-Day landing forces would succeed in all their tasks. Only if the German Army had put up no resistance whatsoever – and probably not even then, given the weather and other confusions – could the D-Day plan have succeeded completely.

It is now necessary to consider how far this 'failure' to take Caen on D-Day – if 'failure' is not too strong a word to use in this context – would contribute to the problems that arose in the weeks and months ahead. To do that we must go back again to the original plan and the reasons Normandy was selected for the Allied invasion.

That there would need to be an invasion of German-occupied western Europe became obvious after the British Army was bundled out of Dunkirk in 1940 and the Germans, having failed to win air superiority over southern England, were unable to follow up that exploit by invading and conquering Britain. Britain fought on after 1940, but to win the war, British armies – supported by their Allies – must one day return to the Continent. When the Americans entered the war in December 1941 – after which the US forces were bundled out of the Philippines with Dunkirk-like rapidity by the Japanese – the US commitment to the war in Europe, the 'Germany First' policy adopted at the Arcadia Conference in 1941, was given on the understanding that the Allies would return to the Continent with the greatest possible speed. This led to an argument on exactly how speedy that return would be.

At American insistence, plans were quickly laid for an invasion of France as early as the summer of 1942. This venture was not on the cards so fresh plans were laid for an invasion in 1943, but various other commitments and necessities – to finish the war in North Africa, drive Italy out of the war and beat back the U-boat menace in the North Atlantic – plus a dawning realisation in Washington that beating the German Army would not be easy, gradually put the invasion date back.

This is not to say that the invasion of France was not constantly under discussion. The build-up of US, Canadian and British forces in the UK in 1942 and 1943 had no other objective than an invasion of western Europe and the only real questions were what force was necessary to achieve a successful landing and when such a force could be mustered, trained and supplied with enough shipping. These problems were analysed in a number of complicated plans which began to take final shape in May 1943 when a British officer, Lt General F. E. Morgan, and his American assistant, Brigadier General Barker, were charged by the Combined Chiefs-of-Staff with drawing up plans for an invasion. Morgan's title was 'Chief of Staff to the Supreme Allied Commander (Designate)' – and 'designate' because the Supreme Allied Commander had yet to be appointed. The rest of these initials form the word Cossac and Morgan's subsequent proposals were therefore known as the Cossac plan.

The decision to proceed with planning the invasion was taken by the Combined Chiefs in Washington in May 1943 and a provisional date for the assault, May 1, 1944, was chosen at the same time. The forthcoming invasion also acquired some codenames. The overall operation would be Overlord, while the naval part of the assault phase – transporting and landing the troops – was codenamed Neptune. It was also agreed that the Supreme Commander of the Allied Expeditionary Force would be an American.

Numbers alone would see to that. After the initial landing the bulk of the Allied forces in Europe would be American and the Americans were anyway notoriously reluctant to put their forces under other generals. Fortunately, the man chosen to command this multi-national force in Europe – Americans, British, Canadians, French, Poles – was a fifty-four-year-old general from Texas, Dwight D. Eisenhower.[4]

Dwight Eisenhower – Ike – was a protégé of General George Marshall, the US Army Chief-of-Staff. Eisenhower graduated from West Point in 1915 in the top third of his class. This class included two other Second World War Army commanders, Omar Bradley, who would command the US Forces in Normandy, and Mark W. Clarke, who in 1944 was commanding the US Fifth Army in Italy. By the time the United States entered the Great War in April, 1917, Eisenhower was serving with the 57th Infantry Regiment in Texas and, to his considerable chagrin, he was kept in the USA to train recruits. After the war he entered the newly formed Tank Corps where he met an officer recently returned from France, a flamboyant and wealthy cavalry officer, George Patton.

Patton introduced Eisenhower to General Fox Connor, then the US commander in Panama, who took Ike on to his staff. This move set the pattern for Eisenhower's career in the inter-war years. He became a staff officer, with wide experience in staff duties in Panama with Fox Connor, then more staff work under MacArthur in the Philippines and later in Washington. Eisenhower was therefore a widely experienced and well-respected staff officer when the USA finally entered the Second World War in December 1941. His first chance for field command came in 1942 when he was appointed Allied Commander-in-Chief for Operation Torch, the North African landings. North Africa was Ike's first taste of action and the place where he first met the British field commanders, notably Alexander and Montgomery, and made many friends.

Eisenhower had been chosen for this task by the head of the US Army and Chairman of the Combined Chiefs-of-Staff, the body directing the Allied war effort, General George Marshall. Marshall sent Ike to London in the summer of 1942 as Commanding General for the European Theatre of Operations – the ETO – although Eisenhower's substantive rank was only colonel. After Torch, though still a substantive colonel, he was promoted to four-star general and appointed Allied Commander in the Mediterranean theatre. Finally, in January 1944 he was appointed Allied Supreme Commander at SHAEF for the Normandy invasion.

Although entirely without battlefield command experience, Eisenhower had three assets that made him the ideal choice for the post of Allied Supreme Commander. First of all, he had a vast amount of experience in staff work – at the highest level. Secondly, he was entirely without national prejudices of any kind – a quality that was not readily found in some of his subordinate commanders, American or British. Finally, he was American and his ready charm contained a steel core.

However, even if some other Allied commander had all the required qualities, the overall commander at SHAEF was destined to come from the USA – military demographics, the fact that the Americans were playing the larger part in the western European war, would see to that. These comments should not be seen as dismissive for Eisenhower had other assets; he was in every sense a big man, an ideal generalissimo, someone who never lost sight of the big picture and could get people to work together. Such men are rare and in 1944 Dwight D. Eisenhower was the right man in the right place.

The Command set-up at The Supreme Headquarters, Allied Expeditionary Force – or SHAEF – was as shown on page 56.

The basic set-up is shown on this plan – an American Chief and Chief-of-Staff but with a British Deputy Allied Supreme Commander and British commanders for the three elements – land, sea and air – of the invasion forces. This seems a fair division of responsibility, but the simplicity of the structure conceals an number of inherent problems and since a significant part of this book will be taken up with arguments between the commanders, the tensions within this structure have to be understood now.

First of all, there was a disagreement between SHAEF and the American

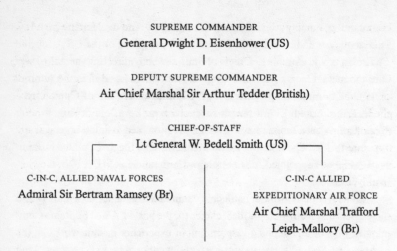

SUPREME COMMANDER
General Dwight D. Eisenhower (US)

DEPUTY SUPREME COMMANDER
Air Chief Marshal Sir Arthur Tedder (British)

CHIEF-OF-STAFF
Lt General W. Bedell Smith (US)

C-IN-C, ALLIED NAVAL FORCES
Admiral Sir Bertram Ramsey (Br)

C-IN-C ALLIED
EXPEDITIONARY AIR FORCE
Air Chief Marshal Trafford
Leigh-Mallory (Br)

GROUND FORCE COMMANDER FOR THE INVASION
General Sir Bernard Law Montgomery (Br)

Army Air Force Commander in Europe, General Carl Spaatz, about the need for a further layer of command at SHAEF in the shape of the Allied Expeditionary Air Force (AEAF). This was probably a valid argument, but it was undoubtedly exacerbated by the dislike felt by many Americans for the AEAF's British commander, Air Chief Marshal Trafford Leigh-Mallory. It has to be added that Spaatz's resistance to the AEAF was mainly over the AEAF claim to control of the *strategic* heavy bomber forces, the US Eighth Air Force and RAF Bomber Command, not over control of the two tactical air forces, the US Ninth and the British Second Tactical Air Force (2nd TAF). These tactical air forces were equipped with medium bombers and ground-attack fighters and were tasked to support the armies in the field. The role of the tactical air forces in the Battle of Normandy cannot be underestimated; in spite of a tendency to bomb and strafe their own troops on occasion, Allied victory in the Battle of Normandy owes much to the skill and dedication of the tactical air force crews.

The air force was also represented by the Deputy Allied Supreme Commander, Air Marshal Sir Arthur Tedder, who, as we shall see, was very anxious to secure the air forces a large share of the credit for the forthcoming Allied victory - a credit which was fully deserved and which no one denied. Tedder had no real grasp of ground operations – and no particular time for General Montgomery.

There was no argument over the naval member, Admiral Sir Bertram Ramsey. Even though the naval member on the US Joint Chiefs-of-Staff Committee and one of the Combined Chiefs-of-Staff, Admiral Ernest King, was a fervent Anglophobe, Ramsey was a competent and popular commander, with wide experience of amphibious operations. Besides, at sea the Anglo-US boot was on the other foot; the bulk of the shipping and naval forces on D-Day and for the subsequent supply of logistical support and reinforcements to the troops ashore would fly the White or Red Ensigns of the Royal Navy or the British Merchant Navy; in every way Admiral Ramsey was clearly the right man for the job.

The air and naval elements were not, however, the main area for potential trouble in Normandy. The area of contention involved the Land Forces Commander for the invasion phase of Overlord, General Montgomery, former commander of the Eighth Army in North Africa, victor of El Alamein, conqueror of Rommel, the most charismatic British soldier of the Second World War, and a man many people detested.

General Sir Bernard Law Montgomery was not an easy man to know – and a very hard man to like. 'Monty's biggest problem was vanity,' says Major General Shan Hackett, who served under Montgomery in the western desert and at Arnhem. 'He had his own way of doing things, thought he always knew best and was not open to criticism. On the other hand, with Monty at least you knew what was going on ... which is not always the case in military matters.'[5]

Monty was a hero to the British soldier, and the British public who saw him as the architect of victory. To the common soldier, the tank crew and the infantryman, Monty was a general who cared about them. Dennis Keen, a private in the Signals platoon of the 1st Battalion, The Worcester Regiment, 43rd Division, puts it like this:[6]

Monty was there. When he was in command you knew you had a commander, that someone was in charge. When we were stuck in the Reichwald in 1945, water everywhere, suddenly there was Monty, driving down the line in his jeep, tossing out packets of fags to the lads. When you were in trouble, Monty was around, not at the rear ... and it trickled down to the other officers. Another time, just after crossing the Seine in Normandy, we were held up by a couple of Tigers, and they were Tigers, not Mark IV's or anything, we had pictures later. We had no armour up, just our 6-pounder anti-tank guns, but up comes our Brigade Commander and then our Divisional Commander to sort things out. And that was because they took their tone from Monty. I am sure he was difficult, but we thought he knew what he was doing, and he did all right by us.

It is curious, and in some ways quite moving, to realise how in an age without television or widespread public relations, this small, neat, brusque general managed to make his presence felt throughout his armies, from divisional commanders to private soldiers. The relationship between a commander and his soldiers is always complex but it seems to come down to a matter of trust. The men trusted Monty with their lives because they knew him to be competent; soldiers much prefer a competent martinet to an easy going officer who does not know his job; an officer who knows his job will be popular.

Montgomery was no martinet and the trust between him and his soldiers cut both ways. 'It is the men who matter, not the machines,' he said in 1945, on leaving command of 21st Army Group. 'If you tell the British soldier what you want and launch him properly into battle, he will never let you down. Never!'

When Monty was around, men felt that matters were under control, that their lives would not be squandered, that their needs were understood. That is not always the case in military affairs – where chaos and shambles seem to rule – and Montgomery should be given considerable credit for his inestimable contribution to leadership and morale. Nor was this indispensable contribution confined to the British Army. In the months before D-Day, Monty visited all the US divisions under his command and US accounts record how well his visits went down with the US soldiers; here was an officer who had seen war at the sharp end and knew what he was doing.

However, most of the US generals did not like Monty. This feeling had its roots in the Anglophobia felt by many senior American officers, a feeling rooted in US history, where Britain – not Germany – is the ancestral enemy, the national opponent in the Revolution and the War of 1812. Mutual acquaintance did not always remedy this emotion; Americans mistook British reserve for snobbery, the British mistook American enthusiasm for brashness; both nationals thought the others rude but in Monty's case the issue often got personal.

Quite apart from the facts mentioned above – Monty's vanity and his brusqueness which many Americans certainly took for rudeness – many of them, especially George Patton, were jealous of Monty's greater experience and reputation, two assets that Montgomery did not labour to conceal. This comment has to be qualified by the fact that the better the US generals knew Monty, the better they understood him. They may not have *liked* him any better but they understood him, respected his abilities and could work with him.

Omar Bradley states that in Normandy, 'he could not have wished for a better or more understanding commander'. General Simpson, commander of the US Ninth Army, which served under Montgomery in the later stages of the campaign in north-west Europe, always got on well with Montgomery and the US liaison officers who served at Monty's headquarters had no difficulty coping with his ways.

That apart, it is fair to say that among the US generals in Normandy, Patton detested Montgomery, Bradley endured him – though their relations deteriorated after the Ardennes débâcle at the end of 1944 – and Eisenhower, knowing him better, tolerated and respected him. Patton's detestation was augmented by envy of Montgomery's reputation as a battlefield commander – and by the unadmitted fact that Patton and Montgomery were not dissimilar. George Patton had more than his fair share of bombast and vanity and Eisenhower would ruefully refer to Monty and Patton as 'my two prima donnas'.

Bernard Montgomery was a front-line soldier with plenty of varied experience in war. Commissioned into the Royal Warwickshire Regiment in 1908, he served on the north-west frontier of India against the Pathan tribesmen and went to France with his battalion in August 1914. In November he was severely wounded at the first battle of Ypres when leading an attack on the village of Meteran, an action for which he was promoted to captain and awarded the DSO, a rare distinction for a young platoon commander. On recovering from his wounds, he was appointed to the staff and spent the rest of the war successively as brigade major, then GSO2, first at a division and then at a corps HQ. He ended the war as GSO1, chief-of-staff of an infantry division.

The First World War taught Montgomery two lessons he never forgot. Firstly, that the battlefield is a confusing place and the task of a commander is to impose order on it, dictating the course of events by careful planning and meticulous staff work. Secondly, that the lives of his soldiers were precious, and must not be thrown away on ill-conceived attacks which offered no possibility of gain. Those other generals and historians, who sneer at Montgomery for being 'cautious' or 'timid' during the Normandy campaign should bear these two points in mind. He had 'been there', up at the sharp end; with a few rare exceptions, they had not.

Between the wars Montgomery served as instructor at the Staff Colleges at Camberley and Quetta in India, interspersing these staff appointments with spells commanding his regiment in Palestine; Monty never lost touch with the ordinary soldiers. During this time he suffered a personal blow from which he may never have recovered, the death of his much-loved wife, a lady who had humanised Montgomery and provided him with both affection and a range of interests outside the narrow world of his military profession. After her death the Monty of legend – incisive, critical, abrasive, self-regarding, more and more intolerant of failure – increasingly appears. Had she lived, it is at least arguable that Monty would not have developed those domineering characteristics that so infuriated his peers and superiors.

When the Second World War broke out in September 1939 Montgomery was a major general commanding a division in Palestine. Back in the UK, he was given command of the 3rd Infantry Division in the Dunkirk campaign. After the evacuation he was given command of II Corps in the south of England where his skill in training and motivating troops was noted by the CIGS (Chief of the Imperial General Staff) Field Marshal Sir Alan Brooke. However, Montgomery's great chance came in 1942 when he was sent to command Eighth Army in North Africa, arriving at the moment when this force had been driven back to Alamein by Rommel's Afrika Korps and disaster was looming.

Whatever his exploits in north-west Europe in 1944–5, the name of Montgomery will always be closely connected – at least in Britain – with the exploits of the Desert Army. Under his command Eighth Army drove the Axis powers back across North Africa to their final defeat at Tunis and then, in conjunction with American forces under Patton and Bradley, overran the island of Sicily and invaded Italy.

In January 1944, Monty returned to England to take up the post of Ground Forces Commander under Eisenhower for the invasion – and stepped immediately into a nest of controversy, much of it of his own making. Even so, whatever his personal flaws, Montgomery was by far the most experienced battlefield commander on the Allied side; compared with Montgomery the American commanders had very little battlefield experience; while it might have been more tactful not to point this out at the time, this is not a point any historian should ignore. Monty knew the score on the Allied command structure and was happy to serve under the American Supreme Commander, Eisenhower.

Dwight Eisenhower was appointed Supreme Commander of the Allied Expeditionary Force on Christmas Day, 1943. Eisenhower was then shown the Cossac plan and did not like it – at all. Eisenhower had the experience to know a good plan when he saw one and in his eyes the Cossac plan would not do. He showed it to Montgomery, who did not like it either and while Ike went to confer with the Allied leaders in Morocco and then with Marshall in Washington, he sent Montgomery to London to take a closer look at the plan and suggest modifications.

The basic Eisenhower–Montgomery objection was not the place chosen for the landings, the coast of Normandy in the bay of the Seine, but the width and weight of the assault. They wanted to attack on a wider front and with more troops, tanks and guns ... and they were right. The limitations of the Cossac plan were not the fault of General Morgan and his staff – a fact that Montgomery would have been wise to acknowledge and commiserate about, rather than dismiss General Morgan's plan as fundamentally flawed. As it was, with his usual lack of tact, Montgomery was scathing about the plan's shortcomings and his open disparagement of Cossac made a lifetime enemy of General Sir Frederick Morgan who was to remain at SHAEF in 1944 as British Deputy Chief-of-Staff to Eisenhower, an ideal position from which to poison the atmosphere when Montgomery's name came up. Morgan was also a close confidant of Sir Arthur Tedder, a man who had similar aims.

What Cossac needed and could not get from the Combined Chiefs – specifically the American admiral, Ernest King – was more landing craft. The prime reason for the short invasion frontage suggested by Cossac was a shortage of shipping, notably landing craft and especially the vital LSTs (Landing Ship, Tanks) which alone could carry the armoured divisions into the beach – and that was not Morgan's fault. The blame should have been laid at the door of Admiral Ernest King who controlled the allocation of ships to theatres and much preferred to send LSTs to the Pacific than to the 'British-dominated' ETO. There was also the problem, one which lies outside the scope of this book, of the US commitment to a landing in the south of France – Operation Anvil – later Operation Dragoon, to which the Americans were totally committed and the British totally opposed.

Eisenhower and Montgomery brooded over this problem for a while and finally decided, not least because it was vital to take the port of Cherbourg, that the front of the invasion must be broadened to include a landing on the Cotentin coast – subsequently Utah. It must also include another airborne division landing in the central Cotentin which would aid the Utah forces in moving north to take Cherbourg. If this meant putting back the date of the invasion and the Anvil/Dragoon operation, so be it. Once the armies were ashore their most vital need would be for a constant supply of reinforcements, ammunition and fuel. When it was all added up it meant that the invasion date must be put back from May to June, 1944 – something General Morgan and his staff had worked out months ago.

Cherbourg was the most obvious choice as the major port, but it was inevitable that after this port was finally in Allied hands it would have to be cleared of mines and booby traps and virtually rebuilt before it could be restored to working order. Until that could happen the invasion forces would be supplied through two prefabricated ports, the famous Mulberry harbours. One of these would be set up at Arromanches to supply the British and Canadian forces, the other off Omaha to supply the American armies.

These, therefore, were the basic parameters for the invasion phase. Get ashore, stay ashore, link up the beaches into one continuous bridgehead, take a port, build up the force ashore in the bridgehead, in the meantime using the Mulberries, then break out and move inland – and on to victory. That was the primary task of Operation Overlord and the job of deciding how to carry it out was handed over to General Montgomery and his Allied command, 21st Army Group.

Montgomery was generally regarded as the master of the planned, set-piece battle; American historians frequently make this point before moving on to state or imply that he was therefore totally useless at any other kind of battle. His plan for the Normandy battle would require the assistance of his American colleagues and its implementation would require the approval of his superior officer, General Eisenhower and the Combined Chiefs-of-Staff; but no one, at this time or at any level, disputed that Bernard Montgomery was the best man for this particular job – getting the armies ashore and winning the initial battle for Normandy. This would certainly start with a set-piece battle, to a plan laid before the first troops went ashore ... after that, who knew what would happen?

When Montgomery was handed this task in January 1944, the date for the landing was already fixed for May 1. He had less than five months to plan and carry out the biggest amphibious operation in recorded history and the extent of his task should not be underestimated. Neither should the problem of supply.

In most popular military histories, there is a natural tendency to concentrate on the battles and the exploits of the fighting troops. This, while understandable, has the effect of taking attention away from the underlying fact that without adequate and sustained logistical support, armies can neither fight nor function for long. Before closing this chapter it is therefore necessary to raise the argument beyond the 'muck and bullets' level and take a close look at the question of *logistics*, that arcane branch of the military art concerned with the problems of supply. This will be covered in some detail later but the importance of supply during the Normandy campaign has to be grasped now.

Consider the day-to-day requirements of three armies in the field. The troops will need everything from fuel, food and ammunition to cigarettes and toilet paper, and the rapid establishment of working ports was the most vital task for the Allied armies once they were 'ashore and firmly established'. The troops that splashed ashore on D-Day carried their weapons, a quantity of ammunition and a couple of twenty-four hour ration packs; that was not going to last them very long. Until proper ports could be set up they relied for supply on what could be landed over open beaches and at the Mulberry harbours, but these were of limited capacity and exposed – as we shall see – to the full force of the elements. It needs to be borne in mind that one purpose of pulling the German forces on to the Second Army front and shielding the US First Army from heavy counter-attacks from the east was to allow the US forces to advance north to Cherbourg and west into Brittany as quickly as possible, where their prime purpose was not to gain ground but to seize ports.

As for threatening or taking Caen, this city was more important to the Germans than it was to the Allies. For Montgomery, the importance of Caen was its importance to the Germans. Without doubt they would strain all their resources to retain it and prevent an Allied breakout to the south and east which would cut off those German forces deeper in western Normandy. With luck and good judgement on the Allied side, this strain would eventually stretch the German resources until they broke.

In Montgomery's calculations – if not those he started with, certainly those he quickly arrived at – the Germans would be most anxious to hang on to Caen. Therefore, to defend it they would be obliged to commit whatever forces they had. There was still an element of calculation here for it was equally important that the Germans did not commit those of the Fifteenth Army, mainly located north of the Seine on D-Day and kept there by Operation Fortitude. If Fifteenth Army intervened in Normandy before the Allied build-up was complete – and perhaps even after that – matters might go beyond Allied control.

There was an inherent if unavoidable snag with this strategy, as we shall see later. The US armies had to seize ports and ground *in the west*, while the direction the Allied armies must eventually head lay north and east. But after the breakout, the further the Allies advanced to the north and east the longer their supply lines would become. For the moment there was no help for this. In the days and weeks after D-Day the troops ashore needed supply simply to hold the ground they already held. This was phase two, where our story really begins, the build-up after D-Day, when the Allied bridgehead and the troops within it began to come under steady and mounting pressure from the troops of the German forces defending Normandy and their doughty commander, Erwin Rommel.

3 THE GERMANS JUNE 7

We must defeat the enemy on the beaches and on the first day
of the landing – that will be the longest day.

FIELD MARSHAL ERWIN ROMMEL Commander, Army Group B, Normandy, 1944

Field Marshal Erwin Rommel, once head of the doughty Afrika Korps and now commander of Army Group B in Normandy was a great general but not a lucky one. When the two great crises broke over his command, Montgomery's attack at El Alamein in October 1942 and the D-Day landings of June 1944, Rommel was absent from his headquarters and unable to exert any immediate influence on the battle. On June 5, having been told by his meteorologists that the Channel gales made a landing impossible, he returned to Germany for his wife's birthday. Had he been at his HQ and fully in charge of events, matters might have been handled very differently in those first, few, vital hours – always assuming he had been allowed a free hand by the German Führer, Adolf Hitler.

The German command structure in France was as shown on page 66.

One point about this structure should be noticed; the looming presence of the German Chancellor and Führer, Adolf Hitler. Hitler took a close and detailed interest in the battle for Normandy, kept four crack divisions – 1 SS Panzer, 12 SS Panzer, and 17 SS Panzer Grenadiers and Panzer Lehr – in OKW reserve, from which they could not be moved without his personal order, and he felt free to interfere with the commanders' decisions, down to the lowest level. Two of these divisions, 12 SS and Panzer Lehr, were moved to Normandy in April 1944 – but they remained in OKW reserve.

The next point to note is that Panzer Group West, which contained most of

OBERKOMMANDO DER WEHRMACHT
Adolf Hitler

OBERKOMMANDO WEST (OB-WEST)
Field Marshal Gerd von Rundstedt

COMMANDER, PANZER GROUP WEST
General Gyer von Schweppenburg

COMMANDER, ARMY GROUP B
Field Marshal Erwin Rommel

Fifteenth Army
North of the Seine

Seventh Army
South of the Seine

the remaining Panzer divisions in the west – 9 and 11 Panzer, 2nd, 116 and 21st Panzer – though under the command of Geyr von Schweppenburg who was in turn responsible to von Rundstedt, could also only be deployed on Hitler's orders. It is fair to add that von Schweppenburg also had a very direct say in how and where the divisions of Panzer Group West were to be deployed thereafter ... and his views varied more than somewhat from those of the Army Group B commander, Erwin Rommel.[1]

Field Marshal Rommel had been posted to France in December 1943. His first task, as charged by the Führer, was a total inspection of the Atlantic Wall defences, the western bastion of Hitler's 1,000-Year Reich. Rommel toured the Atlantic Wall from Norway to the Spanish frontier and was horrified by what he found. In all but a few places, most notably the Pas de Calais and the Normandy coast, the wall did not really exist beyond a few strands of barbed wire, the occasional machine-gun post, a few artillery pieces and a scattering of mines.

If it was to offer any kind of obstacle to the Allied invasion the Atlantic Wall would need to be rapidly developed and supplied with a quantity of troops, guns and tanks but there was, inevitably, a snag. The wall was simply too long for Germany's current resources. To create adequate defences along a thousand miles of coast was impossible but fortunately unnecessary. For a defender to foresee what an attacker will do, it is only necessary to calculate what the defender would do in his place. In the case of Overlord, German calculations revealed that the likely places for an Allied invasion between Norway and the Spanish frontier could be reduced to just two; the Pas de Calais and the Calvados coast of Normandy.

The calculations were complicated but the deciding factor was air power. In the Pas de Calais, twenty miles from Dover, Allied fighters could easily dominate the landing area and beat off any attempts by the Luftwaffe to interfere with the invasion. The Normandy beaches were further away, some eighty miles from the south coast of England but the Allied air forces could still dominate Normandy from English bases, even with fighters – and in 1944 Allied fighter range was steadily increasing. The Brittany coast, further west, had more ports and fewer defences but was beyond the range of fighter cover and exposed to Atlantic gales, while north of the Pas de Calais the landing beaches south of the Belgian frontier led towards the 1914–18 Western Front of fatal memory.

For attacker and defender, therefore, the choice clearly lay between Normandy and the Pas de Calais. These were the areas the Germans opted to defend and which the Allied commanders prepared to threaten: Normandy with the actual invasion, Operation Overlord, the Pas de Calais with a 'spoof' invasion, Operation Fortitude and deciding which was which would be one of the prime concerns of the German commanders. Having delivered his report, Rommel applied for a field command in the west and was appointed to the command of Army Group B under Field Marshal Gerd von Rundstedt, a post which would make Rommel directly responsible for repelling the invasion, wherever the Allies came ashore.

Gerd von Rundstedt was sixty-nine in 1944. He was born near Halle in 1875, the scion of a military family, and entered the officer corps in 1892 at the age of seventeen. By 1914 he had reached the rank of captain in the Imperial Army, having already passed the staff course and served in several staff appointments. In August 1914 he was promoted major but failed to make any further advances in rank for the rest of the war. Staying on into the peace, he was promoted general in 1927 and in October 1932 was promoted to full general and command of the 1st Army Group. A year later, in 1933, Adolf Hitler came to power in Germany.

There is no evidence that von Rundstedt was a great supporter of the Führer but he played a full part in the re-equipping of the Wehrmacht and its training in the tactics of blitzkrieg. In the process von Rundstedt was promoted yet again, to colonel general, but in November 1938 – now aged sixty-three – he left active duty and was placed on the retired list.

Von Rundstedt was not on the retired list for long. He returned to active duty in June 1939 and was given command of Army Group South which he commanded in the invasion of Poland, during which his troops took the city of Warsaw. A month later, in October 1939, von Rundstedt was appointed to Army Group A in the west and led that group in the invasion of France and the Low Countries in the summer of 1940, being rewarded for his success with promotion to the rank of field marshal – a promotion he shared that day with eleven other German generals.

Then von Runstedt's star began to dim somewhat. His next appointment took him back to Army Group South for Operation Barbarossa, the invasion of Russia in June 1941, where his group was tasked with overrunning the Caucasus. When the Führer refused to allow a tactical withdrawal at one stage in the campaign, von Rundstedt resigned and was again placed on the retired list but, as before, his retirement did not last long. In March 1942 he was recalled to active duty and given the temporary post of Commander-in-Chief West. This appointment was confirmed in May 1942 and von Rundstedt was still holding it when Rommel arrived in France in the winter of 1943.

By that time von Rundstedt had largely lost interest in the war. His time in France and the Low Countries over the last two years had not been a happy one. Tasked to build up the western defences by Hitler's Directive No. 40 of March 23, 1942, he was kept short of troops, especially of well-equipped and fully trained front line formations, of armour, artillery and all the wherewithal, in mines, wire and concrete to construct adequate beach defences. There was also constant pressure from OKW. From the day of his appointment von Rundstedt was badgered by Hitler, by Colonel General Alfred Jodl, the Führer's Chief-of-Staff, and by Colonel General Wilhelm Keitel, chief of OKW – a man known in the Wehrmacht as 'Hitler's lackey' – to do better, move faster and ensure the security of the west so that the Führer's staff could concentrate on the steadily worsening situation in the east. Von Rundstedt could not obtain the resources necessary to create a real barrier along the western coast and privately considered Hitler a madman and the war as good as lost. However, if young Rommel wanted to expend his energies in attempting to coax the necessities out of Hitler and fortify the wall for the coming invasion, Gerd von Rundstedt was not going to stand in his way.

Rommel's work in strengthening the Atlantic Wall falls outside the borders of this book; enough to say that he did all that any commander could have done in the circumstances but it was not enough to keep the invaders out. Rommel never believed that the wall alone, however strong and well-defended, could achieve that purpose on its own. The successful defeat of the forthcoming invasion depended on selecting the right strategy and there the choice lay between defeating the invading forces on the beaches or a heavy commitment of reserves to drive them into the sea in the days after the landing – once it had been established that this was the real landing and not a feint.

In the spring of 1944, the German field commanders in Normandy – essentially Rommel and von Schweppenburg – held two basic but conflicting points of view on how to defeat the invasion. Rommel believed that since the Allies had control of the air it would be difficult, if not impossible, to bring up adequate reserves and drive the Allies out once they were firmly established ashore. Rommel therefore believed that the Allies must be defeated on the beaches and ordered his troops to prepare for battle on the day of the landings – the 'longest day', as he called it. His men were to dig-in along the shore and be supplied with all the support he could muster – mines, wire, artillery, machine-guns and tanks – and fight the enemy on the tide line. In Rommel's view, the first day would be vital. According to Major Hans von Luck of 21 Panzer: 'Rommel told me that if the Allies will land and we cannot throw them back into the sea in twenty-four hours, it is the beginning of the end.'[2]

Other opinions held that with 1,200 miles of coast to defend and inadequate resources available, an Allied landing could not be prevented, even in the two most likely areas, which in themselves covered many miles of coast. This being so, it would be as well to let the Allies land, establish exactly where they were and only then hurl all the available reserves, especially a quantity of armour, against the bridgehead and drive the invaders into the sea. The main proponent of this view was Geyr von Schweppenburg but he was supported by von Rundstedt. Von Rundstedt's strategy also depended on hanging on to the major ports – 'fortress positions' in the German plan – thereby denying the Allies the opportunity to swiftly build up their forces while German reserves were mustered in quantity to smite the Allies hard. This aspect of the plan had its less beneficial side for the defence of these fortress ports tied up many troops in garrison and employed a quantity of artillery in static defence.

All these views have merit, depending on the circumstances, but in the circumstances of June 1944, Rommel's decision to fight on the beaches was probably right. However, as we shall see in future chapters, Rommel's decision to do so had unforeseen consequences that were not entirely for the good of his troops, not least that they were thereby exposed to the devastating effects of naval gunfire and tied into static defence to retain ground which the Führer refused to let them abandon.

Rommel and his troops laboured on their defences throughout the spring and early summer of 1944 and in the end they were able to create, in certain parts of the coast, a wall that was extremely tough but very thin. This again provided an inherent problem because the essence of any defence is *depth*. Had time and resources permitted Rommel intended to create a defensive system in Normandy some six miles deep, crammed with troops and strongpoints and carpeted by 200 *million* mines. Fortunately for the Allies, time did not permit the completion of such a system. Beyond the beaches there were few defences apart from those provided by the local terrain although, as we shall see, this terrain – the Normandy *bocage* – was to prove more than adequate when manned by resolute, well-trained and well-equipped soldiers and sown with vast numbers of mines.

Apart from adequate defences, Rommel was short of men and equipment, especially artillery and armour. Army Group B contained two armies, the Seventh Army, stationed south of the Seine, and the Fifteenth Army, largely stationed north of that river, though some Fifteenth Army units were deployed west of Honfleur, on the Seine estuary. We are mainly concerned here with the troops committed south of the river, before or during the battle; once the Seine was crossed, the Battle of Normandy was officially over. The British Official History records,[3] that between June 6 and August 31 – during the Battle of Normandy – the Allies were confronted by a total of four German armies, the Seventh, Fifteenth, Fifth Panzer Army (formerly Panzer Group West) and finally by elements of the First Army, in all consisting of thirteen corps, mustering a total of fifty-one divisions. Not all of these were committed at one time and the main force confronting the Allies for much of the Battle of Normandy was the Seventh Army, commanded at the start of the battle by General Friedrich Dollman.

Dollman's command on the eve of the invasion can best be described from the west. From the Cotentin peninsula to the west bank of the river Orne, Normandy was defended by troops of the 84th (LXXXIV) Infantry Corps. Again from the west, this consisted of the 243rd Division in the Cotentin, the 709th Division in Cherbourg and along the east coast as far as the Vire estuary, followed by the 352nd and 716th Infantry Divisions which defended the coast from the western side of the Vire estuary to the eastern side of the river Orne. Apart from the 352nd, all these divisions were static formations, largely dependent on horse transport; horses were in general use in the German Army throughout the Second World War, only the SS divisions and some select armoured formations being fully mechanised. There were a number of other formations, including the crack 6th Parachute Regiment and the well-trained 91st Air Landing Division, both based at the foot of the Cotentin. A study of the map on page 26 will be helpful at this point in identifying these places.

One chronic problem facing the commanders in Normandy was the steady seepage of their best units to the Eastern Front. These tended to be the armoured divisions, especially SS Panzer divisions and other first-class formations, which were only replaced, if at all, by troops of lesser quality, inadequately trained and without the latest equipment.

This gloomy situation began to change somewhat in the winter of 1943–4 and by D-Day the number of divisions in the west had been increased, in number, equipment and performance, an increase duly reported to the Allied commanders by Ultra, the intelligence information obtained by British cryptographers at Bletchley Park, who had cracked the secret of the German Enigma machines in 1940. Ultra decrypts confirmed that by the end of May 1944, there were only eighteen German divisions in Normandy and Brittany. Only two of these divisions, the 91st Air Landing and 352nd Infantry, were fully equipped and properly trained field divisions and the only infantry reserve close to the beaches was the 6th Parachute Regiment which was held around the town of Carentan.

Normandy had been a backwater of the war since 1940 so in spite of Hitler's decision to reinforce the west in 1944, many of the regiments and battalions in these formations were second-rank, filled with older men or those with chronic health and fitness problems – 'stomach' battalions in the jargon of the time – or had been topped-up with unreliable volunteers from Soviet Russia and the Balkans; in some German battalions various forms of paybook were needed to cope with the Cossacks, Rumanians, Georgians, Serbs and Tartars these units now contained.

The other obvious German failure at the start of the battle was a shortage of armour. The only Panzer unit close to the coast on D-Day was 21 Panzer which had been deployed south of Caen, astride the road to Falaise. There were two more Panzer divisions close by, 12 SS Panzer around Évreux and Panzer Lehr on the plain of the Beauce, close to the city of Chartres. As noted, both divisions had been in OKW reserve but both of these were offered to OB-West – von Rundstedt – on D-Day and were on the move towards the beaches before dawn on D plus 1.

Colonel Helmut Ritgen of Panzer Lehr comments:[4]

> There was to have been a major attack by 1 SS Panzer Corps within 48 hours of the landing, a violent attack by three panzer divisions but for various reasons, notably Allied air power, this did not happen – only 21 Panzer got forward and they had to come back. The beach defences were therefore not reinforced and these were not strongly held. For example, on the British and Canadian beaches, the 716th Division was a static division, almost without transport other than horse-drawn, and made up of elderly soldiers with little or no combat experience.

Nor were these German divisions all up to strength. Some armoured divisions, which should have had 200 tanks, had less than 100 tanks of various types, and the formidable Tigers with their 88mm guns were – fortunately for the British tank crews – very unreliable and required much maintenance. German infantry divisions were now being reduced in establishment from around 14,000 men to about 8,000 men, far fewer than the ration strength in a British or American division. The SS Panzer divisions, on the other hand, were being brought up to a field strength of 22,000 men and equipped where possible with Mark V Panthers or the Mark VI Tiger, although the bulk of their armour was still the Mark IV.

For example, on May 19, Ultra reported the presence close to Normandy of 1 SS Panzer (Adolf Hitler), up to strength with over 20,000 men. This decrypt gave no equipment details for 1 SS but the same decrypt supplied the equipment scale for 2 SS Panzer (Das Reich), then based at Toulouse. This unit had fifty-five Mark IV's and thirty-seven Mark V Panthers on strength with forty-six Mark

IVs and sixty-two Panthers still to be delivered. A month earlier 2 SS Panzer had a ration strength of 17,000 men and at about the same time Ultra reported that the strength of 12 SS Panzer amounted to 22,390 men. An SS Panzer division therefore had almost three times the manpower of a Wehrmacht infantry division and much greater firepower.

Although all these units were to be 'written down' in the fighting the evidence suggests that the SS Panzer units and Panzer units in general were always going to be stronger in manpower and better equipped than any Wehrmacht infantry division. These Panzer units also contained strong infantry elements – panzer grenadiers, motorised infantry. That element apart, the German advantage lay in their equipment which was, in almost every respect, superior to that of the Allied armies, and to the fact that they were good soldiers, fighting on the defensive. The problem for Rommel and his commanders was that they did not have enough of them, and reinforcements and replacements would be hard to come by.

Les Wager, then a rifleman in 'C' Company, 1st Bn, The Queen's Own Rifles of Canada, gives a personal view of these German soldiers:[5]

> The German soldiers came in all types. If we were up against the Waffen-SS, Hitler Jugend or paratroops, we knew we were up against a soldier who might be our superior, man to man. If they were 12 SS, Hitler Jugend, we hated them with a ferocity that still prevails. Why? Because we found several of our Brigade lined up against a wall and shot by the 12 SS Panzer Division and we had an absolute order about them by D plus 12 – no prisoners. This order was verbal, not written. We took SS officers, but only for interrogation purposes. Such Hitler Jugend thugs as I observed or tried to speak to displayed no civilising virtues whatsoever, even in the face of certain execution.
>
> The ordinary German soldier, who might well not be a German, quite often fought only as long as he had an officer or a non com. to answer to. We had no animus for these. They were the same as us, caught in the awful inevitability of a war neither of us wanted or made.

Reg Rolfe of 41 (Royal Marine) Commando also comments on the German infantry soldier:[6]

> Their mortaring was very good and constant, and they had the six-barrelled *nebelwerfer* or Moaning Minnie, which was really bad. My mate Blondie

Thwaites was killed by a mortar fragment at Salenelles. The German snipers were good and they were very adept at booby traps and had strong fighting patrols. When we sent out a patrol it usually consisted of a big section, say 16 men; the German patrols always had about 50 men and lots of automatic weapons. To sum up on the Normandy battle? I think it was a pretty close-run thing.

Ted Morris, a medical orderly with 225 Parachute Field Ambulance was captured by the Germans when attending to some wounded:

I was searched and they made me and the escort carry the stretcher and we set off towards their lines. At a cross road I told the escort to put the stretcher down while I dressed Eddy Walker's stomach wound, having indicated to the Germans what I was going to do. This task was interrupted by a big Jerry officer waving a machine-pistol who kicked me to my feet and made us march on guarded by a small Jerry also armed with a machine-pistol. Later on I was interrogated – name rank and number was all they got – and the German said 'You are Sixth Airborne' and let me go and I was taken to a cookhouse where a German soldier said we were soldiers like them and we were fed. After a day or so I was put in charge of some wounded prisoners and we left for the rear through Yvetot. On the whole the front line troops treated us all right.

Brian Guy, a sapper with 246 Field Company, RE in the 3rd British Infantry Division has his memories of this time:

My abiding memory of Normandy is the noise and the smell. The noise of mortars, shells, tank engines and in the little fields the *bocage* with high hedges and narrow lanes, the mines and the machine-guns. Then there was the smell, wherever you went the smell of death, human and animal. The sound of wounded cattle is painful to recall and the cows, all bloated up, their legs sticking into the air, are an abiding memory.

Our soldiers did not always get buried and the stench of death was overpowering. I still have an impression of the faces of the dead, pale orange when recently killed, then turning black as corruption overtook them. The Germans had a smell of their own, quite distinctive, a sickly scented, pungent smell, probably from his cooking stoves. I also hated the sound of Spandau fire – it always reminded me of someone tearing canvas.

It takes very little time to make a veteran. I remember a night that was typical of Normandy. I arrived back in our area after being in contact with the enemy all day, so tired that I did not dig a hole; I just lay down and fell asleep. When I awoke I discovered that I had dead Germans buried all around me but so shallow that their feet and boots stuck out of the ground. The telling thing about this is that I thought nothing of it at the time.

I recall the superiority of the German weapons while we were armed with weapons like the Sten gun that fired when you did not want it to and would not fire when you did. All over Normandy lay the wreckage of burnt-out tanks, the remains of bodies melted into the ground, remains of battledress, steel helmets, abandoned trenches, rifles, unused shells and mortar rounds, all the detritus of war. Normandy was a murderous place, a murderous place!

To defend this murderous place Rommel needed more divisions, infantry or armoured – and he had to have them on hand before the battle began. Otherwise German reinforcement divisions must be brought down from north of the Seine, from Fifteenth Army or up from the south or centre of France or switched from the defence of Brittany. Apart from the inevitable delay, these units would come under air attack every metre of the way. The swiftest support for Seventh Army should have come from the Fifteenth Army which had twenty infantry divisions and four Panzer divisions deployed to cover the other likely invasion area, the Pas de Calais. On Hitler's orders, this army was kept north of the Seine, largely because he was fooled by Operation Fortitude, the elaborate but highly successful Allied deception plan which had convinced Hitler and most of the OKW staff that the Normandy landings on June 6 were only a feint and that the main landing would come later, astride Calais.

A glance at the map on page 116 reveals that Rommel's plan, to fight the decisive battle on the beaches, was done for even before the battle began. The widespread deployment of German reserves, a complicated command structure and a reluctance to accept that the Normandy landings were serious – plus Allied air power – would cause a critical delay in moving up reserves, and the forces already manning the beach defences were simply not sufficient to prevent the Allies getting ashore. The Battle of Normandy would therefore take place in the hinterland in the weeks after D-Day and this being so it is now necessary to consider the ground over which the fighting would take place and again a study of the map on page 26 will be useful.

The countryside of Normandy is green, rolling and highly agreeable, a mixture of arable and pasture land, dotted with orchards and woods and a quantity of grey stone villages and small towns. This terrain is seamed with gentle rivers and supplied with a number of hills and ridges, rising to heights which, although moderate, still overlook the surrounding countryside and offer extensive views. Some parts, beginning south-west of Caen and stretching towards St-Lô, are made up of *bocage,* small fields surrounded by high banks and hedges, divided by narrow lanes leading to small hamlets and stone-built farmhouses. In peacetime Normandy is a delightful province; in wartime the terrain of Normandy is clearly favourable to the defence.

One point to note are the rivers. The river Seine marks the northern boundary of the battle area but there are plenty of other rivers, large and small, of which the Orne, the Seulles, the Vire and the Dives will be crucial to this story; and the Orne and the Odon, in their steep-sided valleys, present a particular obstacle to tanks. These rivers rise in the high hinterland, some fifty miles from the Calvados coast, and although they meander east and west, their general flow is south to north.

These rivers split the front for an attacker coming south from the Calvados coast, and provide a good defensive line for anyone resisting an attack from the west, especially after the river banks have been breached and encouraged to flood the surrounding countryside. Any attack pushing out of Normandy to the east must either go well south and head east, south of the rivers, along the line Avranches–Mortain–Domfront–Alençon, or face a series of waterlogged river valleys with high ridges, woods and hills, virtually impassable to armour.

Normandy is by no means flat. The area immediately south of Caen, astride the valley of the Orne, is so rocky and steep-sided that it is known locally as the *Suisse Normande* – 'Normandy's Switzerland' – and the area is dominated by high ground running roughly south and east from Vire towards Alençon, ground overlooked in turn by rising ground and a number of hills, of which Hill 112 (112m), the Bourguébus ridge and Mont Pinçon (365m) would provide particular obstacles to the British and Canadian forces in the weeks after D-Day.

Although modern farming methods and the ripping-out of hedgerows has changed much of the Norman countryside – and this factor has to be allowed for by modern historians – a critical examination of the ground reveals little to choose in defensive capability between the ground on the Second Army front and that on the First Army front. The Americans had to face marshes and the *bocage*; the British had to overcome rolling country, with plenty of 'dead ground' and forest, and the steep-sided Odon and Orne valleys, where tanks could make only slow progress and be highly vulnerable in the process. The Second Army front also had its fair share of *bocage* and was also narrowed by the *Suisse Normande* which straddles the country south of Caen and forced the British and Canadians into a south-easterly path which the Germans were able to block with a series of defence lines south of Caen. However, the most formidable type of country was the *bocage*.

Linked to the *Suisse Normande* south of Caen and spreading west to the country north of St-Lô, this dense network of small fields, woods, narrow sunken lanes, stone farmhouses and small villages inland from the coast creates a terrain virtually impenetrable except to soldiers on foot. The *bocage* – the 'hedgerow country', as most American accounts call it – lies behind the beaches and is particularly concentrated in the west of the Calvados department, south of Omaha and in the direction of St-Lô. More *bocage* is found in other parts of the province – villages named Villers-Bocage and Beny-Bocage on the British front indicate that not only the Americans had to fight in the hedgerow country – and this close country was to prove a sore trial to the Allied tank crews and a testing ground for the infantry.

Only after the *bocage* had been penetrated could the invaders reach more open country, where they could flex their muscles, territory where tank forces, artillery and air power could be used with great effect and mobility restored to the battlefield. It is worth noting that none of the Allied units tasked to fight in such terrain were trained in such surroundings; for example, while in England the US 29th and 4th Infantry Divisions were trained on the open, treeless expanses of Salisbury Plain and Dartmoor, whereas the British 7th Armoured Division was trained in Norfolk. Anywhere less like the terrain in which these divisions had to fight in Normandy is hard to imagine.

There was more open country near to the Calvados coast, most notably at Carpiquet west of Caen and on the high plain between Caen and Falaise, ground which the Allied air forces were most anxious to obtain as landing fields, but this ground was well defended, the Bourguébus area with six separate but interlocked defensive lines, while the Carpiquet area led south to the Odon and Orne valleys and the *Suisse Normande*. Open country does not extend far anywhere in Normandy and it was necessary to get beyond Caen and St-Lô, two crucial and well-defended positions, in order to reach it at all.

Beyond these places the Allies could use more of their strength but until they had taken the *bocage* and burst through the German defensive lines on the Odon, the Orne and at Bourguébus they were confined in an area where the enemy could punish them with short effective blows, using tanks and infantry in small units of company size, with the deep and narrow lanes providing plenty of overhead cover against aircraft for the tanks and the hedgerows offering perfect positions for snipers, machine-gunners and men equipped with mortars and the deadly German anti-tank weapon, the *Panzerfaust* – the 'tank fist' – or the *Panzerschreck,* the German version of the American rocket-launcher, or bazooka.

Ground itself is not an obstacle ... unless it is covered by fire. Here too the Germans had an advantage, as Sydney Jary of the Somerset Light Infantry relates:[7]

> Basically, the Germans had more firepower than we did and better weapons. Their tanks were better than our tanks – with the possible exception of the Sherman Firefly. Their 81mm mortar was better than our 3-inch mortar, their machine-guns, the MG-34 and MG-42, being belt-fed weapons, were better in the defensive role than the 28-round-magazine Bren gun, certainly in the attacking role. The result was that we could not hope to suppress their fire with platoon weapons alone and yet suppressing the enemy fire is the essence of the basic infantry tactic, fire and movement. You use your fire to suppress the enemy fire and then you can move – which is a good tactic provided you can suppress their fire. But when you are facing an interlinked combination of dug-in automatic weapons, each with a far higher rate of fire than anything you have, how do you suppress it?
>
> I have lost count of the times we were forced to ground while a massive amount of German firepower descended on us, tearing up the ground, shredding branches off the trees; a section of two MG-42s, the German infantry section weapon, as we had the Bren or the American BAR, could deliver 2,400 rounds a minute. That is not an easy thing to go against. We tried various firepower combinations including carrying two Brens per section but the problems of carting enough 28-round magazines and ammunition about when your sections – which should be ten men – are already understrength, proved insurmountable. In that close country the best asset we had, the only one that really

made a difference, was our artillery and there at least we did have the edge. The British gunners in Normandy – the Royal Artillery – were simply superb.

Beyond the beaches, the *bocage*, the *Suisse Normande* and high ground like Mont Pinçon, the Bourguébus ridge and Hill 112 represented a second line of defence for the German forces. This line would be harder to penetrate than the beach defences because the invader's main assets, gunfire support from warships, artillery and tanks, could not be fully brought to bear; the competing forces were too entangled, too close together. Fighting in the *bocage* and across the Odon and Orne valleys called for troops well-versed in close-quarter infantry fighting; in such terrain the well-trained German soldiers, especially those in the SS units, had a clear advantage.

Strongpoints among these natural defences were formed by the towns and villages. Tilly-sur-Seulles, Montebourg, Carentan, Villers-Bocage, Flers, Mortain, all appear in Allied accounts of the Normandy fighting, as places where battles within a battle were fought, places where German and Allied units, infantry and armour, slugged it out hand to hand, sometimes for days, sometimes for weeks. And then there were positions like Caumont and Évrecy, Mont Pinçon and Hill 112, which provided good observation points to the German artillery observers and had to be taken step by painful step as the battle wore on.

Jack Capell of the 8th Infantry Regiment, 4th US Infantry Division, also mentions the German defences:[8]

On our way up the Cotentin to Montebourg we were cheered one morning by the arrival of nine Sherman tanks in support; by nightfall six of them had been knocked out. The situation at that time appeared grim for we had thought that if the D-Day landings were successful and a good beachhead established the German defences would collapse. By the time we got up to Cherbourg we had begun to realise there was a long war ahead, for the Germans were tough fighters, unwilling to give up ground.

A landing in Normandy gave the Allies the best launching pad for the eventual conquest of the Reich but no appreciation of the difficulties facing the troops – and their commanders – is possible without a full understanding of the difficulties presented by the terrain – and the German Army. It is this combination, of defensive terrain filled with the well-trained and well-equipped soldiers of the German Army, that caused the Allied commanders grave and unexpected problems in the days and weeks after D-Day.

The immediate task of the Allies after D-Day was to link up the beachheads and bring more men and equipment ashore. The task of the German defenders was to drive the invaders into the sea before they could get properly established; whether the Germans succeeded in this task or not depended very largely on their Panzer divisions.

At midnight on D-Day – 2359hrs on June 6 – 21 Panzer was drawn up north of Caen, ready to defend the city after a confused day of fighting which had seen them halt the forces advancing from Sword at Riva Bella, but lose more than 70 of their 120 tanks in the process. 21 Panzer had advanced to the out-skirts of Lion-sur-Mer that afternoon before the massive evening glider drop to reinforce 6th Airborne obliged it to draw back towards Caen and go over to the defensive. Even so, 21 Panzer and the resistance put up by other German troops had prevented Second Army reaching Caen. As we shall see, the effects of that action would be far-reaching.

Colonel Helmut Ritgen of Panzer Lehr explains what happened at this time to some of the German forces outside Caen:[9]

> After the landings on the night of 5/6th June, 21 Panzer had been thrown piecemeal into the battle to counter the British airborne landings north of Caen. This move was halted when more British airborne in gliders landed in our rear and by the evening of D-Day the British had captured a coastal strip six miles long but not very deep. In vain the exhausted German defenders looked for reinforcements but all the local reserves had been used up. However, C-in-C West – von Rundstedt – had ordered increased readiness for Panzer Group West – von Schweppenburg – which included Panzer Lehr, 12 SS Panzer and 17 SS Panzer Grenadier Division, now released from OKW control.
>
> Then 12 SS Panzer was put under command of Army Group B and Colonel Kurt Meyer led them towards a sector east of the Orne. Movement was difficult because of enemy air activity during the day and failures of our radio sets. However, marching at night turned out to be reasonably safe and Panzer Lehr, my unit, made good progress towards the Flers–Vire area, using routes we had previously reconnoitred. We finally went into the line on June 9.

Some idea of the quality of the German forces defending Normandy is set out in this brief account. 12 SS Panzer was a superbly trained and equipped unit, manned by enthusiastic former members of the Hitler Youth – the Hitler Jugund – and led by some of the most battle-hardened and experienced officers in the Waffen SS, people like Colonel Kurt Meyer. These SS units had the pick of the tanks, equipment and training facilities and were noticeably larger than non-SS Panzer units – as already noted, 12 SS Panzer had over 20,000 men. Panzer Lehr, commanded by General Fritz von Bayerlein, was another fine tank unit. The word *lehr* means 'training' but Panzer Lehr was no training formation. This division had been the demonstration unit for the Wehrmacht's tank forces and had new Tiger tanks armed with the 88mm gun, plenty of Panthers and Mark IVs and the pick of the non-SS officers and men. Both divisions were to give a good account of themselves in the Normandy fighting.

As already related, the arrival of airborne reinforcements on the afternoon of D-Day obliged 21 Panzer to call off their bid for the beaches. Had it succeeded this move would have split the British on Sword from the Canadian forces coming ashore on Juno. On June 7, 21 Panzer concentrated on holding the British away from Caen and putting in small localised counter-attacks against the 6th Airborne perimeter which was still consolidating on the Ranville ridge. This enabled 12 SS Panzer and Panzer Lehr to form up alongside 21 Panzer when they arrived in the area during June 7 and on the night of June 7–8.

On June 7, 12 SS Panzer was led into action by Colonel Kurt Meyer of 25 SS Panzer Grenadier Regiment, and quickly collided with troops of the 3rd Canadian Division moving on Carpiquet airfield, west of Caen. These two divisions fought it out for the next two days, German tanks and Panzer grenadiers against Canadian anti-tank guns and infantry. This battle was fought with notable ferocity with few prisoners taken on either side – and little quarter given to those Canadians who did surrender.

The soldiers of 12 SS Panzer were mostly young men, eighteen and nineteen years of age, the same as most of the other German soldiers in Normandy – not children as some have alleged – but all convinced Nazis and men not open to pity. On June 7, Meyer's men shot twenty-three Canadian prisoners at the village of Buron, north-west of Caen, and the division continued to shoot prisoners and French villagers throughout the Normandy campaign – and there is little doubt that the Allied units shot SS prisoners in reprisal.[10]

Tough, ruthless and well trained though they were, 12 SS met their match in the Canadians, who beat off all attempts to break through to the sea and were pushed back in a smart little action by the marines of 46 (Royal Marine) Commando, attached to the Canadians around the village of Rots.[11] Bud Hess of the Fort Garry Horse, a Canadian regiment, gives us an account of the battle for Rots:[12]

Rots is a small village on a river near Carpiquet airport and with a tree-lined valley leading up to clusters of farm buildings, an easy place to defend. The Régiment de la Chaudière and the British Commandos were making the attack, I do not know in what strength, but 'A' Squadron of the Fort Garrys went in as well, in support. During the whole day I cannot recall seeing any tanks apart from German ones – plus the four in my Troop.

We made our way down the valley for a couple of miles against light resistance, some on the right flank, until we reached the bridge into the village where there was a road block and plenty of defenders where we had our first chance to try out our high explosive shells. These would penetrate a building and explode inside so in no time we had cleared the area and taken a few prisoners. This did not clear the road so we went through the back gardens and upon breaking through a row of trees came on a group of Germans setting up a long-barrelled gun about 20ft in front of us. We were looking right down the spout and so close that we could not depress our gun to fire at it so I drove up beside the Germans and slewed the tank round to throw the gun into the ditch; then we proceeded into the village.

Some heavy fighting had taken place in Rots prior to our Troop arriving. We were told that some of our tanks had been lost but we did not see any until we emerged into the open and found a Tiger tank burning so we knew that some of our tanks had passed this way. Then we met two Tigers that were very much alive. Luckily they were going away from us and their guns were pointing the other way so we were able to get in a couple of shots before they turned round. Unfortunately, our guns were not big enough to penetrate the Tiger's armour and their 88mms could slice through ours like a hot knife through butter; it was frustrating to see the armour-piercing shells bounce off their thick hides.

Maguire, our loader, was slamming in 75mm shells so fast that it sounded like machine-gun fire, but every shot would bounce off. They were starting to fire back and one of their shells creased us but Maguire then loaded HE and we scored a hit right by the main gun which went up in the air like a flag pole and the German crew bailed out and left. The crew of the other Tiger had also gone so one of our tanks must have hit it. Then we noticed that this cornfield we were in was crawling with Jerries, herding quite a number of our boys back to their lines as prisoners, a process we were happy to reverse.

We stayed in that forward position all night, along with a platoon of infantry and I don't mind saying it was the longest night of my life. However, nothing developed and at dawn we made our way back to our own lines where the rest of the Squadron welcomed us with open arms, thinking we had been killed. Later that day we recovered the damaged tanks and removed the bodies, your uncle Bob among them.

Another member of the Fort Garry's, Edwin Goodman of Toronto, gives his account of the Rots battle:[13]

I was in the same squadron as Bob and Bud and my tank was the last of the four into the village; as we went in a mortar round landed on my turret but I had half the cupola up and that took the blast; instead of blowing my head off it only gave me a bad headache. As we passed the cross-roads there was a German Panther tank about 50 feet away, which fired its high-velocity gun at my tank. The shell went right through the turret, killed my loader and went out the other side; within a few seconds my tank was on fire. My gunner was scrambling to get out and I pushed him through the top of the tank and on to the engine plates at the rear where a German in the top of a house shot him dead, although that did not become known until the next day.

The tank was now a mass of flames and I threw myself out and on to the road. One of my men in another tank which had been shot up told me that he could see all this from the place where he was hiding and that when I landed I was cursing the Germans with words he had not heard before. I then ran across the road and took cover in what the English call the corn; it was like running through a heavy rain storm with bullets bouncing all around me but I was not hit. The Brigade liaison officer was in a small scout car which was also on fire and as he tried to get out I could see his face and he sank back into the flames. It was grim.

By now I was hiding in the corn beside a Commando corporal, and as we peered down the road we saw some Germans walking up to some Canadians hiding in the corn and killing them. My Commando partner said, 'Let us get a couple of those guys before they shoot us' and I said, 'I have no weapon'. He therefore gave me his commando knife which was covered in blood. He told me he had already got one with his knife and told me how to use it.

At that moment two of my Squadron's tanks about 100 yards out in the field started to fire at the Germans. Unfortunately they almost hit my companion and I so we pushed ourselves deeper in the corn. Not wanting to be killed by my own Squadron I decided we had better get up and take our chances and we started to run towards Jerry Curtin's tanks; by the time we got to them there were 13 of us and we all climbed on to the back of one where the turret was not working.

I then found the Commando colonel and asked him what he wanted me to do. He looked at me – evidently I was pretty badly burned – and said I should take one of the non-working tanks and find my own Headquarters. Once there they sent me back to the Mulberry Harbour and thence to hospital in England where I stayed for three weeks before rejoining my regiment. I really regret having to tell you this grim tale and have no intention of telling you another.

This tough fight at Rots by the Fort Garry Horse and the Royal Marine Commandos drove the Germans back to the Caen–Bayeux road. Even so, the 3rd Canadian Division's advance came to a halt at Authie and Carpiquet, the Division's D-Day objective, was not to be in their hands for several weeks. This was the case elsewhere on the Allied beachheads; on June 7 most of the units, American, British and Canadian, were still attempting to take or secure the objectives listed for June 6 so a short resumé of the situation on the first day of the battle for Normandy will be useful.

On June 7, the British 50th Division completed their occupation of Bayeux and sent patrols probing south along the river Seulles towards Tilly-sur-Seulles and Longues where they would shortly bump into Panzer Lehr. Back on the coast, No. 47 (Royal Marine) Commando had completed the capture of Port-en-Bessin and made contact with American troops of the US V Corps edging east from Omaha. Linking up the British and Canadian beaches would take a few more days, while isolated pockets of resistance were rooted out at Langrune-sur-Mer by No. 48 (Royal Marine) Commando on June 7. It took longer at the radar station at Douvres-le-Délivrance, where the German garrison held out until June 17. Overall, by the evening of June 7, the eastern edge of the invasion area from the Ranville heights to Port-en-Bessin was relatively secure apart from a certain amount of sniping and probes from German fighting patrols.

The same was largely true in the American sector west of Port-en-Bessin.

Although the US First Army 'had not fully achieved any of its D-Day objectives'[14] five divisions were ashore by the morning of June 7. These divisions were short of tanks, artillery and supplies of food and ammunition, but they had moved off the beaches – which were still under artillery fire – and were either moving further inland or digging-in to beat off counter-attacks. The two airborne divisions in the Cotentin were gradually gaining strength as more men trickled in, increasing their grip around Ste-Mère-Église and linking up with the 4th Infantry Division which had now expanded its beachhead inland from Utah. It was now necessary for elements of VII Corps to push south and east, past Carentan to Isigny, and link up with the 29th Division of V Corps, coming west from Omaha. This move was being strongly contested by the German 91st Division, dug in at the foot of the peninsula.

The two assault divisions on Omaha, the 1st and 29th Infantry, were still recovering from the events of D-Day. During the assault they had sustained over 3,000 casualties, about 1,000 for every mile of beach, and taken particularly heavy casualties among the officers and senior NCOs. However, the 29th Division (Major General Charles H. Gerhardt) landed its third regiment, the 175th Infantry, at noon on D plus 1 and both assault divisions began to move south, 1st Infantry keeping east of the St Laurent–Formigny line, 29th Infantry to the west of it. The task of both divisions on June 7 was to reach the points they should have reached had all gone well on the previous day.

At this time, all over the Allied front, men marked as missing on D-Day were returning to their units, among them Robert Sales, an infantryman of 'B' Company, 116th Infantry Regiment, 29th Division:[15]

> D-Day was just terrible. I went in on the first wave with 'B' Company and before we got ashore machine-gun bullets were coming in as soon as the ramp went down. Captain Zappacosta, the Company Commander, was killed, the forward observers were killed ... I caught my heel on the ramp and went off sideways or I would have been killed. To this day I never met another person who was in that boat, the Headquarters boat for 'B' Company. It was just a mixed-up affair.
>
> Then a few minutes later a shell hit in the water and knocked me groggy – I was almost out of it. I met Dick Wright, Communications Sergeant and my friend for many years, lying out on the sand behind a log and Dick raised up on his hand a little bit and a sniper hit him in the head and he flopped down on the sand. Nothing could live on that beach that day. I had lost my radio and

rifle in the water ... it was just terrible but some of us got behind a wall and all day we dragged the dead in, they came rolling in on the waves, shells landing, tanks landing ... they had to land those tanks.

As it began to get dark a launch came in and took us off, all the wounded and we got them on to a hospital ship. By the next day though, I was feeling better, my senses were back to normal, so I went and found a doctor and said I did not want to go back to England. I wanted to go ashore and find my Company, what was left of them, and he said that if I felt like going that was fine with him.

So I went up on deck where there was kit they had taken off the wounded and I found a pistol and a rifle and a pack and then I found a launch to take me back to the beach. I joined up with a recon outfit and spent two days with them, moving about the beachhead, asking where I could find the 116th Infantry Regiment and eventually I found them. When I got back to 'B' Company, they all came running out, thinking I had been killed. They were in a bombed-out area where there was a big church and they had church services that night and everyone went to church ... and then we went into the hedgerow country and pushed towards St-Lô.

At first this advance from the Omaha beachhead went ahead without much trouble. The US Official History[16] records 'slight or sporadic resistance' and 'a marked degree of enemy disorganisation', which had first been observed on the afternoon of D-Day. No enemy reinforcements appeared on June 7, and the morale of those elements of the 352nd Division that had contested the US landings on Omaha fiercely on the previous day now seemed low. The US advance therefore took the high ground at Engrainville although the 3rd Bn of the 26th Infantry seemed unable to take the village of Formigny or get moving to the south, though only opposed by exhausted elements of the German 916th Regiment.[17] The Germans were not finally driven out of Formigny until the morning of June 8.

This lack of resistance to the American advance from Omaha on D plus 1 may have been due to the fact that the commander of the 352nd Division, General Kraiss, had other worries on June 7, most notably the advance of the British 50th Division into and around his right flank at Bayeux. 50th Division should have been resisted by the 716th Division, stationed to the east of the 352nd, but the left wing of this division had apparently collapsed. The fighting around

Bayeux on June 7 was confused and it is not easy to make out where German units were or what they were doing but it is clear that the 352nd Division was in trouble and unable to resist any determined advance by the Allied forces, let alone counter-attack them.

Two battalions of the British 56th Infantry Brigade (50th Division) entered Bayeux early on June 7 and by noon the city was in British hands. This advance, combined with that of the US 1st Infantry Division from Omaha, pushed the remains of the 352nd Division into a pocket along the river Drôme where both Allied divisions came to a halt along the river bank. Meanwhile, the US 29th Division spent the day mopping up enemy resistance just off the beach around St Laurent and Vierville, still under sniper, machine-gun and mortar fire from woods and farmhouses. The reserve regiment of this division, the 175th Infantry, was still offshore on the morning of June 7 and did not land until the late afternoon, when, as related, it was ordered west, towards Isigny.

In the VII Corps area in the Cotentin, the 4th Infantry Division had pushed the enemy back two miles from Utah, overrunning German coastal batteries that were firing on the beach and the offshore shipping, reaching the villages of Crisbecq and Dodainville. The main threat to the US positions in the Cotentin on June 7 came from a counter-attack mounted against the 82nd Airborne at Ste-Mère-Église, a strong infantry attack from the direction of Cherbourg, supported by tanks and self-propelled guns. Rapid support from newly landed tanks of the 746th Tank Battalion from the 4th Division reserve beat this attack off in the late afternoon. The Germans then withdrew to take up defensive positions in front of Montebourg, north of Ste-Mère-Église, barring the road to Cherbourg and bringing up more men, tanks and guns to make further advance difficult.

At the southern end of the Cotentin, the 82nd Airborne Division had difficulty in the flooded ground around the river Merderet where early on June 7 they were counter-attacked by tanks and infantry. This attack was repulsed, but not without heavy losses among the American companies. Meanwhile, men of the 101st US Airborne Division were in combat with Colonel van der Heydte's 6th Parachute Regiment on the river Douve and around St Côme du Mont. In this engagement the US paratroopers managed to capture most of the 6th Regiment's 1st battalion.

On balance, June 7 saw the Allied forces doing as well as or rather better than might have been expected. This can be attributed partly to surprise – the invasion was unexpected largely because of the weather – partly to a lack of grip on the German side, probably due to the absence of Field Marshal Rommel, and partly to the overwhelming Allied superiority in aircraft and naval gunfire. The main problem facing the Allied troops ashore on June 7 was a shortage of supplies. Since this problem was to continue, it would be as well to examine the supply situation again.

The Allied invasion had been planned for two years and that may have been part of the problem. The invasion logistics had been prepared down to the last nut, bolt and jerry-can and in their attempts to get things right the planners had forgotten that in war things inevitably and invariably go wrong. The logistical plan was therefore too tight, too exact, with no margin for error or accident – and it began to come apart on the first day.

The first problem was the weather. The build-up of surf on the beaches on June 6 restricted the landing areas and prevented many craft discharging their cargoes. Other craft ran on to obstacles or hit mines or were sunk or damaged by shell fire, while store trucks stalled in the sea when their waterproofing proved inadequate. In the British sector alone 258 landing craft of various kinds were lost on D-Day and only about half the planned number of vehicles were put ashore.[18] The weight of stores landed on the British and Canadian beaches was about forty per cent less than planned. On Omaha, all attempts to land stores were brought to a halt by German resistance and many landing craft were lost, while on Utah the landing was made in the wrong place; it all helped to slow up the delivery of supplies. For the first two days all the men had was the food and ammunition they could carry with them.

These problems were compounded by the fact that the roads, fields and villages behind the beaches had to be cleared of mines and booby traps. Gaps and craters had to be filled, bridges repaired; all this took time and slowed up the forward movement of supplies. This situation was slightly eased by the fact that the Allied advance was not proceeding as quickly as planned – those damned Germans kept getting in the way – so the Allied supplies had less distance to travel.

However, the factor that compounded all this was the first one mentioned – the Allied logistical plan was too rigid. Only one hundred tons of shipping per day had been put aside for emergency use[19] – roughly one per cent of the total planned – which implies that the planners assumed their loading and unloading schedules would work out ninety-nine per cent of the time, an optimistic assessment to say the least. The end result of this, and one becoming apparent as early as D plus 1, was that the logistic plan began to falter. Store ships and landing craft began to assemble off the beaches later that day demanding places to beach and unload. Back in England, the storemen at the invasion ports were staring anxiously out to sea, looking for ships that should have been back from Normandy by now, ready to reload and sail again, but had somehow failed to return.

Meanwhile, the construction of the Mulberry harbours, one at Arromanches for the British and one at Omaha for the Americans, began on D plus 1 but here again there were problems. The British Mulberry had already lost forty per cent of its component parts and was never able to handle its designed amount of cargo and, as we shall see, the Omaha Mulberry was soon destroyed in a gale. No immediate help there then, but shortages were already worrying the troops ashore, so on D plus 2, the existing logistical plans, so painfully and carefully constructed, were largely committed to the wastepaper basket. Ships were to go in where they could and unload all they had, regardless; it was messy and it caused confusion but it was better than not having the goods on shore at all. By the end of D plus 1 on the American front not more than a quarter of the planned 14,500 tons of stores had actually been landed, fewer than half the 14,000 vehicles had come ashore and the troop build-up was already 20,000 men short.

The saving element on the supply front, at this time and later, was the hard work and ingenuity put into the task of supplying the front-line soldiers by the troops in the supply chain. Whatever 'The Book' decreed as the maximum possible, the service units managed to exceed it, in tons of stores unloaded, in gallons of POL supplied, in miles driven. Allied success in the Battle of Normandy owes a great deal to the unsung heroes in the supply lines, the men at the rear who kept the food, fuel and ammunition flowing to the men at the front.

Their labour and enterprise also compensated for a failure to take ports in accordance with the planned schedule. This schedule had been drawn up in order that the logistical staffs could plan their deliveries but the ports were not taken on time or were unusable when taken. Cherbourg, which the Americans planned to take in a matter of days, came on stream six weeks behind schedule. Granville and St-Malo, which the American commanders hoped to have functioning by D plus 27, were still in German hands on D plus 50. Other ports, Isigny, or Port-en-Bessin, Courseulles, Ouistreham in the British and Canadian sectors, though in Allied hands, were simply too small. These problems would not go away.

To sum up the gains so far, the Allied advances on June 6–7, however limited, had forced the German units away from the coast. The Germans had fallen back, in defiance of Hitler's firm order that every metre of ground was to be contested, because they had no choice; Allied pressure was simply too strong. Shelling from the relentless guns of the Allied fleets, backed from the air by the light bombers and ground-attack fighters of the US Ninth Air Force and 2nd TAF, had rendered Hitler's order impossible but by the evening of June 7 the invaders were starting to flag and their forward push slowed. This too was inevitable, for the men were tired.

The men in the assault and follow-up divisions, American, British, Canadian, had not slept or rested for three days or more, not since they boarded their troop transports on June 4 – it should be remembered that they were supposed to go ashore on June 5 and the assault was delayed by the weather. Crammed craft and sea-sickness do not make rest easy and the euphoria of getting ashore, even where it still existed after the first blast of enemy fire, had long since evaporated. The men ashore were now short of food, extremely short of ammunition and in urgent need of rest, resupply and reinforcement.

They were, however, extremely optimistic and with good reason. Although the beaches had not yet been combined into a single bridgehead, the US Official History is correct when it states for June 7 that: 'in general, it was clear that the invasion had succeeded in gaining a foothold. The build-up race was on.'

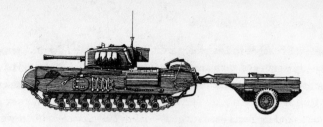

4 THE BATTLE FOR THE BRIDGEHEAD JUNE 8-12

The failure of both V and VII Corps to make any substantial moves toward
the vital joining of the beachheads, together with the general slowness of the
advances on D-Day objectives had become a matter of concern.

US ARMY IN WORLD WAR II *Cross-Channel Attack*

The progress of the Allied armies in Normandy can be organised into a number
of phases. To use such phasing is useful if only in the interests of clarity, for
with hundreds of units fighting in an ever-expanding area along a fifty-mile
front it is otherwise hard to see any pattern in the fighting or gain any sense of
what the various commanders were trying to achieve. The first of these phases
had been accomplished on D-Day when the Allied armies got ashore. The second
phase came on June 7 when no major counter-attack developed and the Allies
were able to consolidate their initial gains and secure their various beachheads.
Now came phase three, the battle to join these five 'beachheads' into one continuous 'bridgehead'. No one knew how long this phase would last but while it
went on it was also necessary to pour troops and supplies ashore.

The post-D-Day build-up phase was essentially a race. While the Allies were
sending troops and supplies ashore the Germans were bringing their reserves
forward from deeper in France and making every effort to prevent the Allied
build-up being completed. They did not, apparently, appreciate that this was
the main, indeed the only landing in the north, and that all their available forces
should have been sent against it; even so, the beachheads were soon being
attacked.

German aircraft, chased from the beachhead skies by day, returned at night to bomb the beaches and assembly areas and drop mines offshore. German E-boats, patrol craft and submarines appeared nightly to take their toll of Allied shipping. Neither should the battle for the bridgehead be seen simply as a matter of linking up the beachheads laterally, along the shore line. It was also necessary to expand the beachheads inland – to 'peg-out' claims – or there would be no space ashore for all the various fighting units and logistical elements needed for the eventual breakout.

Gaining ground inland was therefore a strategic necessity. Possessing ground gave the invaders room to manoeuvre, enabled them to absorb counter-attacks, provided space for more troops and supply dumps and freed the beaches from direct, observed, artillery fire. Within a few days it was found advisable to haul down the barrage balloons over the beaches as these provided German artillery observers with something to aim at. In the face of intensifying enemy opposition the expansion inland would take time but it is notable – see the introductory quote from the US History given above – that as early as June 8 – D plus 2 – the powers-that-be in Britain were already getting impatient with their forces ashore, urging faster progress and failing to realise that expanding the beachheads would not be easy in the face of German resistance and the on-going problems of supply. On that day the US troop build-up was already 20,000 soldiers short, only fifty per cent of the planned number of vehicles had landed and less than seventy-five per cent of the necessary stores had reached the fighting men – and yet people at SHAEF, safe in London, complained about a lack of progress.

Only Montgomery seems to have appreciated this point. 'It was inevitable that after the successful outcome of the assault, the pace of operations slowed down,' he wrote. 'The assault formations needed time for a breather while they reorganised and reabsorbed the echelons which had been left behind for the first days but without which a unit cannot function for long ... the build-up was falling behind schedule and this added to our difficulties'.[1] The build-up fell behind for a number of reasons, some of which – like damage to landing craft, bad weather, enemy action and too tight a time schedule – have been touched on in the previous chapter. Delays should anyway have been anticipated by all concerned. None of these reasons were unusual but none of them were taken into account in the pre-D-Day planning. It was *inevitable* that the original plan would soon get somewhat out of phase but the biggest obstacle to any Allied progress off the beaches was – predictably – the enemy.

In spite of major deception operations such as Fortitude and the destruction of bridges and rail links into Normandy, the German forces in Normandy had been substantially increased in the weeks before the landing, most notably by the arrival of the 352nd and 91st Divisions on the Calvados coast and the introduction of the 243rd Division in the Cotentin. The Germans also had ten Panzer or motorised divisions available to reinforce the defenders around the beachheads and those already mentioned, Panzer Lehr, 21 Panzer, 17 SS Panzer Grenadier and 12 SS Panzer, were to be reinforced by 116 Panzer from Fifteenth Army, north of the Seine, 2nd Panzer from Picardy, 11 Panzer from Bordeaux, 1 SS Panzer from Belgium, 2 SS Panzer (*Das Reich*) from Toulouse and 9 Panzer from Avignon. All these crack divisions were now heading for Normandy. There were also five infantry divisions, including two parachute divisions coming forward[2] so in the build-up race between attacker and defender the defenders appeared to be winning.

12 SS Panzer, Panzer Lehr and 17 SS Panzer Grenadier Division were in the line on June 7, 9 and 12 respectively, but the actions of the first two units resulted from the initiatives of the divisional commanders rather than OB-West and they were committed without any coherent plan. At least to begin with, they simply attacked the Allied forces where found. With the Allies at large across Normandy, from the Bois de Bavant to Ste-Mère-Église, the German defenders were fully occupied in mustering their forces, pouring in reserves and attacking any invaders they encountered. The task of establishing a firm defensive line and preparing a co-ordinated strategy for driving the invaders back into the sea must wait until it was certain where the invaders actually were – and the defenders were also sure that this Normandy attack was the main landing and not a diversion before the major assault in the Pas de Calais.

As a result, the main German effort in the first days after the landings was a series of strong but uncoordinated attacks around the beachhead, spearheaded by 21 Panzer, 12 SS Panzer and Panzer Lehr, largely concentrated against the British and Canadians in the east and the US V Corps pushing south from Omaha. Thanks to Allied air power and naval gunfire support, these attacks, if vicious and pressed home hard, were beaten off. That said, the Germans managed to hold on to Caen and restrict the Allied advance inland in other areas, with the exception already noted, of the 50th Division advance on Bayeux and the advances made by the US VII Corps into the Cotentin from Utah.

In the Cotentin, German efforts to intervene against the parachute divisions and the US troops landing on Utah were largely negated by their own pre-D-Day defences. By landing behind the flooded areas along the Merderet river west of Ste-Mère-Église and around the Vire floods between Isigny and Carentan, the VII Corps units, airborne and seaborne, had a defence line behind which they could muster. The 101st Airborne established a strong defensive position behind the river Vire and the actions fought around Carentan from D plus 1 to D plus 7 cut both ways. The Americans had difficulty taking Carentan and linking up with the troops from Omaha but – on the other hand – the Germans had difficulty feeding forces into the Cotentin from the south, either to reinforce the troops attempting to seal off Utah, or bolster the garrison of Cherbourg.

This being so, the first task for VII Corps, having linked up with V Corps, was to head west, reach the Atlantic coast and cut the Cotentin peninsula. Once the Americans had cut the Cotentin they could turn their full power north and take Cherbourg against no more opposition than the troops already in the Cotentin could provide – and it was vitally important to do this, for Cherbourg was one of the ports needed for supply.

Jack Capell of the 4th Infantry Division tells of this time:[3]

> The fight up to Cherbourg and through Montebourg was hard, for the Germans fought back for every yard of ground and caused heavy casualties. War was seen to be serious and about this time we first heard about the Million Dollar Wound, the one that got you home, but was not serious enough to maim or kill you. That was hard too; Atterbury, one of the men in my wire section, was hit in the buttocks by a piece of shrapnel and since it did not appear serious we gathered round to congratulate him as he lay on the ground smiling, awaiting evacuation to England; next day we asked the medic how he had got on and he told us Atterbury had died in the aid station.

On D plus 5, Colonel Red Reeder of the 12th Infantry Regiment was hit near Montebourg:[4]

> I was talking to some reinforcements who had just arrived from England, young kids, and then a single shell exploded over my head and that was it. My left leg was horribly mangled above the ankle and my left elbow was torn open. I

screamed, I could not help it but Bill Mills, one of my officers, though wounded himself, gave me a shot of morphine from his first aid kit; his own blood splashed on me as he did so. I lay in the dirt for some 15 minutes before a jeep came up carrying six wounded men and eventually I ended up in a hospital, a big black tent, where General Collins loomed up and pinned the Distinguished Service Cross on my shirt.

The four areas of interest for General Montgomery in the days immediately after the landing were (a) the Bois de Bavant–Ranville area on the left flank of the invasion, which must be held in case Fifteenth Army came in; (b) the road from Sword to Caen beside the river Orne; (c) attempts by the Canadians, British and Americans to get inland and peg out claims to the south from Juno, Gold and Omaha, not least to provide suitable ground for airfields and (d) in the west, the US efforts to cut the Cotentin and move north on Cherbourg.

The Bavant–Ranville–Salenelles area was held from early on D-Day by the British 6th Airborne Division, reinforced, as related, by Lovat's 1st Commando Brigade and later by the 4th Commando Brigade as well. These parachute and commando soldiers were assault troops par excellence and in an ideal world would have been quickly replaced by 'heavy' infantry and armoured units and withdrawn to the UK. However, as the beachheads came under increasing pressure, as casualties mounted and Caen remained untaken, this withdrawal did not happen. Like their American counterparts in the west of the beachhead, the British paratroopers and commandos stayed in the line east of the Orne until mid-August and the Allied breakout. Among their number was Lieutenant Bryan Samain of 'E' Troop, 45 (Royal Marine) Commando.[5]

I was a 19-year-old subaltern when I joined 45 in Normandy, one of a small group of replacements sent in after the casualties in the fighting to secure the beachhead. As we drove up to Amfreville, we passed the evidence of battle, smashed and abandoned German guns and tanks, Achtung Minen skull-and-crossbones signs for minefields. As we got closer we began to hear the sound of the guns and across the Orne on the plain were the remains of wrecked gliders, like broken model aeroplanes, lying about at crazy angles.

I met the CO, Nicol Gray and was sent to 'E' Troop where the OC was Major Ian Beadle and because I had done a sniper course in England I was made sniper officer as well as commanding a section of 'E' Troop. There were four snipers in 45, all of them excellent shots with many kills to their credit. Commando snipers were in action daily working singly or in pairs. Marine Cakebread of 45 was one of the most successful snipers in the Brigade – the other was an Army Commando – and he accounted for more than 30 Germans in the course of the Normandy campaign. There was constant mortaring and shelling by the Germans, to which we replied in kind but the emphasis on our side, certainly in the Commando Brigade, was on fighting patrols, raids and sniping, all to maintain the initiative and make it difficult for the Germans to mount an attack.

The Germans were also active snipers and as their line faced west they would snipe at us in the mornings when their backs were to the sun, often concealing themselves in high trees difficult to detect in the foliage; we had to move about with great care.

The heights east of the Orne, which are occupied by the Bois de Bavant and a series of small villages, Ranville, Touffreville, Le Mesnil, Bréville, Salenelles and – lower down – Merville, are not particularly high but they occupy a ridge that runs inland from the coast towards Troarn and this ridge dominates much of the ground between the rivers Orne and Dives. By June 8 most of the airborne troops still alive and uncaptured had rejoined their units in this area and, reinforced by the two Commando brigades, 6th Airborne dug in on the heights, ready to fend off attacks on the left flank of Sword beach, attacks which began, as related, on the evening of June 6.

During the evening tide on June 6, and on June 7, the Second Army followup forces arrived, notably the 7th Armoured Division (Desert Rats) and the 51st Highland Division. These veteran units had served with Eighth Army in the western desert and much was expected of them as the Desert Rats were sent inland towards Tilly-sur-Seulles and 51st Highland were sent east of the Orne to support 6th Airborne. While they were moving forward on June 8, 13 Para were attacked in the 6th Airborne perimeter beyond the Orne and on June 10 a strong force of infantry and tanks from the 346th Division came up from beyond Bréville and attempted to reach the bridges at Bénouville. This attack was beaten off by 7 Para and 13 Para, the latter putting in bayonet charges across the cornfields and causing heavy losses to the German 858th Grenadier Regiment.

These scattered actions were a sign of growing German strength around the airborne perimeter beyond the Orne. From June 10 these attacks continued, many mounted from the village of Bréville which the Germans had managed to retain. Brigadier Hill of the 3rd Parachute Brigade later declared that the fighting for Bréville between June 8 and 12 were 'five of the toughest days of fighting I had in the war,'[6] and the situation was not helped by the fact that the parachute units were very short of men. Lt Colonel Otway of 9 Para had attacked the Merville battery on D-Day with only sixty men; two days later he had ninety men but even by June 12, when more men scattered in the jump had come in, his battalion could only muster 270 soldiers. Nevertheless, these airborne battalions held their ground tenaciously and beat off enemy attacks with loss.

Lt 'Dixie' Dean, the mortar and machine-gun officer of 13 Para, has some accounts of this time:[7]

The morning of June 7 was reasonably quiet with only sporadic shelling on the south side of Ranville and we must have been out of range of any mortars since we were not bothered by them, but it was always artillery from the direction of Ste Honorine, near to Caen, that troubled us. All the action was away to our left as the Ox and Bucks cleared the bridgehead. They cleared the Boche out of Hérouvillette but he was determined to hold on to Escoville and the Light Infantry had heavy casualties in their attempt to take it. We did have a bit of a panic on the afternoon of the 8th when the word came that German tanks were crossing the bridges; if true this was serious because it meant our life line to the seaborne forces was cut and we waited in our slit trenches, gammon bombs in hand – it turned out that the tanks were Allied tanks, much better news. Then we were told that there might be very heavy shelling as the 51st Highland Division were going to attack Ste Honorine and how right it was; we experienced the first heavy bombardment, the attack failed and when I went up later to see what had happened, all I saw were dead bodies.

We had seen no civilians but one evening a middle-aged French woman turned up in the Platoon area and I was just able to understand that she wanted to see her house in the village. I detailed someone to accompany her, just in case she was up to no good, and the house she claimed was one at the end of a row which had received a direct hit and had a great gaping hole at the gable end. She was soon back, ranting and raving at me because of the damage to her property and appeared to hold me personally responsible for the damage, demanding to know why we had come to Normandy to fight the war? All the other wars had been fought elsewhere in France so why had we not gone there? She really meant it, but considering Ranville was in the front line the damage to the houses was negligible, compared with a lot of other villages we saw later.

In an attempt to lance the boil of Bréville, on June 11 Major General Richard Gale ordered 3 Para Brigade, supported by the 5th Bn, The Black Watch from 51st Highland, to clear the village. The Highlanders duly went in, accompanied by their pipers, but were caught in the open cornfields by German machine-guns and promptly cut to pieces, the remnants taking cover with 9 Para. On the following day, clearly encouraged by this success, the Germans mounted an attack on 9 Para, beginning with artillery concentrations during the morning, followed up in mid-afternoon with a full-scale attack from infantry, tanks and self-propelled guns. This attack was finally driven off by a company of the Canadian Parachute Battalion, led forward in person by Brigadier Hill.

General Gale decided that the Germans might well be exhausted by this day of heavy fighting so at midnight he committed his reserve battalion, 12 Para, and a company of the Devonshire Regiment, added a tank squadron of the 13/18th Hussars, and ordered them to take Bréville. The men were briefed for the attack in the church at Amfreville and moved up to the start line at 2200hrs, arriving in time to observe the start of the artillery bombardment supporting their attack. Some of the shells fell short and landed among the assault troops, one wounding Brigadier Lord Lovat of the Commando Brigade and Brigadier Lord Kindersley of the 6th Airlanding Brigade; both survived but had to be evacuated.

Chaos duly reigned, but by dawn on June 12 Bréville had been occupied and came firmly into British hands next morning with the arrival of the 1 Bn Royal Ulster Rifles. The 12th Parachute Battalion was now reduced to fifty-five men, but like the other parachute units it stayed in the line. The fighting on the eastern perimeter of the landing area would continue until almost the end of the Normandy campaign but after June 12 there was no real likelihood that the position east of the Orne would be lost; General Gale of 6th Airborne wrote later: 'There is a turning point in all battles. In the fight for the Orne bridgehead the battle of Bréville was that turning point. Neither in the north nor in the south were we ever seriously attacked again.'[8]

This was fortunate. While Gale and his men were battling at Bréville and securing the left flank of the Allied bridgehead, Montgomery was launching another push on Caen, avoiding the strong northern defences for an attempt west of the city, a continuation of attacks that had been going on since the Second Army came ashore. Second Army's failure to take Caen on D-Day has become one of the great controversies of the Normandy campaign and one might fairly point out that if the 3rd Infantry Division did not take the city on June 6, it was not for want of trying.

These efforts continued until the city fell. A second attempt on Caen was mounted on June 7 and 8. This attack was spearheaded by the 158th Brigade of the 3rd (British) Infantry Division, which thrust directly up the Orne towards Caen and got as far as the village of Lebisey, two miles from the city, before they were driven back with heavy casualties by 21 Panzer. Frontal attacks on Caen were clearly going to be costly so some other way of taking the city had to be found, and after the eastern end of the bridgehead had been secured at Bréville on June 12, the focus of activity switched to another attempt to out-flank Caen at Villers-Bocage.

General Montgomery came ashore on June 8 and established his head-quarters in the grounds of the château of Cruelly, north-west of Caen, reporting to London later that day: 'The Germans are doing everything they can to hold on to Caen, and I have decided not to have a lot of casualties butting up against the place. So I have ordered Second Army to keep up the pressure and to make its main effort towards Villers-Bocage and Évrecy, and thence south-east towards Falaise'.

It his hard to see anything wrong with this decision – though lightly intro-ducing Falaise, a town well south of Caen into this report was probably unwise. The German defences north of Caen were getting stronger by the hour – 21 Panzer, Panzer Lehr and 12 SS Panzer were now deployed or deploying there – and even if the city was taken by direct assault, such success could only lead to days of street fighting, a form of warfare which is notoriously hard on the attack-ing infantry.

This is so for any town, but Caen would be a particularly hard nut to crack. The river Orne runs right through the centre and the Caen canal runs into it, both offering a good defensive line among the narrow streets and old houses, while the medieval castle in the centre seemed impervious to bombs and shellfire. Nor was the city easy to outflank; south of the city lay the tumbled country of the *Suisse Normande* which limited the scope for an attack from that direction so, provided the pressure was kept up in front of Caen to hold the Panzer divisions in place, it made good tactical sense to 'mask' Caen, outflank the defenders and leave them to be dealt with by air power, while the main battle shifted southeast, towards Falaise. This scheme depended on the British being able to break through on either side of the city and the first attempt to do this was made on the western side of Caen, through Tilly-sur-Seulles towards Villers-Bocage.

The prospects of success for a flanking attack west of Caen were not good. By June 7 the 3rd Canadian Division, fighting west of Caen, was having plenty of trouble with 12 SS Panzer, which disputed every metre of ground and – as ordered by Adolf Hitler – counter-attacked immediately to retake any ground lost. Between D-Day and D plus 6, the Canadians lost almost 3,000 men in the fighting for Carpiquet but on June 9, 12 SS broke off their attack. The Canadians' dogged resistance to the German Panzers had taken its toll of attacker and defender and, for the moment at least, the situation on the Canadian division's front was a stalemate.

West of the Canadians lay the British 50th Division which, having taken Bayeux on June 7, was moving south towards Tilly-sur-Seulles – while edging west to keep in touch with the US 1st Infantry Division moving out of Omaha. 50th Division had done very well on D-Day and D plus 1 but was now slowing down. Like the other assault divisions, it had been fighting continuously since D-Day and needed rest and reinforcements before it could push forward aggressively.

Here was the classic post-assault dilemma. The divisions committed on D-Day had been training for months for the landing. They knew, or had been told, that getting ashore was only part of it, and that their battle would continue but inevitably there was a feeling about that if they could punch a breach in the Atlantic Wall, get ashore and stay there, they would have 'done their bit', at least for a while. The advance would then be taken up by fresh, well-ordered, follow-up formations that would come ashore without opposition. This is the classic pattern for any attack; the assault formations take the position and the follow-up formations, kept in reserve, come forward to exploit it; that is what reserves are for. Although they were tired, the problem for these assault divisions was emotional rather than physical; they had been given a task and accomplished it – now they were given another task, one for which they were not mentally prepared and their advance inevitably slowed.

Moreover, the opposition was increasing. From June 7, the German fight-back was being taken up by fresh divisions which, though harassed from the air, had not been pounded by the guns of the fleet, or surprised by the Allied landing or driven out of their positions in the D-Day fighting. By June 8, the Allied assault divisions, tired and somewhat disordered, were being confronted by some of the finest and best-equipped divisions in the German Army; it is hardly surprising if the Allied advance slowed down. On the XXX Corps front, those units moving out of Bayeux in the direction of Tilly-sur-Seulles, due west of Caen, on June 10 ran abruptly into General Bayerlein's crack Panzer Lehr, coming into the line on the left of 12 SS Panzer, and Montgomery's first attempt to outflank Caen came virtually to a standstill in the village of Saint Pierre, just east of Tilly.

The order to advance on Tilly-sur-Seulles came to the 7th Armoured Division (Desert Rats) on June 10 and the division moved forward, led by the 4th County of London Yeomanry (4th CLY) in Cromwell tanks. The enemy was first encoun-tered at the village of Jérusalem, five miles south of Bayeux, where the Desert Rats had their first taste of *bocage* fighting. Since the men of this division were more used to the open deserts of North Africa, it is hardly surprising that they did not like it. Lurking in the dense hedgerows and narrow lanes, small groups of German infantry, equipped with *panzerfausts* and automatic weapons and some-times backed by a tank, brought the 7th Armoured advance to a halt.

There was also a tactical mistake. 7th Armoured's supporting infantry, the Queen's Brigade, had been ordered to bring up the rear, and when the tanks ran into opposition it took time to get the foot soldiers forward to winkle the Germans out of their positions. As a result, little progress was made and at the end of the day the Desert Rats had lost just four tanks and suffered very few casualties – two facts that caused some critical comment when their lack of progress was noted as well.

The division did no better on the following day, June 11, although their tac-tics had improved. Two 'battlegroups' of tanks and infantry were formed, one to advance on Tilly, one to take Lingèvres, east of Tilly, on the road to Balleroy. These attacks got nowhere and a heavy counter-attack that night by German infantry backed with tanks caused heavy casualties – 150 killed and wounded – to the 2nd Bn The Essex Regiment. Many British soldiers were to claim later that the German infantry was reluctant to fight at night but there was little sign of that here and the Germans only fell back when the Essex called down a heavy artillery barrage on their own position.

7th Armoured Division were not the only ones in trouble at this time. 50th Division was making very little progress either while the attack of the 3rd Canadian Division supported by the 6th Canadian Armoured Regiment, is described in the British Official History[9] as 'a costly failure'. The Canadians lost thirty-seven tanks on June 11 and ninety-six of their supporting infantry were killed or wounded. Beating their heads against the enemy defences at such cost was clearly unproductive so it was decided to shift 7th Armoured to the west, outflank the enemy defences in the *bocage* around Tilly and come in on the small town of Villers-Bocage along a high ridge that lay behind Panzer Lehr's main position.

This move began on June 12. By that night 7th Armoured were at Livry, five miles from Villers-Bocage, ready to move in next day and get beyond the town. On the following day the leading tanks made good progress and by noon on June 13 they had entered the outskirts of Villers-Bocage. There had been little opposition so far that morning but a fresh German armoured division, 2nd Panzer, had now arrived in Normandy and the two armoured divisions bumped into each other in the streets of the town where a furious tank and infantry battle developed. One of the first tanks into Villers-Bocage that day was a Sherman Firefly commanded by Sergeant Bobby Bramall of the 4th CLY:[10]

> Most of us were in Cromwells, which I still think was a useless tank, fast enough but without adequate armour and under-gunned. Fortunately, I had a Sherman Firefly, which had the British 17-pounder gun and we could take on anything. As you know, we landed on D plus 1 and advanced on Tilly. From there we were ordered to take Villers-Bocage and the high ground beyond it and had our troubles but ... well, June 13 was the fatal day. We had leaguered the night before at Livry, a bit east of Caumont, and were on the move by first light, against no opposition to speak of, at least at first. Brigade said Villers was clear and although the Colonel wanted to do a recce first, 'Loony' Hinde, the Brigadier, came up and ordered us to push straight on into the town.
>
> So, 'A' Squadron pushed on and got on to the heights beyond the town – so far so good. RHQ and the Recce Troop stayed in the town centre and 'B', my Squadron, stayed out to the west with 'C' Squadron between us. All went well until mid-morning, when I first heard the sound of an 88mm gun – which is

something you don't forget, believe me. A vicious 'crack' and that was the first hint that the enemy were about. The Tiger came out and started to beat us up. First it wiped out the artillery tanks – these were radio-equipped, with no gun, so they could do nothing. Then the Tiger wiped out the Recce Troop and came on until it ran into my colleague, Sergeant Lockwood, who was in a Firefly and he engaged it. He did not do any damage but he certainly scared it off.

However, that was only part of it. By now other German tanks were at work attacking 'A' Squadron beyond the town. They blew up the leading tank in one column and then knocked out the one at the back. Then, having jammed the column, they simply rolled down the line, gunning each of our tanks in turn, knocking them out or setting them aflame, killing or capturing a lot of our chaps. Frankly, Villers-Bocage was a bloody shambles.

The CO was off the air, so 'Ibby' Aird took charge, and ordered my troop – 3 Troop of 'B' Squadron – into the town. Having a Firefly, I was in the lead in case we met Tigers and Captain Bill Cotton, who died a few years ago, was our Squadron OC. Bill was a fearless chap. We got into the centre all right but soon afterwards three German tanks came rolling down the main street. The one in the lead was a Mark IV; you might hear that it was a Tiger but I fired at it and can assure you that it wasn't ... though I missed, incidentally. Fortunately, the 6-pdr anti-tank gunners of the Queen's, our infantry brigade, were on hand by now and they knocked it out.

However, the next tank along certainly was a Tiger. I had reversed a bit and could see it coming through the windows of the corner house in the square and we engaged it through the windows with armour-piercing. This made a terrible mess of the house but we knocked it out. It was now about mid-day, I suppose and there was fighting going on all over the town, tanks engaged, infantry dodging about, anti-tank guns in action in the streets, lots of mortaring and small arms fire, with the Queen's infantry fighting with German tanks, and German infantry coming up from the south. Then another German tank, another Tiger, came up, around the corner of the square. It was too close to get the gun-sight on it but I had already sighted the gun by removing the breech-block and lining up the barrel on a sign stuck on the wall across the road – when the Tiger blocked that sign, I fired, and that was that ... up it went.

We pulled out at nightfall and went back to the village of Amaye-sur-Seulles, near Tracy-Bocage, west of Villers-Bocage, and counted the cost. The Regiment had been mauled; we lost our CO, Colonel Onslow, all of 'A' Squadron, most of the Recce Troop, the RHQ – a lot of good people. Villers-Bocage was a hard battle, believe me, and that night we withdrew to Amaye-sur-Seulles, a little west of Villers and went into leaguer.

For knocking out three German tanks in the streets of Villers-Bocage, Sergeant Bobby Bramall was later awarded the Military Medal. In that day-long brawl in Villers-Bocage, 7th Armoured Division lost twenty-five tanks, fourteen armoured cars and fourteen Bren gun carriers. Much of the damage hereabouts was done by two Tiger tank companies of the 501(SS) Heavy Tank Battalion commanded by Obersturmführer Michael Wittmann, one of the most notable Panzer commanders of the war who was to be killed later in the Normandy battle.

7th Armoured were thrusting into territory held by two German Panzer divisions, Panzer Lehr and 2nd Panzer, and until their 33rd Armoured Brigade came up they could do no more. On the night of June 14–15, 7th Armoured therefore withdrew and took up a position between 50th Division and elements of the US 1st Infantry Division of V Corps which had advanced against slight opposition to Caumont. The British thrust west of Caen had been an expensive failure and, as before, the Germans were quick to mount a counter-attack. This came in against 50th Division on June 14 and was only driven off by heavy artillery concentrations and after some hours of fighting. On the previous day, June 13, another front opened – a strategic one – when German V-1 flying bombs started to fall on London.

The British were not alone in having problems. German units were being sent to the Normandy front from all over France but their movements were restricted by the ever-watchful pilots of the Allied tactical air forces which, on the evening of June 10, struck the headquarters of Geyr von Schweppenburg's Panzer Group West which had been located from information in the Ultra decrypts. Von Schweppenburg had been placed in command of German defences and units on the Caen front but this attack by British fighter-bombers wiped out his entire staff, killing all the transport and operations officers, including his chief-of-staff. For a while, this rendered Geyr von Schweppenburg's command non-operational and command in this sector of the front reverted to Seventh Army.

If the battle on the British front was going slowly in mid-June, matters were going rather better on the American front, where there was less opposition and – as yet – no major Panzer units. The major German effort was still being directed to the retention of Caen and south of Omaha, the 352nd Division, weakened on D-Day, had been distracted on June 6–7 by the advance of 50th Division into its right flank. This being so, while the men of the US 1st and 29th Divisions had also been shaken by the events on Omaha, they were able to make some advances after June 7.

This was in spite of the fact that the Germans were now fully aware of the post D-Day intentions of both the American corps. On the evening of D-Day a complete set of orders for VII Corps had been found on the body of an American officer in an assault boat that drifted ashore at the mouth of the Vire. On June 7, the operational orders for V Corps were found on the body of another American officer killed at Vierville-sur-Mer.

According to the US Official History:[11] 'The Germans thus had in their hands the entire scheme of manoeuvre and order of battle for American units in the first phase of the invasion.' The supply of this information to the Germans was balanced by the fact that Allied units were rapidly made aware of German intentions, strengths and actions through the British Ultra intelligence provided by a daily cracking of the German Enigma codes but since the battle was fluid and not going exactly to pre-arranged plans on either side, such intelligence was of limited value.

The US Official History underlines this point, stating, 'The fact that possession of these (American) plans had no effect on the German conduct of operations throws considerable light on the tactical and strategic problems facing the enemy command.' The Germans were also inhibited by the fact that they did not know what the British were planning – except that they seemed very intent on taking Caen.

From these captured plans OKW did learn that the immediate targets for the US forces were the port of Cherbourg and the road junction at St-Lô, two objectives which they could probably have worked out for themselves. Besides, the main threat to the German position at the moment was the British thrust on Caen. This indicated a possible Allied intention of making a breakout in the east of the bridgehead – which would cut off the German forces further west, or a sudden thrust towards Paris or possibly of pressing south to cut the German lines of communication between the Seventh and Fifteenth Armies. Lacking a copy of British and Canadian plans to make up the set, Rommel was not to know that such a move had not been planned and was not intended. The Allied breakout, when it came, would be made by the Americans, in the west. That had always been the strategic plan and it remained the plan to the end. The problems inhibiting the execution of this plan were the terrain and the enemy.

In spite of these obstacles, 1st Infantry Division pushed east from Omaha to join up with the British near Port-en-Bessin on June 7, and battered their way south towards the high ground north of Trevières and south of the Aure, a river which, unlike most of these Norman streams, flowed west to east across the American front, at least between Bayeux and Formigny; fortunately the Aure was not too wide and could be crossed without bridging equipment. 1st Infantry Division also pushed out patrols towards Caumont, along the planned American-British line, in this on-going attempt to expand the bridgehead and this move went well. According to US reports, 'progress was good against light opposition, no counter-attacks materialised and enemy morale seemed low.'

This was because the main defending formation in this area, the 352nd Division, was fully engaged at this time with the British attack on Bayeux while being harassed relentlessly by the Allied air forces. When coupled with the American advance south from Omaha, the effect of the 50th Division advance was to squeeze the 352nd Division back beyond the Aure, in search of a position they could occupy and defend.

Of the two V Corps assault divisions, the 29th Infantry operated on a line west of a line Omaha to Formigny while 1st Infantry operated to the east of it. The 29th Infantry Division's third regiment, the 175th Infantry, with the 747th Tank Battalion in support, had duly pushed west on June 7, in an attempt to take Isigny and join up with the 101st Airborne around Carentan. The 175th advanced three miles through abandoned coastal defences without resistance before running into German infantry and anti-tank guns outside Isigny. The enemy here were dispersed with the support of naval gunfire and Isigny fell on the night of June 8–9 but only after some sixty per cent of the town had been destroyed by naval gunfire.

On the east flank of V Corps, the US 1st Infantry Division had met up with the marines of No. 47 (Royal Marine) Commando, which had taken Port-en-Bessin on June 7. Thereafter, as the US Official History states: 'Virtually the whole of V Corps, during the week of 8–14 June, was pushing south through the *bocage* country, making rapid progress against a disintegrated German defence.'[12]

The difference between the situation east and west of Caumont is striking. The Americans were moving steadily ahead while the British were making slow progress, either being held or even pushed back. As these accounts in the US History reveal, this rapid progress – along the coast to Isigny and into, rather than through, the *bocage* around Caumont – can largely be accounted for by an absence of enemy opposition. The US advance was to slow down as more German units came up to contest it, a point that was to hold true for much of the Normandy campaign. Units that went ahead did so until they met German opposition; then they slowed down. It was German resistance, not a lack of will or courage, that slowed the advance of the Allied forces in Normandy.

These moves south and west by V Corps prised loose the last grasp of General Kraiss's 352nd Division on the Normandy coast. On the night of June 8–9 he ordered the remaining units of his division to withdraw south of the river Aure and the floods that surrounded it between Isigny and Trevières, and prepare a new defence line behind the wide flooded area south of Omaha. With this resistance removed, the 115th and 116th Regiments of the 29th Division had no difficulty in taking the ground north of the river Aure. The 29th Division were also able to link up with the men of the 2nd Rangers on the Pointe de Hoc and enter Grandcamp-les-Bains on the coast west of Omaha, moving on to the banks of the river Vire on June 9. This put the Allied line comfortably in from the beaches but only on the outside, northern fringe of the Normandy *bocage*.

The units of the US VII Corps in the Cotentin – the 4th Infantry and the two US airborne divisions – which had met comparatively little trouble on D-Day, met plenty of it in the following days. As with the other Allied corps, VII Corps's actions on the days after the landing consisted of attempts to take the positions that should have fallen on D-Day. On June 8 and 9 two regiments of the 4th Infantry Division advanced north for two miles to the villages of Azeville and Crisbecq. There they were held by a strong force of German infantry, well dug-in, with anti-tanks guns and artillery support. Jack Capell again:

> We had our problems at this time and not just with the enemy. One day I saw a man put his foot on the edge of his foxhole, aim his rifle at it and blow the end off; that was the most common kind of self-inflicted wound at this time. We also

found that these Normandy farms had barrels of brandy in them – I still have a glass of that Calvados every D-Day anniversary. Anyway, some men took to drinking this Calvados heavily but whenever a GI drank too much he was usually killed or wounded after a short time. A fellow in my Company who drank too much grabbed his rifle and ran towards the enemy lines, saying he was going to kill every German he could find. We found him dead when we went forward next day.

South of Ste-Mère-Église, the 101st Airborne were engaged in trying to take the village of St Côme-du-Mont from the crack German 6th Parachute Regiment. Van der Heydte's men held on for two days before withdrawing to Carentan, most of them arriving there with all their equipment and still full of fight. On June 8, van der Heydte learned that Isigny had fallen and disposed his men to charge the Americans a heavy price for Carentan, the southern key to the Cotentin.

On June 7, further north, General von Schlieben's forces in the Cotentin mounted one last effort to drive the Americans out of Ste-Mère-Église and into the sea at Utah. This attack was supported by tanks and anti-tank guns but the Americans were now ashore in force and the German attack was beaten off on June 8. Von Schlieben then withdrew to positions close to Cherbourg and prepared to defend that port when the Americans came up. This withdrawal freed the 82nd Airborne for the completion of their D-Day task, the establishment of a bridgehead across the river Merderet, west of Ste-Mère-Église.

At the southern end of the VII Corps bridgehead, 101st Airborne grouped three regiments along the river Douve for the attack on Carentan, with a fourth regiment in reserve at Vierville.[13] The original intention was for an all-out attack by the entire division across the Douve as faulty intelligence led the Americans to believe that Carentan was lightly held. Fortunately, this plan was abandoned for a two-pronged thrust along the Vire from north of Brévands while the 502nd Parachute Infantry Regiment (502nd PIR) would attack directly across the causeway from St Côme.

The Douve is the major river between St-Côme and Carentan but there are several smaller streams as well – the Jourdan, the Groult and the Madeleine – and each of these had to be crossed in the face of opposition. The bridges had been destroyed, so when the 101st attacked Carentan on the night of June 10–11 they crossed the floods either by wading, clinging to the remaining piers of the bridges, or in rubber boats. This attack was contested by German infantry backed with both 88mm guns and the rare support of two German fighter aircraft. As a result the first attack was driven off in the early hours of June 11, after the leading US company had lost fifty-seven men out of the eighty in the company that opened the attack. The Americans renewed their attack across the Carentan causeway at dawn and crossed La Madeleine bridge (Bridge No. 4 in official accounts) where two officers, Lt Colonel Robert Cole and Major John Skopa, led some 250 men of the 3rd Bn, 502nd PIR in a bayonet charge into the enemy positions. [14]

This spirited attack eased the German grip on the town and when the 327th Glider Infantry came in from Brévands later that day, the Germans withdrew. The 327th Glider Infantry Regiment had linked up with the men of the 29th Infantry Division on June 10, and with the fall of Carentan on June 12 all the Allied beachheads on the Calvados coast were finally joined into one continuous, lateral bridgehead. It was still thin but it was solid and further advances could now be made.

This is not to say that the Germans conceded defeat in the Cotentin. Carentan was the vital point and on June 13 the 17 SS Panzer Grenadier Division, a force of lorried infantry supported by tanks and the remnants of van der Heydte's regiment, put in a strong counter-attack from Bapte, a village west of Carentan, their assault supported by no fewer than thirty-seven self-propelled guns. This attack was narrowly repulsed by the 101st Airborne, aided by men of the newly arrived 2nd Infantry Division and an air strike by P-47 Thunderbolts of the US Ninth Air Force. 101st Airborne then stayed in Carentan until relieved by the 83rd Infantry Division on June 29.

While these various formations, American and British, had been attempting to link up the beachheads and move inland, the 4th Infantry Division and other units of VII Corps had been engaged in another vital task, cutting directly across the Cotentin towards the Atlantic coast. Only when that had been done could VII Corps turn north to the capture of Cherbourg, though some VII Corps units were already pushing up towards Montebourg in an attempt to gain ground in the north of the peninsula before the enemy could form a defensive line. The Montebourg area had already been heavily fortified and mined and the first task was to reach the Quineville–Montebourg line, a ridge running west from the coast from which German artillery still had Utah beach under fire. The attack on this ridge line went in on June 8 and made slow but steady progress along the ridge to reach the edge of the river Merderet, north of Ste-Mère-Église.

The Americans met plenty of opposition here. Although the German units in the Cotentin were often scratch forces, drawn from a dozen different formations, they knew what they had to do and had the advantage of using those positions hurriedly prepared by General von Schlieben after the loss of Ste-Mère-Église on the night of June 6–7. Von Schlieben was short of tanks but he had a quantity of heavy artillery, some mobile anti-tank guns, an adequate supply of infantry, and a great quantity of mines. He was also a very determined officer, who would not give up ground without a fight.

As a result, the American attacks on June 9 met with only limited success. Although the 8th Infantry Regiment of the 4th Division took Magneville and got into Écausseville, they were promptly battered by heavy artillery and machine-gun fire. German 88mm guns in Écausseville took a toll of 4th Division's tank support but after the village was outflanked, the defenders withdrew towards Montebourg. By the night of June 10–11 the 8th Infantry Regiment were lined up along the Ham–Montebourg road and dug in there to await the next stage of the push toward Cherbourg, now only fifteen miles away and seemingly well within their grasp.

Meanwhile, the 505th PIR had taken Le Ham and Colonel 'Red' Reeder's 12th Infantry Regiment, having endured some very heavy fighting around Edmondville – where the casualties from shellfire included, as related, the regimental colonel – had reached a line a mile north-east of Montebourg and were now spearheading the advance on Cherbourg. All this was part of a general advance north by VII Corps and by June 12 the forward units were in position around Montebourg and Valognes, ready for the final push north, as soon as the Cotentin had been cut. This penultimate move would take time.

The advance west, to cut the Cotentin, was inhibited at first by the wide floods of the river Merderet, west of Ste-Mère-Église and north of Chef du Pont – and west of the Merderet lay another river, the Douve. The first task was to establish strong bridgeheads beyond the Merderet floods and this task was entrusted to the 82nd Airborne Division. Having failed to establish a jumping-off point at La Fière, west of Ste-Mère-Église, on D-Day, the 82nd had to endure a series of German counter-attacks on June 7–8, before they moved up to the edge of the floodwater and looked for a way across.

Among the airborne troopers at Chef du Pont was Zane Schlemmer, a nine-teen-year-old soldier in the 2nd Bn 508th PIR, 82nd Airborne:

> My big memory is those speckled Normandy cows but the area we landed in was also occupied by the highly disciplined German 91st Division and they occupied most of the farmhouses. Like most of the regiment, I was lost when I landed but I had seen the fire at Ste-Mère-Église and knew I was near Chef du Pont, only one and a half miles from our drop zone, which was not bad compared with the others. There was sporadic small arms fire everywhere and by keeping to the fields I got to our unit rendezvous on Hill 30 which overlooked the river and from where we could in theory control the Merderet crossings.
> I did not know if the invasion had succeeded or not but we stayed there for five days until the seaborne troops came up. We had no resupply of any kind but we could call on 75mm fire to break up German fire on our positions. The lack of medical supplies was felt by everyone and our chaplain was killed while attending to our wounded.

On the evening of June 8 a flooded but passable road was discovered north of La Fière, a reconnaissance patrol crossed without incident and two battalions, one each from the 325th Glider Infantry and the 507th PIR, made it through the floods on June 9. However, once across they were instantly counter-attacked by the enemy and thrown back with severe losses. The Divisional Commander, Major General Matthew Ridgeway, promptly ordered another attack and the task was again given to the 325th Glider Infantry. This attack failed with further losses but it was pressed hard, until the La Fière causeway was clogged with dead and wounded men. Even so, some airborne troopers had got across and they were quickly reinforced by men of the 507th PIR, which managed to gain a foothold at Le Motey, on the west side of the floods where they were able to hang on.

The next step, a development of this Merderet bridgehead and a thrust across the Cotentin to the Atlantic coast, was handed to the 90th Division, (Brigadier General Jay W. MacKelvie) which had come ashore on Utah on the afternoon of D-Day and had originally been tasked to join the 4th Division in the attack on Cherbourg. One regiment of the 90th was devoted to this task but the other two, the 357th and 358th Infantry Regiments, were now ordered to move beyond the Merderet and cross the river Douve, south of the village of St-Sauveur-le-Vicomte. This attack began on June 10 and immediately ran into trouble.

Within the first hour, the 90th's battalions encountered entrenched units of the German 91st Division, whose firepower and aggression drove the 2nd battalion of the US 357th Regiment back in some disorder. The 1st battalion of the 357th was then committed but did no better and the entire 358th Infantry Regiment – equivalent to a British brigade – advancing from Picauville, met some resistance and promptly stopped and dug in. The 90th Division stayed dug in, practically on their start line, for the next two days.

Fortunately, the 508th PIR of the 82nd Airborne Division, advancing to the south of the 90th Division, established themselves without difficulty in the village of Baupt, between the Merderet floods and that of the Marais de Gorges – but could go no further without support. This first attempt to cut the Cotentin peninsula therefore petered out but by June 12 VII Corps was ready to put in their attack towards Cherbourg. If VII Corps could not go west, perhaps they could go north – and their prime task, as stated in the initial plan, was to take Cherbourg.

By June 12, six days after D-Day, the situation in Normandy was as follows. A continuous bridgehead had been formed, fifty miles long and several miles deep. The two Allied armies currently ashore – the US First and the British Second – were now in the sectors they would occupy for the rest of the Battle of Normandy and from which they must expand and advance. The dividing line between the US First Army and the British Second Army was a line drawn south from Port-en-Bessin through Agy and then across the river Drôme to Caumont, which stands roughly central on a line between St-Lô and Villers-Bocage. There was currently a ten-mile-wide gap in the German defences at Caumont, occupied only by the elements of 17 SS Panzer Grenadiers, but buttressed on the east by Panzer Lehr at Longray and the remains of the 352nd Division northeast of St-Lô. The obvious task for the US V Corps would be to exploit that gap, which lay in their sector, and if possible thrust south and prise the German line apart.

This move was thwarted by a growing conviction among the US staff, both at First Army and V Corps HQ, that the Germans were preparing a major counter-attack at Caumont, probably from 11 Panzer and 1 SS Panzer, which were believed to be coming into Normandy from the south and were currently concealed in the Forêt de Cerisy astride the Bayeux to St-Lô road – on June 9, the First Army G-2 (Intelligence) advised V Corps: 'No surprise should be occasioned should this cover produce a major armoured or motorised division.' Some German formations, notably part of the 3rd Parachute Division, did indeed come forward, but the chance to split the German line at Caumont was lost by June 12 when the Americans finally advanced, their attack timed to coincide with the British move already described, that by 7th Armoured Division at Villers-Bocage on June 12–13.

Unlike the fierce resistance the Desert Rats encountered at Villers-Bocage, the US attack at Caumont was – according to their own Official History – 'spearheaded by the 1st Infantry Division on a 3,000-yard front and made good progress against light opposition which rapidly gave way'. Caumont was reached on the evening of June 12 and cleared of enemy by the following morning, when the 2nd Infantry Division came up on the right to occupy the high ground south of the Forêt de Cerisy. Two days of battering then followed, in an attempt to move on to St-Lô but the mood had now changed on the Normandy battlefield. The enemy had got his second wind, the fighting had moved into the *bocage,* and from now on advances would be measured in yards rather than miles. For the moment, says the US Official History:[15] 'The mission of V Corps was to hold its present position while the First Army devoted its main effort to the capture of Cherbourg.'

To sum up – given the fact that no battle ever goes exactly to plan – the first six days of the invasion had, on the whole, gone very well. The enemy had been either contained or driven back, the beachheads had been linked into one continuous bridgehead and most of the D-Day objectives – except Caen – were in Allied hands by D plus 6. The Germans were certainly far from happy. On June 10, the C-in-C West's war diary reported that the Seventh Army was on the defensive everywhere and the Seventh Army war diary recorded that their commander's calculations had been upset by the power of the Allied tactical air forces.

One curious comment in Rommel's report to OKW is that 'the material equipment of the Anglo-Americans is far superior to that of our infantry divisions operating here'. That remark is not borne out by the experience of the Allied infantry; comments on the Germans' abundance of – and superiority in – light and medium machine-guns, automatic weapons, tanks, light mortars and *nebelwerfers* – are made frequently in their accounts. The Germans were fighting hard and well and appeared to be better trained than the Allied troops. They were also highly motivated for if they failed here, the Allies would press on to the Rhine. To defeat the German forces in Normandy was not going to be easy and the Allies had done well to get as far as they had in the first week of the invasion.

General Montgomery certainly seemed satisfied. According to the Official History:[16] 'His general policy remained unchanged', namely 'to increase and improve our build-up through the beaches, to do everything possible to hamper and delay the enemy build-up by air action and other means' and 'to pull the Germans on to the British Second Army and fight them there so that the First US Army can carry out its task easier.'

This overall success was not sufficient to dampen the chorus of complaints at SHAEF. The two 'failures' – of the British at Caen and the Canadians at Carpiquet – were more than enough to cause concern and criticism at SHAEF, where General Montgomery's numerous enemies, both British and American, were already mustering their arguments.

5 EXPANDING THE BRIDGEHEAD JUNE 12-18

My immediate objectives remained to capture Caen and Cherbourg and to develop the central section of the bridgehead to Caumont and Villers-Bocage.

GENERAL B. L. MONTGOMERY *Normandy to the Baltic*

With the link-up of the various beaches on June 12 the Allied bridgehead was complete. The reserve formations of the assault divisions were now ashore, the follow-up divisions were hard on their heels and the next phase of the campaign, the expansion of the bridgehead, was about to begin. This being so, it would be as well to examine the position of the Allied armies on June 12 and see how it compares with the original Overlord plan.

If the phase lines drawn on the maps were any practical yardstick, the Allied plan had already fallen behind schedule. On the Second Army front the end of D-Day should have seen the British and Canadians occupying a line that began on the Channel coast at Cabourg, just east of the river Dives, and swept south and west from there to embrace Caen before swinging north via Norray, south of the Caen–Bayeux road to reach the line where the British linked up with the Americans, somewhere south of Port-en-Bessin. The D-Day line then headed west, just south of Trevières to Isigny and so up to the sea at the mouth of the Vire with US forces well forward south of Omaha. In the Cotentin, no firm line was envisaged for D-Day but it was anticipated that the 101st and 82nd Airborne would have taken Carentan and Ste-Mère-Église that day and the 4th Infantry Division would have linked up with them and started to move north towards Montebourg and Cherbourg.

Broadly speaking, it had taken the first week to achieve these D-Day objectives

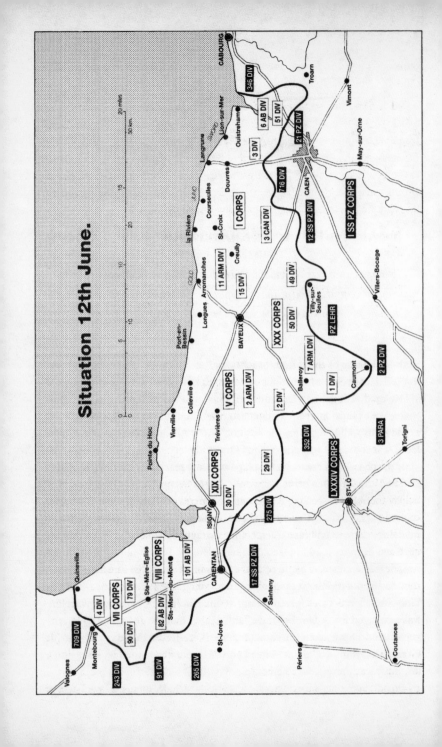

Situation 12th June.

– with the significant exception of Caen and the open country between Caen and Falaise which the Tactical Air Force commanders and the Deputy Allied Supreme Commander, Air Chief Marshal Sir Arthur Tedder, wanted for airfields. When the Second Army failed to deliver this ground the air commanders began to grumble and these grumbles were not mitigated by General Montgomery's response. If the account in his Memoirs[1] is anything to go by, his reply was abrupt, unsatisfactory and calculated to offend:

> 'Maori' Coningham, in command of 2nd Tactical Air Force ... was working with 21st Army Group. 'Maori' was particularly interested in getting his airfields south-east of Caen. They were mentioned in the plan and to him they were all important. I don't blame him. But they were not all-important to me. If we won the Battle of Normandy all else would follow, airfields and all. But I was not fighting to capture airfields; I was fighting to defeat Rommel in Normandy. This Coningham could scarcely appreciate.

Montgomery's considerable talent for making enemies was clearly working well at this time although he goes on to say that the main reason for this dispute with Coningham was that they were not seeing much of each other, and this may well be correct. When they had been in North Africa, the commanders of the Eighth Army and the Desert Air Force had shared a headquarters and worked hand-in-glove, sorting out problems on a daily basis as they arose – but that was before victory in the desert and the public adulation that followed had turned Montgomery's head. There were good reasons for Monty's inability to deliver the country south-east of Caen – the presence of the German Army for one – and if that had been stressed and the various difficulties pointed out to his colleagues with a little more tact, a great deal of subsequent grief might have been avoided.

The Allied air forces had four tasks during this phase of the campaign. Firstly, they had to protect the embarkation ports in England and the massive supply bases close by. Secondly, they had to provide cover for the supply and reinforcement convoys in the Channel. Thirdly, they had to help the ground forces get forward with tactical air support on the battlefield and the interdiction of German supply routes into Normandy. Finally, they had to shoot down any Luftwaffe aircraft that intruded over the bridgehead. This presents the other side to the argument but all these tasks could be handled – and indeed were being handled – perfectly well from the UK. This being so, why were Tedder and his minions so anxious to get their aircraft on to landing fields in Normandy?

The first reason is that they had been promised airfields in the strategic plan and expected the army to deliver on that promise. At his presentation on April 7, Montgomery had clearly stated that he intended 'to assault west of the river Orne and develop operations in the south-east in order to secure airfield sites'. This intention was restated on May 15 when Montgomery again argued for armoured advances south of Caen in order to gain ground for airfields – an argument that later surfaced in Bradley's memoirs as a specific intention to get armour as far south as Falaise on D-Day. According to the plan, by the end of June – D plus 24 – Second Army would have this ground and 2nd TAF would have fifteen operational airfields. These would be used as fighter strips or for emergency landings by battle-damaged aircraft, but their most obvious use would be for reconnaissance aircraft and artillery-spotting Austers – though the Austers could operate perfectly well from grass fields – and by Dakota, (C-47), transports evacuating wounded.

Building these airfields was the task of the Airfield Construction Companies (ACCs) of the Royal Engineers and servicing the aircraft landing on these fields was the task of the RAF Servicing Commando Units (SCUs). The first SCU, Number 3207, sailed from Gosport on D-Day and by the following day was on an emergency landing ground (ELG), B (British) 2 near Bazenville, three miles from Gold beach, where a strip had already been laid out by the sappers. A few days later another one was operational on the bluffs above Omaha and more strips followed. At B2 they refuelled and rearmed Hurricanes and rocket-firing Typhoons and Thunderbolts, before moving on to No. 122 Airfield at Esquay-sur-Selle on the Caen–Bayeux road.[2]

Now comes an interesting incident from the 3207 Servicing Commando log. At 1200hrs on June 11 (D plus 5) a B-17 Flying Fortress carrying Eisenhower and Tedder landed on airstrip B2 near St-Croix and the commanders drove off in jeeps for a three-hour tour of the bridgehead. On the following day, June 12, the head of No. 84 Group, 2nd TAF, Air Vice Marshal L. O. Brown, landed at airstrip B3 and the Servicing Commando log notes that on that day the SCU at B3 refuelled and rearmed thirty-six Spitfires, one Typhoon, four Mustangs and a Lockheed Lightning, from four separate squadrons. On June 13, B3 refuelled an RAF Bomber Command Halifax with 800 gallons of petrol – and an increasing number of other aircraft. On that day, apart from the Halifax, B3 rearmed and refuelled 77 Spitfires, one Mustang, two Thunderbolts and four Typhoons. Other airstrips, B1, 2, 4, 5, 6 and 7, plus those in the American sector – A1, A2 etc. – could do as well or better. The US Official History[3] records that the problems of constructing airfields was, 'much less serious than the planners had anticipated' and that by early July 'about a third of the Ninth Air Force fighters and fighter bombers were based on the Continent'. Where then was the problem with tactical air support and why were Tedder and Coningham making such a fuss about airfields south of Caen when they were well aware that they could manage without them?

Quite apart from any other consideration, the logistical effort involved in transporting and storing the fuel, oil, rockets and machine-gun ammunition and spare parts to supply and maintain this number of aircraft, from a varied number of types, on airfields in France should not be underestimated. Every rocket, bullet, drop of fuel and screw had to be transported to France, landed over open beaches or through the limited facilities of Mulberry, or the small ports of Courseulles and Port-en-Bessin which opened for business on June 12 or eventually collected from the Pluto pipeline in tankers or fuel trucks. That done, these stores and POL had to be carried over narrow dusty roads to the airstrips. The airfield log is clear evidence that these airstrips were now working well and capable of handling large aircraft including heavy bombers and transports. The variation in numbers between the various fighter types using these airstrips is also interesting; the Spitfire was a short-range fighter and needed emergency airstrips but all the rest, the Typhoons, Thunderbolts and Lightnings, as their scanty numbers dropping in to refuel indicates, were perfectly capable of strafing targets in Normandy and then returning to their UK bases.

When the great bulk of the Allied air forces could operate from the UK, or be dealt with in emergency by the SC facilities already in France, it seems strange that the Deputy Supreme Commander – whose remit in that role included services other than his own – should choose to make trouble for General Montgomery by insisting on facilities which were clearly not needed *at this time*, and merely duplicated those already available in the UK.

One possible reason for this agitation over ground is the start of the German flying bomb or V-1 offensive which began on June 13. This clearly alarmed the powers-that-be at SHAEF and made them anxious to get the armies moving out to overrun the V-1 launch sites on the Channel coast, but this is a charitable interpretation; the evidence seems to suggest that certain people at SHAEF were angling for Montgomery simply to make trouble and for no other reason.

Later on, as the front line moved away from the beaches – and the English coast – airfields in France would be certainly be necessary, but to start agitating for them at this stage, in the first days of the landing, seems both short-sighted and petty. Having visited the beachhead only two days before and being therefore well aware that the Normandy airstrips could refuel and rearm hundreds of Allied aircraft every day, Tedder's comment of June 14, (D plus 8), that the failure to take Caen and Carpiquet, 'had the makings of a dangerous crisis'[4] is self-evident nonsense and harmful to the unity of the Allied command.

Tedder's criticisms and Coningham's complaints were soon taken up by Montgomery's other detractors at SHAEF who were more than happy to use Second Army's failure to take Caen and Carpiquet as reasons to question his entire strategy. Monty could have defused a lot of this criticism and disarmed his enemies if he had taken the time to explain his problems in detail and give cogent reasons why the airmen could not have what they wanted – or at least not yet. Instead Monty claimed that everything was going exactly as planned, which was patently not so.

The delays across the Allied front are not surprising for the numerous reasons already supplied. Only if the enemy had put up no opposition at all could the D-Day ambitions have been achieved. However, after a little time has elapsed, it is necessary to accept the existing difficulties and start implementing the original strategic plan, though adapted to accept whatever amendments have been forced upon it by difficulties in the early stage. In the case of Overlord, having got ashore and formed a complete bridgehead, it was clearly necessary to press ahead with other immediate tasks, the capture of Caen and Cherbourg. By D plus 6, June 12, it was already clear that the former was going to be much harder than the latter, for the Germans were very determined to hang on to Caen and had the forces on hand to retain it.

On the other hand, the German defenders of Caen were not finding life all that easy either. Crushing naval bombardments and the scale and ferocity of Allied air attacks, especially from the ground-attack aircraft, the Typhoons and

Thunderbolts of 2nd TAF and the US Ninth Air Force, had already shaken them severely. The war diary of the Seventh Army admits that its intended reactions to the Allied invasion had been made virtually impossible by Allied air power and on June 11 Rommel and von Rundstedt submitted a joint report to Hitler, outlining the events to date and pressing for more reinforcements, especially infantry.

A shortage of infantry was forcing them to use the Panzer units in a defensive role when the tanks could have been better employed attacking around the bridgehead perimeter or spearheading those counter-attacks the Führer was constantly calling for. By forcing his commanders to use tanks as strongpoints or pillboxes to support the defence, Hitler was helping Montgomery's aim of sucking Panzer forces on to the Caen front. On the other hand, the German troops were handling the defensive battle extremely well, and blunting the best efforts of the Allied troops sent against them.

This appeal from his generals produced two answers from the Führer. One reiterated his command that the troops were to hold their ground to the last man and the last round. The other was somewhat more supportive, to order the transfer to the II SS Panzer Corps of two divisions from the Russian front. Infantry reinforcements would be gathered in from Norway, Denmark and Holland, but not from the Fifteenth Army, which was still on alert, awaiting the arrival of George Patton's Army in the Pas de Calais. Every day that Fortitude kept the Fifteenth Army north of the Seine, the Allied forces in the bridgehead increased.

The eastern end of the bridgehead, where any Fifteenth Army intervention would fall, was now firmly in the hand of 6th Airborne and the 1st Commando Brigade which had thickened up their defences and been reinforced by the arrival in the Orne bridgehead of the 51st Highland Division. Between June 10 and 12, as related, a violent battle took place around the airborne perimeter, culminating in the capture of Bréville, but this was as much as the paratroopers and commandos could be expected to do. They could hold the eastern flank of the invasion area; attacking out of the bridgehead against German armour was not within their present capability.

Apart from bolstering 6th Airborne, the Highlanders carried out a series of probing thrusts to the east of the city, trying to hook round the right of the defenders north of Caen. In their first brush with the enemy since leaving the western desert, the Highlanders were brought to a halt with heavy losses. This eastern thrust had been timed to coincide with that thrust by 50th Division and the newly landed 7th Armoured Division of Horrocks's XXX Corps – Operation Perch – the move south and south-east out of Bayeux towards Villers-Bocage which has already been described, and went no better.

On June 13 51st Highland Division attacked Ste Honorine, a village one mile north of the German defences in the Colombelles factory area on the east bank of the Orne. Although they took the village they were unable to hold it in the face of enemy counter-attacks. From then on any attempt to enlarge the Orne bridgehead on the east was immediately resisted by the enemy, while in the centre, west of the canal at Blainville, the rest of I Corps were equally hard-pressed. Some fresh effort was needed, and the arrival of VIII Corps seemed to offer this possibility but the landing of the first VIII Corps formation, the 11th Armoured Division, which began on June 15, rapidly fell behind schedule and was soon two days late. This was largely due to the weather which continued poor, and the disruption in shipping schedules for reasons already described

Meanwhile, in the XXX Corps area, 50th Division were still battling for Tilly-sur-Seulles, and the road to the west through Lingèvres and La Senaudière. Their attack on June 14 was made on a 4,000-metre front and preceded by a fierce attack by rocket-firing Typhoons and Hurricanes of 83 and 84 Groups of 2nd TAF, eleven squadrons in all, plus the divisional and corps artillery and the Royal Navy – and the guns of the US V Corps, firing in from the west. With all this going for it the attack promised a great deal but again, as with 7th Armoured's attack on Villers-Bocage the previous day, it made no great impression on the German line nor did much to help 7th Armoured which, on the night of June 14–15, withdrew to a position close to Caumont. Panzer Lehr had held 7th Armoured back and with the arrival of 2nd Panzer the German position on the Caen front was even stronger than before.

According to Tony King, a lance-corporal in a tank regiment, the 5th Royal Iniskilling Dragoon Guards – the 'Skins' – which landed in France at this time:[5]

On arrival at the reception area in Normandy we were told that our role was to replace the 4th County of London Yeomanry in 7th Armoured Division. 4CLY had sustained heavy losses in the recent tank battles, notably at Villers-Bocage and was no longer operational. The 'Skins' therefore joined the 1st and 5th RTR in 22 Armoured Brigade. We collected mainly new Cromwell tanks from a huge equipment compound outside Bayeux and started preparing them for battle. Two sources of amazement to the newcomer were the immense amount of stores that had been shipped across the Channel and the casual way they were dumped in the fields without camouflage, as the Luftwaffe did not pose much of a threat, though curiously our first encounter with the enemy was a night raid on our laager – our night camp – by German fighter-bombers, one bomb dropping on our tank with a tremendous detonation but doing no damage to tank or crew.

Our Cromwell was hung about with loose track plates to help deflect the 88mm armour-piercing shells from German Tiger tanks and 88mm guns which our armour plating was no match for. The 88 had a longer range and higher muzzle velocity than our 75s which was not very confidence-inspiring. Each fighting troop consisted of three Cromwells and one Sherman Firefly with its long-barrelled 17-pounder gun, the only armament that could cope with the Tiger.

Apart from that bombing I cannot recall anything in those first few confused days of real war except the horror of watching for the first time another tank 'brew up' after a direct hit from a Tiger and the frantic efforts of the crew to escape the inferno. The driver – and I was a driver – sitting down inside the turret, was always the last to escape and this one did not make it. Later in the campaign we became hardened to seeing blazing and burnt-out tanks, often a funeral pyre for their incinerated crews. I once helped pull the co-driver out of a tank which had run over a Teller mine. The impact had broken both his legs and the only way to get him out was to haul on the shoulder straps of his webbing after injecting an ampoule of morphine into him and crushing a chloroform phial wrapped in gauze between his teeth, both primitive methods but unavoidable in the heat of battle.

We were puzzled by the lukewarm reception we got from the local people, not the kind liberators from the yoke of Fascism expected; perhaps we forgot that for many French people the occupation was not rigorous, collaboration was rife and the suffering caused by the fighting and bombing was severe in places. Nevertheless the ladies of the night in Bayeux and Caen extended the welcome mat – or more accurately, mattress, to any interested soldier.

Fighting in the Normandy *bocage* was pretty intense and difficult for tanks because of the small fields, high banks and narrow lanes, all tending to limit manoeuvres and lines of sight. The whole crew was tensed as we approached any bend in the road, wondering if an 88mm had its sights trained on the corner, waiting to take out the first vehicle to show its nose.

Jack Capell of the 8th Infantry Regiment, 4th US Infantry Division, has his memories of this time and they confirm those of his British colleague:[6]

Memories of the fighting in the days after D-Day are confused. I recall the mortaring and shelling, the smell of dead cows – and people – and every night this aircraft that would circle overhead, dropping the occasional bomb or flare to keep us awake. We called the pilot 'Bedcheck Charlie' or 'Washing Machine Charlie', from the sound of the engines. There were plenty of Germans about, stretching wires across the road in attempts to decapitate drivers; eventually all our jeeps carried angle-iron posts, welded to the front fender, to cut these wires. The weather was pretty bad, plenty of rain to fill our foxholes and we were never dry. A lot of mosquitoes too.

Bill Thompson of 'C' Squadron, 9th Royal Tank Regiment (9 RTR) talks of the German and British soldiers at this time:[7]

There is no doubt about the quality of the German soldier in Normandy; they were very good, seasoned troops with very good tanks. We found this out very quickly and tried to match them with what we had, Churchill tanks. Mark 4's and 7's. We had been well-trained for this battle, no complaints there, but the 9 RTR was made up of young, green troops in their late teens and early twenties, like most of the soldiers in Normandy, I suppose. We had been told that this would be a hard fight, kill or be killed, and that is what it was; we needed no further training, just experience of the real thing and that came soon enough, not least on Hill 112.

Although the Allies were pouring troops ashore, the Germans were able to build up their forces, particularly their tank forces, faster than Montgomery could. By June 18 Rommel had four Panzer divisions facing the British on a line between Caen and Caumont, with 2nd Panzer astride the British Second and US First Army boundary south of Caumont. On the American front there were no Panzer divisions but plenty of tank-supported battlegroups (*kampfgruppe*) and the crack 17 SS Panzer Grenadier Division was facing Carentan. More German divisions, all infantry, were coming up from Brittany towards St-Lô, harassed as they came by the French Resistance, the Maquis, and it appeared that, while enemy strength was increasing, Allied progress was slowing down ... and not just because of enemy resistance.

It was becoming obvious, even to SHAEF, that this Normandy fighting was posing unexpected difficulties for some of the Allied troops. It is interesting that, be they new or experienced formation, infantry or armour, American or British, the end result was much the same – a tendency to become 'sticky', a reluctance to advance into close country and engage the enemy in all-out battle. We have seen in the previous chapter how the US 90th Division became very 'sticky' and made virtually no progress beyond its start line. This is understandable because the troops in this division had never been in action before. Although they had been well trained there had been no opportunity to put them into the line in a quiet sector and let the officers and men get used to the exigencies of combat. They got off their ships and within a couple of days these young American soldiers were confronting combat troops of the German Army in battle. It is hardly surprising if they faltered, for they lacked experience.

Reg Spittle of the 2nd Northamptonshire Yeomanry, a Cromwell tank commander in the British VIII Corps understands this problem:[8]

Training is not like the real thing, not at all. We were green troops too and no amount of training, all those exercises in the past years, had prepared us for the reality. You are going along and suddenly there is a tank on fire and you think – Bloody Hell! – how did that happen? I was not afraid, not to begin with, mostly curious about what battle would be like but it was not like I expected and there is no way we were really ready for the reality of seeing what we did see, friends dying in blazing tanks.

There are few absolutes in battle. As we have seen, an experienced British division, 7th Armoured – the famous Desert Rats – had also faltered and fallen back at Villers-Bocage. Another veteran division, 51st Highland, would also falter at first in Normandy, displaying little of its western desert *élan*. The reasons here were different. It was not that these British divisions had seen too little of war but rather that they had seen too much. Both divisions had served with distinction in the North African campaign where many of the men, most of the NCOs, and a majority of the officers had been in action, advance and retreat, defeat and victory, for three long, hard years.

Then they had come back to the UK for the invasion – and relaxed for a while. The married men returned to their families and saw how their children had grown up. Many of the single men had got married. Life had looked good and hopeful for a while but now they were sent back in battle and that rosy future was at risk. Again, it is hardly surprising if many of these men felt, to quote one 7th Armoured veteran: 'We had done our bit and a bit besides, in the desert and in Italy ... we thought it was time for some other bugger to have a go.'[6] But again, there are no absolutes in war. 50th Division was a veteran desert-formation and yet it did exceptionally well throughout the entire Normandy campaign.

Soldiers go through stages in combat. If they are well trained and well led, their opening engagements can be exciting, a chance for young soldiers to prove themselves, at least until the first signs of combat – the noise, the confusion, the dead, the wounds, the loss of friends, the sights and smells – bring on the reality. Some men are exhilarated by battle but these are the rare ones. Others are terrified and cannot take it at all; nobody can know, until the battle starts, which category they will fall into. Everyone is afraid – which is reasonable for there is a great deal to be afraid of – but the vast majority of men will cope somehow, buoyed-up by discipline, personal pride, unit *esprit de corps,* and a grim determination not to let their comrades down.

Those who survive these early encounters become useful soldiers – 'battle-hardened' is the phrase for their new condition – men who know the difference between what is dangerous and what is merely frightening. These men know how to fight and win in war and they will continue in that useful condition for a while. But in time, inevitably, their determination wanes; too much exposure to danger, too many lost friends, too many terrible sights, eventually sap the will to fight. Rest and relief is essential to keep good soldiers going even this far, but eventually the will for battle declines.

While rest and relaxation is important this condition can be exacerbated if the soldiers – like those in the old desert formations – are given a prolonged respite at home, amid their loved ones. The will to *return* to battle is harder to create than the will to *remain* in battle and going back to the war is hard for them ... and who can blame them? They have indeed 'done their bit'. The answer has to be provided by the senior officers, with a blast of discipline and the grinding home of the hard fact that the war is not over and will not be over until the enemy has been defeated.

It may also be necessary to dismiss some senior commanders, *pour encourager les autres*. Many American, British and Canadian officers, of all ranks, would be found inadequate for the task before them, and replaced in the coming weeks. The fall-out among senior officers was a notable feature of the Normandy campaign in all the Allied armies. Overall, it appears that the American commanders were rather too quick to dismiss faltering officers and the British rather too slow to do so – but the same willingness to sack the slow or incompetent was common to both.

The curious thing is that this reluctance 'to get stuck-in' does not appear so often on the German side. Although many prisoners were taken, and deserters – many of them Russian or from other subject states – came in in droves during the early days of the Normandy fighting, the majority of the German soldiers stayed aggressive. They were undoubtedly superior to many of the Allied soldiers in basic fieldcraft, infantry tactics and infantry tank co-operation – enthusiastic soldiers being one of the few benefits produced by a militaristic society – at least to begin with, until the Allied soldiers got the hang of this kind of fighting and began to fight with skill as well as tenacity.

The Germans also had a considerable motivation; they were fighting to keep the Allied armies away from their homeland, to gain time for the Führer to produce his promised miracle weapons and – perhaps – to defeat the Anglo-Saxon forces in the field. Moreover, they had some evidence that the Führer was making good on his promises; the first V-1 flying bombs fell on England on June 13 and the devastating V-2 rocket soon followed – perhaps, if they could hang on, the balance of the war would indeed swing back in Germany's favour?

It also has to be added that these were soldiers of the German Army, an army that had conquered most of the Continent, soldiers with equipment often superior to that of the Allies, notably in tanks and anti-tank guns, soldiers equipped with an abundance of mortars and machine-guns, fighting on the defensive on ground ideal for defence ... and fully determined to make the Allied soldiers pay dearly for every metre of ground gained.

They demonstrated that determination when they beat off the Americans at Carentan and Monteboug and when they repulsed 7th Armoured at Villers-Bocage.

After that reverse 7th Armoured was ordered back towards the Aure, to hold there while 50th Division and the newly arrived 49th Division pressed on to capture Tilly-sur-Seulles. This they did on June 19, after three days of heavy fighting.

With the bulk of the German Panzer forces engaged in defending ground against the British and Canadians east of Caumont, the US V Corps on their right had made good progress south, astride the river Vire. South of Caumont 1st Infantry Division had pushed out patrols as far as Balleroy, though their forward push was inhibited by the divide opening between them and the British, exposing their right flank and creating a gap, one that widened when the British 50th Division turned south-east towards Tilly-sur-Seulles and Villers-Bocage. There was also a gap on the German side, south of Balleroy, where there was nothing but a few scattered strongpoints to check an Allied advance east of Bérigny until Panzer Lehr took up the line again by Longraye, south-west of Tilly.

This was an opportunity for the US troops to gain ground, but south from Caumont was not the direction the US forces needed to travel; their 'axis of advance' now was to the south-west, through Bérigny, west of the Forêt de Cerisy towards St-Lô, which is actually due west of Caumont. 1st Infantry Division were therefore ordered to hold their position at Caumont, while the 29th Infantry and the 2nd Infantry pushed south and west down the river Vire towards St-Lô. This advance was made against stubborn resistance from the 352nd Division and the 3rd Parachute Division, which, says the US Official History,[9] 'turned out to have some of the toughest infantrymen in Rundstedt's armies'.

The effect of this German resistance can be seen by comparing the casualty figures for the US 1st and 2nd Infantry Divisions at this time. 1st Infantry Division, attacking east of the Forêt de Cerisy, lost ninety-two men, killed, wounded and missing; 2nd Infantry Division attacking to the west of the forest lost 540 men, most of them in attempts to take Hill 192, a feature which dominates the road between Bayeux and St-Lô.

The first attack, on June 12, by two battalions of the 29th Infantry Regiment, was stopped at the narrow river Elle. The river was only ten feet wide but the banks were found to be mined, the river seamed with wire and the entire frontage under observed artillery and machine-gun fire, much of it directed by observers on Hill 192. This brought the advance to a halt but the attack was renewed on the following day, the Elle was crossed and the regiment advanced two miles before being stopped by an order from the divisional commander, who did not want any of his units exposed to the possibility of a major German counter-attack by moving too far forward on its own. The advance was then taken up by the 29th Infantry Division which quickly crossed the Elle but soon found itself entangled in the *bocage* – the hedgerow country – where tank support was hard to supply and tank losses, mostly to the *panzerfausts,* mounted steadily. There are also accounts of German infantry sniping tank commanders and then leaping aboard their tanks from the high banks of the road and cramming hand grenades into the turrets.

The already depleted 29th Division lost another 547 men battling in the *bocage,* and on the evening of June 13 General Bradley intervened and ordered the V Corps commander to stop the advance on St-Lô. This was largely due to a fear that supporting the V Corps advance at this time would eat up resources, notably artillery ammunition, needed to support the VII Corps advance on Cherbourg. This order left 1st Infantry Division holding a narrow salient at Caumont, well ahead of 2nd Infantry on their right. Even so, this was the right decision; with a fresh US corps, XIX Corps, becoming operational on June 13 and about to enter the fray, it was time for V Corps to take a breather and build up its strength before pushing on again.

The next phase in the advance on St-Lô began on June 15 when Major General Charles H. Corlett's XIX Corps sent the 30th Division to attack the high ground in front of St-Lô, between the rivers Vire and Taute. This thrust, by a single division, was not expected to achieve much and progress remained slow, although German resistance was weak, largely because it proved virtually impossible for the Germans to move troops in daylight while the Allied air forces occupied the skies; 30th Division losses that day were less than twenty men. By June 16, XIX Corps had taken up a position fronting the Vire–Taute canal and stayed there while the battle was taken up by the 29th Division, now attached to XIX Corps and the 2nd Infantry Division from V Corps; both of these divisions moved again on St-Lô.

This force would be opposed by men of the crack 3rd Parachute Division which had just arrived in the area and taken up positions at Montrabot, and when the Americans advanced they almost immediately ran into fire. The 9th Infantry Regiment of the 2nd Division lost 140 men on June 16 and advanced less than a quarter of a mile; the 23rd Infantry Regiment on their right lost eleven officers and 162 men and still failed to take the summit of that vital feature, Hill 192. They got within half a mile of the crest and stayed there, under machine-gun and sniper fire, for the next two weeks.

The attack put in that day by the 29th Infantry Division did little better after an encouraging start. The orders for the 116th Infantry Regiment were for an advance by battalion bounds to take two hill features, Nos 147 and 150, on the Martinville ridge. This advance ran into artillery fire and was then met in the open by a counter-attack from tanks and infantry close to the village of St André-de-l'Épine five miles north-west of St-Lô. Progress stopped and the division dug in for the night, ready to attack again next day. Colonel Canham was dissatisfied with his regiment's performance and ordered the battalion commanders to make more effort on the second day, stating that: 'It is time to get over the jitters and fight like hell'. Even so, the second day was a duplication of the first; very little progress and a great deal of hard fighting.

On the third day, June 18, General Gerhardt mustered eight battalions of artillery to support the attack of the 115th and 116th Infantry Regiments of the 29th Division, but even this support failed to dampen the German resistance and the 116th Regiment was already exhausted by two days of combat and the constant grinding down since Omaha on D-Day. This division needed a rest, reporting that: 'Everyone is done out physically. No leaders left. No reorganisation possible'.[10] The Americans had now advanced their line in the south and west to within five miles of St-Lô but that was all they could do for the moment. On June 17 General Gerhardt felt able to assure the XIX Corps commander that 'I feel we will be getting to St-Lô before long', but added cautiously, 'It's hard to tell.'

It was indeed. US troops were not to enter St-Lô for another month, until July 18, after weeks of heavy fighting. For the moment these American formations, both the battle-hardened 29th Infantry Division and the newly arrived 2nd and 30th Infantry Divisions, had done all they could do. What the British had discovered before Caen, the Americans were now discovering before St-Lô; if the Germans were determined to defend a position, they could not be easily dislodged.

The US Official History[11] highlights some of the difficulties facing their troops at this time. The basic problem was that the enemy's favourite formation – small groups of infantry backed by a tank or two and some belt-fed machine-guns and mortars, all well camouflaged and concealed in the hedgerows – was one that could only be tackled by very well-trained infantry or at a high cost in lives. As the US Official History comments, 'Tanks could not go forward to knock out the machine-guns, nor could the infantry get forward to knock out the anti-tank guns.' The diary of the 747th Tank Battalion records:

> Tanks were forced to withdraw by heavy anti-tank fire and bazooka (*panzer-schrek*) fire. One tank was knocked out and its five crew wounded. The tanks kept trying to get forward but got stuck. The infantry stayed pinned down. Another tank was hit. Then four tanks forced their way through to the objective but no infantry followed. Only two tanks returned; one was knocked out by anti-tank fire and the other got stuck and had to be abandoned. The infantry could not get forward and withdrew 900 yards ...

What was needed now was better infantry–tank co-operation, a higher standard of fieldcraft to match that of the German infantry and some way of breaking through the high sides of the lanes through the *bocage* so that the tanks could manoeuvre in the fields and over the hedges and were not tied to the narrow and dangerous lanes. A programme was introduced to train the American infantry in these tactics even while they were already in the field, in Normandy, facing the enemy. Until that training could be completed and small unit tactics improved, progress on the V Corps front would be slow.

The US V Corps had been in the line since D-Day and for the moment it could do no more. The leading unit, the famous and resolute 29th Division – 'The Blue and The Grey' – a National Guard division from Virginia which had landed on D-Day, was now within five miles of St-Lô. It was to enter the city only at a terrible cost in lives, a later estimate stating that the twenty-day fight for St-Lô cost the First Army 40,000 men – 2,000 casualties for every mile gained, more than one man per yard.

These delays bothered the staff at SHAEF but they do not seem to have caused any great concern to the Allied Commander in Normandy, General Montgomery. His intention as stated on June 15,[12] was to continue with his overall plan 'to increase and improve our build-up through the beaches, to do everything possible to hamper and delay the enemy build-up and to pull the Germans onto the British front and fight them there so that the First US Army can carry out its task easier'.

This strategy had always been Montgomery's plan. As long as that strategic intention worked out, specific objectives were of secondary importance ... at least to General Montgomery; the grumblings from Tedder and Morgan at SHAEF continued.

To this end the fighting continued, east and west of the US V Corps. On the British front, 43rd Division retook St Pierre from 12 SS Panzer and on June 19 50th Division finally drove the Germans out of Tilly-sur-Seulles and were able to link up with both 7th Armoured at Livry and the US 1st Infantry Division at Caumont. The Germans had been driven back into the *bocage* and their casualties were mounting; by June 17 German losses amounted to over 26,000 men, killed, wounded or captured. This included a large number of officers including a corps commander and five divisional commanders.

By that day the Allies had landed a total of 557,000 men in Normandy – almost exactly half-American, half-British. From now on the American contribution would increase and it should be noted that, impressive as this figure was, the units landing were, on average, coming ashore two days late. Even so, progress was being made in the Cotentin where the US VII Corps were beating their way towards Cherbourg.

We left VII Corps stalled in the Cotentin having pushed the 90th Division and units of the 82nd Airborne across the floods of the Merderet at La Fière, en route for the west coast. The 90th Division remained 'sticky'; when Major General Eugene Landrum took over the division on June 13, he sacked two of the regimental commanders on the same day. On the following day, June 14, the 9th Division (Major-General Manton Eddy) and the 82nd Airborne set out again for the west coast of the Cotentin. These two divisions pushed ahead and reached the Valognes–Pont l'Abbé road that day, but when the 90th Division came up to cover their advance from the north, it stalled yet again – 'virtual paralysis', according to the US Official History.[13]

It took two days for the 90th Division to take the village of Gourbesville and one regiment, the 358th, made no progress at all. Part of this slow progress by the 90th compared with that of the other divisions was probably due to the fact that while the 9th and 82nd Divisions were confronted with the tired and much-reduced 91st Division, the 90th met the fresh 77th Division, a strong infantry formation, and was promptly held.

Fortunately, the 82nd Airborne, with tank support from the 746th Tank

Battalion, was soon powering ahead against decreasing opposition as the 91st Division, now reduced to a *kampfgruppe* – battlegroup – ran out of men and ammunition. St-Sauveur-le-Vicomte fell on June 16 and with the crossing of the river Douve that day, the last physical obstacle in front of the Americans before the west coast of the Cotentin peninsula was removed. General Collins then told these divisional commanders that VII Corps were to go all out and cut the Cotentin in two – and while they were doing that, other units of VII Corps would continue to press towards Cherbourg.

Meanwhile, the US forces in the Cotentin were increasing. A new corps, the VIII, under Major General Troy Middleton, was forming at Carentan where it took the resident 101st Airborne Division under command. This was the first step in a reorganisation of US troops in the Cotentin and was based on the intention that after VII Corps had cut the Cotentin, it would turn north and deploy all its strength to take Cherbourg, while VIII Corps formed a defensive line across the base of the peninsula to protect their backs. While this VIII Corps line was forming, VII Corps set out for the Atlantic coast.

The dynamo in this thrust to the west was the superb 82nd Airborne Division, which put up a notably fine performance throughout its time in Normandy – and was given an abundance of hard tasks as a reward for this effort. Before noon on June 16 the 325th Glider Infantry and the 505th PIR had reached the river Douve and crossed at St Sauveur to establish a bridgehead a mile deep on the far side. The 9th Division also got across and by nightfall on June 16 these two divisions were confronting the German defenders in the Cotentin with a classic tactical dilemma.

With no means to stem the American advance west, and in danger of being driven into the sea if they stayed put, should they retreat north, to join the defenders of Cherbourg ... and therefore be cut off and eventually overwhelmed ... or turn south and attempt to squeeze through the narrowing gap between the advancing Americans and the coast and retreat towards St-Lô? Confusion on which course to take was not helped by the death in an Allied air attack of General Marcks, commander of the 84th (LXXXIV) Corps and by a reiteration of Hitler's order that there was to be no retreat of any kind, in any direction.

Field Marshal Rommel elected to ignore Hitler's order. He decided that two divisions were enough to defend – or lose – in the retreat to Cherbourg where the vital Quineville ridge position at Montebourg had now fallen. He ordered that the 709th and 243rd divisions, with what was left of the 91st, should withdraw towards Cherbourg while the fresh 77th Division – which had just trounced the US 90th Division – and all other German units should move south and muster to defend St-Lô.

Although the Allied commanders at SHAEF seemed concerned with the 'slow' progress of their armies in France, that was not how it appeared to the Supreme Commander of the German Forces, Adolf Hitler. Hitler had already ordered von Rundstedt to take men from all other fronts in the west – except that of the Fifteenth Army in the Pas de Calais – to contain the Allied armies in Normandy, and the units would include four SS Panzer Divisions. The situation in Normandy was clearly seen as serious and on June 16 the Führer flew to Metz and then motored to Soissons, north of Paris, on June 17, for a face-to-face meeting with von Rundstedt and Rommel. The Führer's complaints sound like a reverse echo of those being heard at SHAEF ... the Allied landings had been successful, the local commanders – Rommel and von Schweppenburg and the Seventh Army commander – had not done well; and Cherbourg must be held at all costs.

The two field marshals pointed out in vain that if the Führer wanted the Allies held and then pushed back they must have more troops, especially more infantry, better air cover and – above all – *freedom to manoeuvre*. If they were forced to defend fixed positions against Allied air power and ever-increasing numbers, they must eventually and inevitably be overwhelmed. Their soldiers were better trained and better equipped than the Allied troops but they must be allowed to use this skill to outweigh the effect of superior numbers. It was a case of a boxer against a fighter; unless the German soldiers could use their tactical skills, abandon some positions in order to defend better ones and mass troops and tanks for strong counter-attacks, their defeat in Normandy was only a matter of time. The ever-increasing Allied strength would see to that.

This kind of talk only infuriated Hitler. He saw it as rank defeatism; with his flying bombs already pounding London and the unstoppable V-2 rockets about to fly, how could these much-favoured generals argue with him now? He had done his part and now they must do theirs by holding on to the last man – and especially by holding Cherbourg. This was a dialogue of the deaf and when the Führer returned to Germany he left his field commanders close to despair. Their gloom increased later that day when the new commander of the 84th

(LXXXIV) Corps, General Fahrmbacher, telephoned that the division of forces to defend either St-Lô or Cherbourg must take place as quickly as possible, for he had no means left to stop the Americans reaching the west coast and the Cotentin was about to be cut. Only two companies of the 91st Regiment and some remnants of the 243rd Division now stood between Collins's VII Corps and the Atlantic. Getting across the Cotentin had taken VII Corps ten days of hard fighting but they were almost there.

Rommel's order to split the Cotentin defenders therefore came none too soon ... and then came a direct order from Hitler on June 17, ordering that the 77th Division and all other units were to stay where they were and defend Cherbourg at all costs. The troops under General von Schlieben on the Montebourg line, reinforced by the 77th Division, were to hold there and only withdraw to Cherbourg when unable to resist any longer. This order was still being digested at Seventh Army HQ when VII Corps struck again. Cutting through the remnants of German units, the Americans reached the west coast road on the morning of June 18, arriving there just in time to cut off a large convoy of German artillery and a number of 77th Division units attempting to move south.

Allied fighter-bombers swooped in to take advantage of this feast and Generalmajor Rudolf Stegmann, commander of the 77th Division, was killed in an air strike. Only about 1,400 men of the 77th Division escaped the Americans and got away towards St-Lô, but this advance to the west coast of the Cotentin was the only solid achievement in the week after the linking-up of the beachheads on June 12. Caen remained untaken, Cherbourg was still in German hands – and being comprehensively wrecked – and before another day had passed the elements would add their load to the problems facing the Allied armies in France.

6 SUPPLY AND CHERBOURG   JUNE 19–29

The outstanding administrative problem in Normandy
arose from the unfavourable weather conditions.

GENERAL B. L. MONTGOMERY *Normandy to the Baltic*

Logistics – the supply of the wherewithal for armies to operate in the field and fight battles – may seem dry stuff when compared with the cut and thrust of infantry and armoured warfare or the hand-to-hand combat between the generals, but if the problems of a battle or campaign are fully to be understood, some attention must be paid to the problems of supply. Supply is crucial in modern warfare and the problems of supply never go away.

There is also a tendency among some military historians to attribute failures at the front to poor planning or poor leadership among the commanders or to a lack of zeal and drive by the leading elements – the 'teeth' – of the army. Less attention is paid to the fact that the 'teeth' cannot function for long if the 'tail' has been unable to supply them with the fuel, ammunition, food, water and kit necessary to pursue the campaign. A shortage of these essentials may arise from circumstances beyond anyone's control.

The problems of supply had been exercising the Cossac planners for years and some of the factors they had to take into account have been outlined in previous chapters. The directive to the Supreme Commander from the Combined Chiefs had decreed, (Point 5) that while the ultimate responsibility for logistics organisation and supply rested with the British Service Ministries for the British Forces and with the United States War and Navy Departments for the US Forces, SHAEF would be responsible for co-ordinating the requirements of all the forces

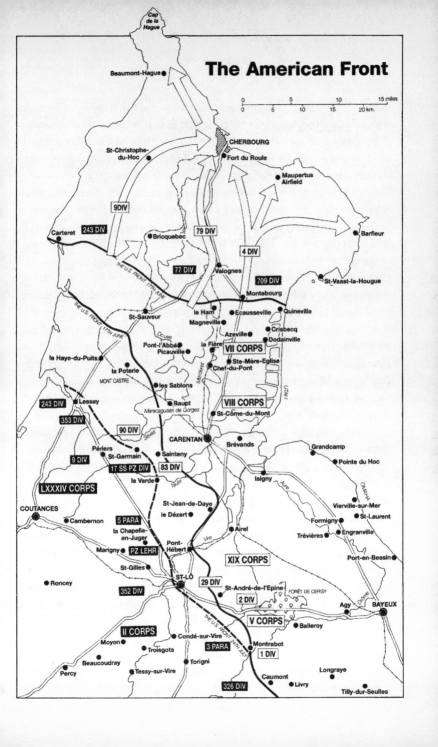

The American Front

0   5   10   15 miles
0 5 10 15 20 km.

Cap de la Hague

Beaumont-Hague

St-Christophe-du-Hoc

CHERBOURG
Fort du Roule

Maupertus Airfield

9 DIV

243 DIV

Carteret

Bricquebec

79 DIV

4 DIV

Barfleur

77 DIV

Valognes

709 DIV

St-Vaast-la-Hougue

THE U.S. FRONT 17TH JUNE

Montebourg

le Ham   Ecausseville   Quineville

Magneville

St-Sauveur

Douve

Azeville   Crisbecq

Dodainville

Pont-l'Abbé   la Fière

VII CORPS

Picauville

la Haye-du-Puits

la Poterie

Ste-Mère-Eglise
Chef-du-Pont

MONT CASTRE

les Sablons

VIII CORPS

243 DIV

Lessay

Baupt

Marécaguses de Gorges

St-Côme-du-Mont

353 DIV

90 DIV

Sèves

9 DIV

Périers

St-Germain

CARENTAN

Brévands

Grandcamp

Sainteny

17 SS PZ DIV   83 DIV

Pointe du Hoc

la Varde

Taute

Isigny

OMAHA

LXXXIV CORPS

St-Jean-de-Daye

Vierville-sur-Mer

COUTANCES

Cambernon

le Dézert

Airel

Formigny   St-Laurent

5 PARA

la Chapelle-en-Juger

Trévières   Engranville

Marigny   PZ LEHR

Pont-Hébert

Vire

XIX CORPS

Port-en-Bessin

St-Gilles

ST-LÔ

Roncey

29 DIV

St-André-de-l'Epine

FORÊT DE CERISY

352 DIV

2 DIV

Agy   BAYEUX

II CORPS

Condé-sur-Vire

V CORPS

Balleroy

Moyon

THE U.S. FRONT 24TH JULY

3 PARA   Montrabot

Troisgots

1 DIV

Beaucoudray

Torigni

Caumont

Longraye

Percy   Tessy-sur-Vire

Livry

326 DIV

Tilly-dur-Seulles

under SHAEF command. The buck, in short, stopped at SHAEF but there was a problem for the American commanders in that their supply organisation COMZ had a separate command set-up and was outside the direct control of SHAEF and Eisenhower's Chief-of-Staff, Bedell Smith; this division of control did not make the supply situation any easier.[1]

Such a division of responsibility would have seemed very clear and logical to the Combined Chiefs and their staff in far-away Washington but the problems of supply during a battle are not necessarily within the competence of a prior plan. It is necessary to look at how the logistical difficulties manifested themselves in the bridgehead once the fighting began, to see the problems that arose, how they were caused and how they were dealt with.

To appreciate the scale of the overall problem, on D-Day the US First Army alone hoped to land the equivalent of 200 trainloads of troops, over open, well-defended beaches. These troops came from 200 individual units and had to be supplied with everything from drinking water – 300,500 gallons of it – to 120-foot long steel bridges and sulfa pills. By D plus 14 the number of US troops ashore would be double the strength of the entire US Army in 1939 and as the battle went on it would double again – and again – with all the necessary stores these soldiers required, much of it in wide variety.

On the most basic item for a fighting soldier – ammunition – the British Army alone needed .45 and .38 pistol ammunition, 9mm ammunition for pistols and Sten guns, .303 ammunition for rifles, Bren light machine-guns and MMG's – two types of ammunition for the Vickers MMG – PIAT ammunition for the infantry anti-tank weapon, 2-inch, 3-inch and 4.2-inch mortar ammunition, 6-pounder and 17-pounder anti-tank gun ammunition, 25-pounder ammunition for field artillery, 5.5-inch ammunition for the heavy artillery and several different kinds of tank ammunition, in various calibres for various purposes, armour-piercing, smoke and high-explosive. To compound the problem, ammunition is heavy and cannot be transported far by hand. This example can be duplicated against every other kind of stores for every front line and supporting arm, for the Signals, Engineers, Ordnance, Supply, RAF – and duplicated in the US and Canadian forces as well ... and all of these troops – 'tail' or 'teeth' – had to be fed.

Supply must get down to the most basic levels. Normandy has plenty of rivers which can provide the armies with water and the summer of 1944 was wet but with hundreds of thousands of men living in the field, hygiene was soon a problem for individual 'field hygiene' – the provision and use of latrines was not always adequate. The rivers soon became polluted, drains were shattered by shellfire and diarrhoea or dysentery spread rapidly among the troops, making the supply of clean fresh water essential as Sergeant Tom Ridley of 233 Field Company RE explains:[2]

An army marches on its stomach but it must have clean water and my task one day was to find clean drinking water for my platoon. This turned into quite a task. To find the right stream we set off into what was termed 'No Man's Land', where there were few soldiers, south-east of Bayeux; the hose on the water truck had a rose on the far end to filter out dead rats and other foreign bodies and having thrown that into the stream, well forward of the other troops and I hoped, clean, so while the bowser was filling I went to look at an abandoned farm house at the top of the slope.

The barn seemed empty but when I heard a rustle, the hair rose on the back of my neck and I called out for one of my lads – and five fully armed Germans came tumbling out of the hay and landed at my feet. They had rifles and potato-masher grenades and what turned out to be a machine-gun but they dropped all those when I pointed my Sten at them. I still have the map case and compass I took from the German NCO and my lads then came running up and took them prisoner. When I told my OC about this, he asked if they had been armed and when I said they had he said I should have shot them – 'that's what you are here for'. All I wanted to do was get some fresh water but finding bottles of Perrier would probably have been easier and a lot less dangerous.

A lack of field hygiene increased the manpower problem in all the armies as Greg Saffiere, a non-medical officer of the RAMC, recalls:[3]

We catered in the main for surgical cases, though I believe there were two hospitals in Bayeux catering for psychiatric cases. Having been operated on, most of our patients went back to the UK as soon as they were able to travel, as even those who might have gone back to their units had become very unfit. A few days in hospital plays havoc with fitness and left the men in no state for heavy work. Then, after some weeks we became a dysentery hospital, when that problem became prevalent and among my tasks was to build a faeces destructor; it did not work and we ended up digging a huge hole and using that but, as you can see, we were capable of change and very flexible.

As the chapter opening quote illustrates, one of the principal causes of logistical delay and problems in Normandy was the weather. The storm that had delayed the initial landings caused some delays, because surf piled up on the beaches, craft were lost and not all the stores got ashore. That was on the first day and these problems were to continue. The weather remained poor for much of June and July, stores had to be put ashore on open beaches, the available ports were too small, shipping turn-round times lengthened and even two weeks after D-Day the Mulberry harbours were not fully operational.

All this, plus Bradley's failure to take Cherbourg quickly – he had antici-pated taking it in eight days[4] – say by June 14 – led to various delays in supply, notably of artillery and mortar ammunition which had at times to be rationed; the US V Corps were limited to twenty-five rounds per gun per day while the US VII Corps were heading for Cherbourg and, as Bradley comments,[5] 'artillery rationing was not limited to the beachhead, it limited the Allied artillery all the way to the Ruhr'. This was one factor that made Eisenhower's later demand – for everyone to attack, all out, all along the bridgehead, all the time – quite imprac-tical; there simply was not enough ammunition to support such a policy, even had it been tactically sensible.

The logistical problem could not be swiftly solved, partly because of the weather and port problem, partly because the size of the force ashore was con-tinually increasing. Bradley comments:[6] 'In Normandy our troubles started with the beaches. For even though we boosted unloading to 35,000 tons a day, three times the capacity of Cherbourg in peacetime, there wasn't enough ammuni-tion to go round and the beaches couldn't carry more.'

By the time the Normandy battle ended in September, the Allied Expedi-tionary Force in France consisted of forty-seven divisions, divided into three Army groups, two American – Bradley's 12th Army Group and Dever's 6th, and one British, 21st Army Group – containing six armies between them. Sup-plying such an ever-expanding force with all it needed to move and fight could never be easy even if all the stores were instantly available but this last require-ment was never possible; at the end of D-Day, for example, not more than a quarter of the planned amount of stores was landed on the US beaches – but then one of those beaches was bloody Omaha – and all the other beaches were being lashed with waves and under enemy fire.

Another illuminating statistic is that the supply of petrol in the first fifteen days of the landing – until D plus 21 – took up no less than twenty-two *million* jerry-cans – there was no other method of ensuring fuel supply until the Pluto petrol pipeline came ashore; it is also notable that by the end of the battle, half these useful jerry-cans had been lost. Nor was it just a matter of stores; delays in supply also affected manpower. The British Official History[7] records that the troops of one British division were still on board their ships offshore, unable to land, two days after they were supposed to be ashore. This delay – an average of two days – was common across all the landing beaches in the first days of the invasion and was not helped by communication problems, a shortage of roads and bridges. Clive Kemp of the 71st Field Regiment, Royal Engineers, describes some of their work in Normandy:[8]

> My unit landed on Sword beach between 0930hrs and 1030hrs on D-Day.
> Our first task was to go to Bénouville and build a bridge there if the airborne
> coup had failed. It was still there so we were ordered to build another bridge
> further up the canal near the château; our stores arrived on D plus 1 and our
> bridge was completed on the 8th, 224ft long, a Class 4 Bailey bridge. The
> Bénouville bridge was used for troops going forward and our Bailey was used
> for traffic heading back to the beachhead for more troops and stores. Inciden-
> tally, this was the first Bailey bridge built in France. The Germans shelled it from
> time to time and on one occasion a German fighter appeared and machine-
> gunned us, probably trying to sink the pontoons; fortunately he only made one
> run. After landing in Normandy we built a total of 22 bridges, including one
> over the river Maas which was 4,008ft long, then the longest bridge in the
> world; in your book, tell them the Sappers did it.

Some indication of how these various delays in the arrival of troops or supplies affected progress or success in battle is provided by what happened to the British forces in front of Caen and at Villers-Bocage:[9]

> If the Queen's Infantry Brigade of the 7th Armoured Division, the 33rd Armoured
> Brigade with its 150 tanks and at least some of the 49th Infantry Division had
> arrived on their due dates, they could have taken part in the later phases of XXX
> Corps operations in the west. Villers-Bocage and the high ground beyond it might
> have been captured and firmly held before the 2nd Panzer Division reached the
> battle ... It seems possible indeed that Caen might have been taken by now
> (D plus 10) if our build-up of formations had kept to the planned timetable'.

Those fatal 'ifs', so common in military accounts, were to muster in quantity as the battle went on. Nor should it be thought that the supply problem stopped with getting supplies and reinforcements *in*; it was also essential to get the casualties and prisoners *out*; from every point of view and at every level, the logistical problem was severe.

Even before the Cossac plan was finally formulated it was obvious that the logistical problems of various kinds which would inevitably confront the Allied armies after the initial invasion would be greatly eased if the armies had the use of an established, working port. However, as the Anglo-Canadian Dieppe raid of 1942 had bloodily underlined, taking a port at all would not be easy and taking one intact and in full working order virtually impossible. If the port facilities were not destroyed in the fighting, they would certainly be demolished by the defenders before the port fell. Faced with this impasse, the Allies were inspired to build their own prefabricated ports and take them with them. This decision to build what became the Mulberry harbours, was taken in May 1942, in a typically pithy memorandum from the British Prime Minister Winston Churchill to Vice-Admiral Lord Louis Mountbatten, Chief of Combined Operations:

> To CCO or Deputy. Piers for use on beaches. They must float up and down with the tide. The anchor problem must be mastered. Let me have the best solution worked out. Don't argue the matter. The difficulties will argue for themselves.

It has been alleged that the Mulberry harbours were created after the failure of the Dieppe raid and that the decision to develop them was one of the few benefits of that costly fiasco, but since the design work for Mulberry was in hand months before the raid took place – in August 1942 – this view is clearly mistaken. Work on the project commenced in June 1943, after the Cossac Operational Staff had been formed to work out the details for the invasion and Vice-Admiral Hughes-Hallett, RN, is credited with coming up with the final workable idea for an artificial port. The resulting Mulberry harbours, each the size of the cross-Channel ferry port of Dover, were one of the wonders of the entire invasion. One was established at Arromanches off Gold Beach and another at Omaha and both were used for the unloading of heavy stores, food and ammunition. Petrol (gasoline) was to be supplied as soon as possible via Pluto (the Pipe Line Under The Ocean) which ran initially from the Isle of Wight to Port-en-Bessin and was later extended to Bayeux and Cherbourg.

The Mulberry components – the blockships and caissons – sailed to Normandy on the afternoon of D-Day and the plan was to have both harbours established and fully operational in fourteen days. The volume of stores landed even without proper facilities was still remarkable. According to the US Official History,[10] by June 18 – D plus 12 – 116,000 tons of supplies, 41,000 vehicles and 314,314 troops had come ashore in the American sector and 102,000 tons of supplies, 54,000 vehicles and 314,547 troops had been landed in the British sector. This is a great quantity of stores and a vast number of soldiers, but the more troops put ashore, the more stores would be needed to support them – and that clearly required the facilities of a major port. Some smaller ports – Grandcamp, Isigny, Port-en-Bessin and Courseulles – were operating and handling useful tonnages. Courseulles and Port-en-Bessin were both open by June 12 – D plus 6 – and between them handled 15,000 tons of stores before June 19 but this was a drop in the growing ocean of demand.

In his memoirs[11] Bradley states that in Montgomery's original plan Cherbourg was to be taken 'with the minimum of delay'. As already related, this was in line with Montgomery's overall view on time phasing; that it was impossible to set targets for capturing objectives until the battle developed and therefore only two target dates were set, Caen on D-Day and the Seine line by D plus 90. Bradley, while sensibly cautious of committing himself to any precise date, naturally set his own dates and although these seem to vary, one estimate – that Cherbourg would fall between ten and thirty days after the landings – seems the most relevant. It actually took VII Corps just over twenty days to take Cherbourg, so it is possible to argue that Bradley either took his first objective ten days early – or ten days late.

The logistical problem during this period was only contained because of the ingenuity and practical steps taken by the supply teams; their first decision, taken on D plus 2, was to dump those carefully worked-out unloading schedules and simply offload the cargo from any ship or landing craft that arrived at the beaches and pile it up on shore. The only limitation to this sensible rule concerned rations, or ammunition, or stores specifically designed for either the American or the British Army, which would be redirected to the appropriate beach; this was sensible because US rifles, for example, could not use British .303 ammunition. These logistical teams also discovered that most ships could be beached at low tide, particularly at Utah and Gold and their cargoes unloaded directly into trucks driven out on to firm sand.

The first of the outer Mulberry blockships, sunk to act as breakwaters, went down on June 7, construction of the Mulberrys went on apace and both ports were already proving their worth when, on June 19, with over 600,000 Allied soldiers ashore in Normandy and supply requirements rising by the hour, disaster struck. The worst June storm to sweep the English Channel for forty years hit the Calvados coast a devastating blow.

The Channel weather is always unpredictable. When the Cossac planners drew up their first schemes for Overlord they were informed by the meteorologists that, on average, the Channel area only enjoyed twelve good days a month, even in midsummer. The high winds and gales of D-Day proved this estimate all too correct; the troops went ashore in the lull between two gales and a number of problems, the dispersal of the airborne forces and the loss of many DD tanks, was directly due to the high winds and stormy weather on June 5–6. Bad as this was, the June 5–6 gale was summer shower compared to the Great Storm of June 19.

Had this been a westerly gale, following the pattern of the prevailing winds, all might have been well; high winds and seas from that direction had been anticipated and the Cotentin peninsula would have provided a measure of protection, certainly for the Omaha Mulberry and the flat sands of Utah. Unfortunately, the June 19 gale came from the north-east, creating high seas and driving waves directly into the bay of the Seine, a gale which swept over the outer breakwaters of the Mulberrys and played havoc with the shipping and small craft within. The weather forecasts had given little warning of this gale and no estimate of its severity so the Mulberry ports and the various beachmasters controlling the landing of supplies were taken completely unawares when the storm struck.

Chaos therefore reigned. Unsecured parts of the ports were soon adrift, smashing into other parts, driving the anchored caissons from their mooring. High tides added to the wave height and sent waves surging over the walls to sink craft sheltering on the lee side. Flat-bottomed craft, the LCAs (Landing Craft, Assault) and the larger LCMs (Landing Craft, Mechanised), and Rhino ferry rafts, were picked up and flung ashore, cargoes were lost, men drowned. Ships which had put to sea in an attempt to ride out the storm in deep water ran out of fuel, lost power, dragged their anchors and were swept ashore. On the second day, the piers of the still uncompleted Omaha harbour gave way and ninety vessels were lost – no trace now remains of the Omaha Mulberry. The Arromanches Mulberry, though badly damaged, somehow survived, but when the storm finally abated on June 22, shipping losses were seen to be severe.

The gale lasted for three days and when it was over a great quantity of wreckage was strewn along twenty miles of coast. Over 800 vessels, large and small, ranging from cargo ships to landing craft and the ubiquitous DUKW (always called a 'Duck'), a kind of amphibious lorry, had been sunk, or driven ashore, or otherwise destroyed. Many vessels remained aground until they could be tugged off on the next spring tide on July 15. By then the extent of the damage had been assessed and it was decided to abandon the Omaha Mulberry and concentrate all efforts on completing the one at Arromanches, which was finished by mid-July. A great variety of special craft were employed at this time including landing barges – LBVs – as Fenton Rutter, a Royal Navy officer describes:[12]

> The V stands for vehicle but in practice we did not carry vehicles but we did carry practically everything else the troops ashore needed. These barges could carry a great quantity of stores and go close inshore so they were very useful.
>
> As with other kinds of landing craft there were various kinds of barge. We had the LBE, the Landing Barge Engineering which carried out repairs on damaged craft and the LBK or Landing Barge Kitchen which would lie off the beaches and supply food to the crews of landing craft when they had the time to eat. I only had time to attend an LBK once. During the storm my cabin was flooded and I lost most of my kit in sea water covered with fuel oil. For a while after that I wore an American Army uniform with Royal Navy epaulettes and cap and slept on netting on top of the ammunition boxes.

Dick Cowlan was with the Mulberry construction teams at this time:[13]

> We landed at 1800hrs on D-Day at Arromanches and spent the first week clearing up the debris, getting ready for the Mulberry. Parts arrived over the next ten days and we sank the blockships and all was fine – warships like HMS *Ajax* and HMS *Warspite* bombarding the enemy inland, until D plus 13 when the storm blew up. That completely stopped the building and the unloading but when the Mulberry was completed it was on the go 24 hours a day, unloading military vehicles, lorries, tanks, food supply trucks, everything for the troops advancing.

We worked 8 hours on and 8 hours off, day and night, round the clock, it never stopped, but in late June we were surprised to see a Salvation Army truck arrive and set up on the beach; that was the first decent cup of tea and sandwich we had had in three weeks and it was much later before we saw the good old Sally Army again, let alone the NAAFI.

Tom Whitehouse was a DUKW driver ferrying stores to the Normandy beachhead:[14]

We went ashore on D plus 1 and parked for the night in an orchard just inland from the beach; that night there was rifle fire from the side of the orchard we parked in and when an aircraft went over all the ships offshore opened up, a real fireworks display. That was the start of it and next day, D plus 2 we went out to sea to pick up stores, which we carried on doing for weeks. The men at the front were to get what they needed first and we were to be seen to later.

The routine was that you drove down to the beach where the beach controlling officer would point out on a black board where the cargo ship was and also its number and we would go out and get the stores, lowered into the DUKW hold on cargo nets. My first load that day was boxes of 'compo' rations. We could carry about three tons of stores and this we would take back ashore and up the beach to an unloading point. By the way, on that day one of our 'Ducks' was blown up on a mine; the story goes that it was laid by a Frenchman who said he had been paid by the Germans to lay mines and wanted to finish the job; if true, I don't know what his fate was. That first day, coming back to the beach, one of the weirdest things I saw was a body in the water, a naval officer, like a tailor's dummy, floating just under the surface.

The beachhead was not quiet, there was shelling and on the next day – D plus 3 – I was sniped at in the orchard by a German trooper, quite smartly dressed. That night we had some commandos come in as a guard and the unloading went on. We carried anything that was needed. Jerry-cans came in various colours, green for petrol, brown for water, blue for diesel, and compo rations in 14-man packs. We even managed to get stores ashore during the Great Storm when there was an urgent call for more supplies.

The real damage caused by the Great Storm was not the losses caused to shipping but the breakdown in the continuity of supply and finding out exactly what had gone missing took some days; one estimate holds that delays caused by the storm cost the Allied armies about 140,000 tons of stores and some 20,000 vehicles. The storm had no effect on the Germans and may even have proved beneficial; air attacks diminished and the Germans were given another four days to build up their forces before the Allied armies struck again. The Mulberry operations were also disrupted by mining, as Reg Plumb, then an officer with 84 Light Anti-Aircraft Regiment recounts:[15]

> Because of the constant mining by the Luftwaffe, in and around the harbour, we had plenty of night firing. One night a hospital ship struck a mine some way north of Port Mulberry and many casualties were caused, the remains drifting in to the north wall where we had the gruesome task of recovering them and locating their identity discs etc; many of the dead were nurses. Our unit casualties remained light; we had one man blown up by a mine when in a jeep ashore and another had a petrol stove blow up in his face but he rejoined later.

The Great Storm had two immediate effects on the Allied forces. Firstly, it obliged Montgomery to delay the start of another bid for Caen where an attack east of the Orne scheduled for June 23, and another west of Caen, scheduled for June 25, had to be postponed, the main reason for delay being a shortage of artillery ammunition. Secondly, this further delay underlined the importance of taking Cherbourg. With the base of the Cotentin cut and VIII Corps deployed to protect their backs, taking Cherbourg was now the prime task of Collins's VII Corps and on June 19 they set about it.

General Collins sent three divisions – the 4th, 9th and 79th – north to take Cherbourg while the 90th was relegated to the role of corps rearguard and maintaining the link with VIII Corps which was blocking any German attempts at interference from the direction of St-Lô. It was known from captured German orders that while General von Schlieben had four divisions in his Order of Battle before Cherbourg – the 77th, 91st, 243rd and 709th – all these had been severely written-down since D-Day and were no longer capable of prolonged resistance.

According to the US Official History,[16] 'this estimate of enemy capabilities turned out to be substantially correct. The 9th Division, beginning its attack at 0550hrs, 19 June, found nothing in front of it.' This was true for a while on the other divisions' fronts for after some initial contact astride Montebourg, German resistance in front of the 4th Infantry Division on June 19 is described as 'no more than a gesture' and by nightfall the 12th and 8th Infantry Regiments of the 4th Division were as close to Cherbourg as Valognes.

This lack of German resistance did not last. General von Schlieben was simply obeying orders and pulling back from Montebourg to the outer defences – the *Landfront* – of Cherbourg, where four regiment-sized battlegroups – *kampf-gruppe* – with tanks and infantry, were already dug in. As the Americans pushed north, German resistance therefore stiffened and the amount of artillery fire directed against the US regiments began to increase. On June 20, the 9th Division were ordered to breach the Cherbourg defences – an optimistic order from VII Corps, probably inspired by the good progress made the previous day – while the other two divisions, the 4th and 79th, were urged to push through the breach into the city.

The US Official History recounts[17] that 'the combat efficiency of all the (German) troops now asked to make a last stand before the port was extremely low'. This comment may well be true for many of the German battalions were fought out and these 'battalions' usually contained fewer than 200 soldiers. Even so, they were German soldiers and they fought back hard and held their ground tenaciously. Until noon on June 19 the American advance went well but in mid-afternoon German artillery fire increased and when the strong *Landfront* defence line was encountered, well manned and supported by fire from 88mm, 20mm and 30mm cannon as well as a plentiful supply of mortars and heavy machine-guns, the US advance came to a halt.

Probing for a way round, the US troops discovered that Cherbourg was protected by an interlinked defence system laid out in a semicircle, at a distance of some five miles from the city centre. Breaking that system was not going to be easy and June 21 was devoted to probing with patrols, an 'extensive reconnaissance', in an attempt to find a weak point while the main force of all three divisions moved up to positions before the defenders' line. While this was going on, the 4th Infantry Division was attacking north-west into the main Cherbourg defences, taking 300 prisoners in the course of the day. By nightfall the VII Corps divisions had closed up on the German line and were ready to put in their assault, one described by General Collins as 'the major effort of the American army'.

General Collins threw a great weight of metal at Cherbourg on June 21–22, starting with the carpet bombing of the main defence line by the Ninth Air Force and aircraft of 2nd TAF. The defenders were also subjected to a leaflet drop in various languages, pointing out the hopelessness of their position, inviting sur-render and giving General von Schlieben until 0900hrs on the 22 June to make up his mind and reply. No reply was received.

The attack began at 1240hrs on June 22 when hundreds of Allied bombers and ground-attack fighters began bombing and strafing the German positions. This was not done without loss; Cherbourg was well supplied with flak guns and twenty-four US and British aircraft were lost over Cherbourg that morn-ing. There followed an air strike by more than 300 bombers and then the VII Corps tanks and infantry went in, making slow progress throughout the after-noon, against stiff resistance. By nightfall little ground had been gained but the attackers noticed that the units they were engaging and the prisoners they were taking contained a wide variety of personnel. The prisoners were not just infantry; they included military police, Todt construction workers and rear-echelon staff, drivers, cooks and signallers. These fought well enough but their presence in the German front line suggested that if the attack was pressed hard the enemy must collapse. This thought may have struck Adolf Hitler for on that day he sent a signal to General von Schlieben reminding him: 'Even if the worst comes to the worst, it is your duty to defend the last bunker and leave the enemy not a harbour but a field of ruins.'

This exhortation did not play too well with General von Schlieben. He was a professional soldier, not a professional martyr, and his response was to ignore the Führer's demands and send a signal to Rommel at Army Group B spelling out the state of the defences and demanding reinforcements. Rommel was preparing to send the 15th Parachute Division up from Brittany by sea but the presence of the Allied fleet, which was now off Cherbourg and shelling the defenders, rapidly put this scheme out of court. General von Schlieben and his men were on their own and they dug in, determined to hang on as long as possible.

During June 23 and 24 the American tanks and infantry crept slowly and painfully into the city, gaining ground but plagued by snipers who had stayed behind in the ruins to harass them. These had to be winkled out one by one and mainly by the infantry, for the piles of rubble in the streets caused difficulty in bringing up the tanks which could otherwise have been used to blast the sniper positions and machine-gun nests. Even so, by the evening of the 23rd, the Amer-icans were within the city and the enemy were pulling back. By evening on the

24th the defences were clearly collapsing, though there was plenty of resistance at various points around the city, especially around the port, most noticeably at La Glacerie and under the bastion of the Fort de Roule, while the sound of explosions from the quays indicated that the work of demolishing the port facilities continued apace. On June 25, the last defence line collapsed and troops from all three US divisions were able to overrun the city – but by no means all the defenders.

Although there were some large surrenders that day – the 12th Infantry took 800 prisoners on June 25, another 350 surrendered to their 1st Battalion on the following day, and the 9th Division took a further 1,000 prisoners – scattered German units and individual defenders continued to offer resistance within the city, especially in the harbour area. Larger units up to company strength, some with tanks, held out in the surrounding countryside, in villages like Barfleur and at other points along the coast until the end of the month.

General von Schlieben surrendered the garrison on June 26 – D plus 20 – but the city arsenal resisted until June 27. Even after the city had fallen, some 6,000 German soldiers continued to hold out in forts out in the harbour where some stubborn defenders had to be rooted out of their bunkers by platoons of infantry equipped with flame-throwers. Only when these defenders were finally subdued on June 29 – D plus 23 – could the victors examine the port and estimate how quickly it could be repaired and put into commission.

Cherbourg fell, not according to some prearranged time plan but simply when it did – as soon as possible after the landings. It would be a further three weeks before the first ship unloaded a cargo in the outer roads and the port began to make its contribution towards reducing the Allied supply problem.

The report on the state of Cherbourg's port facilities when it fell makes grim reading:[18] 'The demolition of the port of Cherbourg is a masterful job, beyond a doubt the most complete, intensive and best-planned demolition in military history.' This was almost an underestimate. Hundreds of mines – some anti-personnel to deter navy clearance teams – littered the quays and the sea bed. Sunken ships, often booby-trapped, blocked the harbour entrances and slipways, cranes had been toppled, gantries destroyed, quay walls demolished, trackways torn up, warehouses set afire ... the port of Cherbourg was a shambles.

The original American estimate, based on the clearance of Naples in 1943, that the port could be open for business in three days, was now seen to be a pipe-dream, but what was actually achieved, in getting many of the facilities working within three weeks, still seems a miracle of effort and organisation. The minesweeping of the outer harbour alone took three weeks and it was not until July 16 that the first cargo was landed, delivered by DUKWs from ships anchored offshore. It would take a couple of months before the port was fully operational and by that time the Allied armies would be far away to the north-east, on their way to the German border.

This fact, the departure of the armies to the north-east, was one of the great supply dilemmas that faced the Allies, and particularly the American divisions, for their supply line came from the west, from the United States, but their objectives lay in the east, in the Low Countries and Germany. Lengthening supply lines inevitably caused delay and limited the Allied advance, and as more troops landed, the problems of supplying them would increase.

By June 30, the day after Cherbourg finally fell, the Royal Navy had landed no fewer than 850,279 men and 148,803 vehicles, American, British and Canadian since D-Day.[19] To support these troops and keep the vehicles moving they had also landed 570,505 tons of stores – a colossal amount but far less than the quantities they would need to land from now on. The more troops, tanks and trucks landed, the more food, fuel and ammunition they would require, so more ports were desperately needed – and as quickly as possible.

The taking of Cherbourg, shattered as it was, marked a definite turning-point in the battle for Normandy. Capturing the port had been one of the prime objectives in the initial plan and the German commanders – or at least von Rundstedt and Rommel – were in no doubt that the loss of Cherbourg spelt the end of any real hopes of hanging on to Normandy. Once Cherbourg opened for cargo and troops, the Allied armies would build up their strength until they would overwhelm anything the Germans could bring against them.

The capture of Cherbourg also put an end to any plans for a major German attack along the Allied line, one planned in response to a demand from the Führer for offensive action. The aim had been to strike at the junction of the British–American armies at Balleroy, south of Caumont, and then drive east, along the inter-Allied boundary as far as Bayeux, rolling up any Allied units encountered on the way. Meanwhile, another attack would drive in the left flank of the landing area, east of the Orne, overcoming the positions of 6th Airborne Division. This plan had been prepared at OB-West on June 20 and called for the deployment of six armoured divisions. Three of these – the crack 1 SS Panzer, 9 SS Panzer and 10 SS Panzer – had not yet arrived in Normandy and two – Panzer Lehr and 12 SS Panzer – were already heavily engaged with the British and Canadians at Caen. The only German division on hand for offensive action was 2 SS Panzer – *Das Reich* – which had now arrived having survived the harrowing passage north from Toulouse, with the French Maquis and British SAS troops doing everything to slow them down along the way. *Das Reich* had paused briefly en route to massacre some 600 French civilians at Oradour-sur-Glane and was now in Seventh Army reserve near Torigni-sur-Vire.

This grandiose plan reflects the dichotomy between the views taken at OKW and what was actually going on in Normandy. The situation on the ground made this plan a complete impossibility, not least because of the problems of supply, which were affecting the Germans as well as the Allies. In artillery, for example, the Germans had plenty of guns but were very short of shells. The twelve heavy artillery battalions in OKW reserve could muster 150 guns and the various divisions another 487[20] but it was estimated that such a German offensive would require the expenditure of an additional 14,000 *tons* of artillery ammunition – a logistical impossibility given the difficulties of moving supplies of any kind while constantly under air attack.

Even so, von Rundstedt was obliged to go through the motions of compliance and he duly reorganised the Panzer forces for an offensive. Panzer Group West had now recovered from that shattering attack on their HQ and all the available armour was again concentrated under Geyr von Schweppenburg who was now to take over the sector between the rivers Seine and Drôme with four corps – I SS Panzer Corps, II SS Panzer Corps, 67th (LXVII) Panzer Corps and the 87th (LXXXVII) Infantry Corps, this last unit operating east of the Orne. Von Schweppenburg took up this command on June 28. This left SS General Paul Hausser, the new commander of the Seventh Army – General Dollman having died of a heart attack – with just two corps, the 84th (LXXXIV) Infantry and II Parachute. The main enemy forces in Normandy – in terms of both manpower and equipment – would therefore be in Panzer Group West, while Seventh Army was demoted to a largely defensive role from in front of St-Lô to the west coast of the Cotentin.

Von Rundstedt knew what he was doing and this regrouping had a sound tactical base. The biggest threat came from the British at Caen and a fresh attack there – following the British reverse at Villers-Bocage on June 13 – could not be long delayed. That attack must be met with armour, certainly if it reached the Caen–Falaise plain. As for the American sector, von Rundstedt had no doubt that Cherbourg would fall and was now taking steps to deal with what would inevitably happen after that – the Americans would turn their strength south and lunge at St-Lô. St-Lô, however, lay behind the *bocage* and here infantry held sway – with two infantry corps in the *bocage,* taking St-Lô would take time and cost the Americans a quantity of men.

This might not be the problem von Rundstedt supposed because the Allied armies were landing more men all the time. By the end of June, Bradley's First Army contained four corps, a total of eleven infantry and two armoured divisions, while Dempsey's Second Army mustered four corps containing ten infantry divisions and three armoured divisions. This was impressive but there was a snag; all these forces were crammed into a bridgehead that had not expanded much since June 14. There was no space to deploy many of these units against the enemy in order to stretch his front until it snapped and the problems of supplying these forces was placing a great strain on the logistical facilities. What it came down to was that until these troops could be used in combat it was probably better to leave them in the UK.

This action was not contemplated but in mid-June Montgomery asked that more combat troops should be included in the supply serials and the number of support troops reduced. The flow of trucks also gave way to more tanks and armoured vehicles. This decision soon had an effect, at least in the US sector – the British were already running out of troops to send. The US 83rd Infantry Division was sent to Normandy and units of XV Corps from Patton's Third Army began to go ashore in the Cotentin ... and so the build-up continued.

The capture of Cherbourg was a great fillip to the Allied commanders in Normandy and a great relief to their superiors at SHAEF, in Washington and in London, where a new concern had arisen over the V-1 offensive, which was causing considerable damage and some loss of life in the British capital. Beginning on June 13, when just four bombs fell on London, killing six people, these attacks soon escalated. On June 15, 244 V-1s were fired from the Pas de Calais and seventy-three bombs reached London, killing more than fifty people. On June 17, thirty-seven people were killed by V-1s and on Sunday, June 18 a V-1 fell on the Guards Chapel at Wellington Barracks in London, killing 121 of the congregation. By the time Cherbourg fell at the end of the month, some 1,600 British civilians had been killed by V-1 flying bombs in just two weeks and these attacks would continue. Since the air forces and the anti-aircraft defences could not provide an absolute defence against the V-1 weapon, fresh demands arose, that the breakout from Normandy should come without delay, and the Allied armies proceed up the Channel coast to overrun the V-1 launch sites in the Pas de Calais.

On June 18 – two days after Operation Perch, the 7th Armoured Division's attempt to outflank Caen at Villers-Bocage, had finally been called off – Montgomery issued a new directive, ordering the Second Army to launch a pincer attack on either side of Caen and encircle the city to the south – a plan made risky by the rough terrain of the *Suisse Normande,* along the Orne south of the city. The first idea was to break out east of the Orne but the cramped state of the bridgehead there forced an alteration to the plan; the Orne attack would therefore be a minor attack to extend the Orne bridgehead south, and the major attack over the river would go in west of the city – Operation Epsom.

Epsom had been scheduled to start on June 22 but the Great Storm put this back until June 25. The operation had therefore started during the VII Corps battle for Cherbourg. We must now switch to the British part of the front where two corps of Dempsey's Second Army – XXX Corps and VIII Corps – had been making yet another attempt to expand the bridgehead and take Caen.

7 OPERATION EPSOM JUNE 18-30

To win any major campaign there usually has to be at least one bloodbath

BELFIELD AND ESSAME *The Battle for Normandy*

While the American VII Corps were battling their way up the Cotentin to Cherbourg, fifty miles away to the east the British and Canadians were still battering at the defences of Caen. The American historian Stephen Ambrose has written:[1] 'The difficulty centred round the taking of Caen. Gen. Bernard Law Montgomery had said he would take the city on D-Day but he had not, nor did he do so in the following ten days. Nor was he attacking.'

Professor Ambrose is quite right – or at least half right. The difficulty did indeed lie in the taking of Caen – or rather in the determination of the German Army to hang on to it – but where this notion that the British and Canadians were not attacking comes from is rather harder to determine. A cursory examination of the British Official History: *Victory in the West* reveals that the British and Canadians were attacking Caen continuously from the morning of D-Day; subsequent study indicates that they would continue to attack Caen until the city was taken while attacking at other points along the Second Army front. Montgomery – though surely Professor Ambrose means General Dempsey – had not *taken* Caen, but the Second Army was certainly attacking.

Where is the evidence that Second Army were not attacking? By the end of June, three weeks after D-Day, the British and Canadians had lost 24,698 men – an average of 1,000 men *per day* in the various battles for Caen. These attacks were made down the centre on the axis of the Caen canal, from the Orne bridge-

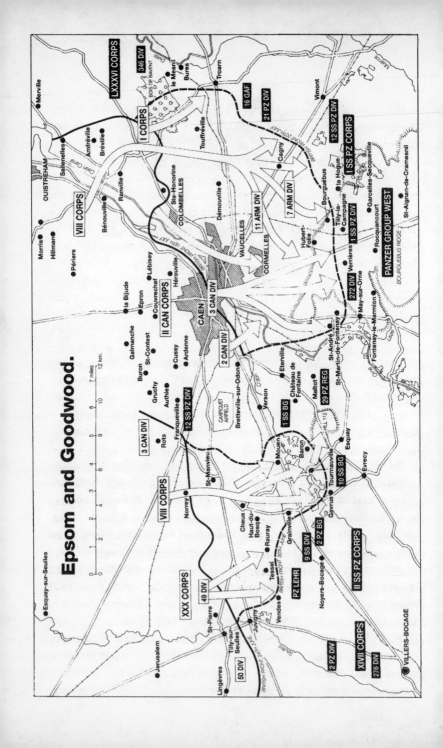

Epsom and Goodwood.

head on the east and from the west via Carpiquet, Tilly-sur-Seulles and Villers-Bocage, and they went on even though the real objective of the battle for Caen had changed.

Monty had quickly realised that actually *taking* Caen, while useful, was of no real benefit to the campaign at this time and would cost a quantity of lives. The strategic aim – yet again – had always been to hold the east front secure against any incursion from Fifteenth Army and keep the German armour there so that the Americans could build up their forces in the wide spaces of the Cotentin and break out in the west. If this purpose could be achieved by merely *threatening* Caen, why lose men in an all-out attempt to take it?

The problems with the failure to take Caen came at the time from Montgomery's critics at SHAEF and later on from historians who, given one firm deadline to hold on to – Caen on D-Day – have used it as the peg on which to hang a long list of accusations relating to Montgomery's 'timidity' and 'caution' and a British and Canadian reluctance to get 'stuck in' and take the place by storm. Bernard Montgomery was not a 'one-note' general; he orchestrated his strategy according to the situation at the time, not according to previous plans which present experience showed to be outdated.

Nevertheless, in the initial plan, Caen and Cherbourg were the first Allied objectives after the initial landing, so when the Americans took Cherbourg, speculation – even criticism – as to why it was taking the British so long to take Caen began to come into the open at SHAEF. This criticism was aided by the antipathy shown to Montgomery by Tedder and Coningham who were increasingly agitated over the failure to gain ground for airfields. It may also be that this Air Force agitation was caused by the dawning realisation that their still-strident demands for airfields was being proved unnecessary on a daily basis by the fact that the tactical air forces could manage perfectly well without more French airfields than they had already. When Trafford Leigh-Mallory claimed before D-Day that the dropping of parachute troops in the Cotentin would lead to heavy losses among the airborne forces and was proved wrong in the event, he had the courage and decency to write to Eisenhower after the landings and apologise for adding to the Supreme Commander's worries at a difficult time. Not everyone at SHAEF was as willing as Leigh-Mallory to admit that their initial predictions had been disproved by subsequent events.

Various reasons account for the 'failure' to take Caen and a comparison with the taking of Cherbourg is not accurate. Caen was much more heavily defended than Cherbourg and a far more difficult place to attack since the front was narrow and hemmed in by rivers. Another part of the answer lies in the varied state of the opposing forces at these two places. Collins's VII Corps were faced with troops – not all of them German – fighting with their backs to the wall and already 'written-down' by the D-Day fighting, roughly formed into *kampfgruppen;* even so, as we have seen, they fought well and continued to fight in the surrounding countryside after the city fell, when there was no hope of either rescue or relief. This being so, the resistance put up by the divisions of crack SS and Panzer troops opposing the British at Caen can only be wondered at.

Besides, if the taking of Caen had been easy, as Montgomery's critics imply, the British and Canadians would surely have taken it. In any event, to compare the scratch German forces fighting under von Schlieben in the Cotentin with the large, well-equipped and strongly motivated troops deployed against the British and Canadians astride the Orne north of Caen, is not comparing like with like.

One indication of the poor quality of troops facing the Americans is the number of prisoners taken. The total of prisoners taken by the Americans far exceeds the numbers surrendering to the British and Canadians which is used by the less well-informed as another indication that the British and Canadians were not trying hard enough. The real reason is that the SS troops and those in crack divisions like Panzer Lehr or 21 Panzer facing the British Second Army were not given to surrendering. Anyone who fought the Waffen-SS or has listened to those who did knows that for a fact.[2]

Nor is it fair to maintain, as some historians do, that the British were letting the Americans do all the fighting while the British leaned gently on the German line east of Caumont. On the Second Army front, attack followed attack in the attempt to take Caen. On D-Day there had been the direct thrust down the Orne from Sword, an attack blunted by the German defences at Morris and Hillman and the presence of 21 Panzer. Then came the attempt to break out on the east of Caen by 51st Highland at Ste-Honorine which had been followed on June 13 by Operation Perch, the attempt by 7th Armoured to reach Villers-Bocage. This attack had ended by June 16. Then came the Great Storm, on June 19, which put everything back by a couple of days before the British attacked again west of Caen, in another attempt to cross the river Odon – Operation Epsom. If the British had not yet taken Caen, it was clearly not for want of trying but so far every attempt had been frustrated by strong, even fanatical, German resistance.

Even so, there were some grounds for disquiet at SHAEF. These attempts to take or encircle Caen had failed, yet one or other solution, either to drive the Germans out of the city by a direct assault or avoid it by an outflanking movement on to the Caen–Falaise plain and leave the garrison of Caen to rot, should have been successful by now. As it was, while the British and Canadians seemed able to contain any German attempt to break through to the coast, when they moved against the German lines they soon came back again with a bloody nose. The disquiet arose over why these attacks had not succeeded. The common element is the power of the defence.

This should not be too surprising. It cannot be emphasised too strongly or too often that the countryside of Normandy is ideal for defence; all the Allied Histories, American, British and Canadian, stress this fact. This topographical benefit was balanced by two opposing military factors: on the German side the superior armour of the crack Panzer divisions and well-trained panzer-grenadier infantry, on the Allied side, air power, an abundance of artillery and the guns of the Fleet; against these combinations whichever side attacked was soon thrown back with loss – and the people who had to do most of the attacking were the Allies. Heavy losses could also be a problem, for the British and Canadian Armies could not sustain losses of any magnitude, not because of any reluctance to fight but because their manpower resources were almost at an end.

Added to this demographic factor was the legacy of the 1914–18 Western Front when a whole generation had been lost in fruitless attacks against an entrenched enemy, the infantry decimated repeatedly for no territorial gain over four long years. Britain had not forgotten those years and if American generals or historians sometimes chided the British for their 'slowness' or 'caution' – being too polite to employ the words 'timidity' or 'cowardice' – the more limited American experience of total war at this time probably had something to do with it.

The American front-line experience of the Great War was limited to a few months in 1918 and the USA did not enter the Second World War until 1941, when it already had been going on for more than two years – and six months after the Russians, having been allied with Nazi Germany since 1939, had finally come in on the British side to tilt the balance in a way that would lead to Allied victory. The United States had not 'stood alone' for years against a formidable enemy as the British had done between 1939 and 1941. For the British, this war was a long game and while they wanted to win, and end it, they had no intention of forcing the pace with costly and unnecessary attacks.

It is notable that the US military has become considerably less 'gung-ho' since the 1960s and 1970s when Vietnam taught them that they were not invincible and that throwing men and *matériel* at a military problem is not always the answer – and can lead to terrible losses of the brave American soldiers tasked to make such a philosophy work, one lesson the British had learned on the Somme. The selection of the right tactics for a particular situation is a task for the generals, and generals are expected to use their brains or what use are they? Although American historians and military men have had many hard things to say about General Montgomery since the Second World War ended, nobody has ever said that he was stupid.

All that said, the circumstances of June 1944 were difficult. However effective Montgomery's long-stated and firmly held strategy might be and however often that strategy was explained – which clearly was not often enough – unless some progress was made around Caen, the powers-that-be would remain unhappy. This unhappiness was made manifest by the airmen, notably Air Chief Marshal Tedder and his crony Coningham who, as related, had been promised Carpiquet and space for airfields on the Caen–Falaise plain and were now hotly demanding that Monty supplied it.

There was a third reason, accurately summed up by that astute American officer, General Omar Bradley:[3]

> He (Monty) left himself open to criticism by over-emphasising the importance of this thrust towards Caen. Had he limited himself simply to the containment, [of enemy forces] without making Caen a symbol of it, he would have been credited with success instead of being charged, as he was, with failure. For Monty's success should have been measured in the Panzer divisions who rushed against him while Collins sped on to Cherbourg. Instead, the newsmen clamoured for a place called Caen which Monty had once promised but failed to win for them.

Reading the plethora of memoirs and histories on the Normandy campaign, it is striking how much attention was paid at the time to the opinions of the press. After a lapse of fifty years – and in spite of the fact that media interference in the running of campaigns and critical comment on the actions of the commanders has greatly increased in the decades since – one can only wonder if all the time and attention spent at SHAEF agonising over press comment in the United States or the United Kingdom could not have been devoted to a more useful purpose.

Providing journalists with dramatic headlines is no part of a general's duty but what the papers said was read by the public and the politicians had to answer to that public. Pressure for results was duly applied down the line and the lives of the generals in the field became uncomfortable ... and the generals discovered that a new field of opposition had to be tackled, in the daily press. The golden days when Lord Kitchener, campaigning in the Sudan in 1898, could greet the assembled press corps with a gruff, 'Get out of my way, you drunken swabs', were long over by 1944. Some generals realised this; General Mark Clark – another prima donna – the commander of the US Fifth Army in Italy, travelled around with his own private press group and would return any newspaper copy that did not mention his commanding role – not simply 'With the Fifth Army' but 'With General Mark W. Clark's Fifth Army' – to the relevant journalist for correction.

All this pressure, from the media and from SHAEF – plus a need to keep the German armour fully occupied before Caen – meant that action was called for and as soon as the Great Storm abated Monty struck again with a double blow, a thrust by the 152nd Brigade of the 51st Highland Division out of the Orne bridgehead, followed by a major Second Army attack across the river Odon, west of Caen–Epsom.

The Orne bridgehead attack, another attempt to capture the village of Ste-Honorine, went in before dawn on June 23 (D plus 17), spearheaded by the 5th Bn The Cameron Highlanders, supported by tanks of the 13/18th Hussars. The advance went well, the tanks and infantry got into the village before the defenders were fully awake and a counter-attack later that day by a force of German tanks and infantry commanded by Colonel Hans von Luck was driven off, the Germans losing eighteen tanks in the fight for the village. This neat little operation was a prelude to the main attack – Operation Epsom – mounted across the Odon west of Caen two days later by the newly arrived VIII Corps, supported by XXX Corps. It will be noted that these attacks went in while the Americans in the west were heading up towards Cherbourg; there was no delay on the British front.

The river Odon runs north-east from the centre of Normandy towards Caen where it links with the river Orne. The basic plan for Epsom employed VIII Corps and consisted of three divisions as yet untried in battle; 15th Scottish, 11th Armoured and 43rd Wessex. This corps was commanded by Lt General Sir Richard O'Connor, a Desert veteran who had been captured in 1941 and returned to the fray after the fall of Italy. VIII Corps was not yet complete as some of its elements had been held up by the Great Storm but with the addition of two independent tank brigades, 31st Tank and 4th Armoured Brigade, the corps could muster some 600 tanks, Shermans, Churchills or Cromwells. Epsom would clearly be a major attack for which VIII Corps really needed more infantry to match its great weight in tanks and artillery.

For Epsom, VIII Corps artillery mustered 300 guns *plus* the support of some 400 guns from the 3rd Canadian Division or XXX Corps and I Corps, which would fire on the VIII Corps front, *plus* the naval gunfire from three cruisers and the monitor HMS *Roberts*, *plus* ground-attack fighters of 2nd TAF and a preliminary drenching of the attack area by RAF heavy bombers. Some 60,000 men were involved from VIII Corps alone, so Epsom was clearly envisaged as a massive thrust, deploying great strength on a limited section of front – a Second World War replica of the attacks used on the Western Front in the Great War.

VIII Corps would advance on a four-mile front west of Carpiquet, cross the Caen to Villers-Bocage road and thrust across the Odon to the high ground overlooking the assault area beyond the river, which rises to a point called Hill 112, north-east of Évrecy. That height achieved, they would press on to Bretteville and so to the river Orne. Meanwhile, XXX Corps would cover their right flank with an attack – Operation Dauntless – a southward thrust along the high ground from Rauray to the village of Noyers-Bocage which lay three miles north-east of Villers-Bocage. XXX Corps would take the high ground overlooking VIII Corps' attack area, while I Corps prepared to exploit to the north of Caen – if all went well. Unfortunately, all did not go well.

'The course of the battle,' says the British Official History,[4] 'was largely influenced by the nature of the ground', a comment that could hold good for the entire Normandy campaign on both the British and American fronts – and most other battles. Like the ground confronting the Americans before St-Lô, the country north of the Odon was, says the Official History, 'difficult country through which to attack and its broken contours and abundance of cover make it almost ideal for defence'. Added to this was a problem not yet encountered by the American forces, the presence in this ideal defensive terrain of crack Panzer units: 12 SS Panzer – Hitler Jugund – together with units of Panzer Lehr and 21 Panzer. These units had been in this area for two or three weeks. They knew the terrain in detail, had prepared their defences and were soon to be joined by two more SS Panzer units – 9 SS and 10 SS from the II SS Panzer Corps.

The Epsom offensive began on June 25 with preliminary attacks by XXX Corps. Their first move was to take Rauray, a task handed to the 49th Division as its first venture in battle. The 49th Division would be supported at the start by a great deal of artillery including the guns of VIII Corps and would need all the help it could get. The villages in front of Rauray – Juvigny on the river Seulles, and Vendes – were occupied by the right flank formations of Panzer Lehr and the left flank formations of 12 SS Panzer – and apart from their own resources these units had some sixty to eighty 88mm guns from III Flak Corps in support. This was a great deal of opposition for one infantry division to take on but to begin with the attack went well.

The 49th Division went in at around 0400hrs on June 25, their advance covered by a thick ground mist. On that day the 49th Division succeeded in taking the village of Vendes and the larger village of Fontenay, though Fontenay was not finally in British hands until dawn on the 26th. This attack was pressed home with great persistence as the Army Group B war diary records: 'After heavy fighting on the severely weakened left flank of 12 SS and the right of Panzer Lehr, attacks by successive waves of enemy troops succeeded in tearing open a gap 5 km (3 miles) wide by 2 km (1 mile) deep.'

This was a good start and on the following morning, June 26, 49th Division moved on to attack the high ground at Rauray, just as the main VIII Corps attack began towards Hill 112. On the day Epsom was launched, bad weather restricted flying and for the first time since D-Day there was no air support for the ground troops.

Even so, supported by all that artillery and naval gunfire, the VIII Corps attack began when the 15th (Scottish) Division set out from their start line, heading for the Odon bridges between Gavrus and Verson, five miles to the south of the line. When those bridges had been taken, tanks of the 11th Armoured Division would cross and seize the Orne bridges and so open the way to the plain south of Caen round the western side of the city.

A tactical change will be noticed here; on Perch, the 7th Armoured Division's thrust at Villers-Bocage, the tanks went first and the infantry came up later. This was found ineffective, so on Epsom, the infantry led the way and the tanks came later. Unfortunately, the Germans had an answer to the infantry tactic: firepower.

The VIII Corps attack began at 0730hrs on June 26, with a bombardment from over 700 guns. After this had flayed the enemy positions for a while, the Scottish infantry, supported by 31st Tank Brigade, advanced across open cornfields ... and ran into heavy opposition. The Germans were well dug-in and had suffered very little from the shelling. From concealed positions in the villages, farmhouses, copses and woods on the north bank of the Odon, a heavy fire from machine-guns, mortars and anti-tank guns began to take its toll of the advancing infantry and their supporting tanks. Even so, the battle for the Odon position was not all one-sided; one German account tells of their infantry emerging from their dug-outs to find their positions, 'surrounded by furious Scotsmen throwing grenades'.[5]

Beyond the open cornfields lay more *bocage,* thick hedgerows laced with wire, littered with mines, well provided with enemy troops, tanks and anti-tank guns, a country where every village – La Gaule, St Manview, Cheux and Le Haut de Bosq – was stoutly defended. British attack was followed by German counter-attack and the fighting went on all day, most of it conducted at close quarters. By the evening of June 26, 15th Scottish had punched a shallow hole about two miles deep into the German defences; they had not, however, reached their first objective, the bridges over the Odon.

The follow-up division, 11th Armoured, had come forward as planned and attempted to reach the Odon bridges at Gavrus and Tourmauville but ran into 88mms and *panzerfausts* long before they got there. The narrow Norman lanes were a considerable obstacle to the tanks and a great traffic jam soon developed in the ruined village of Cheux. Cheux contained the main road junction in this part of the front with seven roads leading into it and was therefore under constant shell and mortar fire. 11th Armoured soon realised that they were not going to cross the Odon that day or even reach the bridges at Tourmauville and Gavrus – and as night fell the front was drenched by torrential rain that turned the churned-up ground into a swamp. Even so, the battle continued and began to concentrate around a ridge beyond the river, Hill 112.

The fight for Hill 112 was to continue for some weeks and the following varied accounts from the veterans will give some idea what the fighting there was like. Among the young tank troopers taking part was Bill Thompson of the 9th Bn The Royal Tank Regiment (9 RTR):[6]

We had about a year of training before we embarked for Normandy, landing in tempestuous weather between the 19th and 22nd June as part of the 31st Tank Brigade in VIII Corps. This corps was made up predominantly of peacetime weekend soldiers – the TA or Territorials – and conscripts, green troops in the main, and we arrived in time to participate in Operation Epsom, which aimed to punch a two-mile gap in the German lines across the Orne and Odon. It was not an easy job and the Germans brought in no less than six Panzer divisions in the end, to hold us back.

My baptism of fire came on June 26 at Cheux, when our squadron of 18 Cromwell tanks moved into the village. The countryside was ideal for defence, made up of sunken roads and thick hedges – it was not only the Yanks who had the *bocage* to cope with. Snipers would pick off the tank commanders who had to keep their heads and shoulders out of their turrets to see what was going on and in the lanes there was no way to turn left or right and it was almost certain that a German tank, a Panther or Tiger would be somewhere ahead – or a *panzerfaust*.

That first day my squadron lost 13 tanks out of 18; fortunately, a number of the tanks were recoverable and the loss among the crews was not too great but the first one killed in my regiment was Sidney Chapman, our Troop corporal. I remember thinking that he was married with two kids and it seemed sad that a husband and father had to be killed in battle; at least we younger ones – I was 20 – had no dependants.

In that first action 'C' Squadron supported the 1 Bn The Gordon Highlanders of the 15th Scottish and being half-Scots I was proud to be fighting alongside them. They took a lot of casualties and that night I remember quite clearly the sound of the bagpipes as the Gordons and the other Scots battalions played laments – *Flowers of the Forest* – to honour their fallen. It made the hair stand up on the back of my neck. Then came Maltot and Hill 112, but around Caen that summer it was attack and counter-attack, all the time. There was not a lot of love lost between us and the Americans at this time. The Americans thought that the British and Canadians were not moving fast enough but we had around seven

Panzer divisions on our front most of the time and they only had one – and that makes a difference, believe me.

Ernie Cox of the 141st Regiment, RAC, has another account of this time:[7]

Hill 112 was not very high but it was the key to this part of Normandy as from its summit every move in the surrounding country could be observed. I belonged to a flame throwing unit of Churchill tanks and it was our job to take out the strongpoints with flame. Farmhouses would be turned into strong points by the Germans and with the enemy well dug-in just shelling would not move them. The mortaring and shelling never stopped and several men were wounded in the open when they did not get to cover quick enough. There were also Tigers moving about – and the first time I saw one my heart missed a beat.

It was not fifty feet away, but on a second glance I saw the crew were hanging out the hatches where they had been shot; a 17-pounder anti-tank gun hidden in the hedges had done for it but there was German infantry in the hedges so we went along, flaming the hedgerows. When our infantry had been over the ground one of their Majors came over and asked if we wanted to inspect our handiwork. We declined.

Peter Shepherd was on Epsom with the 25th Field Regiment, Royal Artillery:[8]

We had been tasked to take part in the opening barrage on Cheux. The battle began at 0730 but the infantry made slow progress mainly because of the deep minefield at Le Mesnil-Patry; our guns were also held up by several traffic jams at the entrance to the minefield and 'A' Troop were hit by rifle fire on reaching the far side, forcing us to dismount and seek cover until the enemy had been cleared from the woods to our front. Two small patrols were formed from the battery personnel and entered the wood. They had hardly gone in before heavy machine-gun and rifle fire was opened and no more was heard of them. Of the men who entered the wood, only one man, Gunner Erskine, returned.

Help was sought from a platoon of infantry who also entered the wood and came under heavy fire and we eventually obtained help from some Shermans and Honey tanks which gave the wood a good plastering before another party of gunners went in, returning with forty-three German prisoners, including a wounded officer. The other batteries of the regiment had also been in close contact with the enemy and mopping up our position was not completed until the evening.

There is little doubt that, like the 49th Division of XXX Corps, the VIII Corps formations, 15th Scottish and the Tank Brigades, pushed home their attacks on June 26 with considerable persistence and courage; the casualty figures are a bleak confirmation of that fact with 2,720 men lost – killed, wounded or missing – in the 15th Scottish Division for that day alone. The British attacks were delivered in a text-book fashion, the infantry attacks pressed home with grenades and at the point of the bayonet; but it is fair to say that the Allied forces in Normandy – British, Canadian and American – had yet to get a grip on the Germans and were not getting ahead as quickly as they might have done.

Tom Stokes of the 15th Scottish Division gives some reasons why:[9]

227th Brigade of 15th Scottish had been moving forward hoping that by the evening of June 26 the two bridges over the Odon would be secured but the villages of Cheux and other villages were heaps of ruins, roads were blocked with rubble or so narrow that tanks could not get through. Off the road, after pouring rain, the fields were well-nigh impassable to cross with trucks, carriers or tanks. 10th HLI (Highland Light Infantry) under Lt Col Young pushed forward but soon ran into dug-in German tanks which had to be knocked out by anti-tank guns and they were then pinned down by intense mortar fire.

At Tourmaville, a German tank was shooting-up our tanks as they turned into the main street. At Grainville the Cameronians got in and consolidated despite accurate mortar and shellfire as well as counter-attacks by SS so their casualties were heavy. Despite gains on the flanks, this salient, the Scottish Corridor, south of Cheux, was only about one and a half miles wide and the enemy were gathering around the flanks.

On a man-to-man basis the German soldiers, especially in the well-equipped and fanatical SS units around Caen, were simply better soldiers – or at least better trained soldiers than the Allied troops – at this time; the fact that they fought so well when completely without air cover is just one indication of this fact.

As time went on all that would change. Soldiers learn fast in battle – or they die – and it is noticeable from the many accounts of American, British and Canadian veterans that although they are willing to acknowledge the skill and ingenuity of the German soldier, they were also quite willing to attack and take the battle to the enemy. On Epsom the British attacks were fiercely resisted by the Germans; so were German counter-attacks against the British infantry, soldiers who are famously stubborn in defence and very reluctant to give up ground they have taken or been ordered to defend.

The Germans also had much better kit than their opponents, an abundance of automatic weapons, notably heavy machine-guns deployed down to squad or section level, where their greater firepower overwhelmed the platoon weapons of the British. The German infantry anti-tank weapon, the *panzerfaust* – the 'tank fist' – was lethal in the close country of the *bocage* and German mortars, both 81mm and multi-barrelled *nebelwerfer*, were a real scourge and German snipers ranging along the front, took a heavy toll of Allied officers, who quickly learned not to wave their arms about, display maps or carry revolvers.

Ernie Cox tells of meeting a Panther tank:[10]

I was a Driver/Operator in 'A' Squadron, 141 RAC, (The Buffs) in Crocodile flame throwers but we were used as gun tanks to start with until the infantry realised we were useful. Hill 112 seemed to dominate the battle front and we seemed to be attacking it every few days. The Odon country was well suited to defence and we took up a position on a ridge overlooking the river valley and for once we could see for about 2,000 yards and that is how we saw five Panthers and two Tigers. We were told to hold our fire until they got closer, no use engaging them otherwise and they had not seen us; we had two troops and a command tank, seven tanks in all, and I had an AP round up the spout.

When the range came down to 800 yards the command came to open fire and our gunner lined up and fired at the nearest Panther. It was a good shot on the front plate and I expected it to burst into flames, as our tanks did, but it just kept on coming so we quickly fired the next shot only to see it bounce off the Panther armour.

At that point I stopped looking and concentrated on pushing more rounds into the breach, at least until I got to number six which stuck there and I could not get it out; after some shoving and pushing the shell case came out but not the shell and the floor of the tank was covered in cordite; nasty stuff at the best of times and as I looked out of the periscope the Panther seemed awfully close and had not yet fired a shot. All we could do was watch it come on, unstoppable.

Then, suddenly, it burst into flames as a Sherman Firefly on our flank opened up with its 17-pounder; no one got out and then another Panther went up and they began to turn away. One of our tanks hit a Tiger right in the drive sprocket and stopped it, the crew took to the ditches and got away, and then another

Panther went up in flames; if only we had had the 17-pounder instead of these useless 75mms – but for the Sherman Fireflys they would have rolled right over us. Later on a recovery tank came out and dragged the damaged Tiger into our lines and we had a look at it. That 88mm gun made ours seem like popguns and the score marks showed how many times it had been hit but none of our shells had penetrated it. By the end, our casualties were over 100 per cent and by the war's end we were on our fourth tank.

The Allied troops would learn how to cope with these German advantages but they were taking heavy punishment in the meantime. All these factors were to play a part in the Epsom offensive but on the evening of June 26 the German intelligence officers at Army Group B were correct in their claim that the defenders had obtained 'a clear defensive success' along the Odon river.

On the other hand, the same report admits that this success had cost the I SS Panzer Corps its last reserves, 'with the forces of 12 SS and Panzer Lehr taxed to their utmost'. In anticipation that the British attack would continue, a counter-attack was planned, involving II SS Panzer Corps, plus a tank battalion of 2nd Panzer and the 8th Werfer (Mortar) Brigade, a plan encouraged by the foggy weather which spared the German units from Allied air attack. Their attack should have gone in on June 27, but the assembly of forces had been delayed by the destruction of the French rail network by the RAF and the French Maquis, so VIII Corps had time to come on again, moving forward at 0500hrs on June 27, through another thick ground mist. Overnight, the 43rd Infantry Division of VIII Corps had taken over the ground won by 15th Scottish, freeing that division to push on again at first light.

By mid-morning, 15th Scottish had reached the river Odon, found an undamaged bridge at Tourmauville and crossed over. This division was now spearheading the advance while 49th Division of XXX Corps had secured the right flank of the advance by taking Tessel-Bretteville, north-west of Rauray. 11th Armoured provided close support to the advancing Scots and 43rd Division deployed to hold the left flank against probes from tanks and infantry from I SS Panzer Corps. As 15th Scottish pushed across the Odon, the effect was to create a salient reaching south across the Odon, its point resting on Hill 112.

Hill 112 is not much of a hill; it is best imagined as a rise in the ground, rather like a long ridge between the Odon and the Orne, barely noticeable from the east or west, but a distinct obstacle to any forces coming up from the steep-sided Odon valley on to the open plateau. The fighting for Hill 112 marked all the forces engaged there and features strongly in the veterans accounts as Ernie Cox of the 31st Armoured Brigade confirms:[11]

> Hill 112 was an awful place. Dotted with small hamlets that were just piles of rubble, the debris of war blew across the battlefield, letters from home, photos of loved ones, all that is left of a casualty, each one a story. Wrecked and burnt-out tanks – did the crews get out on time? Few did. Ammo boxes, rifles, blankets, equipment of all kinds, the putrid stink of death and the carcases of dead farm animals. There were times when we drove over them in the dark and then the vile-smelling mess would revolve around in the tracks while inside we would be trying not to vomit.
>
> One thing we knew, the enemy tanks were better than ours and virtually all the Panzer divisions faced us and could see us from the top of Hill 112; they shelled us, they mortared us and we sat there, hanging on and taking casualties. Pyrotechnics of burning lorries, exploding trucks of ammunition, and still we stayed there.

Once through the woods on the south side of the Odon, their advance followed closely by 11th Armoured's tanks, 15th Scottish gained the north slopes of Hill 112, east of the village of Esquay ... and there they held and were held. Time and again the British infantry surged up to the open crest of 112 but the Germans held that crest and the reverse slope and declined to give them up. They also held both flanks of the narrow salient the British thrust had established from the river towards Hill 112 and now had this salient under fire from three sides.

Hill 112 is the ideal spot from which to view the battlefield west of Caen. To the north lie the runways and hangers of Carpiquet airfield which was still in German hands; so was Caen to the north-east. To the north lie the woods along the Odon valley and the higher ground beyond; much of this too was still in German hands. To the south, flat, open and west of the Orne, lies the object of this Epsom attack, the start of the Caen–Falaise plain. Finally, just to the south-west stands the town of Villers-Bocage and another local summit, Mont Pinçon. It takes no military experience or expertise whatsoever to realise the value of Hill 112.

Jack Woods, a trooper in 9 RTR, fought at Hill 112 on Epsom:[12]

We sailed for Normandy during the storm and I was as sick as a dog; all I wanted to do was die as the LST we were on did everything but sink. The day after we landed we were told-off to support the 15th Scottish at Cheux on Epsom, which did not mean much to me at the time. Then I was told to report to the Recce Officer as his driver had injured his hand in the top hatch. His replacement was me and so I went into battle for the first time in my life.

It was a lousy day, pouring with rain, and just to cheer us up we passed some 7 RTR Churchills being taken back with ominous holes in their hulls and tur-rets. We then spent the rest of the day stuck in traffic-jams finally getting up to the tanks late in the day and witnessing a scene which has stayed with me for the rest of my life. Some of our tanks – which we had been told in the UK were impenetrable – were blazing away merrily on the skyline, giving out clouds of black smoke or a firework display of exploding ammunition; those of the crews who survived were coming back, their faces registering the shock of what had happened to them. The infantry, not having reached their objectives were also coming back, those that were left anyway – and regrouping by the road.

We stayed there awhile and there I saw my first dead Germans, a group led by a sergeant and freshly killed; the Jocks who had done the job were still crouching in the hedgerow. Further on we passed a burning half-track, its infantry component hanging dead over the side; then we bellied the armoured car and had to be extracted by a Bren-Gun carrier while a Spandau stitched a line of bullets up our back. It transpired afterwards that this road was the front line; how green we were, standing there while the Recce Officer went off to do his bit and us waiting there with not a personal weapon in sight and the Bren gun stowed.

Then German tanks were coming up and we elected to abandon the car and bail out, making our way back across the fields. What I remember of the rest of the day was a Panzer Mk IV being knocked out by an infantry 6pdr and our radio operator crouching at the door of the armoured scout car, desperately trying to raise the squadron 'Hello Sugar Niner, report my signals, over' and then the squadron coming over the horizon like a cavalry charge. So the day ended.

On June 29, the Germans made a determined attempt to take back the north-ern slope of Hill 112 and push the British back across the Odon. The British bridgehead south of the river was untenable unless it could be expanded, for it was surrounded on three sides by high ground from which fire could be poured down on the river crossings and on any troops attempting to reinforce the British foothold on the northern slope of Hill 112. The British were reluctant to give up this ground and the fight for the hill at the end of June became one of the epic struggles of the Normandy battle.

Two SS Panzer divisions, 2 SS (Das Reich) and 10 SS of the II SS Panzer Corps, backed by 9 SS Panzer, which had been holding the ground south of the Odon, were flung into this counter-attack against the salient south of Cheux, deploying Tiger tanks and concentrating their efforts on the 29th Armoured Brigade around Hill 112. Their first attack was driven off but enemy pressure only intensified, with heavy artillery concentrations and plenty of 'stonking' from *nebelwerfer* multiple-barrelled mortars.

The rain cleared away on June 29 and 2nd TAF were active, with Typhoons swooping down to attack German tanks with rockets and cannon fire. Still the German pressure on Hill 112 and the Odon salient continued as the 11th Armoured Division crossed the Odon and attempted to enlarge the 15th Scottish bridgehead south of the river. The pounding of Hill 112 by artillery, German and British, now reached Great War proportions; shellfire scoured the trees and grass from the slopes, infantry and tanks attacking and counter-attacking all round the bridgehead perimeter, where both sides were now feeding in more troops and tanks.

On the British side this included the first elements of the Guards Armoured Division, the 32nd Guards Brigade, which was put under command of the 43rd Division and positioned along the Caen–Bayeux road, west of Carpiquet. The village of Mouen, north of the Odon and to the left of the salient, had been taken on June 28 but the woods between there and the river remained in German hands. Bad weather prevented much Allied air support reaching the Odon bridge-head and the Luftwaffe appeared again only to be taken on at once by the arrival of fighters from 83 Group, 2nd TAF, which shot down a number of enemy aircraft and then strafed targets on the ground.

Heavy fighting continued all that day. German pressure was coming in all around the salient, especially on the top of Hill 112, though a major attack by newly arrived units of the II SS Panzer Corps – 9 SS and 10 SS – was disrupted by Allied air strikes and artillery concentrations. However, it was clear to General O'Conner that the Germans were gathering their strength for a major counter-attack by several SS Panzer divisions against the Odon salient. He there-fore decided to break off any attempt at a further advance, pull back from the northern slope of Hill 112 to a narrow bridgehead east of the Odon and dig-in to resist what was coming.

The anticipated German attack did not come in on June 30 – mainly because naval gunfire and artillery concentrations fell on the German forming-up posi-tions – but early on the morning of July 1 the Germans attacked the southern end of the Odon bridgehead at Gavrus with infantry, and thrust infantry and tanks into the right flank of the salient at Grainville. Both attacks were halted by artillery concentrations and air strikes without which the British infantry would have been in considerable trouble. German attacks were resumed later and con-tinued throughout the day and were only broken off after the Germans had lost between thirty and forty tanks. British infantry, aided by Crocodile flame-throw-ing tanks then hunted down pockets of enemy infantry within the salient and had restored their lines by nightfall. Once again the advantage in the Normandy battle went to the defenders – in this case the British.

The slender British salient across the Odon had been battered by this attack, but it still held. On the other hand, it was not expanding and maintaining it was proving expensive. The British advance was now being held between the Orne and the Odon rivers and more German divisions were coming up to seal off the salient; 9 SS Panzer had already been identified in the attacks on the right flank astride Grainville and 10 SS Panzer had been involved in the attack on Gavrus.

The only apparent advantage accruing to the Allies by holding the Odon bridgehead was that to contain this British attack these strong Panzer divisions had been forced to expend effort and tanks which might have been better employed in a strong counter-offensive against the Allied line elsewhere or been sent west to aid the defenders of St-Lô. It can also be claimed that these two experienced SS Panzer divisions – 9 SS and 10 SS – expended their strength here to defend the Caen front and were never used, as Hitler originally intended, in a strong attack to break the Allied line at Caumont. This being so, it can also be claimed that Montgomery's strategy, to contain and write down the German Panzer divisions on the British front, was working well; as the Panzers came up, so they were consumed.

Even so, further progress with the Epsom offensive or across the Odon at this time was deemed to be impossible, other than at great cost. There were now eight Panzer divisions covering the Second Army front between Caumont and Caen and some 200 tanks, plus a quantity of panzer grenadier infantry were directly confronting the British 11th Armoured Division along the Odon. In view of this, says Montgomery,[13] 'It was decided that VIII Corps should concentrate for the time being on holding the ground already won and regrouping started with the object of withdrawing our armour into reserve ready for renewed thrusts.'

On the night of June 29, therefore, the troops still clinging on the shell-torn slopes of Hill 112 were withdrawn. The Epsom offensive was over. It would be charitable to call it a draw, since the objectives of the attack were not achieved and the losses, especially in 15th Scottish, were severe, but if the aims of Epsom are compared with the results it is hard not to conclude that the Germans had the best of it. The Orne had not been crossed, the Caen–Falaise plain was still out of reach, Caen and Carpiquet were still in German hands and Hill 112, drenched in blood, had been given up after days of heavy fighting.

In the short term, the Germans had enjoyed the best of it locally but there is also the strategic factor to consider. German losses, especially in tanks, were considerable. Panzer Lehr and 12 SS had received another drubbing. 9 and 10 SS Panzer had been committed to a fight which not only cost them tanks but also diverted them from the purpose for which they had been called from the Russian front, an attack on the junction of the Anglo-American line at Caumont. The Germans had been forced into another heavy commitment against the British when they should have been redeploying to resist the Americans now moving on St-Lô – although in the event the German forces in the west proved quite sufficient to bring the US advance to a halt. Finally, the new, untried, troops of the British VIII Corps had been flung in battle against the pick of the Wehrmacht and given a good account of themselves.

It was now the end of June, more than three weeks into the Normandy battle. Apart from getting ashore and staying ashore, and linking up the beachheads, the only concrete success had been the belated capture of Cherbourg. On the other hand, territorial objectives were not everything. The German Army had been brought to battle in the west and if the losses were not on the scale of those suffered by the German armies fighting on the Eastern Front they were not inconsiderable as the casualty figures from D-Day to June 30 indicate:

KILLED, WOUNDED AND MISSING

British and Canadian...... 24,698

American........................ 37,034

Allied total..................... 61,732

German Total................. 80,783

These figures require some analysis. At this stage the US total is inflated somewhat by the heavy losses taken by the 1st and 29th Infantry Divisions at Omaha on D-Day and by the losses in the two US airborne divisions. The German total is inflated by the large number of prisoners recently taken at Cherbourg but the notable difference is the one between the British and Canadian casualty figure and the American one. The losses of D-Day may inflate the US total but the difference – almost one-third – is too wide to be bridged by the events of D-Day alone. While every army and corps was carrying out its allotted task, the Second Army had been engaged in a series of offensives against crack German formations – as the Epsom offensive illustrates and the casualties taken by the 15th Scottish Division alone underlines – while the Americans had kept up a steady pressure in the Cotentin and on the west flank, but against far less well-equipped or well-trained formations.

Why then the difference? Up to this stage in the battle the British and Canadians had roughly the same number of men ashore as the Americans and since both the Allied armies were attacking, it might appear reasonable that their casualty figures would be roughly the same.

The first answer – one popular with a certain type of historian – was that the Second Army was not doing its fair share of the fighting, or that the British and Canadian troops were not pressing their attacks home but sitting in safety, drinking excessive amounts of tea; American historians are particularly given to mentioning tea. As evidence, these historians point out that while there was some fighting every day on the Second Army front, Second Army was putting in a series of specific, set-piece offensives – Perch and Epsom, for example – with intervals between each one, while the American divisions were attacking all out and all the time.

This scenario is not entirely correct. As we have seen, the US V Corps had stopped before St-Lô, while on the VII Corps front there were delays in sealing off the peninsula and in the advance up the Cotentin to Cherbourg. This is no criticism of either corps or the American soldiers; after attacks all units need to reorganise, re-equip and reinforce; and the problems of supply and the Great Storm had obliged both armies to call off or delay attacks. Before attacking, units need time to plan and prepare, issue orders, rest their men, carry out reconnaissance, agree a fire plan and bring up ample supplies of artillery ammunition to support the attack; the idea of 'continuous' attacks, all along the line, all the time, is rarely feasible in practice.

It is true that some British formations, 7th Armoured and 51st Highland, seem to have lost their western desert verve at this time but – on the other hand – the US History lists formations – the 90th Division, for example – that had also failed to deliver the required amount of 'get up and go'. In both armies generals were to be sacked for their perceived failures in command. In terms of performance there is little to chose between the Allied armies and chauvinistic comments by historians do little to illuminate the true position at the time – and yet we have this interesting difference in casualty figures.

A careful study of the available information and discussions with the veterans would suggest that the reason for the difference in casualty figures lies not in any particular British unwillingness to fight but because many US infantry formations were simply not well enough trained for the sort of fighting Normandy required and therefore took heavy casualties in the *bocage*. This is particularly noticeable among the two Omaha divisions, the 1st Infantry and the 29th Infantry. They were well-trained formations which lost heavily on D-Day and had to be topped up with reinforcements; these new soldiers were not well-trained and were not well assimilated by the D-Day veterans. By the end of June casualties in these divisions topped 100 per cent in some of the rifle companies – as they did in some of the British units.

Take, for example, this account from A. L. Hayman, a nineteen-year-old infantryman in the 7th Bn Somerset Light Infantry, 43rd Division:[14]

I was a corporal in 10 Platoon, 'B' Company. Hill 112 when we attacked it later was like a second Verdun. We attacked at 0400hrs and reached our objective at 2000hrs covering about 1,500 yards that day and by that time I was the senior rank in the Company which had just 23 men left. We were then counter-attacked and reduced to just 18 men but we held the hill.

I can tell you about the Caen area where we were constantly putting in attacks but not going far and had to endure a lot of artillery and mortars. We lost three Commanding officers in two weeks, two killed and one wounded. We needed replacements and we got a lot of Royal Artillery men who had been on light anti-aircraft sites where they were not needed so they were transferred to the infantry – they were not pleased, I can tell you!

We did not like working with tanks as they drew shellfire and we could not hear the sound of the shells coming with the engine noise and tanks were anyway not much good in that close country. After Hill 112 my section of ten men had just three in it, so I got seven replacements. Our OC was Major White-head, a finer officer there never was. He always carried a rifle, and when he was wounded he would not leave until the hill was taken. Then he was wounded again, in the jeep taking him back down the hill, when it was hit by shell splinters but he survived and came back to use later. I hope this gives you some idea of what it was like.

Good training reduced casualties and it is noticeable that within days of the landings General Bradley was insisting on more training for his troops, and this for divisions that were actually 'in-theatre' at the time and – one would hope – were already fully trained and ready for combat. This difference in battlefield capability is pointed up by the superb performance of the two US Airborne divisions in the Cotentin, the 82nd and 101st – good training and leadership seem to be the vital factors here, rather than combat experience, because the 82nd had been in action before and the 101st had not.

The US Official History[15] records: 'All during the rest of June training took place in the V Corps zone to perfect tank-infantry tactics which could set the attack rolling once more towards St-Lô *when the time came*' (author's italics). This tends to confirm the view that the US units were *not* attacking 'all the time' and were in need of more training. It has also to be remembered that the hedgerows of Normandy would be strange indeed to the young soldiers in units newly arrived from the USA and therefore totally unused to enemy action of any kind – or even the wartime atmosphere of Britain. Such troops would be particularly open to casualties in the early days when everything was strange to them.

Then there is the matter of basic US military philosophy. This dictates that it is better to fight all along the line, all the time, at whatever cost, rather than get involved in a prolonged campaign. That philosophy had been the basis of US military thinking since General Grant attacked Robert E. Lee in the Virginia

Wilderness during the US Civil War eighty years before the Normandy battle and for the same reason; the side that has more troops can afford heavy casualties to get the job done and the war over. The name for this kind of strategy is attrition.

A policy based on attrition can be very expensive in lives, especially if the enemy has troops of the calibre of the German formations now fighting in Normandy, on ground of their own choosing and ideal for defence. It is at least arguable, for example, that US losses at Omaha might have been fewer had the US assault plan included more DD tanks and the employment of the British-designed 'special armour', such as mine-clearing flails, flame-throwing tanks or petard, pillbox-busting tanks, to help get their embattled infantry off the beach. This equipment was offered but declined, largely on the technical ground that it was mounted on Cromwell tanks which the US Army did not employ, but also because these defence-busting devices were regarded by Bradley as an unnecessary frill.

The British, with far fewer troops, simply could not afford to expend them in such a fashion – and doing so is anyway not part of British military thinking. The possible losses in an attack are always factored in and the maximum available support, in guns and aircraft is – as at Epsom – always provided to minimise infantry losses. Letting an offensive degenerate into a battle of attrition is simply not the way the British do it; that is one lesson the British generals learned from the million casualties of Passchendaele and the Somme during the Great War, a war in which many of the British generals, including Montgomery, had served in the front line.

It is also fair to repeat that the Allied casualties in Normandy would have been fewer – and Allied progress quicker – had it not been for the skill, courage and tenacity of the Germans. It is *not* fair to hint, or allege, as some historians have done, that the smaller British casualties indicate a lack of a British will to fight. As we shall see, by the time the battle ended, in percentage terms on the basis of troops committed, the casualty figures, British and American, were almost exactly the same – around ten per cent. The Allied troops in Normandy, serving in front-line formations – American, or British, Canadian or Polish – did not flag or fail. Nor did they look too far into the future. When the Normandy battle ended hardly mattered; it would end in an Allied victory but the true cost would be paid by them in the valleys and the *bocage*.

Von Rundstedt and Rommel were certainly under no illusion about the eventual outcome of the Normandy campaign. Their chance to defeat the invasion had been lost on D-Day and now it was only a matter of time before the Allied build-up led to a massive German defeat. However, Rommel and von Rundstedt also felt that this defeat could be delayed for some time if they were given a free hand to manoeuvre their troops, to fall back to more defensible positions and make the Allies pay dearly for every metre of ground. This belief was one they shared with the other German generals in Normandy, including Geyr von Schweppenburg and the new commander of Seventh Army, SS General Hausser. Hitler's insistence on holding every position and making fruitless counter-attacks to regain any position lost was eating away at Army Group B's manpower, tanks and supplies while the Allied build-up continued and would grow at a faster rate once Cherbourg was open for shipping.

German discontent with Hitler, however, was more than matched by the Allied High Command's unhappiness with Montgomery. The issue at SHAEF was Caen; June had gone and Epsom had been called off and Caen was still untaken and who could now deny that the battle for Normandy had become a stalemate? Well, General Montgomery could ... and did.

On June 30, as the Epsom offensive ended, he issued a new set of orders to Dempsey and Bradley, orders aimed at getting another phase of the campaign under way without delay. The Canadians were to take Carpiquet – which would shut up Air Chief Marshal Tedder, Coningham and the RAF – while Bradley's First Army, which had bustled north to take Cherbourg, where the last elements of German resistance had been snuffed out on the previous day, was to turn about and capture St-Lô. The orders to Bradley on what happened then were the blueprint for the later Cobra operation – the 'St-Lô Breakout' as the American soldiers call it – which would then follow.

Tedder's campaign against Montgomery had been provided with fresh ammunition by the calling off of Epsom and the air chief marshal was again roaming the corridors of SHAEF spreading alarm and despondency and dripping more poison into Eisenhower's ears about the state of affairs at the front in Normandy. Nigel Hamilton's comment[16] that 'Tedder's intrigue, as Deputy Supreme Commander of the Allied Expeditionary Force, must rank as one of the most reprehensible performances by a senior Allied Commander in modern battle history', seems entirely accurate.

There seems to be a common thread in Tedder's attacks. On June 22 Tedder recounts how Coningham was complaining to him about Montgomery's 'dilatory' methods. On July 1, again according to Tedder's memoirs, it was Eisenhower who told him that he was worried about Montgomery's 'dilatory' methods.[17] The question that now arises is, if everyone at SHAEF – Eisenhower, Tedder, Morgan, Coningham, and apparently also Bedell Smith, Ike's intelligent and sensible Chief-of-Staff – were worried about Montgomery's 'dilatory' methods, why did they not do something about it? Could it be, perhaps, they did not know what to do, or what alternatives to propose to what Montgomery was already doing? They could criticise, certainly, but as for cast-iron guaranteed ways to push the German Army out of the way, they had no suggestions to make, except to propose more attacks against entrenched German opposition, attacks that might keep the SHAEF commanders happy but led to no apparent strategic gain.

Eisenhower was the Allied Supreme Commander; if he really was dissatisfied with Monty's performance, why did he not act? He had a dozen courses open to him, ranging from giving Montgomery a direct order to attack – and go on attacking until something broke – to taking personal charge of the land battle. If he was unwilling to get a grip on Monty himself, he could have asked Alan Brooke, the British CIGS, to do it for him; Monty was always careful not to disobey Brooke. If Ike felt there was no help there – for Brooke understood the strategy and agreed with what Montgomery was doing – he could have appealed to Churchill for another general or taken the entire matter to the Combined Chiefs-of-Staff in Washington where Marshall would certainly have backed him to the hilt. Eisenhower did none of these things; he simply listened to the whinges of Tedder and Coningham and then started whinging himself.

It should also be remembered that both the Allied armies were part of Montgomery's 21st Army Group and working to Monty's strategic plan at this time. It is therefore a little unfair to criticise Montgomery for the so-called 'stalemate' at Caen and not give him due credit for the success of his plan in the Cotentin; first take Cherbourg, then turn on St-Lô. In spite of the on-going claims of American historians, the Battle of Normandy was an Allied battle, not a purely American show.[18]

Monty's directive to Bradley and Dempsey on June 30, which will be discussed further in the next chapter, is worth noting. It states clearly the position which Montgomery was to maintain about his overall strategy for the Normandy campaign; to pull the German armour on to the Caen-to-Caumont front in order to let the Americans break out in the west. Having done so the Americans would then head south, send forces into Brittany to take the ports there, then head east to encircle the German forces west of the Seine. This was the plan that eventually succeeded but it may not be the exact, original Montgomery plan with which the Allies entered the battle. By declaring that it was Monty again provided his critics with knives to plunge into his back.

It was *always* the intention that the eventual breakout should be made by the Americans, in the west. The later tale, that Montgomery intended to break out at Caen and that – when he failed to do so – Bradley and Patton saved his bacon by breaking out at St-Lô, is simply not true. A breakout in the east had been part of the Cossac plan which Eisenhower and Monty had rejected months before D-Day but the notion that Monty intended to break out in the east, at Caen–Falaise, remains part of the popular myth which will take some time and a great deal of objectivity to remove. Another method is simply to refer again to the facts.

The strategic plan of campaign for Normandy was laid out by Montgomery on April 7, 1944 and has been discussed before. Regarding events *after* the taking of Cherbourg the plan reads as follows: 'In its subsequent operations, the Second Army will pivot on its left and offer a strong front against enemy movements towards the lodgement area from the east.'[19] In his account of the campaign planning, Montgomery states that: 'The general strategic plan was to make the breakout on the western flank, *pivoting the front on the Caen area,* (author's italics) where the bulk of the enemy reserves were to be engaged'.

This states that the Caen *area* will be the hinge for the Allied armies as they swing south and the word 'area' is interesting; we are not talking about the square in front of the Abbaye-aux-Hommes. That hinge might swing at Caen or somewhere further east, perhaps at the mouth of the Seine, or perhaps further west at Caumont or Vire, but on that hinge the entire Allied force was to pivot and turn east. That was the declared intention in April 1944, two months before the invasion, but the important point is – and was – that the breakout would come *in the west*. Now, one month into the invasion, Monty was coming up with a new – or slightly revised – plan, based on the current situation, which certainly called for some revision.

The immediate task of the British Second Army now, he stated, was 'to pin and fight the maximum enemy strength between Caen and Villers-Bocage ... while the main American thrust swung south and then east to the Le Mans–Alençon area and beyond'.[20] US First Army was required to begin on the right flank with an offensive southwards on July 3 and then, *pivoting on its left at Caumont* (author's italics), to swing eastwards to the general line Caumont, Vire, Mortain, Fougères; that is north-east to south-west, from Normandy into Brittany. (A look at the map on page 26 will be helpful.)

> When the base of the Cotentin peninsula was reached near Avranches, the right-hand US Corps, (VIII Corps) should be turned westward into Brittany ... Plans must now be made for the rest of General Bradley's command to ... direct a strong right wing in a wide sweep south of the *bocage* country to successive objectives as follows, (a) Laval-Mayenne (b) Le Mans, Alençon.[21]

The current situation was that the German Panzer divisions were containing the Second Army at Caen – or being kept there by British pressure around the town. This created a situation where Second Army could not pivot at Caen but could press hard against the enemy forces in the east, while the US armies in the west did the pivoting, perhaps at St-Lô or – as stated in Monty's June 30 directive – from the junction of the Allied line at Caumont; and having pivoted, they then came east, south of the restrictive grip of the *bocage,* on an axis of advance from Avranches through Mortain, Domfront, Argentan and Alençon (see map on page 26), a strategy which, if speedily executed would put the Seventh Army in the bag as the British and Canadians came south.

There is nothing wrong in any of this. It is more or less what actually happened two months later at the end of August and – mostly – this plan worked. The problem came later, when Monty claimed that idea of pivoting at Caumont had been his intention all along. This claim is debatable – on the basis of how big is the 'Caen area' – but in the context of the campaign as a whole, it hardly matters. The Allied armies had to pivot *somewhere* for their strategic objectives lay north and east not south and west. To dismiss an entire strategy – and a successful one – because the pivot point has moved twenty-three miles to the south-east, from Caen to Caumont, is wilful nit-picking. It is also highly desirable that generals should change their minds, and their plans, if the situation has changed and requires it; why a change of mind should be seen as some kind of failure in a commanding general escapes this writer, but this too is a point to which we shall return.

For the moment the future strategy was clear and in spite of later claims made by his enemies, it was Montgomery's strategy and nobody else's; the Americans were to take St-Lô and push on south and west to clear Brittany and open the Breton and Loire ports – Brest, Lorient, Nantes and St Nazaire. Second Army were to carry on with their constant attacks at Caen and Carpiquet but must, above all, maintain maximum pressure on the German positions in the east to hold the enemy forces defending that flank in position. To this hard and thankless task Dempsey and his men – British and Canadian – now returned.

8 ATTRITION OR STALEMATE? JUNE 30-JULY 9

*The most consistent mistake made by the Allied Commanders in
North West Europe was a failure to realise – despite repeated examples – the
will and tenacity of the German Army to resist against overwhelming odds
and in the most appalling conditions.*

CARLO D'ESTE *Decision in Normandy*

According to many people at SHAEF, by the end of June 1944, three weeks
after D-Day, the Allied armies were getting nowhere in the battle for Normandy.
Apart from the capture of Cherbourg, the Allied front line had hardly moved
since the beaches had linked up on June 12 and some of the senior officers, most
of them British – Tedder, Morgan, Coningham – were becoming extremely
impatient with General Montgomery and critical of his methods.

Nor were they alone in this. In his memoirs, General Eisenhower comments:[1]
'Late June was a difficult time for all of us. More than one of our high-ranking
visitors began to express the fear that we were stalemated and those who had
prophesied a gloomy fate for Overlord were being proved correct.'

This statement is somewhat at variance with the facts. The Allies had now
been in Normandy for twenty-four days, having successfully carried out the
largest amphibious operation in history. On June 29, one of their armies had
taken the vital port of Cherbourg and another one was currently engaged on a
major battle with five German Panzer divisions astride the Odon. More troops
were coming ashore, more air strikes flown, more enemy soldiers were being
killed and their tank forces destroyed. The German forces in Normandy were
being written down and according to the agreed strategic plan the Seine crossing

was not due to take place for another two months. When the battle is calculated to last three months is there any reason to cry stalemate after just three weeks?

Eisenhower's account goes on to point out that an invading force must not be penned up in its beachhead, that it needs room to bring in more troops and prepare for the breakout, two blinding glimpses of the obvious that provide little enlightenment on how this should be done – or reasons why it was not being done. Eisenhower's impatience with General Montgomery is revealed in something he does *not* say: 'I spent much time in France conferring with General Bradley and General Montgomery concerning the timing and strength of projected battle operations. Such visits with Bradley were always enjoyable ... '.[2]

Perhaps Eisenhower's meetings with Monty were less enjoyable because General Montgomery did not tell Eisenhower what the Supreme Commander wanted to hear, that the armies were attacking all along the line, all the time – a logistical impossibility but an encouraging prospect – or that Monty declined to make any comment on the current situation at all, other than that in his opinion it was going well. One of General Montgomery's less-endearing characteristics was his complete faith in his own ability, a factor irritating to both his American colleagues and the powers-that-be at SHAEF.

The problem was one of character – or attitude. Montgomery was an extremely able and widely experienced general. He seemed to know what he was doing and where this campaign was leading but a few explanations to his superiors would not have gone amiss, since they could not be expected to share his vision. Refusing to attend meetings, sending his chief-of-staff, Freddie de Guingand, to represent him when Eisenhower came to confer with his commanders was not a good policy – although often taken as arrogance instead of what it really was, sheer bad manners.

That said, it could be argued that Monty was acting in accordance with standard British Army practice: the senior commander always goes forward to see the situation, the junior commander does not come back to report on it. Here again, if Eisenhower did not like this practice he should not have tolerated this; Monty was an officer who had to be 'gripped' and would respond to a firm hand – Alan Brooke, the British CIGS, told Eisenhower as much. If Eisenhower had 'gripped' Monty many problems might have been avoided and Eisenhower might have gained a better understanding on the way the battle was going.

Montgomery asked that his superiors take his views on trust because he thought it obvious that he knew what he was doing. Perhaps he did but they would still have welcomed some hints as to why he believed his plans were working out or why, whatever the present state of play, all would turn out well in the end. Had he deigned to provide them with his views and explain his policies in person, a great deal of misunderstanding and bad feeling might have been avoided, at the time and later.

Unfortunately, this was not Monty's way, not with his subordinates, not with his colleagues, not with his senior commander. He had been placed in charge of the land campaign in Normandy, he intended to run it his way and he expected everyone to back him up. There is merit in this point of view; a commander is appointed to do a job; he then has to be trusted to do it, given the necessary resources and supported every step of the way. If he fails, or loses the trust of his superiors, he must be sacked.

There is, of course, a middle way. When the original master plan – the strategy – does not seem to be working or has to be changed, the superiors are entitled to an explanation. This Montgomery not only declined to provide at the time, he later claimed that the original plan had worked out in every detail, a claim which even the most objective observers find hard to accept.

Montgomery seemed unable to appreciate that complete faith in his overall strategy was a lot to expect from his superiors unless he shared his views with them and gave sound reasons for his actions – and explained lack of results in territorial terms. This was especially necessary at this time because Eisenhower had still not been able to establish his headquarters in France. Staying in Britain kept Eisenhower at one remove from the day-to-day action, hearing a constant drip of criticism at SHAEF from Tedder and Morgan, while coming under constant pressure from Marshall, the Combined Chiefs-of-Staff, the politicians and the press in Britain and the USA who were becoming increasingly critical over the lack of progress in Normandy.

Less was heard about the shortage of airfields; there were now twelve airstrips in the British sector and another eleven in the American sector, including one above Omaha beach from which some 15,000 US casualties had already been evacuated in C-47 transport aircraft to hospitals in England. By July 5 all of No. 83 Group, 2nd TAF, and nine fighter groups of the US Ninth Air Force, were operating from French airfields – and over 6,000 RAF and USAAF aircrew had already been lost in the battle for Normandy. One of them was Flt Lt Bill Yunker of the Royal Canadian Air Force, whose story is another reminder that this battle was costing a quantity of lives:[3]

> On the night of 4/5 of July they had dropped their bombs on a mission to Villeneuve-St-Georges and turned for home when they were hit by anti-aircraft fire. Another report says they were hit by a night fighter. An engine caught fire and the fire spread to the wing. Flt Lt Yunker then ordered the crew to bail out which they all did except the tail gunner, P/O Bill Gracie, whose legs had been injured and who was unable to extricate himself from the turret. It is reported that Yunker, who was getting ready to bail out, heard of Gracie's predicament and decided to try and land the aircraft. He took it down to an open field but the damage had spread and both men were killed in the crash. Their bodies were taken by the local French people of Tronchet and buried in the churchyard where the graves were well-tended.

Monty's reticence over his intentions was both misguided and unnecessary. There were good reasons for the current hold-up, most of which have been spelled out in previous chapters. Another reason for delay at the end of June, and a perfectly valid one, was a need to regroup. The US VII Corps, having mopped-up German resistance in the Cap de Hogue around Cherbourg, needed to turn about and head south, pushing out of the Cotentin to open up a path to Avranches and the Brittany ports. Lacking these ports, some materials, like artillery ammunition, was still in short supply and large amounts of ammunition were needed to support any attack against the sort of defences the Germans had established in the *bocage* before St-Lô.

The US History states that the offensive on St-Lô would have started sooner but for a shortage of ammunition, especially artillery ammunition, which was being used up rapidly in supporting attacks. By now 850,819 Allied soldiers had come ashore, 452,469 of them American, and the strain on the supply services was growing. On June 22 there had only been one day's supply of 25-pounder artillery ammunition and 4.2-inch mortar ammunition in the British dumps and rationing had to be imposed; such was the effect of the Great Storm but hard work by the supply teams soon eased that particular crisis. By July 1 the British had nine days' supply of artillery ammunition – at normal usage – and fifteen days' supply of mortar ammunition.[4]

Some explanation on these points and the offer of sound reasons for delay by Montgomery would have quietened the moans of complaint at SHAEF and enabled the Normandy battle to be pressed without this continual carping from on-high. Nor were lengthy explanations needed. The reason the Allied armies were not making faster progress could be summed up in four words – the *bocage,* supply, the weather and the enemy.

As June ended US V Corps were still stuck in the *bocage,* five miles north-east of St-Lô while on the Second Army front the XXX and VIII Corps were licking their wounds after Epsom – but both armies were preparing to attack again. According to General Montgomery's instructions of June 30, while the Second Army were to continue to hold the main enemy forces between Caen and Villers-Bocage, 'and develop operations for the capture of Caen as opportunity offers ... and the sooner the better', US First Army was to begin on the right flank an offensive southwards on July 3 and then, pivoting on its left at Caumont, swing eastwards to a general line, Caumont–Vire–Mortain–Fougères'.[5] Montgomery's instruction of June 30 should be borne in mind when claims surface later about the origins of the Cobra breakout.

To keep up the pressure at Caen, the Canadians were to thrust again for Carpiquet on July 4 and the British were to attack Caen on July 8, just after the attack of US VIII Corps down the west coast of the Cotentin came to an end. Pressure was being applied at either end of the Allied line constantly to stretch and reduce the German resources.

That said, there was a need to press on, especially on the western flank, where the breakout would eventually take place. US V Corps were stalled in front of St-Lô and their advance south from Caumont had come to a halt against the bastion of 2nd Panzer. In the Cotentin, US VIII Corps had started their push on the west coast while on the east the British and Canadians were still battering fruitlessly – and expensively – at the defences of Caen where the German position had stabilised after Epsom. However, as Bradley pointed out (see Chapter 7), if the Second Army kept the German Panzer divisions busy defending Caen, that was as good as possessing it. Even so, with much promised and less delivered in the early weeks of the campaign, the commanders at SHAEF had some reason to be querulous.

Anxiety was also present on the German side. The British Official History[6] comments: 'While the fighting was being conducted with skill by the local

(German) commanders and with stubborn bravery by their troops, the battle as a whole was being conducted by Hitler; not even a division could be moved without his concurrence'.

This seems to be quite true and when the command situations of the two sides are compared, it can be argued that the Allied High Command had rather less to worry about than the situation appears to present – although General Eisenhower may have sometimes envied Hitler's wide-ranging powers over his subordinate commanders.

On July 3, Hitler sacked Field Marshal Gerd von Rundstedt, the commander at OB-West, allegedly because of his handling of the Epsom offensive but more probably because the Führer and von Rundstedt had a fundamental disagreement on how the Normandy battle should be handled. Out, too, on July 4 went Gerd von Schweppenburg, command of Panzer Group West passing to General Eberbach ... but at this point, to put the German end-of-June situation in perspective, we must go back a little.

Since the invasion, von Rundstedt had been appealing to OKW for permission to order 'extensive adjustments to the front' of Seventh Army and freedom, should the need arise, to withdraw the German forces from around the Allied beachhead to a more favourable defensive line somewhere inland, beyond the range of naval gunfire. The answer to this request was a firm and constant 'no' but von Rundstedt – backed by Rommel – continued to press this point ... and irritate the Führer.

Von Rundstedt had also been urging a strong armoured counter-attack to split the British–American line at Caumont – a very sound tactical scheme. This proposal attracted the Führer's approval and plans to implement it were in hand when Hitler suggested that an attack should also be mounted against the rear of the American forces moving on Cherbourg. This too was a worthwhile initiative, but on June 26 von Rundstedt pointed out that he lacked the force to do both, at least with any possibility of success, and insisted that the Caumont attack must have priority – which is probably correct. Two newly arrived divisions, 9 SS and 10 SS Panzer, were to spearhead this attack but – as we have seen – the British then launched the Epsom offensive across the Odon and these two divisions were soon sucked in to resist it.

Arguing with Hitler was fruitless but on June 28–9 von Rundstedt and Rommel motored 700 miles to the Führer's retreat at Berchtesgarten where

Hitler and his senior advisers, Keitel and Jodl, held a conference with the two field commanders. No meeting of minds appears to have taken place. When the field marshals left for Normandy, they were followed by another Führer Directive, insisting that they hold every metre of ground, as before. The last development came three days later on July 3, when, in the course of a telephone conversation on the Normandy difficulties, Keitel asked von Rundstedt what could be done? 'Make peace, you fools', von Rundstedt replied, 'what else can you do?' Keitel rushed to pass this titbit on to the Führer and on July 7, von Rundstedt was sacked.[7] His replacement was Field Marshal Gunther von Kluge, a devoted supporter of the Führer – or so it was generally believed.

Von Kluge served as an artillery officer in the First World War but he also learned to fly, an activity which gave him an early grasp of the importance of air power. He remained in the army after 1918, rising steadily in rank and reputation and when Hitler came to power in 1933 von Kluge was a Major General. He was then prompted Lt General and in 1936 given command of the Sixth Corps. This rapid promotion did not endear Hitler to von Kluge, who participated in a plot to overthrow the Führer in 1938 – a plot that came to nothing when the Munich crisis gave Hitler all he wanted.

Hitler's anti-Semitic policies were anathema to von Kluge but he could not deny the success of the Führer's strategy or fail to approve the expansion of the German Army and his attitude towards Hitler from 1939 on has rightly been described as 'ambivalent'.[8] Commanding the Fourth Army he took part in the Polish campaign in 1939 and the invasion of France in 1940, after which he was promoted to Field Marshal.

He then took part in the Russian campaign and stayed in the East until 1944. Now he was given the command in the West and was expected to do what the Führer wanted; hold every metre of ground and then drive the invaders into the sea.

Von Kluge was not a fool. He had seen the gradual collapse of German power in Russia, seen the destruction of Germany from the air and knew that – whatever was done in the field, East or West – Germany was eventually doomed and that by the summer of 1944 Germany's defeat was only a matter of time. Like a number of officers who had served on the Eastern Front, he was also convinced that the war in the West was a softer option, waged against a less aggressive foe. Shortly after arriving in Normandy he had reason to change his mind on that point.

The situation in Normandy at the end of June was as follows. The senior Allied commanders, with the probable exception of Montgomery, believed that the Battle of Normandy had degenerated into a stalemate, a grinding battle with no sign of rapid progress; they judged success in terms of territory gained, not in the 'writing-down' of enemy forces. The commanders in the field, Dempsey, Bradley and their various corps commanders did not share this view because they saw the battle as an on-going concern with only necessary let-ups. Dempsey was preparing another thrust after Epsom, Collins's VII Corps was about to break out of the Cotentin and Gerow's V Corps was preparing to move on St-Lô. The front-line commanders may not have been moving much but they were doing plenty of fighting and preparing to do plenty more.

Rommel and von Rundstedt would have agreed with the commanders at SHAEF that the battle for Normandy had now become a grinding process; and they were most unhappy about it for they believed that the Normandy battle was not a stalemate but a battle of attrition, and one they could only lose. This outcome was largely due to Adolf Hitler who – like many of the commanders at SHAEF – judged success in terms of ground and would not permit his generals to manoeuvre and still less to fall back.

However, in the circumstances of June–July 1944, Hitler may have been right. The best battleground in Normandy – the 'killing ground' in military parlance – was in the *bocage*. Once the Allies had broken out of that, they would have space to deploy their strength and mobility and run the slower German forces into the ground. On the other hand, if the Führer wanted his generals to fight in the *bocage* he should have given them the wherewithal to fight flexibly, which meant more infantry to hold the ground so that their superior armour – in quality if not quantity – could be used for powerful thrusts and counter-attacks. That said, whatever the eventual outcome, hanging on in the *bocage* was a good tactic for the Germans and one they took every opportunity to exploit. As a result, Allied losses were heavy, especially in the infantry.

Richard Harris of the 1st Bn The Suffolk Regiment, 3rd British Infantry Division, describes his battalion's action at the Château de la Londe, near Caen, on June 28:

> We moved up on the morning of 24th June and the plan was that the South Lancs should take the château and the E. Yorks and Suffolks would follow through and capture the villages of Epron and La Bujude. It all sounded quite

simple and straightforward for the Lancs had taken possession of the château in the first attack but been driven out by a German counter-attack backed by tanks. Anyway the South Lancs attacked but had to withdraw after suffering heavy casualties. We in 'B' Company of the Suffolks waited all afternoon for the word to attack and that period of suspense is one which only those who have experienced it can know. We tried to dig-in as 88mm shells and mortar bombs kept coming over but the ground was chalky and we could make little impression. We stayed there that night, soaked in dew, and my first recollection of the unhappy day was the toe of my section mate's boot and the words, 'Get your kit on, mate, we're going in soon'.

The whole Company moved forward and I think there was no man who was not afraid. Forward through the soaking corn as close as we dared to the curtain of death from the supporting artillery falling ahead of us. Realising that this fire preceded an attack, the Boche were sending over artillery and mortars and casualties were inevitable, cries of 'Stretcher-bearer' were soon heard and men began to fall, their mates sticking his rifle in the ground to mark where he was, before moving on.

I found myself walking forward with one of the corporals and the Company Commander, having no idea where the rest of the section had gone. One of the platoon officers shouted for his sergeant to carry on and came back, his right arm dangling limply at his side. As we passed a group of blazing farm buildings I could see that the Company line was much thinner and straggling than it had been. From the burning farm came four figures in German helmets, a Sten barked and they fell. On for what seemed like hours, sometimes running, sometimes crawling, sometimes waiting and praying for the barrage to lift. There seemed even less of us now but the Major was still in front, bellowing words of encouragement to those remaining, a leader of men if ever there was one; I followed like a dog at its master's heel.

Then it was tea time, but there was no tea and men from Battalion HQ came up, men who are not usually combative and we left our holes and went forward through the fields towards the château. So that day passed and the day was ours and the château was taken and took us that much nearer Caen.

There was nothing spectacular about it. It was just one of the many battles which took place in Normandy but the old spirit of the Company had gone for ever. We were made up but the reinforcements after June 28 could never replace old and well tried friends. One member of my platoon, writing to me from hospital later, had reason to remember that day for he is still paralysed from a piece of shrapnel embedded in his spine. There must have been many more wounded, who died in the corn before they could be picked up.

On D-Day, my Platoon numbered 33 men. After that day, June 28 there were six of us left. Of that six, one was evacuated with severe shell shock in July, three were killed and two, Wakeling and myself, were wounded and evacuated. They got us all in the end.

A battle of attrition is, put simply, a trial of strength, a gamble. In a battle of attrition victory goes to the side that can afford – and is willing – to lose large numbers of men as long as the other side loses more men. The parallels with the 1916 Franco-German battle of Verdun, already so apparent at Caen, were now appearing across the entire Normandy front. If the German commanders were right and the Normandy battle was indeed a battle of attrition, it was one in which the long-term advantage went to the Allies or certainly to the Americans who had plenty of troops to commit and were prepared to accept heavy casualties. So far the Allies had lost 61,000 men and received 79,000 replacements, more than making up for the losses incurred. German losses so far totalled some 80,000 men and although the German replacement figures are not complete, they certainly do not even approach the number of men lost.

US divisions were now landing in Normandy at the rate of one a week. So many troops were arriving that it was becoming hard to find places to put them and harder still to find ways to supply them, given the shortage of ports. There was no space to use them in the line but they still kept coming and the long-term signs were clear. American military muscle – those awesome, overwhelming, United States resources in men and *matériel* – was now being brought to bear in Europe in a fight the German generals could not hope to win. By the end of the Normandy battle the Americans would have landed sixty-one divisions in France and more kept coming until the war ended – though even American manpower began to run out before the European war ended.

This benefit to Allied manpower was restricted to the US armies. The British and Canadian armies were already at full stretch and their front-line numbers could not be increased. By the end of June the British and Canadians had just six divisions left in England as reinforcements for 21st Army Group and before the battle ended the British would be forced to break up one division in Normandy

– the 59th Division – and several armoured regiments, in order to reinforce the rest. If the Normandy battle developed into a battle of attrition the British contribution was likely to get smaller.

Tilting the balance of power on the Normandy battlefield therefore depended on the US armies. The US armies could be expanded considerably ... on July 5, the millionth Allied soldier landed in Normandy and he came from the United States. Hundreds of thousands more would follow and, given this increasing Allied manpower, what could the Germans do in order to maintain the struggle?

One answer to sheer manpower is better technology and here the Germans had some hopes; the V-1 flying bombs were already falling on London – where they seem to have bothered the staff at SHAEF rather more than the civilian population – and the V-2 rockets would shortly follow. At sea, the introduction of snorkel-equipped U-boats promised to restore the effectiveness of the submarine wolf packs and result in higher shipping losses; these gave the Germans hope but, fundamentally, they fought on and fought well because they were good soldiers ... and because they had no other choice.

At this point it is necessary to recall that appeal made to Hitler by von Rundstedt and Rommel for more flexibility in handling the ground battle ... and consider the effect of the Allied tactical air forces. Allied air power was the key to victory in the Normandy fighting, *if it could be brought to bear*. In the close country of the *bocage,* still in the full leaf of summer, the German units, both armour and infantry, could remain concealed if they remained in fixed positions. It was when they moved that they revealed themselves to the Allied pilots. Then in came the *jabos*, as the Germans called the Allied fighter-bombers, scourging the ground with rockets and cannon-fire. This being so, what was the advantage, never mind the possibility, of the German commanders fighting a battle of manoeuvre across the countryside of Normandy?

Hitler's and his cronies at OKW – Jodl and Keitel – believed that a defensive battle, which reduced the advantage in numbers enjoyed by the Allies, was the best German option; that the defenders need fewer men than the attackers is common to all battle, wherever fought. However, in Normandy the *bocage* and the tumbled countryside of the Odon valley and the *Suisse Normande* offered additional advantages to the defence and if the Germans gave it up voluntarily in order to fight a mobile, offensive battle, *à la* western desert in more open country, as Rommel appeared to prefer, surely it would be an entirely different matter? Indeed, had the depth of the bridgehead permitted such a tactic, one can see an astute Allied commander pulling back from the tank and troop-eating *bocage* country, in the hope of enticing the Germans into the open – though that assumes the Germans would have taken such bait, which seems unlikely.

That option, a strategic withdrawal, *reculer pour mieux sauter*, did not exist in Normandy; close behind the Allied armies lay the sea. What it comes down to is that by July 1944, the best hope of the Allies was to batter their way forward through the *bocage* and the *Suisse Normande* on to the open country beyond Caen or St-Lô and the best German option was to stay in the *bocage* and shatter any attempt to evict them.

The powers-that-be at SHAEF could complain that this was taking too long and they may have had a point but – however long it took – it was the only option and for the Allies not a bad one. Pressure against the German line was building in the West, while German forces were being contained in the East; sooner or later something had to give.

For the Germans, however, this battle was developing into a 'zero sum game'. In the end the Allies were bound to win and by any measure of military judgement the situation of the German armies in Normandy was unsustainable. If they moved, the Allied air forces would shatter them. If they stayed where they were, they would be ground down in a battle of attrition or overwhelmed and surrounded by the eventual breakout. There was no hope whatsoever that they could push the Allies back into the sea. For the moment, however, the Germans were hanging on grimly, their professional tenacity helped by the terrain and the weather, as Montgomery points out. Writing of the US V Corps' attempt to reach St-Lô, he states.[7]

It was moreover apparent that the American operations, designed to secure the general line of the Périers–St-Lô road as a preliminary to the main assault to the south, were going to take time. The terrain gave the German defenders every advantage; there were few very good roads across the extensive marshlands and floods; the *bocage* country was extremely thick; the weather was atrocious and not only restricted mobility and caused great discomfort to the troops, but seriously limited any attempt to give them support from the air; and owing to maintenance difficulties, ammunition remained in short supply.

This situation dictated a pause for the moment, with the certainty of an Allied victory before too long, either through attrition or a breakthrough as this constant Allied pressure on the German line finally proved decisive. There was, of course, the other scenario mentioned above, one much favoured by Adolf Hitler, that while his armies in Normandy kept the Allies in play, his terror weapons, the flying bomb and V-2 rockets would destroy London, his snorkel-equipped submarines would again ravage the Atlantic convoys and this combination would compel an Allied surrender or a negotiated settlement – sheer madness perhaps, when viewed with hindsight – but 1944 was not a year for rational thought in Germany.

Besides, the German flying bomb and rocket offensive which began a week after D-Day, *did* influence the powers-that-be at SHAEF, mainly in providing some of them with yet another reason to whinge about the slowness of the Allied armies under General Montgomery. Putting the Overlord plan aside, these armies, they felt, should by now be surging up the Channel coast and eliminating the V-1 launching sites which had proved largely impervious to Allied bombing. The first of these weapons, the V-1, or flying bomb – 'buzz bombs' to the British, 'doodlebugs' to the US troops in Britain – appeared over southern England on June 13, a day after the Allied bridgehead in France was completed.

Thereafter the tempo of attack speeded up considerably and casualties mounted, greatly alarming the authorities who – for no apparent reason – feared a sudden collapse in civilian morale. The flying bomb was a dangerous, indiscriminate weapon and while Allied fighters and anti-aircraft guns shot down a good number and Allied bombers flying Crossbow or No-ball missions destroyed many of their launching sites on the Channel coast, the only certain way to stop the V-1 offensive was for the Allied armies to advance up the Channel coast from Normandy and overrun the launch-sites. That, however, was going to take time and meanwhile the battle in Normandy continued.

While the flying bombs droned over southern England, the arrival of Von Kluge at OB–West led to some changes in the German command structure, as shown on page 197.

The most significant changes – all at Hitler's behest – were the placing of Panzer Group West directly under Rommel, and its transformation from a headquarters reserve into an operational command, with four Panzer divisions. The other major change was the removal of Fifteenth Army from Rommel's Army

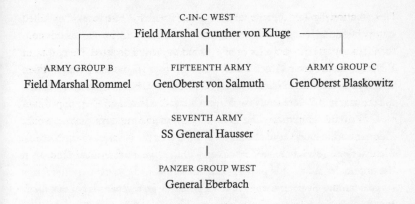

C-IN-C WEST
Field Marshal Gunther von Kluge

ARMY GROUP B   FIFTEENTH ARMY   ARMY GROUP C
Field Marshal Rommel   GenOberst von Salmuth   GenOberst Blaskowitz

SEVENTH ARMY
SS General Hausser

PANZER GROUP WEST
General Eberbach

Group B to the direct command of von Kluge. Geyr von Schweppenburg now vanishes from the scene – for arguing with OKW that the Panzer forces must be allowed to fight in a more flexible manner, that more infantry was needed and that tanks must not be used as pillboxes. Panzer Group West would eventually – from August 5,1944 – be renamed the Fifth Panzer Army.

Von Kluge's first stop in France was at Rommel's HQ at La Roche Guyon on the Seine where he discussed the situation and the Führer's demands with the Army Group B Commander. Their discussion became so acrimonious that their staff officers were ordered to leave the room. Von Kluge was a Hitler man through and through – or so it was widely believed – and after some hours of argument, simmering with rage at Rommel's pessimism and apparent disloyalty to the Führer, von Kluge departed to tour the front-line units.

He returned after two days, somewhat subdued by all he had seen and heard. His professional conclusion – that Rommel's dire assessment of the situation was all-too-correct – was honest and in the circumstances, courageous. From then on Rommel was allowed to fight Army Group B as he saw fit, while von Kluge took up the thankless task of trying to talk some sense into the Führer.

Meanwhile, Fifteenth Army remained north of the Seine. The failure to employ this army against the left flank of the invasion is either an indication that the Germans were confident they could hold their line in Normandy without calling in Fifteenth Army units or a credit to Operation Fortitude or to the stamina of the German forces defending the Allied 'hinge' at Caen. Either way, retaining most of the Fifteenth Army beyond the Seine shows a failure in German tactical planning – the infantry divisions of Fifteenth Army would have been invaluable in the *bocage* and their presence would have released the Panzer units for short, savage, counter-attacks of the kind the Führer wanted. Instead, their Fifteenth Army with 250,000 well-trained troops, equipped with plenty of artillery and a useful number of tanks, sat looking south across the Seine, unable to take part in the Normandy battle until it was too late.

On balance, therefore, and however dim their long-term prospects, the German commanders could be fairly satisfied with the progress of the battle so far. Cherbourg should have been taken within a week or so of the landing; it did not finally fall until D plus 23. Bradley had hoped to send the First Army surging through St-Lô at the end of June but made no real progress in that direction for another three weeks. His advance was hindered by the floods around Carentan which had been augmented by the heavy and persistent summer rain, by the increasing density of the *bocage* and, as always, by the enemy. Poor weather also limited the operations of the tactical air forces and frequently denied the Allied forces that support on which they had come to rely. Meanwhile the German troops had dug in for a prolonged siege of St-Lô, where the next battle in this campaign was due to take place.

A glance at the map on page 26 reveals why St-Lô was the key to success on the western part of the bridgehead. All roads from the US beachheads at Omaha and in the Cotentin led towards St-Lô. South of St-Lô lay the open country that would give the large American armies space to deploy their massive strength and mobility. From St-Lô the Americans could power ahead to the base of the Cotentin, then head west into Brittany and south towards the Loire. Unfortunately for Montgomery and Bradley, the Germans were equally aware of this fact and fought tenaciously to retain St-Lô and the country round about. As at Caen, when the Germans elected to defend a position, the Allies had trouble in taking it.

This was the situation in early July and while it hardly amounts to a stalemate, it was clearly vitally important for the Allies to keep the initiative, always to be attacking somewhere, whatever the territorial gain, if only to prevent the initiative passing to the enemy. Montgomery embodied this belief in his directive to Dempsey and Bradley on June 30, the one quoted briefly above, in which he reiterated that his strategic plan was to develop the breakout situation by pinning and fighting the maximum enemy strength between Caumont and Caen, i.e.

in the British and Canadian sector, 'while the main American thrust swung south and then east to the Le Mans–Alençon area and beyond'. 'Beyond' Alençon was the river Seine.

Dempsey was to maintain the pressure at Caen to keep the Panzer divisions there. First Army was to begin an offensive on the right flank, V Corps heading south but pivoting on its left at Caumont to swing eastwards on a general line Caumont–Vire–Mortain–Fougères (see map on page 26). When the VII Corps had reached the base of the Cotentin at Avranches, VIII Corps – which actually belonged to Patton's Third Army but was currently attached to Bradley's First Army – should head west into Brittany, towards Rennes, St-Malo and Brest. Brittany was important because of its ports – Brest, St-Malo, Lorient – but plans must now be laid, said Montgomery, for the rest of Bradley's command 'to direct a strong right wing in a wide sweep, south of the *bocage* country, to successive objectives, Laval, Mayenne, le Mans, Alençon'.

Here again it would be as well to study the map on page 26 and understand clearly what Montgomery was now proposing. Montgomery was looking ahead and directing the First Army on to a broad front line that would set it up for a sweep right across Normandy to the Seine, with the dreaded *bocage* outflanked, with the British and Canadians poised to come down on the German armies from the north, with Patton and his US Third Army sweeping east along the Loire to the south, on the right flank of First Army. This is the plan that eventually drove the Germans out of Normandy and if indeed it is somewhat different from the one proposed in Britain on April 7, in that the Allied hinge was further east than Caen, what of it? With this as the next phase of the campaign, the Army commanders issued their orders for the forthcoming round of battle.

First into the fray was Dempsey on July 4, committing the 3rd Canadian Division of I Corps in yet another bid for their D-Day objective, the Carpiquet airfield west of Caen. This was never going to be an easy battle. Carpiquet, village and airfield, had been turned into a strongpoint, mined, seamed with wire, dotted with pillboxes, the open ground of the airfield covered with machine-guns and anti-tank positions and ranged to the inch by mortars and artillery. These positions were manned by 26 SS Panzer Grenadier Regiment with some tanks of 12 SS Panzer, all well dug in.

The assault on Carpiquet was to be made from west to east by the 8th Canadian Infantry Brigade attacking from Marcelet and supported by the 16-inch guns of the battleship HMS *Rodney,* an additional infantry battalion, three squadrons of 'Funnies' from the 79th Armoured Brigade, a battalion of machine-guns and no less than twenty-one regiments of artillery and two squadrons of rocket-firing RAF Typhoons.

On the evening of July 3, HMS *Rodney* fired fifteen rounds from her 16-inch guns at Carpiquet, a supposedly stunning blow against the defenders' positions. At 0500hrs next day the field artillery opened up, drenching the airfield with fire for fifteen minutes before the infantry went forward, supported by tanks. This advance over the open airfield was immediately confronted by heavy fire from dug-in tanks and machine-gun posts. Two of the Canadian infantry battalions pressed on and took the village of Carpiquet and some of the airfield hangars but the third infantry battalion lost all its supporting tanks to the 88mms and was forced to withdraw. The fourth battalion then went in through Carpiquet village but ran headlong into a German counter-attack backed by tanks, which first threw them back and then drove the Canadians out of their positions around the airfield hangars. Attack followed by counter-attack was the pattern and this set the tone for the rest of this battle for Carpiquet which raged until the evening of July 5.

R. W. Dunning was there with the 4th Field Regiment, Royal Canadian Artillery:

> As you know, it was early July before Caen was captured. The 4th Field Regiment was deployed in the reverse slope of a hill near Carpiquet airfield. We had been experiencing heavy artillery and mortar fire and during the nights German aircraft had appeared and bombed and strafed our positions. We had acquired a battery pet, a small chicken which had had its feathers blown off by a shell burst. Christened *Hard Tack*, it became very popular – and kept out of the pot. That was the only light relief; otherwise it was shelling and being shelled, all the time.

Another Canadian gunner, Lt Norm Richardson, confirms this last point:

> When I joined the 14th Field Regiment in July, they were at a place nicknamed Hell's Corner, on the northern outskirts of Caen and about 300 yards from a cross-roads which Jerry kept under harassing fire. Some of the shells landed close by so we all dug-in but on the day I arrived a couple of the gun crews had taken advantage of a quiet period and were lying out in the sun when Jerry put

four rounds right beside the guns, killing two sergeants and a gunner and wounding a bombardier and five gunners – by that time the Regiment had lost 16 killed and 26 wounded. I must confess I was nervous. Not so much from physical fear although from time to time there was a good deal of that, but because I was joining a group who were more experienced and I did not want to let them down.

The end result of this fresh attempt on Carpiquet was brief success followed by failure. The Canadians managed to get on to the airfield but were unable to take the German strongpoints around the hangars and were eventually driven back with loss by artillery, mortar and machine-gun fire – and tank attacks. Bad weather prevented the RAF Typhoons assisting until the afternoon of July 4 when they went into action against the seventeen German tanks dug in on the east side of the airfield. Several tanks were knocked out with rocket fire but it is hard to argue with the conclusion of Panzer Group West that, 'the attempt on Carpiquet has failed'. Both sides went back to shelling and mortaring their opponents while I Corps prepared for yet another attack on Caen.

The defenders of Caen had now held up all progress south on the eastern end of the Allied line for a full month. By now it was abundantly clear that any attempt to take the city of Caen by direct assault, or by outflanking thrusts to the east or west, was not going to succeed unless it was delivered with over-whelming force, a force that would involve the virtual destruction of the city. This force was applied four days after the failure at Carpiquet, on the evening of July 9, when 267 aircraft of RAF Bomber Command dropped over 2,500 tons of bombs on the city centre and reduced this fine and historic Norman city to rubble.

As the dust cleared and night fell, I (British) Corps with three infantry divisions, 3rd British on the left, 59th Division in the centre and 3rd Canadian on the right, supported by two brigades of tanks and the now-usual massive gunfire back-up from artillery and warships, prepared to move forward and root out the German defenders of Caen, street by street, house by house, room by room, if need be. Whatever had happened in the nine days since the end of Operation Epsom and the fall of Cherbourg, any 'stalemate' on the Normandy battlefront was over.

9 CHARNWOOD AND JUPITER JULY 7–11

Hitler's personal and, as it proved, fatal interference in the strategy and even the tactics of the battle for France was unchecked.

GENERAL B. L. MONTGOMERY *Normandy to the Baltic*

At the end of June the Second Army was still three divisions short of its planned strength. This was largely due to the effect of the Great Storm and those various other problems and delays already described in previous chapters. Nor had the advance inland gone to plan; the lodgement area still was well short of its hoped-for extent for July 1. According to the pre-D-Day logistical estimates, the Allied front line should by now have taken in Lisieux, Alençon, Rennes and St-Malo. These estimates had been prepared mainly for the benefit of the supply services but the ground actually taken did not amount to twenty per cent of this area. As a result various problems arose.

Two of these were severe congestion within the bridgehead and growing agitation for more ground at SHAEF. On July 7, Eisenhower put this agitation in writing, telling Montgomery that, 'we must use all possible energy to prevent a stalemate'. This comment received a confident reply from Montgomery: 'On one thing you can be sure: there will be no stalemate.' Whether this comment was entirely true depended on the swift conquest of Caen by the British and Canadians and some progress up to and beyond St-Lô by the US V Corps.

Whole books have been written on the 1944 battle for Caen. The fight for this city had begun on D-Day with the 3rd British Division thrust south from Sword beach. That was followed by a series of attempted outflanking moves on both sides of the city and steady pressure along the German defensive line in the north, between Caen and Caumont. All of this had proved useful in writing down the enemy forces and keeping them engaged in the east, but Caen was still in German hands.

The pattern of the Normandy fighting, not just at Caen but right across the Allied bridgehead, had now become apparent. There would be no sudden victories in Normandy, no great advances all along the front, no early and entirely fortuitous German collapse. This was going to be a grinding battle, to wear down the opposition until something gave and the Allied grindstone would be applied yet again to Caen by land, air and from the sea – and with unprecedented force. The city was to be hit with all the power at General Sir Miles Dempsey's command and this power would be employed without ceasing until the defenders of Caen either retreated or lay dead beneath the ruins.

The aim this time was not to outflank the defences as on Perch or Epsom, but to thrust directly into the city centre from the north, down a broad axis west of, but parallel to, the Caen canal. This attack, Operation Charnwood, began with those preliminary moves by the 3rd Canadian Division at Carpiquet described in the previous chapter, moves which, it had been hoped, would take the village and airfield and so free the western approaches to the city. The stout resistance put up by 12 SS Panzer at Carpiquet brought this attempt to a halt on July 5 and obliged the attacking forces to pause for a couple of days before coming on again.

This fresh setback at Carpiquet is hardly surprising. The defences around Caen had been stiffened considerably in the weeks since the invasion, underlining the earlier point that, difficult as it might have been to take the city on D-Day, that task could only get harder in the weeks ahead. East of Carpiquet, the city was now protected by wide minefields, anti-tank ditches and machine-gun nests, all woven into an overlapping belt of fire some two miles wide; the essence of defence is depth and on this part of the front the defenders' positions were deep indeed. All the villages in this belt – La Bijude, Cussy, Couvre-Chef, Franqueville, Gruchy, Galmache and Lebisey – had been turned into tank-proof strongpoints, with 88mms to deal with the advancing British and Canadian tanks, while *nebelwerfers* and machine-guns drenched their supporting infantry with mortar bombs and machine-gun fire as they picked their way through the minefields.

Nor were these defensive positions short of tenacious troops. These came from the 16th Luftwaffe Field Division, backed by tank units of 21 Panzer, plus units of I SS Panzer Corps, 12 SS Panzer, elements of 1 SS Panzer and the 7th Werfer (Mortar) Brigade. Near the Orne, some miles south of the city, were the rest of 1 SS Panzer and a regiment of III Flak Corps with more 88mm guns and 10 SS Panzer of II Panzer Corps, now facing the 43rd (Wessex) Division across the Odon. To back-stop this position, west of the Orne lay more elements of Sepp Dietrich's I SS Panzer Corps deployed between the Orne and the Odon. Some of these units had been involved in the Odon offensive, the fight for Hill 112 and then for Carpique, and had been written-down in the fighting, but they were fully prepared to go on fighting when that last attack at Carpiquet petered out on July 5.

During the brief pause after the Carpiquet battle, the British 59th Division came ashore and went into the line north of Caen; and responsibility for the next phase in this on-going battle was handed to Lt General Crocker's I British Corps – now mustering 115,000 men. I British Corps would attack on July 8 with three infantry divisions 3rd British on the left, or east, 59th British in the centre and 3rd Canadian on the right, or west. This assault infantry would have two armoured brigades, the 27th and 2nd Canadian, in close support and another armoured brigade in Corps reserve, ready to exploit forward if the chance arose.

To overcome fixed defences, minefields and pillboxes, there would be the petard, flail and flame-throwing tanks of the 79th Armoured Division, plus the usual abundance of artillery support from the guns of the 51st Highland and Guards Armoured Divisions, as well as from two Royal Artillery regiments. As this attack went in, the 43rd Division of VIII Corps would launch another attack south of Caen, in an attempt to cross the Orne at St André – a move that must involve another costly attack on Hill 112.

Added to this artillery support were the 16-inch guns of the battleship HMS *Rodney* and the monitor HMS *Roberts,* plus the guns of the two cruisers, HMS *Belfast* and HMS *Emerald.* HMS *Rodney* would deliver a pre-attack bombardment on the key position at Point 64, a low hill just north of Caen, which Dempsey and Crocker – and their German opponents – believed to be the key to the Caen defences. Finally, the Caen assault would be preceded by a devastating attack from 467 Lancaster and Halifax bombers of RAF Bomber Command dropping 2,562 tons of bombs among the defenders' positions on the northern outskirts of the city.

Personal accounts of the Normandy battle, especially from ground troops and tank crews, are full of grateful memories of the support the soldiers received from the air forces, mingled with some ironic accounts of being bombed or strafed by their own aircraft – the Germans having very few aircraft over the bridgehead, other than at night. Both the Allied air forces seem to have attacked their own troops to a greater or lesser degree; one bridgehead story alleges that: 'When the Germans come over, the Allies take cover. When the RAF come over, the Germans take cover. When the Yanks come over, everyone takes cover'. This mild slander on the US Ninth Air Force should not conceal the fact that 'short bombing' or strafing of own forces was an all-too-common occurrence in Normandy by all the Allied air forces, strategic as well as tactical, and steps to mitigate this evil were therefore taken at the highest level and built into the assault plans. This necessary caution had snags as well as benefits

For the bombing of Caen it was considered that since this was the first time the heavy Lancaster and Halifax aircraft of RAF Bomber Command had been used in a tactical role in direct support of ground troops, the bombing should take place at least *6,000 metres* in front of the Allied lines; 6,000 metres is almost four miles and covering that distance, even without opposition and in good going, would take a infantry soldier loaded with equipment and weapons at least two hours. That was assuming everything went to plan – which it rarely did. It was more than probable that the ground the troops advanced over would be cratered by shells and bombs, and certain that any enemy troops surviving the bombing would rake the attacking British and Canadian formations with suppressive fire as they came on.

All this was bad enough but the bombing support plan contained a basic tactical flaw. While it is hoped that a heavy bombardment by bombs or shells will destroy enemy positions and kill soldiers, at least half the benefit comes from the fact that a heavy bombardment will leave the enemy dazed and in no condition to resist while the attacking troops move in; but such benefit depends on the attacking infantry arriving on the enemy position as soon as possible after the bombardment ends. That rule is absolutely basic, but on this occasion it was decided that the bombing would take place on the night of July 7, between 2150hrs and 2230hrs. The ground attack, however, would not go in until 0420hrs the following day, July 8 – not for another six hours. Granted, the bombing would be followed up by constant shelling from the artillery, but when the time taken for the infantry to advance is factored in, the time-lag between the bombing and the infantry actually getting into Caen still comes to around eight hours.

This delay was a serious tactical mistake. However heavy and accurate the artillery bombardment, the Germans were used to artillery fire and their defences were proof against all but direct hits. Heavy bombing was a different proposition, but if the defenders were given all that time to pull themselves together, the attacking troops would reap little benefit from the pounding delivered by the RAF. Even though the shelling continued for most of the night, this objection remains valid; there was little point in RAF Bomber Command delivering such a heavy blow – and then giving the enemy time to get over it.

Charles Bedford of Victoria, British Columbia was then serving with 'B' Company, the 1 Bn The Manchester Regiment:[1]

> We travelled to Normandy in a transport, the *John L Sutter*. There were 12 Canadian generals on board and our CO, Major Woolsey, was given command of all the military personnel – including the generals. He was the Ship Major. At the time of the great RAF raid on Caen, July 8, we had taken over Carpiquet airfield from the Canadians and were slap-bang in the middle of the field with orders to dig everything in – two trucks, a jeep and a Bren-gun carrier – with just our entrenching tools; a bulldozer would have been quite useful. On the northern edge of the field, tanks had been dug in, hull down, facing south towards the enemy, and Major Woolsey told us that we were facing dozens of German tanks who the Brass hoped would attack us so we could knock them out.
>
> This never happened but we were attacked by fighter aircraft which caused much damage and chaos. A few hundred yards to our left, at Maltot, the Germans had bayoneted some Canadian prisoners to death in an orchard and more were killed in the abbey near Caen. Worst memories? The snipers, the dust, the smell ... and burying a company of the Duke of Cornwall's Light Infantry, killed in the Odon bridgehead. That was the worst.

The taking of Caen on July 8–9 has become established as a 'Canadian' battle, although the bulk of the forces were British and all the forces engaged came under the command of General Crocker of I British Corps. The 3rd Canadian Division were to come in on the right flank and on their left flank, astride the road from Caen to Bayeux, lay the 8th Canadian Infantry Brigade. This would move through the village of Carpiquet and on to Caen with the rest of the 3rd Canadian Division advancing on a line from the Caen–Bayeux road, north and east to Vieux-Carioun. From there the 59th (Staffordshire) Division was to sweep south towards Caen through Glamache and St-Contest and La Folie. East of there, north of Lebisey and occupying the line as far as the Caen canal, was the 3rd British Division, which would come into the city via Lebisey and Hérouville, on the west bank of the canal. On July 7, before the attack, the Second Army line lay about three miles outside the city and the last mile of the advance into the city centre would be taken up with street fighting.

Nor would it be possible to sweep quickly through the city once the outer defences had been overrun. Apart from the inevitable damage caused by bombing, with rubble blocking the streets, the Caen canal ends in the city centre, which is occupied by an extensive dock area. Added to that is the river Orne which, after curving into the city from the east and making an S-bend in the city centre, continues out to the north and extends back into the rugged *Suisse Normande* where it is joined by the Odon, coming in from the west.

The Caen canal and the Orne therefore provided any force defending the city with a natural defence line in the city centre and the possibility of withdrawing across the river, if pressed, to carry on the fight in the southern suburbs. This being so, the aim of this attack, Operation Charnwood, on July 8 was not to overrun the entire city but take that part of the town that lies north and west of the Orne and establish bridgeheads over the river to the suburb of Vaucelles. The attackers would advance to this point through the bombed area north of the city, an area shaped like a rectangle, 4,000 yards (metres) wide by 1,500 yards (metres) deep while defences in the outlying villages, north and west of the city, would be reduced by shellfire.

The two British divisions would strike first, from the north. After they were on the move and drawing enemy fire and attention, the 3rd Canadian Division would come in from the west. When all three divisions were inside the city, the Canadians were to finish the capture of Carpiquet airfield and mop-up any remaining enemy resistance in the city itself, while the two British divisions took the bridges over the Orne and the Caen canal – assuming they were still intact – and established those bridgeheads in the Vaucelles suburb.

Charnwood duly began at 2150hrs on July 7 when RAF bombers pounded the northern outskirts of the city. They were followed by light bombers and ground-attack fighters which roamed over the Caen–Falaise plain and attacked any movement detected on the ground at night, notably trains on the railway lines south of the city. An hour later the artillery of I and VIII Corps opened up, supported by naval gunfire, again concentrating on the village strongpoints north of the city. This steady barrage went on all night and increased in intensity from 0420hrs, on July 8 when the infantry and their supporting tanks went forward.

The attack went well although reports soon came in of heavy opposition, especially against the 59th Division in the villages north of the city. This opposition indicates that the defenders had already recovered from the bombing and shelling and were both alert and aggressive; in fact, although they had lost tanks and equipment in the bombing, the SS troops of the Hitler Jugend division had been well dug-in and suffered very few casualties from the bombing; one account claims that 12 SS lost just two Mark IV tanks and fewer than twenty men; 1 SS lost even fewer. The 3rd Canadian Division was now on the move, following up the British attack and the Canadian History[2] reports that 'the 25th SS Panzer Grenadier Regiment was fighting with the bitterness expected of the 12 SS Panzer Division'.

Neal Hamilton was at Caen with the artillery of the 3rd Canadian Division:[3]

Artillery support was essential to knock out these SS positions. We called down artillery fire on the German lines which might only be a matter of yards in front of our position and often the shells would fall short but that was better than not having it or risking being overrun in a counter-attack. We advanced into Caen behind a bulldozer; that was the only way as the streets were blocked with rubble from the bombing. I remember seeing a church complete with steeple, which was the only place I recall standing. The Germans had fled the city by then except for snipers who were active in the ruins and had to be rooted out. There were plenty of dead, men and horses, overturned tanks and vehicles and crowds of people – French townsfolk – coming out to meet us.

Close air support from Second Tactical Air Force arrived at dawn, followed at 0700hrs by light bombers of the US Ninth Air Force, attacking the village strongpoints and any traffic on the roads. July 8 saw some extremely heavy fighting, especially for Point 64 in the 3rd British Division sector which was struck repeatedly by shells from HMS *Rodney* but still managed to produce a heavy volume of defensive fire. The second phase of the advance – to the villages of Épron and St-Contest on the British front and the Canadian attack on Buron, commenced at 0730hrs. On the left, around Lebisey, the attack went well but on the centre and right the British and Canadians had much more trouble, the SS resisting stubbornly and putting in constant counter-attacks with tanks and infantry. The attack in the centre by 59th Division was held up in the villages of Épron and St-Contest and by a suddenly discovered German trench line west of La Bijude. General Crocker therefore decided to reinforce 59th Division, sending tanks on to Point 64 on their right and putting the corps reserve, the 33rd Armoured Brigade, under 59th Division command.

Meanwhile the Canadians and their regular opponents, 12 SS Panzer, were locked in combat in the village of Buron, north-west of St-Contest. This day-long battle followed the familiar pattern – attack followed by counter-attack – but the Canadian soldiers had the measure of these SS troops by now and after a battery of 17-pounder anti-tank guns came up to deal with the Panzers – knocking out thirteen German tanks in the course of the day – the Canadians took Buron and held it against several attempts by the SS to take it back. The SS finally pulled out in the evening but Canadian losses had been high; in the fight for the village of Buron, the Highland Light Infantry of Canada lost 262 men, of whom sixty-two were killed, their highest single-day loss in the entire Normandy campaign.

The village of Gruchy, west of Buron, fell after the Canadian infantry had stormed through the centre in Bren-gun carriers, but German resistance was strong everywhere and the Charnwood attack began to fall behind schedule. Buron was not secured until after dark, the village of Cussy was not taken by the Canadians until 1830hrs, and Ardenne, on the western edge of the bombed zone outside the city, did not fall until the following morning. A similar story can be told about the attack of 59th Division. Progress was steady but slow; although St-Contest fell, other places held out and it was soon apparent that when the SS troops were evicted from one village strongpoint, far from retreating, they simply fell back to reinforce the troops holding another one.

As a result, the opposition to the Second Army attack grew rather than diminished as the day wore on. One clear success was the capture of Point 64 by the 3rd British Division – which thereby reached the point they had hoped to occupy on D-Day – and that night the division sent patrols into the city. Crocker then decided to hold 59th Division where it was, leaning on the northern defences, and leave the clearing of the city to the two flanking divisions, 3rd Canadian and 3rd British.

The Germans too had taken a pounding. That evening Kurt Meyer, now commanding the 12 SS – and a man the Canadians were very anxious to get their hands on – reported to Sepp Dietrich that the 16th Luftwaffe Division had collapsed, that his right flank was dangerously exposed and that the British had penetrated the outskirts of Caen.[4] 1 SS Battalion had been forced out of La Bujude, Épron was about to fall, Gruchy, Franqueville and – at last – Carpiquet airfield were all in Canadian hands and the 1st SS Flak Battery, whose 88mm guns had taken a heavy toll of Canadian tanks, had been overrun and wiped out. General Crocker could be well pleased with the achievements of his corps on July 8.

Heavy fighting continued in the northern suburbs of Caen throughout July 9. There was a particularly heavy battle around Ardenne abbey on the western suburbs of the city where Kurt Meyer had his headquarters. Just as the position looked like falling, Meyer summoned up more support in the shape of a company of Panther tanks and elements of 1 SS Panzer Grenadier Regiment from the 1 SS Panzer Division. A fierce tank and infantry battle went on around the abbey until well after dark but although Mayer hung on to the position until midnight, by dawn he and his remaining troops had withdrawn.

In spite of this opposition and heavy losses in tanks and men, the British and Canadian assault on Caen therefore went well but their advance slowed perceptibly when the troops entered the city. However valid – or debatable – accusations about British 'slowness' might be on other occasions, they were not justified in the shattered streets of Caen. The centre of the city was a ruin, the houses destroyed by bombing and shelling, the narrow streets filled with rubble and blocks of quarried stone – sometimes to the level of the first-floor windows – the wider avenues blocked by fallen trees and toppled lamp-posts.

Progress, even on foot, was inevitably slow and in tanks or armoured cars virtually impossible – the main requirement in Caen on July 9 was for bulldozers. Among these broken buildings and tucked into the rubble, snipers lurked, picking off the officers and tank commanders, stalking the tanks with *panzerfausts*. The Germans might have made a good fight for days in the wreckage of Caen but following Rommel's order to Panzer Group West on the night of July

8–9, General Eberbach had moved all the tanks and heavy guns out of Caen to a line on the west bank of the river Orne around the village of Bretteville-sur-Odon, south of Carpiquet.

It was now apparent to the German commanders, even to the dauntless Kurt Meyer, that Caen was about to fall. This being so, Meyer requested permission to pull his men back across the Orne – a request that Sepp Dietrich reluctantly refused. Dietrich had a problem; in view of Hitler's demands that every metre of ground should be held and Caen must be held at all costs, he could not order a withdrawal. On the other hand, if they stayed where they were they would soon be overrun. It was eventually decided that if Meyer's men were thrown back to the south of the Orne by superior numbers, the Führer could not consider that a retreat.

Mayer's men duly pulled back, having lost 423 men, killed, wounded and missing, in the previous two days, as well as ten Panthers and twenty-two Mark IV tanks. 12 SS still left plenty of infantry and anti-tank guns to hold the streets and take a steady toll of the attackers when they came on again at Vaucelles. Crocker's corps resumed the advance at dawn on July 9 and found the resistance put up by the Germans far less troublesome than the rubble-filled and cratered streets left by the bombing. The advance went ahead, if slowly, and by evening all three divisions were within the city and up to the west side of the Orne. After four weeks Caen had finally fallen ... but the southern suburbs beyond the Orne were still in German hands.

The last two days had been expensive to both sides. In taking Caen I Corps had lost 3,500 men, the 59th British and 3rd Canadian Division losing about 1,000 men each; eighty British or Canadian tanks had also been destroyed. On the other hand, the Germans had not escaped lightly either; the 16th Luftwaffe Division has lost seventy-five per cent of its men, including all the battalion commanders, while the infantry strength of 12 SS Panzer Division had been reduced to a battalion – about 600 men. Very few of these SS troops had surrendered. Only about 600 prisoners entered the I Corps cages; those who were not dead or wounded were as ready as ever to fight another day.

The bombing of Caen on the night of July 7 was accurate and according to the Canadian Official History,[5] extremely impressive: 'Smoke and flame wonderful for morale. Everything on our front seems to be in flame. Cannot get anything more accurate.' As a bonus, no RAF bombs had fallen among the waiting

British and Canadian troops – but whether the bombing did any great harm to the German defenders in their deep dug-outs is debatable.

Again according to the Canadian Official History,[6] 12 SS Panzer said they 'suffered only negligible casualties although numerous bombs fell in the assembly area. Some tanks and armoured personnel carriers were toppled over or buried under debris from bombed houses but after a short while most of them were again ready for action.' On the other hand, interrogation of captured prisoners seems to suggest – according to reports at 21st Army Group – that the bombing was 'decisive' and the morale effect 'considerable'; those who fought the SS over the next few days might doubt that claim. What is not disputed is that the bombing did terrible damage to the old city of Caen.

Although the number of civilian casualties – at around 400 – seems mercifully low, when the Allied troops entered the city the inhabitants came out cheerfully to greet them, but the city was in ruins. The warm reception the inhabitants of Caen gave the Allied troops was welcome, for the country people of Normandy had given sour reception to the Allied troops and seemed far from willing to be liberated; at least the Germans had not killed their cattle or shelled their farmhouses. The peasants blamed the inevitable destruction of the battle on their American, British and Canadian liberators – though due praise must be given to the help and support given to the Allies by the men of the FFI – the French Resistance, the Maquis.

The fall of Caen was a great relief to all the Allied commanders, not least to General Montgomery. The capture of Caen, he stated,[5] 'greatly simplified our problems on the eastern flank, as we had now eliminated the German salient west of the river and were well placed to continue operations by extending our bridgehead to the west of it'.

With Caen now – mostly – in his hands, General Dempsey elected to tidy up his line west of the city by finishing off the attack over the Odon at Hill 112. This was a renewal of the bloody battle at the end of June and this time the task was entrusted to the 43rd Division. With the usual massive support from the air and artillery, their attack – Operation Jupiter – went in at 0500hrs on July 10, the day after Caen fell – there was no let-up in the fighting on the Second Army front.

The task of the 43rd Division was to break out of the Odon bridgehead, which now lay between Verson and Baron, take Hill 112, and advance south-east to the Orne. Major General G. I. Thomas – known as 'Butcher' to his men – decided that his infantry division, with tank support, should take Hill 112 and the village of Maltot just to the east, while the 4th Armoured Brigade and the 46th Highland Brigade, which were attached to 43rd Division for this operation, would exploit forward to the Orne at St André. Artillery support would be provided by the guns of two artillery groups and the two other divisions of VIII Corps, 15th Scottish and 11th Armoured, and the 43rd Division attack opened at 0500hrs on July 10.

The initial advance went well. By 0800hrs the leading troops were on the slopes of Hill 112, advancing over ground still littered with the débris of the previous battle, had got into the village of Étreville and were fighting their way into Maltot. It gradually became clear – as in the previous Odon crossing – that this village and the country around it could not be taken and held while the Germans occupied Hill 112. On Hill 112 the British infantry were at close quarters with the defenders and the 4th Bn Somerset Light Infantry had managed to get up the north slope and halfway across the crest before they were held up by heavy machine-gun and mortar fire.

Douglas Proctor, then a corporal in the 4th Bn The Somerset Light Infantry writes about his experience on Hill 112 on July 10:[8]

> The battalion had failed to clear and capture the forward slope of Hill 112 so while we firm based on our hard-won gains, the 5th Cornwalls (5th Bn The Duke of Cornwall's Light Infantry) attacked through us with the intention of clearing the entire feature. Within a matter of hours, they had been decimated. Their attack reached just over the brow of the hill to a small wood where they were cut to pieces by murderous machine-gun and mortar fire. Enemy tanks occupied the wood and they had a field day, slaughtering the hapless Cornwalls. Eventually survivors trickled back to the safety of our line and were formed into one company to help defend our slope. That night and all the next day we held fast, suffering under intense German mortar fire.

Corporal Proctor's officer in 18 Platoon was a twenty-year-old second lieutenant from the Hampshire Regiment, Sydney Jary, who arrived just after this first engagement:[9]

> The 43rd Division's major battle had been Hill 112. On July 5, three officers and 62 other ranks were required as reinforcements. Between 14 and 18 July, a

further 12 officers – of whom I was one – and 479 men arrived and still the Somerset battalion was below its full strength of 36 officers and nearly 800 NCOs and men. This will give some idea of the appalling level of infantry casualties which had to be accepted to enlarge the slender and vulnerable Normandy beachhead.

Despite not being a Somerset or even from one of the other excellent Light Infantry regiments, I was at once made welcome and therefore decided not to ask for a transfer to the 7th Hampshires in 130 Brigade ... and I was soon sucked into the real infantry battle as commander of 18 Platoon, 'D' Company. In 1944 the war establishment of a British infantry platoon was 36 men. It consisted of three rifle sections, each of ten men including a Bren gunner, each commanded by a corporal or sometimes a lance-sergeant. There was also a small Platoon HQ with a 2-inch mortar detachment, a PIAT (anti-tank weapon) the Platoon Sergeant and the commander's batman/runner. On 31 July, 18 Platoon consisted of 17 all ranks, twelve of them recent replacements; Hill 112 and Briquessard had claimed the rest.

Another account of the fighting for Hill 112 comes from Field Marshal Lord Carver, then commanding the 4th Armoured Brigade:[10]

Thomas's plan was for two brigades of his division to capture the ridge (Hill 112). 4th Armoured Brigade were then to thrust through six miles to the Orne and try to capture a bridge. It looked like Balaclava all over again. The only stipulation I insisted on was that before launching my leading regiment over the crest the square wood on its reverse slope must be firmly in our hands. If it were not, my tanks would be shot up from the rear as they went forward. After further heated argument and objections from the infantry this was agreed.

The infantry attack was launched, with the tanks of the 9 RTR, supporting the final phase of the attack being almost all knocked out by anti-tank fire from this wood, which the infantry had not cleared. Having confirmed this myself, I said I would not order my leading regiment over the crest until the wood had been cleared, as agreed ... Thomas then came on the set and said that his information, from the infantry brigadiers, was that all objectives had been secured and I must start my forward thrust. I said I was on the spot, as his infantry brigadiers were not, and that if he did not believe me he could come and see for himself.

This, not surprisingly, did not please him. He insisted that I should *order* my tanks to advance over the crest. I said that if I did, I expected the leading regiment to take at least 75 per cent casualties. He asked me what regiment I proposed to send. I told him it was The Greys. 'Couldn't you send a less well known regiment?' he replied ... at which I blew up. Finally he accepted my arguments.

Brigadier Carver's view was all too accurate; an officer of the Greys reported that:

The skyline (of Hill 112) was dominated by Churchill tanks brewing-up, not a pretty sight. They had gone too far over the ridge and been knocked out by the enemy who were in extremely good positions. There were dead and wounded men lying all over the ground in the long grass, rifles stuck in the ground marking the positions of their owners, a gruesome sight.

Fortunately, matters went better elsewhere in the 43rd Division area. The 5th Dorsets got into the Château de Fontaine soon after dawn but were held there until the afternoon. The 4th Dorsets, advancing with tank support during the morning, had reached Étreville from which the 22 SS Panzer Grenadiers and the 2 SS Panzer Grenadiers had been forced to withdraw. The 7th Hampshires had taken Maltot but could not hold it when a German counter-attack came in. By mid-morning nine of the tanks supporting the Hampshires had been knocked out and then Tiger tanks came rumbling into the village with plenty of supporting infantry; by early afternoon the Hampshires had been driven out and losses were mounting.

This reverse called for a British counter-attack, which was mounted by the 4th Dorsets and a squadron of the 9 RTR at 1620hrs that afternoon. The battle for Maltot swayed to and fro for the rest of the day, attack following counter-attack; by dawn on July 11, Maltot was back in German hands and the 9th Cameronians – which had relieved the battered 4th Dorsets – held Étreville. Casualties were heavy on both sides; one company of the 3 SS Battalion lost forty-four men on the night of July 10–11; the Glasgow Highlanders lost eighty-five men in the space of two hours in Étreville, and still the fighting continued.

Charles Bedford of the 1st Manchesters took part in this fighting on the Odon:[11]

We took over from the 15th Scottish sometime in early July near Cheux, the forward part of the forward area, and were greeted with a heavy stonking from

German *nebelwerfers* and suffered heavy casualties. The whole battalion was in slit trenches and the visits to the MMG platoons – three Vickers platoons, each with four MMGs – had to be timed to when the enemy was otherwise engaged. The 'Moaning Minnies' were our biggest worry; on one occasion a No. 1 gunner was half-way into his slit when a mortar bomb exploded two yards away and almost cut him in two. The shelling was pretty horrendous and it was far more dangerous in wooded areas when the shells detonated above in the branches and shrapnel cascaded downwards. Airbursts exploded about 6ft from the ground and sprayed shrapnel like an umbrella. Very nasty.

On one attack on Hill 112 the enemy waited until the infantry reached the top and then opened up on them from Évrecy with everything they had and forced them back to their start line; we fired all our Vickers guns in support of this attack which led to the enemy locating 'B' Company and mortaring them; all three platoon commanders were killed.

That night, July 10, the Germans on the southern half of Hill 112 – most of them from 1 SS Panzer – put in attacks which began just after midnight on July 10–11, continued for much of the following day and succeeded in retaking about half of Hill 112; in this battle the 5th DCLI (Duke of Cornwall's Light Infantry) lost 240 men, a casualty rate of forty per cent. This sharp battle around Hill 112 cost the 43rd Infantry Division over 2,000 casualties and very little ground was gained; Étreville had fallen but the Germans held Maltot while Hill 112 was half-British, half-German, both sides of the ridge were now littered with dead and the débris of war.

Brian Clarke, commanding a troop of Churchill tanks, took part in this battle with the 147th Armoured Regiment, part of the 34th Armoured Brigade:[12]

Hill 112 was a mess. If you ever want to see what a battlefield was like this was it. The entire area was covered with burnt-out tanks, dead bodies and all the wreckage of war, usually under a pall of smoke from shell and mortar bursts. The Germans seem to have been at the bottom of the hill, certainly when I was there, but they were always ready to have a go, always aggressive, so you had to be aggressive back or they would have walked right over you.

We moved up towards Évrecy on 15 July, and the attack was to start at Baron. We were now with I Corps and we saw the RAF raid on Caen on July 10, sitting on our tanks. We also inspected a Churchill which had received a direct hit, probably from an 88mm and been blown apart – not an encouraging sight. It was a night move black as pitch, but eventually we met the tanks of our sister regiment, the 153 and we knew we were in the right area. We followed a flail tank into a minefield but it then blew up on a mine so we had to reverse out as the infantry were coming up and the mortar bombs were coming down. The mortaring went on most of the time we were on Hill 112 and caused a lot of casualties.

My Squadron commander then ordered me to take my troop of tanks up 112 and let the Germans know we were there by firing into Esquay, but not into Bon Repos, the next village. By this time both villages were heaps of rubble but we went up 112, myself leading, followed by Sergeant Frampton and Corporal Shipman; in my regiment the officer always led. The side of 112 was pock-marked with shell holes and there was a lot of smoke drifting about but we were able to move up behind three shot-up Sherman tanks and into the 'turret-down' position, just below the crest.

On the way there I had been struck by the most dreadful smell. You got used to smells in Normandy, mostly dead cattle that were lying about, their legs in the air like overturned vaulting horses, but this was quite different. Then, on the left, I saw some slit trenches with British infantry, dead infantry, grossly bloated and leaning out of their slits, and this was the source of that terrible smell.

From our turret-down position we worked out which heap of rubble was Esquay and fired about 15 rounds of HE into it to let the Germans know we were there. From where we were we saw German Panther tanks firing on our 153 Regiment as they moved through an area we called the Gully, by Gavrus. The German tank commanders were standing on the backs of their tanks direct-ing the fire and many of the 153 Regiment tanks were on fire or knocked out; by the end of the day they had lost 29 out of 54 Churchills. We tried to help out by firing HE at the Panthers – it was too far for armour piercing – and we may have shook them up a bit.

The only benefit was that this attack, together with the taking of Caen, obliged the Germans to keep crack forces and tank units on the Second Army front and wear them out fighting for Caen and Hill 112 which General Eberbach had told Sepp Dietrich of I SS Panzer Corps was 'the pivotal point of the entire position ... in no circumstances must it be surrendered.'

This role, fights for position to write down the enemy strength, seems to have become the role of the British in Normandy; their task was to pin the Germans in position and wear them down – often at terrible cost. Corporal Douglas Proctor of the 4th Somersets again:[13]

> Our assault on Hill 112 was a set-piece battalion attack but due to the enemy's overwhelming superiority in men and firepower it was only partially successful. The cost in casualties ... was too awful to comprehend. The battalion as we had known it no longer existed – out of the 36 men in 18 Platoon who so bravely went into battle only 9 remained; a 75 per cent casualty rate.'

The results of Charnwood and Jupiter were mixed. Caen had fallen; well, half of Caen had fallen; the Germans still held on across the Orne, even if their position was fundamentally untenable. The British had also extended their bridgehead across the Odon and taken half of Hill 112 but in both cases these gains had been made in the face of fierce opposition and at terrible cost.

German losses were also high but the writing-down of their forces by the British and Canadians before Caen was not the only problem currently facing von Kluge and his commanders. On July 3, the US First Army, following Monty's directive of June 30, struck out again for St-Lô. Here, as with the British before Caen, they met stiff resistance and were soon entangled yet again in the *bocage*, but they kept going and St-Lô was soon being threatened. On July 7 this growing threat forced von Kluge to move Panzer Lehr west to meet the Americans moving on St-Lô, replacing Panzer Lehr in the British front with the 276th Infantry Division. Panzer Lehr arrived on July 11 and went into action that day alongside 2 SS Panzer (*Das Reich*) which had been opposing the Americans for the last week.

It is frequently alleged that the British made little or no progress in the east and that this lack of territorial gain was a clear sign of hesitation, or failure. The reasons why they made so few territorial gains and why that 'failure' was strategically unimportant have been covered already but will be discussed again, for the argument continued. It might also be asked, in view of this fact – that the bulk of the German armour and the powerful and aggressive SS divisions were on the Second Army front – why American progress in the western sector had been so slow?

To which the short answer is the *bocage,* the weather, and the enemy. However,

Montgomery's overall strategy was sound; the British and Canadians kept the Panzers busy in the east so that the Americans could make progress in the west. This being so news that a crack unit like Panzer Lehr had been sent west was not one Monty would welcome. The Panzer divisions must be kept in the east and if the only way to keep them there was by constantly attacking, then another attack there must be.

This 'continuing operation' referred to above would therefore be the next major phase in the eastern bridgehead, another effort to hold the Panzer units in the British and Canadian sector, but before we look at that attack – Operation Goodwood – it is time to move to the west and see how the American divisions were getting on as they battered their way out of the Cotentin and towards St-Lô in the early days of July.

10 THE FIGHT FOR ST-LÔ JULY 3–18

*St-Lô itself, disfigured and lifeless, became a memorial to those who had
suffered and died in the battle of the hedgerows*

THE US ARMY IN WORLD WAR II: *Breakout and Pursuit*

To cover the American moves in the west in July we must now go back to the
end of June, after the US VII Corps had taken Cherbourg. In early July, while the
British Second Army had been battering at Caen, Bradley's First Army, having
snuffed out the final opposition around Cherbourg on June 29, had been edging
south across the Carentan swamps. With four corps – from the west the VIII,
VII, XIX and V – Bradley was now preparing to take up a line between Caumont and Coutances, a position that would be the start-line for the move up to
the eventual breakout, as defined in Montgomery's directive of June 30. This
breakout would take the US armies south to the Loire and west into Brittany
once Patton's Third Army was deployed in the bridgehead but the road to Brittany and the Loire was barred by the town of St-Lô. Before Bradley could make
his breakout, it was first necessary to take St-Lô .

As elsewhere, the necessary steps towards this end had fallen behind schedule – the notion that only the British and Canadians were failing to keep up to
some alleged 'timetable' is another Normandy myth. The US Official History
claims[1] that 'The Americans had secured Cherbourg on schedule', but this statement is difficult to reconcile with the fact that the supposed timings seem to
vary. In some accounts Cherbourg was supposed to be in Allied hands by D
plus 8. Other accounts say that Cherbourg was due to fall between ten and thirty
days after the landings. Bradley thought that D plus 15, say ten days after the

landings, would be realistic and the city centre finally fell on D plus 21 – June 27 – although local opposition was not finally quelled until two days after that on June 29. Since Monty's plan only required Cherbourg to be taken, 'as soon as possible', it could equally well be argued that there was no 'schedule'.

The plain truth is that *all* the Allied forces in Normandy fell behind their self-imposed deadlines and for the same reasons – the terrain, the weather, the problems of supply and the enemy. This is not to say that the generals in Normandy, American or British, neglected to factor these chronic problems into their plans but subsequent commentators have frequently neglected to take them into account; these factors – particularly the last one, the enemy – have to be kept constantly in mind, not least when evaluating the difference between the proposed plan for any attack and what the attack actually achieved.

Nevertheless, in spite of a general lack of territorial gain, a certain amount of progress was being achieved in the west and by early July, from their current line north of Lessay, the US forces could look back up at a broad expanse of cleared territory in the Cotentin with a certain amount of satisfaction. The next step was to push south to a line between Caumont and Coutances and that attempt began in early July with a thrust towards La-Haye-du-Puits by Major General Troy Middleton's VIII Corps. This corps, which actually belonged to Patton's Third Army, had arrived in the bridgehead on June 15 for initial service with the First Army and Bradley had intended to send it thrusting south, out of the Cotentin on June 22. That plan was delayed by the Great Storm of June 19–21. A shortage of supplies and especially of artillery ammunition, meant that the advance on Cherbourg and this southern advance could not be handled at the same time; the VIII Corps attack was therefore delayed until July 1 – two weeks after the corps arrived in the battle area – and was then further delayed until July 3.

The centre ground in the Cotentin, where it was not occupied by floods or marshland, was held by Collins's VII Corps, on a narrow front astride Carentan. East of the Vire lay V and XIX Corps which had done very little since the middle of June – 'remained inactive' – according to the US Official History[2] not because of any lack of zeal but because all the necessary resources for a sustained advance were rightly devoted to the attack on Cherbourg.

However, by July 3, Bradley was ready to strike at St-Lô and gain the breakout Start Line, using all four US Corps. VIII Corps was to advance down the west coast of the Cotentin, through La-Haye-du-Puits to Coutances, and would move first. Their advance would be followed down the line Carentan–Périers by VII Corps while XIX Corps and V Corps, east of the Vire, would head on a broad front for St-Lô . This advance would take all the US divisions through the *bocage* and out to more open country.

Bob Sales of the 29th Division took part in the advance on St-Lô:[3]

All the fighting from the beach to St-Lô was in the hedgerow country and it was well into July before we got to St-Lô . We had to take these hedgerows one at a time; sometimes you were one side of the hedge, and the Germans were on the other and you could hear them talking. But finally we made it to St-Lô but the losses had been heavy and we were really shot up. Some of the men coming in, the replacements, had not had much training, just the usual basic training and sent right over, and these men were at a great disadvantage in that country.

Harper Coleman of the 4th Infantry also recalls this time:[4]

After we had been in Cherbourg for some days we were sent in trucks to Carentan and into the hedgerow country where we took over the positions of the 83rd Division. It was all hedgerow and swamp and we were often facing SS troops who would fight you for every inch of ground. The first day we made only 400 yards and during the next week only about four miles.

Certain accounts of the Normandy fighting give the impression that the highly defensible *bocage* country – small fields, deep cut lanes, thick hedges – only appeared on the American front. The US History[5] has a map which shows the *bocage* only infringing slightly on the British and Canadian front – significant names like Tracy-Bocage, Beny-Bocage or Villers-Bocage – on the British front not being marked on this American map. In fact, the *bocage,* being man-made, appears in all parts of Normandy, though the introduction of modern farming methods since 1945, methods which require large fields, has done away with the small fields and most of the hedgerows have been uprooted. In 1944, much of Normandy, north of a line between Avranches and Alençon was *bocage* country – hence the idea of breaking out to the south and then wheeling east *below* that *bocage* line. This again is basic military strategy; every commander's battle plan begins with a consideration of the ground.

Given that much of the area through which these US units were to advance was *bocage,* the US divisional commanders had spent a great deal of time in the last weeks, working out small-scale tactics for use in this terrain, based on the use of tank and infantry teams and then training those teams in their use. While the other three corps were pushing south out of the Cotentin, V Corps would maintain the line at Caumont – where the US sector joined the British – until needed for any final push.

The Allies were now faced with two separate German forces in Army Group B. From June 28, the British were opposed by the eight Panzer divisions of Panzer Group West, now under General Eberbach; Panzer Group West mustered some 400 tanks, Mark IV, Panthers and Tigers, and a considerable amount of infantry; this force was fully mechanised. The Seventh Army, opposing the Americans, was 'awaiting the arrival of a single armoured division'[6] and preparing to oppose US First Army with just two corps, II Parachute Corps and the 84th (LXXXIV) Infantry Corps, the latter corps facing the American forces emerging from the Cotentin, the former – a much tougher formation – defending St-Lô. Seventh Army could currently muster around seventy-five tanks. This presented the Americans with a great opportunity for the forces opposing their advance were neither well equipped or numerous. The chief German asset was the terrain – *bocage* and swamp – and the US advance south into this terrain began on July 3 when VIII Corps moved forward down the Cotentin coast.

Troy Middleton's corps contained three divisions, the 79th Infantry on the right, the crack 82nd Airborne in the centre and the 90th Infantry on the left. Their first task was to take La-Haye-du-Puits, a village on higher ground – around 130m (300ft) – and a road junction due west of Carentan. This high ground formed a causeway some seven miles wide, between the marshes of the Marécageuses de Gorges, dominated by the higher ground at Mont Castre, and the Ay river estuary at Lessay. The 82nd was down to half-strength and due to return to England and was therefore given a limited objective and charged with taking the high ground north of La-Haye-du-Puits. The other two divisions were to attack on either side of La-Haye and converge to pinch out the advancing 82nd after the hills had been cleared. Intelligence estimates suggested that the Germans in La-Haye were no longer capable of much resistance and the advance began with a great air of confidence. This soon evaporated; the enemy struck back fiercely, aided by low cloud and heavy rain which curtailed Allied air support for the US divisions.

The advancing Americans soon discovered that the La-Haye-du-Puits position was extremely strong and held in depth – a hard nut to crack. Mines, artillery fire, tenacious infantrymen well supplied with automatic weapons, all played a part in holding up the US advance. Getting on to the high, dry ground north of La-Haye-du-Puits, some three miles from the US front line of July 2, took *five* full days. On July 7, the three attacking divisions were still heavily engaged although the defending force at La-Haye-du-Puits, drawn from the 91st Infantry Division, amounted to no more than 150 men but their tenacious resistance was buttressed by heavy flanking fire from German forces on Mont Castre. This continued resistance prevented the early relief of the 82nd Airborne Division. The division was eventually relieved by the newly arrived 8th Division, after the American paratroopers had rounded off their brilliant performance in Normandy by taking the Poterie ridge, north of La-Haye-du-Puits, and wiping out the defenders.

By the time they pulled out, 82nd Airborne had taken heavy losses; the 325th Glider Infantry Regiment, which had fifty-five officers and 1,245 men on July 2, had only forty-one officers and 956 men left three days later. The capture of La-Haye-du-Puits was then entrusted to the 79th Division, which elected to attack the town with armour and a battalion of infantry, supported by plenty of artillery and tank destroyers. This support proved necessary for the German company defending La-Haye-du-Puits put up a savage resistance throughout July 8 and the town – by then a ruin – did not finally fall until noon on the following day.

The 82nd Airborne – as usual – had done extremely well but the other divisions of Middleton's corps, the 90th and 79th, had been less fortunate. The travails of the 90th Division in the early fighting have already been recorded and matters had hardly improved. This was compounded by the need for the 90th Division to take Mont Castre, a low hill east of La-Haye-du-Puits, which the German soldiers were most anxious to retain. In the process of doing so they gave the 90th Division one hell of a beating.

On the first day of the attack, July 3, the 90th advanced less than a mile and took 600 casualties – a figure which tends to suggest that whatever was wrong with the 90th Infantry Division, it was not a lack of courage. One of the 90th's regiments, the 358th Infantry, was taken in the flank by self-propelled guns and the advancing battalions were then struck by shellfire, machine-gun fire, tanks and infantry, which halted the regiment in the hamlet of Les Sablons just north of the

TOP Men of the US Rangers prepare to go ashore in LCAs (Landing Craft Assault), June 6, 1944. (*IWM EA 25357*)

ABOVE The Mulberry Harbour at Arromanches – as large as the ferry port at Dover. (*IWM MM 2405*)

ABOVE Black American troops of the supply services unload ammunition from DUKWs (ducks) on a beach in Normandy. (*IWM AP 26559*)

RIGHT US General Dwight D. Eisenhower, Supreme Commander of the Allied Expeditionary Force. (*IWM NYP 31355*)

LEFT Lieutenant General J. N. Bradley, General Montgomery and Lieutenant General M. C. Dempsey in Normandy, June 10, 1944. (*IWM B 5323*)

BELOW General Montgomery with his Second Army commanders.

Front row: Major General Keller, 3rd Canadian Division; Lieutenant General G. C. Bucknall, XXX Corps; Lieutenant General Crerar, Canadian First Army; General Bernard Montgomery, 21st Army Group; Lieutenant General M. C. Dempsey, British Second Army; Air Vice Marshal Broadhurst, 83 Group TAF; Lieutenant General Ritchie, XII Corps;

second row: Major General Thomas, 43rd Division; Major General D. A. H. Graham, 50th Division; Lieutenant General R. N. O'Connor, VIII Corps; Major General E. H. Barker, 49th Division; Lieutenant General J. T. Crocker, I Corps; Major General D. C. Bullen-Smith, 51st Division;

back row: Major General G. H. A. McMillan, 15th Division; Major General G. P. B. Roberts, 11th Armoured Division; Major General R. N. Gale, 6th Airborne Division; Major General G. W. E. J. Erskine, 7th Armoured Division. (*IWM B 5917*)

ABOVE Infantry of the 6th Battalion Royal Scots Fusiliers advance into a smoke-screen, June 26, 1944. (*IWM B 5952*)

RIGHT British troops in the Normandy bocage: a rifle section engages the enemy, June 26, 1944. (*IWM B 5959*)

BELOW Led by their pipers, men of the 2nd Battalion Argyle and Sutherland Highlanders march up to the battle area, Normandy, June 1944. (*IWM B 5988*)

ABOVE An ammunition lorry of 11th Armoured Division hit by shellfire, June 26, 1944. (*IWM B 6017*)

LEFT German dead lying alongside the roadway in the Tilly-sur-Seulles area, June 28, 1944. (*IWM B 6153*)

ABOVE Sherman tanks
lined up in position
with their guns ready
at La Bivude, near and
north of Caen, July 10,
1944. (*IWM B 6869*)

RIGHT A wounded
German sniper is
evacuated by British
medical staff, July
1944. (*IWM B 6806*)

ABOVE A German machine-gunner of the 25 Panzer Grenadiers lies dead beside a trench in Malon, July 1944. (*IWM B 6807*)

BELOW Men of the 1st Dorsets firing 3 inch mortars. (*IWM B 6937*)

ABOVE The Royal Artillery in action near Tilly-sur-Seulles, July 11, 1944. (*IWM B 7005*)

RIGHT Major General Gale of 6th Airborne Division is decorated by General Omar Bradley, July 13, 1944. (*IWM B 7045*)

LEFT A Mark IV Panzer knocked out by the Canadians at Carpiquet, July 13, 1944. (*IWM B 7056*)

ABOVE Typhoons can be seen taking off from an RAF airfield in Normandy, with a Bofors 40mm gun and crew in the foreground, July 14, 1944. (*IWM B 7267*)

LEFT Sherman tanks moving up through cornfields to attack the enemy soon after dawn on Sunday, July 16, 1944. (*IWM B 7419*)

ABOVE British infantry seated on tanks as they move off for the Goodwood attack, July 18, 1944. (*IWM B 7516*)

LEFT A young German soldier cheerfully allows himself to be taken prisoner during the Goodwood attack, south of Caen, July 19, 1944. (*IWM B 7674*)

BOTTOM American tanks of First US Army advancing to start the Cobra offensive, July 25, 1944. (*IWM PL 31235*)

LEFT The wreckage of Villers-Bocage on the Second Army front, August 5, 1944. (*IWM B 8635*)

BELOW Allied bombers clear a path for the Canadians south of Caen, August 8, 1944. (*IWM B 8817*)

ABOVE British infantry and armour moving in to the fighting south of Mont Pinçon, August 1944. (*IWM B 8886)*

BELOW Thousands of German prisoners from the Falaise pocket, August 22, 1944. (*IWM B 9624*)

LEFT These Germans did not get away from the Falaise pocket. (*IWM B 9657*)

BELOW German horse transport caught in the Falaise pocket, August 25, 1944. (*IWM B 9668*)

TOP A Churchill tank memorial on Hill 112, Normandy. (*Author*)

RIGHT German 88mm gun, Falaise: this dual-purpose gun, used against tanks and aircraft, was the most feared German artillery piece of the Second World War. (*Author*)

BELOW The US military cemetery at Colleville-St Laurent, by Omaha beach. 9,286 American soldiers are buried here. (*Author*)

ABOVE The large British war cemetery at Bayeux. This contains 4,144 graves – and is just one of eighteen major British CWGC cemeteries in Normandy. (*Author*)

LEFT The remains of the village church, now a Canadian war memorial, at Carpiquet. (*Author*)

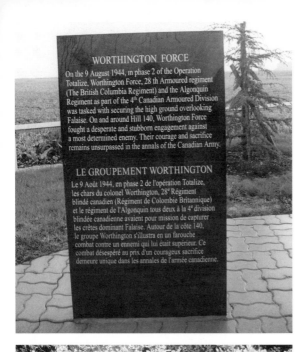

WORTHINGTON FORCE

On the 9 August 1944, in phase 2 of the Operation Totalize, Worthington Force, 28th Armoured regiment (The British Columbia Regiment) and the Algonquin Regiment as part of the 4th Canadian Armoured Division was tasked with securing the high ground overlooking Falaise. On and around Hill 140, Worthington Force fought a desperate and stubborn engagement against a most determined enemy. Their courage and sacrifice remains unsurpassed in the annals of the Canadian Army.

LE GROUPEMENT WORTHINGTON

Le 9 Août 1944, en phase 2 de l'opération Totalize, les chars du colonel Worthington, 28e Régiment blindé canadien (Régiment de Colombie Britannique) et le régiment de l'Algonquin tous deux à la 4e division blindée canadienne avaient pour mission de capturer les crêtes dominant Falaise. Autour de la côte 140, le groupe Worthington s'illustra en un farouche combat contre un ennemi qui lui était supérieur. Ce combat désespéré au prix d'un courageux sacrifice demeure unique dans les annales de l'armée canadienne.

TOP The Canadian memorial to Operation Totalize, on the Caen-Falaise plain. (*Author*)

LEFT Memorial to the US 30th Infantry Division at Mortain, Normandy. (*Author*)

Marécageuses marshes, from which they had to be extricated later that day. The 359th Infantry got going after a ten-minute barrage from their supporting artillery but were halted by German fire from Mont Castre after only a few hundred yards and did not move again. Clearly, the key to the advance of the 90th Division was possession of Mont Castre on their right flank. The fight for that position continued on July 4 with a further loss of men, even more than on the previous day – and still no ground was taken.

On July 5, the 357th Infantry Regiment took up the battle for Mont Castre and managed a useful gain, getting on to the north slopes of the hill. By July 6 the 90th Division had managed to get four battalions on to the hill and take a high point on the ridge line, Hill 122. These positions were counter-attacked by the enemy on July 7 but here the 90th Division soldiers gave no ground. Elsewhere it was the same old story; the Germans came on again with infantry and tanks, smashing into the 357th Infantry at Beaucondray where, after a terrible, close-encounter battle in the flooded fields and swamps, several companies were overrun. The remnants of these companies – just seven men – fell back and the 357th were driven out of the Beaucondray position by daylight on July 8.

The capture of Mont Castre represented the only advance made by the 90th Division during five days of fighting during which the division lost over 2,000 men and displayed, says the US Official History[7] 'fumbling and ineptitude'. This seems a harsh judgement and it is fair to add that the 90th's soldiers had shown great stamina in the fight for Mont Castre. On the right of the VIII Corps line matters were handled rather better.

While the 90th had been fighting for Mont Castre the 79th Division had been forcing its way down the west coast of the Cotentin. The 79th had been 'blooded' in the advance for Cherbourg and in efficiency lay somewhere close to that of the 82nd Airborne Division. To get to their first objective, the Montgardon ridge west of La-Haye-du-Puits, the 79th had to cross six miles of *bocage,* under the eyes of the Germans on the ridge and then make a frontal assault. Their attack began on July 3 and went well though the opposition was considerable and the planned timings were not maintained. One German strongpoint, Hill 121, north of the ridge, fell on the morning of July 4 to the 314th Infantry Regiment and the advance continued, the division making contact with the 82nd Airborne Division that evening.

On the following day, the task got harder. Opposition mounted but the 79th

Division pressed on and by July 7 had taken the Montgardon ridge. Hanging on to the ridge would be a different matter for the German forces at La-Haye had been reinforced with small elements of 2 SS Panzer Division – the notorious *Das Reich* – which had just arrived in the bridgehead from Toulouse.

On the afternoon of July 7, elements of this SS division formed part of a two-battalion force, backed by armour, which struck the 79th Division with great power and drove it back across the ridge. There the Americans rallied and fought back, regaining their position and knocking out four tanks. The fighting on this day alone cost the 79th Division around 1,000 men and in the five days of fighting until July 10 the 79th lost over 2,000 men. By then the troops were exhausted, by the incessant rain as much as by the equally incessant German shelling. Nor had these American losses achieved much for La-Haye-du-Puits was still in German hands.

There is no need to continue this sad tale of the early stages in the advance on St-Lô , for it becomes repetitive. When the 8th Division came in to take part in their advance – during which the division appears to have made little actual progress – the US Official History[8] lists 'hesitation, inertia, disorganisation, inaccurate reporting of map locations, large numbers of stragglers, poor employment of attached units ... the usual symptoms of inexperience', but the account goes on to state that ' the division also demonstrated a particular ineptness in the realms of organisation and control' – an accusation which points the finger directly at the 8th Division commander and his staff.

Clearly, the US VIII Corps was in some difficulty hacking a path towards St-Lô and Major General Middleton reacted by sacking the commander of the 8th Division and several regimental commanders; General Ludrum, the commander of the 90th Division, was also replaced.

This action demonstrates a difference between the American and British methods; the British tended to hang on to failing commanders too long; the US Army tended to sack failing commanders rather too quickly. According to the US Official History,[9] Major General William C. McMahon, the 8th Division commander, had, 'one of the best-trained divisions in the European Theatre' – and yet after just four days in battlefield command, General McMahon was sacked; had he been given the chance to 'play himself in', and get used to the situation, he might have done very well.

In spite of the claims made for the 8th Division's battlefield readiness, the fundamental problem with these US forces – at this time – appears to be one of training. The 'hedgerow country' was dense and claustrophobic, where visibility was rarely more than a few yards. Fighting forward called for first-class infantry skills, especially in fieldcraft and snap-shooting by the infantry, who needed mortars and automatic weapons above the usual scale and plenty of support from tanks and engineers, the latter to clear mines. This close country also caused command difficulties for it was hard for the commanders to get reliable information on what was going on or plot the position of their units on the map.

The hedgerow country prevented the deployment of American muscle and firepower. Until they got out of it the US troops and their commanders were at a considerable disadvantage, one which should not be either underestimated or blamed on any lack of commitment or courage by the front-line American soldier. Nor were the senior officers reluctant to go forward; in these early battles Brigadier General Nelson M. Walker of the 8th Division was killed in the front line when leading an infantry battalion forward for an attack.

Harper Coleman of the 4th Infantry again:[10]

> The artillery barrages on the advance to St-Lô were some of the heaviest of any time that I remember. There were these German rockets we called 'Screaming Meemies' (actually *nebelwerfer* mortars), the 88mm, the German guns, tanks and others; this went on for three weeks and we lost a lot of good people. I saw one of the battalion commanders killed by a sniper and as I was on the machinegun a bullet came across the top of my shoulder and cut my hand, nothing serious but too close.
>
> During one barrage we came across a column of German troops that had been caught by our shells and their bodies were thick in the road. There was no time to move them as the tanks came through and that was not a pretty sight, though I don't think we gave much thought to it at the time. Another time I saw an officer shoot a wounded German who asked him for water, took out his pistol and just shot him in the head; he said 'Water, hell', and just fired. Nothing we could do about it, just keep moving on.

The VIII Corps advance continued but slowly and at some cost. To reach the river Ay near Lessay cost the corps 2,000 casualties. After twelve days of fighting VIII Corps had advanced seven miles beyond La-Haye-du-Puits – which fell on July 8–9 – to the Ay and Sèves rivers at the cost of some 10,000 casualties, the enemy, says the Official History,[11] 'giving ground only grudgingly'. The line achieved by July 14, the Lessay–Périers line, was only about one-third of the way to Coutances and, says the US Official History, 'When the grinding attack through the hedgerows ceased, at least temporarily, on July 14, Coutances, four-teen miles to the south, seemed as unattainable as Berlin.'

Meanwhile, over in the centre, Major General Joseph – 'Lightning Joe'– Collins's VII Corps was breaking out of the Cotentin, heading down the isth-mus between the Taute and Marécageuses marshes on the axis of the road between Carentan and Vire. This meant an advance over flooded or marshy ground and against first-class opposition; the 6th Parachute Regiment, the 7 SS Panzer Grenadier Regiment and artillery and Tiger tanks of the 2 SS (*Das Reich*) a unit that was every bit as formidable – and almost as ruthless – as 12 SS (*Hitler Jugend*).

Having just arrived, 2 SS was up to strength, fresh and full of fight. Although weary and much reduced in numbers, the other German units fought with intel-ligence and tenacity – their use of tank and infantry fighting patrols, one tank and fifteen to thirty infantrymen in each one[12] was particularly significant. They were not about to give way, even before a full corps attack backed by abundant Allied air power – when that air power could be deployed during brief breaks in the relentlessly poor weather.

Collins's VII Corps now contained the 4th, 9th and 83rd Infantry Divisions. Their task was to barrel down the road from Carentan, take the high ground at Saintany, a mile ahead of their current line, and reach the Périers–St-Lô road which ran across their front, seven miles from their existing front line at Carentan. Their initial progress was neither fast or significant in territory. According to the US Official History:[13] 'At the rate of advance made in the preceding week, the final objective was at least a month and a half distant.'

The problem was how to overcome the fatal combination of enemy and terrain. A narrow front through the marshes prevented VII Corps deploying its full strength until it reached the Périers–St-Lô road, so Collins attacked on a two-division front, the 4th on the right of the road, driving towards Périers, the 83rd Division on the left along the Taute river. Major General Barton's 4th Division front was a swamp of soggy ground , criss-crossed with small streams, deep drainage ditches – each a tank trap – and inundated marshes, without a single, hard-surfaced road other than the axis of advance, the

Carentan–Périers road, which the German gunners had ranged to the inch. In such a situation says the Official History,[14] 'General Barton was unable to concentrate the power of his infantry and supporting arms into a sustained effort.'

Even so, slowly and painfully, their close air support hampered by the continual low cloud, the 4th Division crept forward down the road from Carentan until, on July 15, when still four miles short of Périers, the 4th Division was taken out of the line, having sustained over 2,300 casualties in the last ten days for very little territorial gain. These casualties included three battalion commanders and nine rifle company commanders.

On the left of the 4th Division the 83rd Division was having two major problems; enemy tanks – and leadership. The German units to their front were using tanks as mobile forts to support local counter-attacks or back-up defensive positions. It was also apparent that, again to quote the Official History,[15] 'weakened by attrition and fatigue, units failed to press towards their objectives, even after eliminating the tanks that barred the way'. More sackings seemed called for and the regimental commander of the 330th Infantry was relieved of his command on the evening of July 9.

The 83rd Division clearly had a very bad time in early July. By the time it reached the west bank of the Taute on July 14, the division had taken the staggering total of some 5,000 casualties in twelve days – 1,400 on the first day alone – and been further disrupted by these changes in command. The 331st Infantry Regiment had no less than five new commanders in one week and only when Colonel Robert H. York – the *seventh* man to take command – arrived on July 13 did the regiment begin to function properly. The US Official History[16] devotes a full page to the various failings of the 83rd Division in the first days of this offensive but also records that by July 7 the division was beginning to find its feet and General Collins was able to remark that – on the whole – the 83rd Division had done 'pretty well'. Even so, by July 15, German resistance had brought the US advance in the Carentan–Périers isthmus to a halt.

Clearly, the German forces opposing VII and VIII Corps had resisted stubbornly, caused heavy losses and only fallen back when unable to sustain their positions. Against General Corlett's XIX Corps, on the right flank of Joe Collins's VII Corps, their resistance was equally fierce. Corlett had a small corps of two divisions, the 30th Infantry and the veteran 29th Infantry Division, the latter back in the line after a short rest and considerable reinforcement. Bob Sales of 'B' Company, 116th Infantry Regiment, 29th Division, was still with them:[17]

> The fighting in the hedgerow country was fierce, the worst I had seen to this time. One morning a sniper hit several of our men and I managed to pick him up. I knew where he was and I spent two hours working my way behind him in a sunken road. When I got up to him, moving slow, until I was maybe 50ft from him, and then I laid that M1 rifle on him and put a whole clip into him and he fell over and rolled back into that road, dying.
>
> He made that he wanted a cigarette and I gave him one, put it in his mouth but he died in the next couple of minutes. I went through his pockets and found a picture of him, which I still have. He was a young boy, 16 or 17 years old, and had been decorated and was an SS, determined to fight to the death which for him came early. Snipers were bad, they can kill many men in a day with one of those rifles and a good scope. Then there was the 88mm, that was a devastating gun and their tanks were big – all the way to St-Lô it was hard going.

Corlett's corps was soon to be reinforced by the 35th Infantry Division which had just arrived in the bridgehead. Before the advance on St-Lô began, his existing divisions held the line astride the river Vire, which split the corps in two – and placed the left-hand division, the 29th Infantry, some distance in advance of the 30th Division. The XIX Corps' task was to take the Coutances–St-Lô–Bayeux road between the villages of St-Gilles and St André l'Épine and the high ground south-west and north-west of St-Lô .

Since their advance was split by the Vire, it is as well to consider the divisional tasks separately, beginning with the 30th Division. The first problem for the division was to cross the Vire-et-Taute canal. This was not deep and the troops could wade but it was a considerable obstacle to their supporting tanks, as was the marshy ground beyond. The Vire further south was a far more serious problem, sixty feet wide, hidden behind high banks and from nine to fourteen feet deep; on the other hand, the Vire could be crossed in assault boats, which might well be quicker than wading across the canal. Careful preparations were made to tackle both obstacles and the 30th Division attacked at 0300hrs on July 7 and met very little opposition – at least to begin with.

This was sheer luck. The defending unit here should have been 17 Panzer Grenadier Regiment but this had been taken away to oppose the attack of

VII Corps at Périers. The only forces left were from Kampfgruppe Heinz – a *kampfgruppe* is equivalent to a British brigade group or a US combat command – basically an infantry brigade, reinforced with some artillery and armour. This force, small as it was, had the advantage of terrain and knew well how to use it.

The Vire was crossed – in assault boats – before 1000hrs. The bridge at Airel was taken, tanks and tank-destroyers got across, and apart from poor weather which grounded the expected air support, all was going well: by the afternoon six American battalions, from the three regiments, were across the Vire and into a bridgehead at the village of St-Jean-de-Daye. This was deep in the hedgerow country but XIX Corps were doing well and the troops kept pushing on. To help them to carry on doing so Bradley gave Corlett the 3rd Armored Division from Army reserve and Corlett told the 3rd Armored commander to cross the Vire at Airel and get on to the high ground east of St-Lô. If the two corps on the right of First Army had stalled, it appeared that XIX Corps were getting quickly into their stride, having taken fewer than 300 casualties on the first day and pushing ahead with skill and speed. Then the Germans counter-attacked.

This XIX advance, if it continued, would soon outflank the German units holding up the advance of VIII Corps at La-Haye-du-Puits, and in V Corps, the Caumont–St-Lô sector. It was therefore essential for the Germans not merely to contain Corlett's advance but to push XIX Corps back. The Germans north of St-Lô were rapidly reinforced and by July 9 consisted of elements of the 17 SS Panzer Grenadiers, all that could be spared from the Taute river line, a battle-group of tanks and infantry, Kampfgruppe Heinz, and units from the II Parachute Corps and 2 SS Panzer. This was still not enough so on July 9, following the fall of Caen, Rommel sent Panzer Lehr west with orders to mount a major counter-attack against the American line in the bridgehead west of the Vire.

This move by Panzer Lehr would take several days and meanwhile XIX Corps pushed on. There was now, however, a small but growing problem in the American camp, a difference of opinion between the corps commander, General Corlett, and one of his divisional commanders, on exactly what XIX Corps were trying to do.

General Corlett wanted to get the 3rd Armored Division into the lead, back it with the 30th Division and take the high ground east of St-Lô . Unfortunately,

General Corlett was now ill and confined to bed and when he told Major General Leroy Watson, commanding the 3rd Armored Division, to cross the Vire and keep going, he neglected to tell him where to stop. General Bradley had only anticipated a build-up of forces in the bridgehead across the Vire, not an all-out advance on St-Lô by one division of XIX Corps. Order and counter-order inevitably lead to disorder, and taking St-Lô clearly called for a major effort. Chaos therefore took over when Combat Command 'B' of the 3rd Armored and the 30th Infantry Division set out for St-Lô on July 8 – and ran headlong into 2 SS Panzer Division.

On the morning of July 9, units of 2 SS struck the 30th Division near Le Désert, south-west of St-Jean-de-Daye. Although the first German attack was driven off, they soon came back and brought the American advance to a halt, knocking out a number of tanks and causing a certain amount of alarm and despondency in the ranks of the 30th Division. This confusion seems to have continued and was aided by an Allied air strike which strafed some tanks of Combat Command 'B' but luckily did no damage.

The XIX Corps advance went on but was no longer going as planned. Further delays and confusion led to more sackings; Brigadier General Bohn of Combat Command 'B' was sacked for 'extreme caution' on July 9, but Colonel Dorrance Roysdon, who then took over Combat Command 'B', did well – as did the entire command – leading General Hobbs of the 30th Division to regret the sacking of its former commander. Matters were therefore improving when Panzer Lehr arrived on July 11 and drove directly into the XIX Corps flank.

XIX Corps had now been effectively reinforced by the arrival of the battle-hardened 9th Infantry Division, which had fought in North Africa, Sicily and most recently at the taking of Cherbourg and was regarded by General Eisenhower as one of the best combat divisions in the ETO. This division was placed at first in Collins's VII Corps but on July 8 Collins persuaded Bradley that – since he had no room to deploy it – it could be more usefully employed if it was attached to XIX Corps and used to protect the right flank of that corps. Bradley did not want to move the 9th Division to another corps, so he moved the corps boundaries, giving part of the XIX Corps front to Collins who then had space to deploy the 9th Division across the Vire-et-Taute canal and send it south to cut the Périers–St-Lô road.

On taking up position, the 9th Division took under command Combat Command 'A' of the 3rd Armored Division and the 113rd Cavalry Group. Holding this armour in reserve, General Manton S. Eddy, the divisional commander, proposed deploying his three infantry regiments in line abreast and advancing westward from the Vire to the Taute. This advance by the 9th Division across the Vire-et-Taute canal began on the morning of July 9, after the ground ahead had been blasted by US bombers and artillery. The division still ran into immediate opposition and two regiments could only manage to advance through a couple of hedgerows before coming to a halt. The third regiment did better and cleared a section of country between the Taute river and the Taute canal, meeting little opposition or artillery fire.

That night German artillery fire began to fall on the 9th Division's positions and patrols reported movement to their front, the sound of tank engines and of infantry digging in. The divisional staff, in their wisdom, decided that these sounds were those of the enemy retreating and that the artillery fire was part of a bluff. This was also the view held at Bradley's First Army headquarters. The 9th Division and its supporting elements were therefore preparing to move forward again on the morning of July 11 when, just before dawn, General Fritz Bayerlein's crack Panzer Lehr division struck the 9th US Infantry Division with everything they had.

Panzer Lehr had been reinforced for this attack by elements of the 17 SS Panzer Grenadiers, 2 SS Panzer and various other units. Although tired and much reduced in tanks and manpower, these units were as ever still full of fight and gave valuable support to Bayerlein's attack. Bayerlein's plan was to put in a strong thrust towards the high ground overlooking the US positions at the Vire-et-Taute canal and the Taute river, north-east of the village of St-Jean-de-Daye, the panzer-grenadiers riding on tanks. While this was under way, the II Parachute Corps would mount a feint attack north from St-Lô, along the east bank of the Vire.

Panzer Lehr fell on the 30th and 9th Divisions on a wide front between Pont Hubert and Le Désert. This attack forged ahead but appears to have caused little alarm at 9th Division HQ, even though by 0500hrs the Germans appeared to be all around their trucks and tanks and German panzer grenadiers were seen approaching the positions of the divisional artillery some distance *behind* the US front-line positions. Then a US infantry battalion HQ was overrun. Only then did the 9th and 30th Divisional commanders grasp that they were being counter-attacked ... at which point all the telephone lines from the regiments to division went dead. This caused a certain amount of alarm but not enough for the 9th division staff to wake their commander, Major General Eddy, who was still in bed.

When roused, General Eddy found his command in a considerable state of confusion. Communications to the regiments were his first concern and these were quickly restored, enabling information to come in and orders sent out. By then the subordinate commanders were starting to fight back, infantrymen using bazookas against the German tanks or digging in to fight off the advancing panzer grenadiers. The divisional artillery, having beaten off the enemy infantry prowling around their positions, dropped concentrations of fire on the Panzer Lehr tanks around Le Désert. The guts and resilience of the American soldier has never been better illustrated than by the fight of the 9th Division on July 11 ... 'We were caught with our pants down, but we pulled them up and got going', as one account puts it.

There had also been some miscalculation on the German side; Bayerlein did not know about the presence of the 9th Division and found himself faced with two US divisions instead of one. Once the Americans got organised and began to fight back, the odds were against him and by mid-afternoon on July 11, the German advance had been contained. General Eddy was now ready to launch his own counter-attack, having first established a new defence line buttressed with plenty of anti-tank guns. By the end of the day Panzer Lehr had lost around fifty tanks and been brought to a standstill.

Panzer Lehr had found, as the Allied divisions had found previously, that fighting forward in the *bocage* was a very difficult business: defence was much easier and caused fewer control and communication problems. Therefore, on the evening of July 12, Panzer Lehr took up a defensive position and prepared to hold its ground. Although Bradley felt that his troops had given Bayerlein's division a bloody nose, the 9th and 30th Division troops, who had met Panzer Lehr in the hedgerows felt that these Panzer soldiers were 'big husky boys ... and not beaten at all'.[18]

By July 12, having contained this counter-attack, XIX Corps and VII Corps could go forward again. By July 14, Eddy's 9th Division were finally in sight of the Périers–St-Lô highway, just four miles ahead. With the objective in his reach at last, General Eddy lined up his regiments on a line between La Vincentrie and Le Désert and sent them plunging forward for the road. Once again the terrain – and the enemy – intervened.

Ditches, hedgerows, snipers, machine-gun posts, *panzerfausts*, an abundance of mines, artillery, dug-in tanks and a deluge of mortar fire from units of 2 SS Panzer and 17 SS Panzer Grenadiers struck the advancing American infantry. When night fell, and German infiltration began, the 9th Division was still firmly stuck in the hedgerows.

The 30th Division, on the left of the 9th, were doing no better and were by now fought out. Even by July 11, before Panzer Lehr came in, they had lost 1,300 men and the rest were exhausted, their ammunition low, their supporting tanks in need of maintenance. They clearly needed relief but there could be none for the moment and by July 15 the 30th Division's casualty list had soared to 3,500 men and they could go no further. It was not until July 17 that the 9th Division reached the St-Lô–Périers road. Getting there had cost that fine division some 2,500 men – and they were still a quarter of a mile short of the road, though able to cover it with fire.

It had taken almost two weeks and a great quantity of lives to advance some ten miles but at last the First Army were in position to move on St-Lô . Before that happened there were more changes in the corps boundaries as everyone shifted to the east. Collins's VII Corps passed the Carentan–Périers isthmus to VIII Corps, and took charge of the front between the Taute and the Vire. East of the Vire, XIX Corps and V Corps were making that final bid for St-Lô – a city which by some calculations should have been in American hands by D plus 9. It was now D plus 41 and the city had still to be taken.

St-Lô had been attacked from the air on June 6 and the original American intention – or at least their profound hope – was to take the town by June 15. Now, in mid-July, more than a month after the landing, a combination of bombing and shelling had reduced St-Lô to smoking rubble, a shambles which contained the bodies of the 800 or so French citizens killed in these constant attacks. Now the American ground forces were about to make their final bid for the city ... and the Germans were prepared to put up a fight to retain it.

The defenders consisted of the doughty II Parachute Corps, deployed between the Vire and the Drôme, bolstered on the west by three *kampfgruppe* from the 353rd, 266th and 352nd Divisions and on the east by the 3rd Parachute Division with the 12 Assault Gun Brigade in reserve. The attackers in this final phase came from the US XIX Corps which had taken over the prime task from Gerow's V Corps, though in the event both corps were to participate in the final battle. V Corps opened the attack with an assault by the 2nd Infantry Division on Hill 192, just north of the St-Lô–Bayeux road and the key position east of St-Lô – the river Vire sweeps close to the west side of St-Lô so that any attacks on the city were best made from the north or the east.

The 2nd Infantry had tried to take Hill 192 some weeks before; an assault in June had lasted three days and cost them 1,200 casualties for no territorial gain. The soldiers of 2nd Infantry knew they would have to attack the hill again and had spent the intervening weeks shelling the hill continuously and training their squads in close-quarter fighting, the hand-to-hand kind involving grenades, automatic weapons and the bayonet – and close infantry tank co-operation – that would all be necessary when their infantry went forward again. Supported by tanks, the 2nd Division attack went in at 0600hrs on July 11.

Hill 192 had been constantly shelled but the American advance was met with a hail of machine-gun fire and German *panzerfausts* knocked out all six Sherman tanks supporting the 1st battalion of the 38th Infantry Regiment. That training in close-quarter combat paid off and by noon that day the 38th Infantry had gained the top of Hill 192. By late afternoon they had descended the far slope and, joined now by the 23rd Infantry Regiment, were pressing on down towards the Bérigny–St-Lô highway. That night was spent in consolidating the ground gained and repelling small counter-attacks. By dawn it was clear that the enemy had abandoned the ground around 192 and withdrawn to another defence line somewhere beyond the Bérigny–St-Lô road. The 2nd Infantry Division had taken around 500 casualties but gained a good position for a further advance.

The attack was now taken up by General Gerhardt's 29th Infantry Division and the newly arrived 35th Division of XIX Corps. They were already in position four miles north-east of St-Lô and after the 2nd Division advance had secured their flanks on June 11, these divisions were able to move forward towards the next obstacle, the Martinville ridge, two miles north-east of the town. This attack had been delayed by that diversionary attack mounted by II Parachute Corps in support of Panzer Lehr's counter-attack on the 9th and 30th Divisions, but on July 11 the 29th and 35th advanced through the hedgerows over the Martinville ridge position and down the slope towards St-Lô . This advance was stoutly contested and made in the face of heavy artillery and mortar fire which cost the 29th Infantry Division some 500 men.

Although they were still fighting well, the defenders of St-Lô were running out of steam. The Panzer Lehr attack on the 9th Division had been halted, the 3rd Parachute Division had lost around seventy-five per cent of its men and the 353rd Division *kampfgruppe* had been reduced from 1,000 men to less than 200. Even so, the survivors were German soldiers, very resolute in defence, not afraid to die. They fought on, taking a heavy toll of the attackers and on July 12, the 29th Division, still thrusting directly down the Martinville ridge for St-Lô, made very little progress ... and took *another* 500 casualties.

Later that day, General Corlett and General Gerhardt decided that before they took St-Lô they must eliminate the other hill feature, Hill 122, a mile from the northern suburbs of the city. This view was reinforced when a thrust at the city by the 175th Infantry of the 29th Division, supported by tanks, was brought to a grinding halt by German artillery and tank fire directed from the hill. On July 13 the task of taking Hill 122 was delegated to the 35th Division which was given no time to survey the position and found it a hard nut to crack.

Their attack began on July 14, when the 137th Infantry Regiment advanced to the St-Lô–Pont Herbert road and loosened the grip held by the 352nd Division *kampfgruppe,* which had suffered no less then forty American attacks, large and small, in recent days and was running out of men and ammunition. With resistance finally crumbling, the 35th Division formed a task force around the 135th Regiment, put it under the assistant divisional commander, Brigadier General Sebree and, on the night of July 15, sent it against Hill 122. It was a mile uphill to the crest but by midnight the task force were on the top and digging in to await the inevitable counter-attack.

The Germans put in two counter-attacks on July 16 and the second one, backed by artillery fire, almost succeeded in pushing the 35th Division off the hill. Somehow the American infantry hung on, supported by artillery and tanks and encouraged by the sight of St-Lô, which was now less than a mile away ... at which point the focus of the advance switches back to the 29th Division.

When the 29th Division halted on July 14, St-Lô lay about three kilometres – a mile and a half – from their forward positions. The division went forward again on July 15, striking first down the Isigny–St-Lô road and then along the crest of the Martinville ridge. This advance was immediately opposed by the enemy and in spite of support from fighter-bombers of the US Ninth Air Force, their attack here stalled for a while. Fortunately, two battalions of the 116th Infantry Regiment had made good progress on to the Martinville ridge and one of them, commanded by Major Sidney Bingham, pressed on without orders and only stopped when it had got to within a kilometre of the city. This put Bingham's battalion well outside the regimental lines but it stayed firm, the nearest American unit to the city. As it held on, the Germans in St-Lô finally began to pull out.

This was not before time. The American position in front of St-Lô in mid-July did not appear encouraging. By midnight – 2359hrs – on July 15, the 35th Division were only just hanging on to Hill 122 while the 29th Division appeared to have been halted on the Martinville ridge and on the Isigny–St-Lô highway. This situation did not improve on July 16, because both divisions were exhausted. It would have been good to relieve them and get fresh troops forward but that would have meant delay and encouraged further German resistance.

Besides, the 29th Division had fought towards St-Lô all the way from Omaha and the city had always been their target. The Virginians of the Blue and the Grey felt they were entitled to the town which they had been battling towards with the remains of their strength for the last six days. Now, with any luck, one last shove might do it. That shove came at dawn on July 17, when Major Thomas D. Howie of the 3rd Battalion, 116th Infantry, led a column of infantry out to reach Bingham's isolated battalion on the outskirts of St-Lô .

The regimental commander of the 116th Infantry hoped that these two battalions would have enough strength to push on into the town but Bingham's battalion, short of men and ammunition, was too reduced for further effort. That left the task of entering St-Lô to Major Howie, who told his men that he would lead them into the city. Howie duly advanced at the head of his battalion but had hardly gone a hundred metres before he was killed by shellfire. The command of the 3rd Battalion devolved on a company commander, Captain William H. Puntenny, who ordered the advance to continue.

The 3rd Battalion pressed on until halted by mortar fire and the Germans continued to attack these two isolated and much-reduced American infantry battalions for the rest of the day. All attempts by the regiment or division to reach them failed and contact was not re-established until early on the morning of July 18. Early that morning General Gerhardt of the 29th Division contacted General Baade of the 35th Division and told him he was going to try to push into St-Lô that day. 'In that case, so will I,' said Baade.

Meanwhile, SS General Hausser of Seventh Army had been in conversation with Army Group B, requesting permission to withdraw from St-Lô to the high ground south of the city. In spite of Hitler's orders forbidding any withdrawal, Army Group B told Hausser that he could take whatever action he saw fit. Who gave this order is not clear but it was certainly not Field Marshal Rommel. On the previous afternoon, July 17, his staff car had been strafed by a roving Spitfire and the field marshal was now en route to Germany, seriously injured and out of the war. The decision was eventually relayed back to Field Marshal von Kluge but he had no reserves left to offer and on the night of July 17–18, the Germans began to withdraw from St-Lô .

And so, finally, on the afternoon of July 18, 1944, six weeks after D-Day, the Americans finally entered St-Lô. At their head marched the remnants of the 3rd Battalion of the 116th Infantry Regiment, 29th Infantry Division, the first platoon carrying the body of their battalion commander, Major Thomas Howie, whom they laid in the ruins of the church of St-Croix. Thomas Howie had told his men he would lead them into St-Lô, and he did.

11 GOODWOOD JULY 18-21

We were now on the threshold of great events.
We were ready to break out of the bridgehead.

GENERAL B.L. MONTGOMERY *Normandy to the Baltic*

The Goodwood battle took place at the crux of the entire Normandy campaign, caused a great deal of controversy, at the time and since, and requires some careful dissection if the various elements are to be fully understood. The first two points are that Operation Goodwood was linked with Operation Cobra, the US breakout at St-Lô, and was part of the strategic policy Montgomery had been following since shortly after D-Day – the British to hold the eastern flank and pull the German armour on to that front, while the Americans built up their forces and broke out in the west.

Since this strategy has frequently been misunderstood, misinterpreted or overlooked, it has to be pointed out – yet again – that this had always been the plan. Other than arguments about where the eventual 'hinge' for the swing east might be, no one at the time disputed it and in mid-July the bulk of the German armour were indeed facing the British around Caen. By the third week of July, as related in the previous chapter, there were eight German divisions facing the fifteen divisions of the US First Army between St-Lô and the west coast of the Cotentin; Panzer Lehr, 2 SS Panzer and six infantry divisions. Facing the British, on the shorter front from Caumont to Caen, were seven strong Panzer divisions; 1 SS Panzer, 2nd Panzer, 10 SS Panzer, 9 SS Panzer, 12 SS Panzer, 21 Panzer and 116 Panzer, plus five infantry divisions, a total of twelve divisions, over half of them armoured and most of the armour

SS. More than 600 German tanks faced the British and Canadians; fewer than 200 tanks faced the Americans.

This being so, it is rather surprising that it is *still* claimed that Montgomery intended to break out in the east, or is smeared by continuing odium for not breaking out, or for being 'cautious' and 'too slow'. If the strategic plan was to work, the people being 'too slow' in July were the American units in the west who had fewer enemy to contend with. The German armour was in the east, the US forces had completed their build-up in the west where the breakout was to take place – and in the end did take place – so what was the reason for delay?

This is not chauvinism. The US Official History makes the same point. Writing on the advance to St-Lô[1] it sums up the result as follows:

> Heroic exertion seemed, on the surface, to have accomplished little. With twelve divisions, the First Army in seventeen days had advanced only seven miles in the region west of the Vire and little more than half that distance east of the river. Not only was the distance gained disappointing, the newly established Lessay–Caumont line was less than satisfactory. The VIII Corps physically occupied neither Lessay nor Périers; the VII Corps did not actually possess the Périers–St-Lô highway, and the city of St-Lô remained under enemy artillery and mortar fire for more than a week after its capture by XIX Corps.
>
> To reach this position along the Lessay–Caumont line, the First Army had sustained approximately 40,000 casualties during July of which 90 per cent were infantrymen.

The US History goes on to comment:[2] 'The majority of casualties were caused by shell fragments while many men were now suffering from combat fatigue which, though not always reported in the casualty returns, nevertheless totalled an additional 25 to 35 per cent of the men physically wounded.' The US History then compares the state of their forces with that of the enemy:[3] 'The German troops were good. Not invincible, the Wehrmacht units nevertheless had staying power while SS forces and paratroopers were a breed apart; elite troops, with an unshakeable morale, they asked no quarter and gave none.'

Given the allegations of slowness and timidity made against the British and Canadian troops it is again worth pointing out that the bulk of these élite, 'breed apart' SS troops were facing the British Second Army although most of the equally resolute German parachute units were facing the Americans.

By now, halfway through the campaign – and rather more than halfway through this book – Montgomery's strategy in Normandy should be abundantly clear. It was his mistake not to reiterate the details of this strategy at the time and foolish later to argue that it had worked out in every respect, but the actions of the Allied armies since D-Day make his overall purpose obvious – and unlike words, these actions are irrefutable. The British Second Army had mounted a constant series of strong attacks at or around Caen since D-Day and had thereby sucked in the German reserves while the US First Army had captured first Cherbourg and eventually St-Lô. Everything was now ready for the next phase, the breakout.

Cherbourg was coming on stream to provide a port for reinforcements and supplies and the road from St-Lô to Périers and Lessay in the west would provide Bradley with the start line for the Allied breakout – and provided there was an Allied breakout only a chauvinist would complain about who made it. These British and US attacks on the east and west of the Allied line had either been co-ordinated to stretch the German line to its utmost or where the shortages of fuel or artillery ammunition did not permit two offensives at the same time, had either followed each other in rapid succession, or overlapped. In the end this growing pressure caused the German line to snap.

This had been the pattern of events since D-Day. It is hard to imagine that it was accidental or developed by the two army commanders, Bradley and Dempsey, without reference to the Allied Ground Force Commander, General Montgomery. Although some American accounts seem to ignore his existence – other than for the purposes of denigration – Montgomery was the field commander in Normandy and it was *his* plan that Bradley and Dempsey were implementing with considerable success and no particular objections at the time. Now at last, the British had Caen and the Americans had St-Lô. This put the Allied forces in line for the breakout, but before moving on to the next major Allied efforts – Goodwood and Cobra – it is necessary to take a look at some of the other events taking place at this time, notably those affecting the Germans.

The first, on July 17, 1944, was the wounding of Field Marshal Rommel in an Allied air attack. The battle on the Caen front had now reached a position south of the city and the main German defence line lay astride the road to Falaise, on a position known as the Bourguébus ridge, one of several German defence lines spanning the plain between Caen and Falaise. The Bourguébus ridge was occupied by troops of 1 SS Panzer who were preparing to beat back the next Second Army thrust and on the afternoon of July 17, Rommel left his headquarters at La Roche Guyon on the Seine to see how these preparations were coming on. Moving on Norman roads in daylight was extremely hazardous, and an account written at the time, by one of the staff officers who accompanied Rommel, speaks of seeing 'transport in flames' and of the need to 'divert on to lanes and second class roads' – all this giving the field marshal a vivid, first-hand demonstration of Allied air power. Getting across Normandy when the skies were full of Allied fighters required luck and at the village of Ste-Foy-de-Montgommerie, south of Liverot, Erwin Rommel's always-uncertain luck finally ran out.

The aircraft spotter sitting on the back of Rommel's staff car reported that two RAF Spitfires were flying along the road in their direction and the driver was ordered to increase speed and turn off on to a side road. Before they could reach it, one of the Spitfires, coming in at low level some twenty feet above the road, sighted the oncoming staff car and opened fire. Both the driver and Rommel were hit, the car overturned and the field marshal was thrown out. He lay in the road for some while until help could be found and was then carried into Ste-Foy.

The attacking Spitfire was flown by a South African, Squadron Leader J. J. Le Roux – who had twenty-two confirmed enemy aircraft to his credit. Sqn Ldr Le Roux was lost over the English Channel in September and never knew whom he had strafed near Caen that summer morning. Rommel's wounds were dressed by a pharmacist from Liverot and he was then taken to a Luftwaffe hospital at Bernay before being sent back to Germany and hospitalised. He was out of the picture when, three days later, on July 20, 1944, an attempt was made on the life of the German Führer, Adolf Hitler.

Plots against the Führer were not new. Attempts had been made to put a bomb on his private aircraft or plant one at his headquarters, but all such attempts had either failed or been detected in the early stages by Himmler's security service, the SD. Those suspected of plotting against Hitler suffered a grisly fate in the cellars of the Gestapo headquarters in Berlin but as the war situation deteriorated, certain officers, many of them members of the High Command, finally decided that Hitler must go. The man selected to carry out this new attempt –

Operation Walkyrie – was a German aristocrat and staff officer, Colonel Count von Stauffenberg, an officer on the staff of the Commander-in-Chief of the Home Army, General Fritz Fromm.

The assassination plan was elaborate and need not concern us, except that many of the figures who appear in these pages, including Rommel and von Kluge, were either involved in the plot itself or in preparing to move against the Nazis after Hitler was dead. The plot proceeded undetected and around midday on July 20, von Stauffenberg was able to place his briefcase containing a bomb under the table in Hitler's conference room at Rastenburg. At 1230hrs, the Führer and many of his staff, including Jodl and Keitel, entered the room and with a score of other staff officers gathered round the table to study the map. At that point von Stauffenberg primed the bomb and left the room, claiming he needed to make a phone call. He was about fifty metres from the building when the bomb went off.

The effect on the wooden building, which virtually disintegrated, led von Stauffenberg to believe that Hitler and his cronies must have been killed. He immediately flew to Berlin while all over the Reich the other plotters proceeded to put the rest of the plan into execution, arresting SS officers and taking over command centres inside Germany and France. One of the people affected was Field Marshal von Kluge. He had known of the plot and on hearing that it had succeeded, suggested an immediate halt to the V-1 offensive and contact with the Allied commanders to discuss a cease-fire. However, within a few hours, before any of this could happen, doubts arose, doubts confirmed by a phone call to von Kluge from Rastenburg. 'Nothing more can be done', von Kluge told a fellow plotter, General Blümentritt, as he put down the telephone, 'the Führer is alive'.

Hitler was not even seriously injured. The heavy oak conference table had absorbed most of the blast, the wooden building had allowed the effect of the explosion to disperse and although several officers were killed and a large number injured, the Führer was still unharmed and crying treachery. Over the next weeks and months he took a terrible revenge on his opponents. Senior officers were arrested, interrogated by the Gestapo, given a brief and humiliating trial and strangled to death, hanging from hooks in nooses of piano wire; over 5,000 Germans were executed in the next few months, many of them after torture. Rommel, who knew of the plot but took no direct part in it, was left alone for a while, but in October 1944 he too was murdered, as his son Manfred Rommel later described:

> My father died on October 14, 1944, in Herrlingen, near Ulm. We lived in a house we had rented from the town of Ulm and my father had himself brought there after being seriously wounded in Normandy in July. At the time I was 15 years old and serving as a Luftwaffe auxiliary in a Home Defence battery at Ulm. On the morning of October 14, I went home for a spot of leave and on arrival was told by my father that two generals from Army Personnel had said they would be calling at lunchtime in order to discuss his next posting.
>
> He thought he would be arrested that day as the Gestapo had been keeping a 24-hour watch on the house for weeks. At about midday the two generals arrived and asked to speak alone with my father so my mother and I withdrew to the first floor. After a time my father came upstairs and went first to my mother's room and then came into mine.
>
> He said both generals had, in Hitler's name, accused him of treason. They had brought poison with them as Hitler was inviting him to kill himself. If he accepted this invitation his family would not be subjected to the usual measures taken against a family for crimes committed by one of its members. He said he had decided to take this way out as it was the most reasonable solution. He had no chance of receiving a trial. Hitler would not have him sentenced in public as Hitler was afraid of the high esteem in which people held my dad.
>
> We would receive a telephone call in twenty minutes telling us he had died of a stroke. They wanted to give him a state funeral, either in Berlin or Ulm. He then gave me a few personal things and his keys – he was very calm. Then, together with his aide-de-camp, Herr Aldinger and me, he left the house where both generals were expecting him and we accompanied him through the garden to the road, where the car was waiting. Twenty minutes after the car left we had the phone call telling us that my father had had a stroke and on being taken to the hospital in Ulm was found dead on arrival.

The effect of the Hitler plot on the morale of the German soldiers in Normandy is hard to estimate. Whatever the worries or fears of the senior commanders as the search for conspirators came ever closer – and a film showing the trial and execution of some senior plotters was shown to troops all over Europe – the plot seems to have had little effect on the lower ranks or on their willingness to go on fighting. They had enough to do containing the Allied armies, for on the day the bomb went off at Rastenburg they were into the third day of a yet another British attack on the Caen front, Operation Goodwood.

To trace the origins of Goodwood we have to go back to that meeting between Montgomery, Bradley and Dempsey on June 30, after the fall of Cherbourg. At that conference it was agreed that 'the immediate task of the British Army was to hold the main enemy forces between Caen and Villers-Bocage ... and develop operations for the capture of Caen – and the sooner the better'.[4] US First Army were to begin an offensive on the right flank on July 3 – the drive on St-Lô – and then, as already described pivoting on its left at Caumont eastwards to a general line Caumont–Vire–Mortain–Fougères. When this move was complete the right-hand corps (VIII) should be turned westward into Brittany and directed on Rennes and St-Malo. Plans must now be prepared for the rest of General Bradley's command to 'direct a strong right wing on a wide sweep south of the *bocage* country to successive objects as follows: a. Laval–Mayenne, b. Le Mans–Alençon.'[5]

The US Official History does not dispute this account but also claims,[6] that 'By July 11 General Bradley had conceived the idea; two days later the idea became the First Armies plan. It was called Cobra.' Bradley may indeed have developed the plan for Cobra; as the commanding general of the forces employed that was his duty, but it was certainly not Bradley who conceived the idea. This is a small point but it should not be allowed to go unremarked for it conceals a larger one; the connection between Cobra and Goodwood – and the aims of the latter offensive.

Goodwood began on July 18, immediately after the First Army had advanced into St-Lô. The aims of Goodwood were similar to those of previous Second Army attacks – to tidy up the battlefield and finish any left-over business from the previous offensive; to keep the enemy armour occupied and 'write it down'; and, if possible, to gain some ground. It should be noticed that the need to gain ground was the last objective. In his Operational Order for Goodwood, issued on July 15, Montgomery is very specific on this point:

> 1. Object of this operation; to engage the German armour in battle and write it down to such an extent that it is of no further value to the Germans as a basis of the battle. To gain a bridgehead over the Orne through Caen and thus to

improve our positions on the western flank. Generally to destroy German equipment and personnel, as a preliminary to a possible wide exploitation of success.

Regarding the operations of the various units involved, Monty states that XII Corps and the Canadian Corps were (Point 4) 'to make the Germans think we are going to break out across the Orne between Caen and Amaye.' Then (Point 5), 'The VIII Corps – the three armoured divisions, were to fight and destroy the enemy on the Bourguébus–Vimont–Bretteville area although, armoured cars should push far to the south *towards Falaise* (author's italics) and cause alarm and despondency'. While this is going on (Point 6) 'the Canadian II Corps must capture the Vaucelles suburb in Caen and get a very firm bridgehead over the Orne.' Only when this has been done (Point 7) can VIII Corps 'crack about' as the situation demands. 'But not before 6 is done.' The orders stress that the capture of Vaucelles and that bridgehead over the Orne were vital – pressing on to Falaise was; if it had been it would have required a lot more than a thrust by armoured cars.

All this is laid out in the British Official History[7] and there is nothing in any of this even hinting at the overrunning and holding of the Caen–Falaise plain – *or a breakout*. Indeed, the word 'Falaise' appears just once, in Point 5 of the order when Monty suggests that, if all goes well and the other objectives have been achieved, then armoured cars could push towards Falaise and 'spread alarm and despondency' – in other words to exploit any success. In view of the outcry at SHAEF where – in spite of all the evidence – the impression seems to have arisen that Monty was planning a breakout in the east, this fact should be noted, and remembered.

The US Official History,[8] compounds this error when it states 'As a hush fell over the American front after the capture of St-Lô, intense activity began in the British sector. The Second Army launched a strong attack, (Goodwood) that promised the Allies an excellent chance of achieving a breakthrough. Had it succeeded Cobra would probably have been unnecessary.'

Apart from confirming that Goodwood–Cobra were linked, this statement hardly stands close inspection and flies in the face of every move in the strategy the Allied armies had followed in Normandy so far.

Goodwood had three purposes; firstly, to follow-up the Charnwood attack of the previous week and take the suburb of Vaucelles, south of the Orne. Secondly, alarmed by the transfer of Panzer Lehr to the west, Second Army must at least threaten a breakthrough south of Caen, which would hold the other Panzer divisions in place and, perhaps, force the recall of Panzer Lehr. Thirdly, to write down the German armoured forces south of Caen, as a *preliminary* to exploitation – the later advance on Falaise. All of this would help the American breakout at St-Lô .

As further evidence on this point there is the matter of timing. Goodwood began on July 18; Cobra was supposed to begin on July 20. The reason the two attacks were not scheduled for the same day was the availability of air power; both attacks were to be supported by a massive bombing programme and this could not be managed at two places at the same time. This proximity indicates that Montgomery, who had suggested the objectives for Cobra on June 30, intended the Goodwood–Cobra operations as part of a two-part plan which the US Official History accurately describes as follows:

> By launching Goodwood, the British would throw a left hook at the Germans; by following quickly with Cobra, the Americans would throw a right cross. Whether the primary intention of Goodwood was to aid Cobra by forcing the Germans to engage their mobile reserves and the secondary intention was to achieve a breakthrough, or whether the reverse was true ... later became a matter of doubt and controversy.[9]

Indeed it did, and in view of the evidence given above one can only wonder why. Montgomery's intentions for Goodwood are perfectly clear and it is hard to imagine that Martin Blumenson, the author of this volume in US Official History, published in 1961, had no access to the papers available for the British Official History, then in preparation and published in 1962. As we shall see, Montgomery himself managed to muddy the waters over the *results* of Goodwood, but his *aims* did not change.

The problem with that 'left hook followed by right cross' tactic was that the US First Army could not start Cobra until 7 days *after* Goodwood, because they still did not possess the necessary start line along the St-Lô–Périers road. This American delay was also due to the weather, which remained poor, to a need to regroup, and to bring in replacements to cover losses caused in taking St-Lô. With the preliminary moves completed and three British armoured divisions shifted to the Orne bridgehead, Goodwood could not be delayed, not least because of that on-going fear that the Germans might shift more armoured divisions on to the American front and disrupt the hoped-for breakout. Although the US forces could not manage the necessary follow-up with Cobra, the Goodwood attack went ahead anyway.

US First Army had lost a lot of good men getting to St-Lô and it would be at least a week before it could attack again. That space must be filled by Second Army for one task remained constant, to weaken the German forces in Normandy in preparation for the breakout. A breakout *somewhere* was now becoming essential if only to keep SHAEF, the politicians and the press happy ... and because the German Fifteenth Army across the Seine would not stay on the sidelines much longer once the Germans discovered that Patton, now supposedly commanding an invasion group poised in Kent opposite the Pas de Calais, was actually commanding the Third Army in Normandy. As Montgomery points out, when writing of the situation on July 18:[10]

> The sooner we got going on the western front the better, while the setting for the breakout remained favourable. Apart from the local conditions in Normandy, it seemed impossible that the enemy should much longer continue to anticipate an invasion in the Pas de Calais ... he must surely soon give overriding priority to the Normandy battlefields and when he took that decision substantial reinforcements would become available from Fifteenth Army.

At this time neither army, not the British Second nor the US First, were making much speed over the ground and the Americans who were ultimately responsible for the breakout, were trying to get into position to launch one. Like their British and Canadians comrades in the east, the Americans were constantly attacking and taking extremely heavy casualties in the process. The losses among company officers in recent weeks before St-Lô had been extremely high; the US Official History[11] quotes one regiment that in mid-July, after a month in the line, had only four lieutenants left, all of them now commanding rifle companies; this shortage of infantry officers contributed to the rising losses among the men.

Bradley comments on this:[12]

> Prior to the invasion we had estimated that the infantry would incur 70 per cent of the losses of our combat forces. By August we had boosted that figure to 83 per cent, on the basis of our experience in the Normandy hedgerows. In the 15 days of fighting for St-Lô , the 30th Division sustained 3,934 battle casualties. At first glance this might seem to imply 25 per cent losses for the division. That

figure is deceptive. Because three out of four of those casualties occurred in the rifle platoons, the rate of loss in those platoons exceeded 90 per cent.

These are appalling figures and need some explanation. One part of the explanation is surely that the men in these rifle platoons were not adequately trained for this kind of fighting, a point which Bob Sales of the 29th Infantry Division, one of the units caught up in the advance on St-Lô, would confirm:[13]

> We were committed back to the front line in the hedgerow country and the fighting there was fierce and we continued to lose men. We'd get a few replacements and they would come in overnight and we'd jump off on an attack next morning and they would get killed or wounded, and nobody knew who they were in many cases.

With casualties at this level there was no option but to feed in replacements as they arrived, but this compounded the problem. These replacements were lonely, scared, without friends in the unit – not because of any personal animosity but because they were new and had not 'been there' on D-Day or during the previous action. With no one looking out for them, these replacements were very vulnerable. When the number of raw troops in the rifle companies amounted to between eighty-three to ninety per cent the casualty rates were bound to be high.

Casualties were also extremely high in the British and Canadian units. Sydney Jary, who won the MC in Normandy as a nineteen-year-old subaltern in a rifle company recalls that casualties in his battalion reached Great War levels. Even so the regimental system in the British Army did keep losses below the US level and replacements found it easier to fit in with the old soldiers – 'veterans' – those who had been in Normandy for a couple of weeks.

Most of the casualties came from shell and mortar fire, mines and in close-quarter fighting in the hedgerows, though the weather that July – plenty of rain and low cloud – greatly reduced the support the infantry and tank commanders should have been getting from the tactical air forces. Nothing could be done about this; all the generals could do was keep on attacking, do their best, and hope for better times.

So the campaign continued with two big, co-ordinated offensives in train, one in the east, one in the west, both planned to achieve that long-required and now-urgent breakout in the west. In accordance with the strategic plan, Goodwood would go in first and be followed by Cobra a day later. Monty makes this quite clear in a letter he wrote to Eisenhower on July 13, after another conference with Bradley and Dempsey on July 10:

> Second Army will begin at dawn on the 16 Jul and work up to the big operation on July 18 when VIII Corps with three armoured divisions will be launched to the country east of the Orne. Note changes of dates from 17 to 18 July. First Army to launch a heavy attack with six divisions about five miles west of St-Lô on July 19. The whole weight of air power will be required for Second Army on Jul 18 and First Army on Jul 19. Have seen Coningham and explained what is wanted.

It seems perfectly clear from this that Monty was planning a two-fisted attack and that Goodwood was designed to help the American attack at St-Lô on the following day. For some reason Eisenhower appears to have taken this the other way round, assuring Monty that the US troops would, 'fight like the very devil, 24 hours a day, to provide the opportunity your armoured corps will need', though exactly how they would do this is not stated and is not immediately apparent because the American attack would come *after* the British one. The aim of the American attack was to break out at St-Lô; the aim of the British attack was to keep the Panzers on the Caen front and/or write them down while the Americans were doing this or – following the American delay – to help them do so, by engaging the enemy at Caen. Once again – one wearies of repeating this – that had *always* been the aim.

The problem is that Monty also made statements or comments that led Eisenhower to believe that he was planning a major offensive in the east. In early July Monty had rejected the stalemate complaint by stating that he intended to 'set things alight on my eastern flank'. On July 14, Monty told Brooke that 'the time has come to have a real showdown on the Eastern flank'. On the same day he wrote a letter to Tedder, stating that 'if successful, the *plan* promised to be decisive and it is therefore necessary that the airforces bring their full weight to bear'. The 'plan' in question was (see above) for an attack on *both* flanks, not just south of Caen. The 'if successful' is interesting but Tedder chose to ignore both points when the chance to attack Montgomery arose again.

There is a natural tendency for people – even generals – to hear what they want to hear and believe what they want to believe and Eisenhower was no exception to this rule. He had long wanted an all-out attack, all along the front, and in spite of the Field Commander's orders – which he knew – and in spite of the importance of the overall strategy – which he also knew but apparently did not understand – Eisenhower came to believe that an all-out attack *and a break-through* on the eastern side was what Montgomery intended. Had he read Montgomery's orders with the attention they deserved, or asked Brooke for clarification, he might have been better informed for Brooke had no doubts about Montgomery's intentions – and approved of them.

Perhaps anticipating some misunderstandings, or wary of further criticism at SHAEF, after delivering his plan of attack in writing, Montgomery took the somewhat unusual step of sending his Military Assistant, Lt Colonel Kit Dawnay, over to London to explain the plan verbally to the CIGS, Alan Brooke and answer any questions. In Dawnay's words:[14]

> The real object is to muck up and write-off enemy troops. On the eastern flank he is aiming to do the greatest damage to enemy armour. Caen–Falaise is the only place this can be done. If the proposed plan can be completed, the next British move will be westward, in order to ring round Évrecy, (*Hill 122 again* – author's italics) ... having broken out in the country south-east of Caen, he (Monty) has no intention of rushing madly eastwards and getting Second Army so extended that that flank might cease to be secure. *All the activities on the eastern flank are designed to help the (American) forces in the west, while ensuring that a firm bastion is kept on the east* (author's italics). At the same time, all is ready to take advantage of any situation which gives reason to think that the enemy is disintegrating.

This seems clear, logical and sensible. The presence of Fifteenth Army across the Seine to the east is all too often forgotten in accounts of the Normandy fighting. If Fifteenth Army came in from across the Seine – and it might do so at any time – then it would be the British Second Army's task either to stave it off if directly attacked or advance to block it if it came in further south and headed for the Americans. American accounts stress how the US commanders were willing to take risks. Perhaps this is so; with the British taking on the bulk of the enemy forces and guarding their backs, they could afford to take risks; their British and Canadian colleagues guarding the eastern flank were not so fortunate.

Since D-Day, one prime task of Second Army was to shore up the eastern end of the front against any thrust from north of the Seine. If Fifteenth Army came in the British would have Fifteenth Army on their left flank, Panzer Group

West before them and Seventh Army on their right flank – and if the American breakout succeeded and the German front in the west collapsed, then the Fifteenth Army had to come in – surely even Hitler would see that it must. With all this to consider, 'rushing madly eastwards' and taking risks on that flank was not an option.

Goodwood was the first part of a two-part plan – Goodwood *and* Cobra – but it had to appear to be an all-out attack – and if it succeeded or went further than planned, all well and good; as Dawney pointed out, the commanders must be ready '*to take advantage of any situation which gives reason to think that the enemy might be disintegrating*'. What is the problem with that?

Goodwood certainly employed a considerable force but the attacks around Caen had shown that considerable force was necessary. For Goodwood Montgomery employed three armoured divisions, Guards Armoured, 7th Armoured and 11th Armoured, all under VIII Corps command. This force could muster some 750 tanks, Cromwells, Churchills and Shermans, with some specialised armour from the 79th Armoured Division. When the other elements were added in, Goodwood employed about half of Second Army and the movement of this large armoured force into the Orne bridgehead eliminated any possibility of surprise.

The armoured divisions were to advance south out of the Orne bridgehead, but were not to go very far. Their orders stated that they were not to advance beyond Vimont, Garcelles-Séqueville, Hubert-Folie and Vérriers – about four miles south of Caen at the most – without the express permission of General Dempsey. Dempsey wanted to be sure that the main aim – to take the Vaucelles suburbs – had been achieved and that the Canadians were firmly established south of the Orne *before* the VIII Corps armour made any further moves. This point again refutes the notion that Montgomery was aiming at a breakout.

The US Official History[15] states that 'although neither Montgomery or Dempsey mentioned Falaise specifically in their orders, they and other commanders were thinking of Falaise, and even of Argentan, as objectives perhaps quickly attainable if the battle developed favourably'.

Three points can be made about this comment. Firstly, given that none of the British commanders were mind readers, they would still need specific orders if they were to plan and mount attacks aimed at Falaise, (twenty-one miles south of Caen) or Argentan, (thirty-six miles south of Caen). Secondly, objectives twenty-one and thirty-five miles from the offensive's start line were not 'quickly attainable' at any time in the Normandy battle.

Thirdly – see Dawnay's report to Brooke given above – Monty was indeed prepared to exploit any gain achieved in this offensive. Being ready and willing to exploit success is standard military procedure and is only to be expected of any competent commander. Even so, given the distances involved and two months' bitter experience in the problems of gaining ground, it is inconceivable that Montgomery seriously intended to do more with this offensive than what he said he intended to do – and if possible exploit any result. A great many misconceptions on this point would never have arisen if historians had taken the trouble to read Monty's orders fully – and look at the map.

The infantry divisions – from the east, 51st Highland, 3rd British, 3rd Canadian and 2nd Canadian – which last, with the 1st Canadian Division, now formed the II Canadian Corps under an excellent Canadian commander, Lt General Guy Simonds – supported by 350 tanks, would follow up the armour, widen the breach created, and mop-up. Meanwhile, I British Corps was to establish the 3rd Infantry Division on the east flank between Bures and Troan to Touffreville and hold that line against any attack from the east or south-east. There would seem to be a tactical flaw in this plan, namely that the infantry divisions were tasked to *widen* the breach. The problem with making a breach at all was the presence of German strongpoints on the Bourguébus ridge, in the other defence lines and in the many villages and farmhouses on the plain; these strongpoints, well-equipped with dug-in tanks and anti-tank guns, could only be cleaned out by infantry. The tanks needed infantry in close support, not bringing up the rear.

However, if the stated objectives given above could be achieved, Montgomery would be very satisfied – and, who knows, if all went well it might indeed be possible to press on to Falaise? Monty was well aware that battles seldom go as planned, but they sometimes, if rarely, go better than expected and he was quite willing to see how things went and take advantage of any opportunities to push on, or fall back if the cost of pushing on got too high. Not everyone seems to appreciate this fact – an omission which displays a woeful lack of understanding among military historians about the nature of military orders. As a result, those last directions – to send armoured cars 'far to the south towards Falaise' or to 'crack about as the situation demands' – embodied as points 6 and 7 in the Goodwood orders – would be dissected to haunt Monty's reputation in the years to come.

The point is that *all* attack orders should include some mention of exploitation – on what to do if the enemy folds and where your forces should 'crack on' to if the opportunity arises; this is standard military procedure. Orders that do not contain an exploitation clause hang in the air. In various post-war critiques, the British are frequently accused of failing to exploit success or of sitting on the objective instead of pushing on (i.e. exploiting it). Now, when Monty puts a clear exploitation clause in his orders, his detractors state later that he promised more than he delivered.

However, to the battlefield. Goodwood would be supported by the RAF, both 2nd TAF, RAF Bomber Command and USAAF. Over 2,000 aircraft, mostly bombers, would pound the area over which the tanks would advance, using fragmentation rather than high-explosive bombs to avoid cratering the ground, and this time there would be no delay before the ground troops went in. The attack would also be supported by 750 pieces of artillery, the guns of the fleet and another 2,500 fighters and ground-attack aircraft. Big as this appears, this amount of support was similar to that given to the Charnwood attack on Caen but, clearly, this Goodwood attack would be a truly shattering blow.

As a result, much – perhaps too much – was expected. As the British Official History points out,[16] 'Although he, (Montgomery), had made it clear to the CIGS (Alan Brooke) and the War Office that Goodwood was not an attempt to break out eastwards, he hoped it might appear so to the German command'. 'It will be seen later,' the account continues dryly, 'that not only the Germans misread his intentions.'

It is certainly possible that Eisenhower never did understand the aims of Goodwood. In his report to the Combined Chiefs a year later, in July 1945, when the European war was over, Eisenhower states that the aim of Goodwood was 'a drive across the Orne from Caen towards the south and south-east, exploiting in the direction of the Seine basin and Paris' ... which is light years away from Montgomery's oft-stated intentions.

The intentions – and the subsequent disappointment – were also heightened by Montgomery's incautious and extravagant claims for the battle, made while it was still in progress and the outcome as yet uncertain. Once again, if Monty had kept his mouth shut and refrained from raising expectations before the attack and then claiming good progress during it, a great deal of subsequent trouble might have been averted ... and his plan did contain a few unavoidable snags which might have dictated caution.

The first problem was that Second Army could not achieve surprise. The armoured divisions had to cross the Orne and Caen canal into the airborne bridgehead and this move could be observed by the Germans still clinging on in the Colombelles factory area north of Caen. Even after dark, the rumbling of British tank engines – the aero engines in Cromwell tanks were notoriously noisy – could be picked up far across the Norman countryside. Nor could the move across the Orne be done quickly; there was a shortage of suitable bridges and roads. Then there was the second problem, the small matter of the German defences.

The German defences south of Caen and around Bourguébus, a village on an open, commanding ridge, three miles south of the city, were in great depth. They consisted of five defensive lines, all well provided with infantry from the 346th, 16th Luftwaffe and 272nd Divisions, closely supported with deadly, tank-busting 88mm guns and some tracked, Hotchkiss anti-tank guns. Across the narrow line of the British advance the enemy could deploy seventy-eight 88mm guns, twelve heavy flak guns – all equipped with armour-piercing as well as high-explosive ammunition – 194 pieces of field artillery and no less than 272 six-barrelled *nebelwerfer* mortars. The Bourguébus ridge was a formidable obstacle and gave perfect observation for artillery fire from guns positioned behind the ridge. It is sometimes forgotten that 'good tank country' is also good anti-tank country, and the German 88s outranged the British tank guns by over 1,500 yards and had far greater hitting power, as Reg Spittle of the 2nd Northamptonshire Yeomanry points out:'[17]

In the *bocage* you had a chance for the ranges were short but out there on the plain when the 88s out-ranged us by a thousand yards or more, and had a clear field of fire you did not have a chance. Out there in the Bourguébus ridge or by the railway line it was chaos, lots of smoke and mist but open country. We lost 52 tanks in two days and our regiment only had around 60–70 tanks at best. At Hubert Folie three of us in the turret were wounded and that was the problem later, a shortage of men – we had hundreds of spare tanks, but you could not replace the crews.

Another defensive zone was organised in the villages and farmhouses beyond the Bourguébus ridge. These had been transformed into strongpoints, wired in, surrounded by minefields and manned by six battalions of SS Panzer Grenadiers from 1 SS Panzer. Behind that line were two battlegroups of 1 SS, each with forty tanks, including Tigers and forty-five Panthers positioned as a mobile reserve. It was estimated that the Germans also had some 230 tanks, Mark IV, Tigers and Panthers, many of them dug-in, ready to counter the British advance. More than a thousand tanks would take part in the British advance, 750 in the VIII Corps tank divisions and 350 supporting the infantry but the deployment of this massive force was hampered by the narrow front and the open terrain which made the attacking tanks sitting targets for the German guns.

Apart from the villages and farmhouses, every one a strongpoint, there were two other physical obstacles to the attackers, the embanked railway line running across the front from Caen to Vimont and Lisieux and the Bourguébus ridge, five miles south of Caen. The attack front was also hemmed in by the Orne river gorges north and south of Thury-Harcourt, by the *Suisse Normande*, by the river Dives and yet another railway line, running south from Mezidon to Argentan. As a preliminary to this push south, Second Army – in this case the Canadians – had to take Vaucelles. To do that, break through the German defences at Bourguébus and overcome tough opposition further on, the Second Army attack would have to go very well indeed.

Unfortunately, all did not go well. The first moves began on July 15 when XII Corps and XXX Corps attacked to their front on a line between the west of Caen and Tilly-sur-Seulles. XII Corps were again thrusting at Évrecy, aiming to reach the Orne and Thury-Harcourt in the *Suisse Normande* while XXX Corps were thrusting at Noyers and the high ground north of Villers-Bocage. The result of these attacks was a two-day-long, ding-dong battle, where attack was followed by counter-attack. Very little ground was gained but three German panzer divisions – 1 SS, 10 SS and 2nd Panzer – plus the newly arrived 276th Infantry Division, were sucked in to hold the line. XII Corps and XXX Corps took 3,500 casualties in two days, but at least they had diverted German attention away from the east bank of the Orne. This was not enough to get Goodwood off to a quick start but it reduced the chances of a German shift west to the Cotentin.

John Sharp of 2 Platoon, 'A' Company, 2nd Bn Middlesex Regiment, 3rd Infantry Division, gives an infantryman's view of Goodwood:[18]

On July 14 orders were issued for the division to move east of the Orne and our new battleground would be the triangle between Caen, Troarn and the mouth of the Orne. There was a fantastic traffic jam east of the Orne where three armoured divisions were forming up for the attack; our task was to clear the woods and villages of Le Pré-Barnon, Touffreville and Banerville, to exploit to Troarn and in general protect the left flank of the armoured thrust.

The attack began on the morning of July 18 with a second great bombing attack and the spectacle was fantastic with bombers droning in for over two hours and dropping 8,000 tons of bombs. This was followed up by artillery fire and our own mortars took up the task and fired 3,500 bombs in support of 8 Brigade in ninety minutes. So far it seemed that the attack was going well but the Germans in the woods near Troarn were a tough proposition; they pulled themselves together, gathered their guns and Moaning Minnies – *nebel-werfers* – and held out in the woods against the KOSBs and the Royal Ulster Rifles. 12 and 13 Platoons were firing mortar concentrations on Troarn, but casualties were high and very little progress was made – and we were being eaten alive by mosquitoes, shelled, mortared, sniped and harassed by machine-gun fire.

Touffreville and Sannerville were just within German mortar range but it was easier to get about in Sannerville as the ground was so pitted with bomb and shell craters there was always somewhere to jump into when something came over. The Germans had left behind great quantities of kit, and not booby trapped it and their deep dug-outs were very comfortable and full of wine, cameras, field glasses. In the woods were four wrecked Tiger tanks, one of them completely upside down, plus one Panther, seven Mark IVs and seven self-propelled ack-ack guns.

It was still a problem getting forward for the enemy simply beat down the forward battle area with his artillery and heavy machine-guns. We saw nothing of the Luftwaffe by day but my memory of July is of the most intensive bombing we ever had at night; they came over after dark, dropping flares, heavy bombs, anti-personnel bombs – one fell on a trench of the driver-operators and killed five out of ten. In the field I would say that the fighting men, British and German, were now about equal – I cannot say about the rest of the Allied troops – but the German 88 was the best gun in the war and their tanks were really good.

Eric A. Brown MC, was an anti-tank Royal Artillery subaltern commanding a troop of M10 tank-destroyers and describes the effect of German anti-tank fire during Goodwood:[19]

From behind a building a Panther emerged, surrounded by enemy infantry. Its prominent gun was not pointed in my direction but its flank was and I ordered the layer to aim on to it. Difficulty in discerning its shape confused him, so he moved over and I was able to direct the telescopic sight right on to it. I ordered 'Fire' but the solenoid switch did not respond, so I grabbed the emergency cord and we opened up, hitting the Panther squarely and stopping it in its tracks. We then swung our machine-gun round to engage the infantry, they scattered and with no immediate enemy follow-up I decided to re-deploy.

This we did – then disaster. Seconds later the M10 received a direct hit from behind – and it instantly burst into flames with a catastrophic roar. I was in the turret and had been talking to Driver Donaldson and Wireless Op. Norton. I was literally blown out of the turret on to the corn stubble below with my clothes burning; Donaldson and Norton had no chance as their hatch covers were covered by the external mantlet of our gun and they could not get out – they perished. We had been told that with clothing alight, the only answer was to roll over and over and put the flames out. This I did but my left leg was askew and blackened skin hung from my hands and face up to my forehead; luckily my steel helmet was still on and my hair did not catch fire.

I sat in the stubble trying to work out what had happened when I heard Sergeant Todd's voice; as Troop Sergeant of an adjacent Troop he had seen my 'brew-up' and without thought of the danger had raced over to pick me up. He got me on to the bonnet of his jeep and somehow to a Field Dressing station.

I remember a surgeon saying, 'You are going to be OK' and replying, 'Thanks, but don't overdo the morphia.' I could not see anything and lapsed into unconsciousness and it was three or four days later when I heard a Canadian voice saying that although I could not see, I was in a Canadian hospital – face masked, hands bandaged, both legs in plaster, but a lot of people had been looking after me since the shell hit the M10. Incidentally, all this took place three weeks before my 23rd birthday.

Goodwood began on July 18 and was a chapter of accidents from start to finish. The first problems arose in the move to the start line for which all three armoured divisions had to make their way around the north of Caen and across the Caen canal and the Orne. This move was closely observed by the enemy in the Columbelles factory area north of Caen because most of it could not be done at night. Nor could all the divisional elements get up to the start line before the attack. The cramped space east of the Orne meant that some reserves and support elements – including the artillery – must pass over the bridges after the battle started, with the risk of considerable congestion at the bridge approaches. By July 15 the Germans were therefore well aware that the next big British push would come in east of the Orne, though they did not appreciate that the axis of advance would be to the south. They too anticipated a move to the east, towards Paris and the Seine, but this view disappeared at dawn, 0530hrs on July 18, when a thousand RAF bombers dropped a huge tonnage of bombs on the German positions east of the Orne.

The first bombing lasted forty-five minutes. As it ended medium bombers of the US Ninth Air Force came in to drop their bombs on the German front line. That raid lasted until 0745hrs and as the dust drifted away the Shermans, Churchills and Cromwells of the 11th Armoured Division moved forward to the attack, close behind a bombardment from hundreds of guns. This initial bombardment from aircraft and artillery had its effect; for the next two hours the advance met little opposition and penetrated some three miles into the strongly held German lines ... but then matters began to go awry.

The tanks and infantry were now moving beyond the range of their supporting artillery which for lack of space in the Orne bridgehead had been positioned west of the Orne. It also became apparent that, for all its weight and spectacle, the bombing had left large parts of the enemy position untouched. This bombing had been concentrated on the enemy front line, the air commanders failing to appreciate that the enemy had deployed his defences in great depth. Since depth is the essence of good defence, this should have been obvious, but the end result was that instead of the resistance lessening as the British advanced, the opposition grew stronger – and the attack started to congeal.

The German defensive positions began to engage the tanks of the 11th Armoured Division at a time when their artillery support was held up in the vast traffic jams on the six bridges over the Orne and while the Guards Armoured Division were still deploying to their rear. The 7th Armoured Division, delayed in these traffic jams and the last one across the bridges, took no significant part in the first day of the Goodwood offensive. What it came down to on July 18 was that this supposedly shattering blow by three large and well-supported armoured divisions, became a scrambling advance by two divisions, which the defenders had no real difficulty in dealing with in detail.

This opposition made itself felt on the tanks of 11th Armoured at the Caen –Vimont railway embankment at Cagny, which was overlooked by the higher ground of the Bourguébus ridge. Most of the enemy positions here – occupied by 21 Panzer, with the 503rd Heavy Tank Abteilung (Tigers) under command and 12 SS Panzer – had escaped the bombing and shelling. When the Shermans and Cromwells of 11th Armoured and then Guards Armoured came in range, they opened up with field artillery, mortars and 88mm guns.

The Tiger and Panther tank guns outranged those of the Sherman and Cromwell and before long the fields in front of the embankment were littered with hundreds of shattered and burning British tanks. More British tanks moved forward, the infantry pressed on, aircraft came in and by nightfall the British advance had got beyond the railway embankment, but at some cost; 200 British tanks and around 1,500 men had been lost – and after about 1100hrs very little progress had been made in the centre at all.

The 3rd Infantry Division, tasked to guard the left flank, had moved forward at 0745hrs, supported by tanks of the 27th Armoured Brigade. The bombing had again reduced the opposition, at least for a while, and Troarn on the Dives was reached without difficulty. Then their troubles began. The 346th Division and elements of the 16th Luftwaffe Division, supported by Tiger tanks, put up a stiff fight for the villages along the Dives and by the end of the day their resistance had cost the 3rd Infantry Division 500 casualties and eighteen tanks.

The battle in Caen, to clear the enemy out of the Vaucelles suburb and the Colombelles factory area, had been entrusted to the Canadian II Corps. The 8th Canadian Infantry Brigade moved on Colombelles from the Ranville heights and spent most of the day clearing the factory area, aided in the task by a brigade from the 3rd Canadian Division. Within Caen, the 2nd Canadian Division got across the Orne into Vaucelles by dark and were ready to move on again at first light. German losses here had not been insignificant; 21 Panzer had started the day with around 100 tanks, thirty-nine of them Tigers, but lost most of these during the day to bombing attacks or rocket-firing Typhoons. Yet the Germans were still full of fight and the battle was by no means over.

At this point General Montgomery made a big mistake – not a professional one, but one that provided fresh fuel to his critics and greatly damaged his reputation. At 1640hrs on July 18, when none of details on the progress of the battle could be known, Montgomery sent a message to Alan Brooke at the War Office:

> Operations this morning a complete success. 11th Armoured reached Tilly-la-Campagne. 7th Armoured passed Demouville and moving on La Hogue. Guards Armoured passed Cagny and now in Vimont, 3 Div. moving on Troarn ... Have issued a very brief statement for tonight's 9p.m. BBC news ... situation very promising and it is difficult to see what the enemy can do just at present. Few enemy tanks met so far and no (repeat no) mines.

Very little of this enthusiastic message was true. The British Official History is being charitable when it calls this signal, 'inaccurate and misleading'. 11th Armoured had not reached Tilly-la-Campagne and lost 126 tanks trying. 7th Armoured had passed Demouville but were miles from La Hogue, and Guards Armoured never got within three miles of Vimont that day and lost sixty tanks when they tried to get there on June 19. Everywhere along the line the Germans were fighting back strongly and most of their options were still open.

The really sad part about this unfortunate signal is that it was so unnecessary. The gains on the first day were not insubstantial, the ground gained was useful and there was enough in that for a communiqué if Montgomery really felt obliged to issue one. Caen had been cleared of the enemy and if only the German line around Bourguébus could be penetrated, the way ahead did indeed lie clear. For a few hours on the night of July 18–19 it all seemed possible but the gains of July 18 were the only ones made during Operation Goodwood.

The German defenders had been anticipating an attack; only its scale and ferocity surprised them. When they had recovered from that surprise, with the bulk of the Allied support expended and Allied air cover again restricted by poor weather – torrential rain was to turn the Caen–Falaise plain into a morass – they prepared to hang on and resist any further advances. Dug-in behind a screen of 88mm anti-tank guns and *nebelwerfers*, this they did, and the persistent British and Canadian attacks over the next two days only increased the loss in men and tanks. The stone farmhouses and small villages south of Caen became strongpoints which the SS defended with great skill and tenacity, while the

Bourguébus ridge became notorious for the excellent observation it afforded over the Allied line and the volume of artillery and mortar that those observers brought down on the British and Canadian tanks and infantry.

Harry Secretan was a lance-corporal, a Bren gunner in the 2nd Bn King's Royal Rifle Corps:[20]

By mid-day on July 19 the artillery and tanks of my brigade were in a good position to offer some flank protection to the leading British tanks as they came down to the Bras–Hubert-Folie area, being fairly open country and very suitable for tank actions. There seemed to be very little German infantry and so the way seemed relatively clear for the armour to push up to the Bourguébus ridge which was their main objective.

However, as the tanks got near the ridge, all hell broke loose. Tanks were going up in flames all over the place. These tank formations were supposed to go between the two villages of Bras and Hubert-Folie because both were sup-posed to be outside the German defence line but both were in fact strongpoints, well-equipped with anti-tank weapons. In fact all the villages on the Bourguébus ridge, even Soliers and Foure, were likewise heavily occupied. On the ridge itself very heavy anti-tank fire was taking its toll of the British tanks, now caught in the open. Out of the great array of armour that had moved out that morning 106 British tanks now lay crippled, on fire and out of action in the cornfields. Our own support, from the Fife and Forfar Yeomanry, had lost seven tanks.

'O' – Orders – Groups that night put us back in the frame. There was to be a joint effort to clear Bras and Hubert-Folie with armour and infantry and the brigade began to move at 0500 on the 20th with my battalion attacking the southern outskirts of Hubert-Folie. We advanced behind our armour and it was hard to see at first, with the dust and smoke shells fired by the artillery. Enemy retaliation was light at first but soon got stronger as we reached the piles of rubble which had been cottages a few hours earlier. Machine-gun fire was coming from several places and there was lots of small arms fire being returned by our own infantry.

What we could see as we pushed through was complete devastation. German tanks and other vehicles, guns etc, just a twisted flaming mass, with the dead horses which we knew would be there for Jerry used horses all the time for shifting guns. Our artillery had certainly done their job here and done it well.

As we moved into the centre of the village and came up the main street, there was still some resistance, small-arms fire which was soon brought under control, more or less, and then white flags began to wave from doors and windows and a trickle of Germans began to walk into the middle of the road with their hands in the air. There seemed to be a lot happening in the northern end of the village, firing had increased and heavy stuff too, so our tanks began to move off in the direction of the fire, while the infantry began to move up, throwing grenades in doors and windows, keeping a good look out for snipers.

We then came face to face with three German Panthers, using the same road we were on, a most frightening experience. There was a mad scramble for cover before the leading tank opened fire, my carrier crashed into a shop front and I got my Bren and jumped out of the carrier into the shop, where Sergeant Pierce and a young officer were trying to get on to HQ which they did after a few minutes, and send for help. The plan he worked out was that a 17-pounder anti-tank gun would be brought up to attack the rear two tanks while we here took on the leading one.

Finally two PIAT operators got behind the tanks, moving through the back gardens and then, when the anti-tank guns had arrived, there were two tremendous explosions as the rear tank burst into flames, then two more, smaller bangs and the track of the front tank was blown off. When it tried to move it slewed round and jammed itself against the buildings. And so, after an age, the turret slowly opened and a young German officer poked his head out, and all four of the crew surrendered, as did the crew of the second tank. Only two were able to escape the fire on the last tank, which is a dreadful thing to see, something which one never gets used to. That night the rains came again and turned the ground into a swamp.

That persistent low cloud which had inhibited the Ninth Air Force helping the First Army into St-Lô also prevented the 2nd TAF rendering much assistance to the British south and east of Caen. A prolonged downpour on July 20 turned the battlefield into a tank-track churned morass but the Canadian 2nd Division, getting into its first fight since the Dieppe raid of 1942, attacked the Verrières ridge, west of the Caen–Falaise road and held it in the face of heavy counterattacks. But with that advance by the Canadians, the Goodwood offensive came to a halt – after just two days. It is hardly surprising that the commanders at SHAEF were outraged.

Fighting did not cease but Goodwood was effectively over and the results

seemed scanty indeed, although in Normandy terms they were not inconsiderable. After two days and at the cost of around 400 tanks, forty per cent of those
committed – though many were later recovered and repaired – the British and
Canadians had advanced about seven miles. They had got on to parts of the
Bourguébus ridge and although the German tank losses had been far less than the
Allied tank losses, these were tanks the Germans could ill spare and would find
hard to replace.

Moreover, the Goodwood offensive had kept the German eyes fixed in the
east while the Cobra operation geared up in the west. A greater advance would
have been better, but the strategic aims of the battle had in fact been achieved.
Besides (see above) this seven-mile advance by six British and Canadian divisions in two days is as far as twelve US divisions had recently advanced towards
St-Lô in seventeen days. This fact was obscured by the row that developed at
SHAEF in the aftermath of Goodwood, and the blame for that lies evenly
between Montgomery, for sending that hasty claim of progress on July 18 – and
his vocal detractors at SHAEF.

Had these difficulties and gains been appreciated it is probable that Goodwood would not have aroused so many critical comments – until we refer back
to that communiqué and to Montgomery's casual declaration in his initial order
that if all went well his armoured cars could advance *towards Falaise*. When put
together, these two statements provided useful ammunition to Morgan and
Tedder at the time and Monty's numerous detractors in the decades since. As
with his declaration of taking Caen on D-Day, Monty had made another extravagant claim and given his enemies a stick to beat him with.

The British Official History says mildly: 'Some dissatisfaction had been
expressed over the slow progress made by the Allies in Normandy.' This is a
considerable understatement; it is fair to say that all hell broke lose at SHAEF in
the aftermath of Goodwood. Most of the outcry came from the RAF commanders, Coningham and Tedder over the army's failure to get them that long-
promised open ground on the Caen–Falaise plain which they now had another
chance to bleat about.

According to Eisenhower's aide, Butcher, the air chiefs were 'completely dis-
gusted with the lack of progress' and their mood was not improved by British
newspaper reports, based on Monty's rather less extravagant claims of June 18
– simply that 'his forces were operating further to the south and south-east' –

that he had achieved a great victory south of Caen and that, so trumpeted the London *Times*: 'Second Army Breaks Through – Armoured Forces reach open country'. The effect of these media exaggerations, although ignored by Montgomery, took further toll of Eisenhower's patience.

Ever anxious to pour fuel on the fire – the better to cook Monty's goose – Tedder, according to Butcher, then phoned Eisenhower and alleged that Monty 'had stopped his armour from going further'.[21] Ike was certainly less than pleased with this news and Tedder, quickly seizing his chance, told him that he was certain the British Chiefs-of-Staff would 'support any recommendation Eisenhower might care to make with respect to Monty' for not going places with his big, three armoured division push ... a strong hint that Monty's sacking would be the logical answer to the current lack of progress on the British front. To stir the brew further, Tedder sent a copy of this note to Air Marshal Peter Portal, the Chief of the Air Staff and a member of the Joint Chiefs-of-Staff Committee.

Some generals were sacked in the aftermath of Goodwood, notably Major General Erskine and Brigadier Hinde of the 7th Armoured Division and the Commander of the 51st Highland Division. These sackings were long overdue and other sackings would follow but many of the senior officers at SHAEF were now pressing Eisenhower to take over direct control of the land battle, which he was for the moment reluctant to do. Besides, even if he did so he would still have to deal with Montgomery, whose strategy was under attack but was certainly not without merit.

The emerging fact is that Eisenhower simply did not understand Montgomery's strategy. Had he simply disagreed with it, he was the Supreme Commander and could have ordered Montgomery to do something else – according to Eisenhower's astute Chief-of-Staff, Bedell Smith, Eisenhower wanted 'an all-out, co-ordinated attack by the entire Allied line, which would at last put our forces in decisive motion. He was up and down the line like a football coach, exhorting everyone to aggressive action.' Once again the question has to be asked: since Eisenhower was the Supreme Commander and if this is what he wanted, why did he not try orders instead of exhortation?

The fact that neither of the Allied armies had been able to achieve such action – or, indeed make a great deal of progress in the supposedly easier attacks they were currently making – proves two points. Firstly, an all-out attack by both armies, all the time, could not be that easy or they would have already done it. Secondly, the overriding factors listed again and again in this account – supply, terrain, the weather, the enemy – made such an all-out offensive impossible or impossibly expensive in lives. The Germans needed to be eased or manoeuvred out of their defences before the full power of the Allies could be unleashed upon them.

On July 20 Eisenhower visited Montgomery in Normandy and was surprised – and, it appears, not a little put out – to find Monty quite satisfied with the results of Operation Goodwood. Details of their private conversations are not available – their chiefs-of-staff were not invited to participate, at Monty's request – but on the following day Eisenhower summed up his thoughts in a letter.

In this letter Ike told Monty that there was a discrepancy between some of his statements and the execution of his policy; for example, if the Allies were indeed as Monty claimed, 'strong enough and so well-situated they could attack the Germans hard and continuously in the relentless pursuit of our objectives', why was this not happening? Monty should 'tell Dempsey to keep up the strength of his attack', adding that 'in First Army, the whole front comes quickly into action to pin down local reserves and to support the main attack'.[22]

This last statement is certainly incorrect, as any First Army Corps commander could affirm. The US History itself clearly confirms[23] that 'a hush fell over the American front after the capture of St-Lô', V Corps had stayed quiet while Cherbourg was taken by VII Corps and had done very little while XIX Corps was fighting towards St-Lô; and the VIII Corps were moving down the west coast, not because the V Corps commanders were hanging back but because of a shortage of supplies and artillery ammunition.

It is also a matter of fact that the Second Army, by its continual attacks, was now containing most of the German armour – seven divisions – and four of the new infantry divisions – the 271st, 272nd, 276th and 277th – which had arrived in Normandy since July 3, compared with only one and a half new infantry divisions, 2 SS Panzer, and a much-weakened Panzer Lehr, which had arrived on the American front in the same period.

Eisenhower sent a copy of his letter to Tedder – one wonders why, since they shared an office – and the air marshal was soon on the warpath again writing to Eisenhower on July 23 (the thought of these two officers, sitting at desks a few yards apart and writing each other letters, is one of the most curious images of the Normandy campaign) to dispute Montgomery's strategy. 'I have no faith in such a plan,' wrote Tedder, 'I have every faith in General Bradley and his commanders and in their impending attacks, but I do not feel we can expect rapid moves in that area owing to the nature of the terrain.'

This is a grovelling, disloyal and rather stupid letter, an example of the perils of inviting an airman to comment on a land battle. Tedder appears to be arguing for an attack in the east, where one had just – in his opinion – failed and where the bulk of the German forces had been assembled, while claiming that an attack by Bradley and his commanders in the west could not succeed, *because of the terrain*. One wonders exactly where the air marshal felt an attack would succeed – or whether this was simply a continuation of his on-going campaign to get Monty sacked, a campaign in which the facts must not be allowed to get in the way of the aim. The fact that an attack in the west *could* swiftly succeed would be amply demonstrated just two days later on July 25 when the US First Army struck out of St-Lô in Operation Cobra.

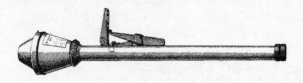

12 COBRA JULY 25-30

The word 'breakout' was often employed to describe the results of Cobra,
and meant variously leaving the hedgerow country, shaking loose
from the Cotentin, acquiring room for mobile warfare –
good bye Normandy, hello Brest.

THE US ARMY IN WORLD WAR II: *Breakout and Pursuit*

The roots of Cobra can be traced back to that conference between Montgomery
and Bradley on June 30[1] but the development of the actual plan of attack dates
back to another meeting between Monty, Bradley and Dempsey on July 10. At
this meeting[2] Bradley admitted that he was discouraged with the slow progress
made in the hedgerows towards St-Lô since July 3 and was brooding about the
way to mount some new and more decisive offensive once the city fell.

Montgomery told Bradley to 'take all the time you need' in order to develop
such a plan and following that meeting the idea of a major British attack – which
eventually became Goodwood – to aid the US advance, was suggested by
Dempsey. Plans for Goodwood and Cobra were then put in train and when
Bradley produced his initial plan for Cobra on July 12 it had one factor in
common with those concurrent British attacks around Caen; in both cases, the
lever to prise open a way through the German lines was air power.

As related in a previous chapter, Goodwood and Cobra should have been a
double blow on successive days to utilise all the available air power in successive strikes but, for reasons already explained, this did not happen. First Army
could not mount another attack immediately after taking St-Lô, so Cobra was put

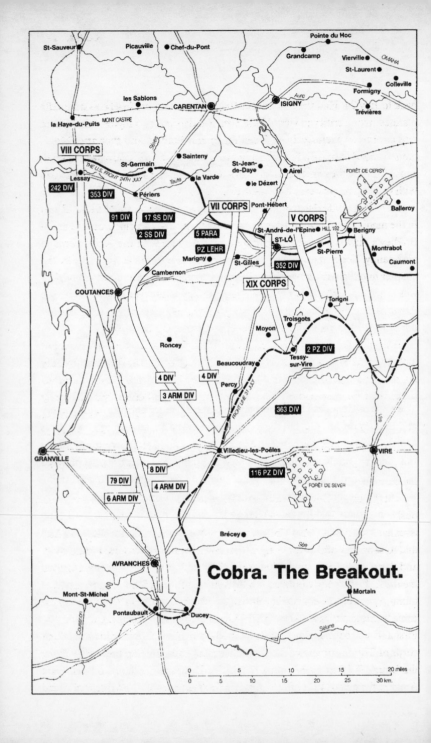

Cobra. The Breakout.

back to July 24. Had the two attacks followed each other closely, as originally planned, much criticism would have been avoided and two myths – that Cobra was conceived exclusively by Eisenhower and Bradley and that after Montgomery failed to make a breakthrough with Goodwood, the exasperated Americans took over the conduct of the Normandy battle and forced a breakthrough with Cobra – might never have gained credence.

As it was, while the grumbling over Goodwood continued at SHAEF and in the media after July 20, all eyes switched to the St-Lô sector where General Bradley's First Army were preparing for the next stage of the Allied battle in Normandy. The first point to make about Operation Cobra is illustrated by the chapter quote given above; that while the common opinion holds that Cobra was designed as the final breakout from the Normandy beachhead, allowing American armies to spill all over France, its original purpose was simply to get out of the *bocage,* round the Avranches corner and into Brittany.

It would take a careful plan, a great deal of force and a certain amount of luck, to break out of the Allied bridgehead south of St-Lô. However, by July 20, the major preparations had been made, the bulk of the German armour sucked east and moves to reach a start line on the St-Lô–Périers road had finally succeeded. Even so, everyone knew that breaking the German line was not going to be easy. A study of the Caen attacks revealed two snags that must not appear in Cobra – a long time delay after the bombing before the infantry went forward and heavy cratering of the ground by high-explosive bombs, which would impede the passage of the armour.

This being so, General Bradley wisely decided to take his time – and, curiously, was never accused of slowness for doing so. Twelve days separated the issuing of the initial Cobra plan and its actual implementation, a delay filled by that long and painful advance up to the start line at St-Lô and the Périers road, and the aim of Cobra was to break the German line west of the city. Once on the move, First Army would continue to swing south and then east to the Caumont–Avranches line, ready to fend off any threat to Patton's Third Army as it came bursting out of the Cotentin. Having debouched out of the Cotentin, the First and Third Armies would storm past Coutances to Avranches where one corps of Third Army would head off west into Brittany and the rest head for the Loire. The first steps to this end would be a thrust by VII Corps of First Army in the centre, backed by a drive for Coutances by the VIII Corps of Third

Army. 'If all goes well', said General Bradley to General Collins of VII Corps, 'we ought to be in Avranches in a week.'

The US Official History – *Breakout and Pursuit* – most sensibly, is at some pains to point out that the Cobra plan was designed to achieve a breakthrough, not a breakout – to make a breach in the enemy line, not necessarily to exploit it – and states[3] that 'it was a reasonable hope that Cobra would participate a breakthrough that might be *exploited into a breakout*, (author's italics) but a justifiable hope did not constitute a firm intention' – a phrase that seems to echo Montgomery's thoughts before Goodwood on 'cracking about' at Falaise – another justifiable hope of exploitation.

Bearing in mind the fierce resistance already encountered in the hedgerows, General Bradley was far too canny to commit himself to such a declared aim. Besides, what the Americans had to do first was to seize a sound start line for their attack. For this Bradley selected the St-Lô–Périers–Lessay highway but to get there some obstacles had to be removed, most notably the German strongpoints at la Varde and St-Germain-sur-Sèves, two salients in the US line between VIII Corps and Coutances.

These were to be attacked by the 83rd and 90th Divisions, the 83rd going in first against Varde, on the far side of the Taute river flats, on the evening of July 17. The 331st Infantry Regiment put a battalion across the river and through the swamps but could not support it and on July 18 the battalion came back. On the following day, July 19, the 331st went in again, this time with support from the 330th Regiment, and were again repulsed, having sustained heavy casualties and lost one battalion commander. This reverse can be attributed to difficult terrain, bad weather and plain bad luck but, the US Official History adds,[4] 'more basic was the ineffectiveness of the 83rd Division'.

It is fair to point out that the 83rd had only been in Normandy a month and in that short time had incurred more casualties and received more replacements than any other US unit in Normandy. Casualties are not always a result of enemy resistance, pushing forward against odds, or bad luck. A lack of training, poor fieldcraft and faulty handling in the field can increase the casualty list equally well. It appears probable that the 83rd Division's high casualty rate was due to poor training and indifferent leadership, so while the generals took another look at the VIII Corps role in Cobra, the 83rd was pulled out of the line to train and absorb reinforcements. As Colonel York of the 331st Infantry Regiment remarked after this battle,[5] 'We have quite a few new men and they are really new. They don't know their officers and the officers don't know their men'.

The ill-fated 90th Division were in no better case and this offers yet another illustration of the point made above. The 90th had achieved very little, yet after six weeks in Normandy the division's enlisted infantry replacements (i.e. private soldiers – pfc's and non-coms) numbered more than 100 per cent of authorised strength – and officer replacements totalled almost 150 per cent! The problems of the 90th Division were compounded by this situation, because the replacements, being neither as well trained or as well motivated as the original members of the division,[6] they were sent to squads and platoons where nobody knew them, just pushed in where needed, often on their own; a soldier without buddies is in a difficult and demoralising situation.[7]

The preliminary objective for the 90th Division was the village of St-Germain-sur-Sèves, which occupied an 'island' of high ground, two miles long and half a mile wide in the marshes in front of the divisional line. This position was held by one understrength German battalion, which was well dug-in on a commanding feature and had several assault guns and some light tanks in support. A feature of the otherwise excellent German performance in Normandy – one rarely made use of by the Allied generals – was an apparent reluctance to fight at night, but Major General Eugene Landrum, the 90th Division commander, did not consider his men well enough trained for a night attack on the German position. He therefore decided to send the 90th in daylight, supported by the entire VIII Corps artillery and tactical air strikes.

This attack was planned for July 18 but after various delays finally went in on the morning of July 22. The weather was poor, which prevented both air support and observation of the artillery bombardment, but this did not inhibit the actions of the German artillery. Their guns had the range to a metre and subjected the US troops to fierce shellfire which prevented the assaulting troops from crossing their start line for the first three hours. The attack was led by the 358th Infantry Regiment. The first battalion to reach the 'island' suffered fifty per cent casualties before reaching dry land but the attack was pressed home – again demonstrating that whatever this division lacked in performance, its young soldiers were not short of courage.

Another battalion was sent in but only one company reached the island – and the battalion commander was relieved of his command on the spot. The

Germans were now pounding the island with artillery and sweeping the marshes and open ground around it with machine-gun and mortar fire, and the 400 men of the 358th who had got across to the 'island' were on their own.

General Landrum's attempts to feed in reinforcements that night failed. Dawn on July 23 brought more German shelling and then an assault by German infantry backed up with three armoured vehicles, and a self-propelled assault gun. The American defenders fell back to the edge of the 'island' and there, trapped between the advancing enemy and the shell-swept marshes, they surrendered. A check revealed that of the 1,000 on the island, some 100 men had been killed, 500 wounded and 200 captured. After an investigation into the events of the 22–23 July, the divisional commander, General Landrum, was replaced, as previously related, though it is hard to see what else he could have done in the circumstances.

The American First Army took many casualties in Normandy, far more than the British Second Army. Many reasons have been advanced to account for this variance, including the suggestion that the British were holding back and letting the American soldiers do all the fighting. This is tantamount to saying that the British soldier lacked guts. This line can play well with the more chauvinistic historians, but readers may care to note that *none* of the *hundreds* of American veterans interviewed by this author over the years has ever made such a suggestion.

This may be simple courtesy but a significant number of American veterans, including those who endured the landing on Omaha also went out of their way to urge that full attention be paid to their British and Canadian comrades in Normandy – and the same urging has come from British veterans over their American comrades. This author can recall that one British veteran, recalling the American tank crews taking on German 88mm's in the *bocage,* had tears in his eyes when talking of 'those bloody Yank fools – but they were *brave* bloody fools'.

As this book has already revealed, the fighting – and the delays – in Normandy seem to be evenly spread among the Allied armies. This opinion is not fuelled by chauvinism but based on official accounts from national sources. Still, the discrepancy in casualties remains and it needs to be accounted for. Poor training must have made a significant contribution to US losses – and not only in the 90th Infantry Division.

The 83rd Division, the 90th Division and some other American units were simply not well-enough trained for the sort of fighting they were swiftly plunged into when they came ashore in Normandy. Motivation and leadership must also have something to do with it. The fine performance of many excellent US divisions – the 82nd and 101st Airborne, 1st Infantry, 29th Infantry, 4th Infantry and 9th Infantry Divisions, to name but a few – are evidence of the importance that must be given to these essential factors. However, the real answer to the basic problem of high battlefield losses was discipline, motivation and more training in the right tactics for the battle the troops were currently fighting. Hedgerow fighting called for *individual* infantry skills, tank and infantry, fieldcraft, camouflage, fire and movement, plus the use of grenades and light support weapons, especially mortars, at very close range.

Individual skills and infantry–tank co-operation are not much practised at the training camps and battle schools, where small unit tactics at squad (section) or platoon level tend to take up most of the time. In the *bocage,* the young American infantryman was often on his own, out of sight of his comrades, facing an enemy who was not afraid to come to close quarters, who could always manage a counter-attack and attacked with automatic weapons, grenades, mortars, even the sharp-edged infantry spade – and had close support from tanks, while using the *panzerfaust* to keep the US tanks at bay. It is also more than possible that the US infantry units could have used more support. As at Omaha on D-day, studying the Normandy battle imparts the feeling that, again and again, too much was left to the infantry soldier, and more support, from tanks, artillery and aircraft might have reduced their losses. There was also pressure on the US commanders to produce results *quickly* – the all-too-rapid sackings of divisional commanders is evidence of this fact – and this may have led these commanders to take chances which pushed up the casualty figures.

It may also be that the Americans were less 'casualty-conscious' than the British. Having more manpower, they were willing to take higher losses in attempting to get the job done quickly. The growing shortage of British manpower was another inhibition to such attrition on the Second Army front but there was another factor, less often mentioned, which may have had a bearing on this matter. The British generals often had first-hand experience of the carnage of modern war, dating from their time as subalterns on the Somme or in Flanders during the Great War; the American generals' attitudes to war were not coloured by that dire experience.

Fortunately, American ingenuity and 'get-up-and-go' came at least partially to the rescue of the beleaguered US infantry in the *bocage* with the invention of the Rhino, the *bocage*-busting tank. The US Official History[8] attributes this useful invention in early July to Sergeant Curtis G. Cullin Jnr of the 102 Cavalry Reconnaissance Squadron. Cullin conceived the idea of welding steel bars and ploughshares to the front of a Sherman tank. Allied tanks suffered heavy losses from *panzerfausts* when crossing hedgerows, because the vulnerable, poorly armoured belly of the Sherman tank was fully exposed when the tank reared up to mount the hedgebank. Sgt Cullin's invention cut directly into the bank and held the tank down as it broke through, thus clearing a wide gap for other tanks to follow.

This invention was inspected by General Bradley on July 14 and orders for more Rhinos were issued that afternoon. Within days, welding teams were at work fitting this device to tanks, self-propelled guns and tank-destroyers, right across the US line. This was the one example of specialised armour produced by the Americans, who might have profitably employed the range of mine-clearing, flame-throwing and gap-bridging tanks used by the British 79th Armoured Division – but one wonders if a British general would have been so quick to accept an idea from a mere sergeant.

Steps were also being taken to improve air-to-ground communications between the troops and the tactical air forces. Short bombing, ground strafing of their own troops and positions were still occurring, and poor communications – plus poor training on both sides of the radio link – were making tactical air support less effective than it might have been. This support was increasing as more airstrips were opened and USAAF fighter groups and RAF ground-attack Typhoon squadrons were now moving to France at the rate of two a week. This increased the amount of support available because aircraft no longer had to return to the UK to refuel and rearm; on the other hand, the need to bring in aviation fuel, bombs, rockets, and spare parts for a range of aircraft, increased the already heavy demands on the RAF and USAAF supply and logistical units. These arrangements, the training, the Rhinos, the greater availability of tactical air support, were all on stream for Cobra – the 'St-Lô breakout'.

For Cobra, General Bradley assembled fifteen divisions in four corps of First Army, although one of these corps – Middleton's VIII – and the 90th Division, actually belonged to Patton's Third Army. More units were arriving; eight US divisions, four infantry and four armoured, arrived in Normandy in July bringing the US total to twenty-two divisions, fourteen infantry, six armoured and two airborne. Four more divisions – one a week – were expected in August and as many again in September. Patton's Third Army HQ had arrived in the Cotentin in July, and Third Army was only waiting for the breakthrough to become operational. In anticipation of having two US armies in France, the HQ of the US First Army Group, which Bradley would command, began to move to France on July 5 and was on station by the start of August. Meanwhile, on the Caen front, the Canadian First Army became operational on July 23 under General Crerar.

On July 12, Bradley presented his Cobra plan to a conference of his staff and corps commanders. The start line for the attack would be the Périers–St-Lô highway, and the 'breakout', led by Collins's VII Corps, would take place on a four-and-a-half-mile front across the Coutances–St-Lô plateau, south of the highway – a slight problem because even on the night before the attack two US divisions, the 4th Armoured and the 83rd Infantry, were not on their start line. Once on the plateau – which was *bocage* country – the divisions of VII Corps were to veer west, towards Coutances, a move which would trap any German units left in the Cotentin unless they were quickly withdrawn.

For this task VII Corps would be beefed-up virtually to army size; Collins would have five divisions, three infantry, and two armoured. The attack would be preceded by a massive bombing of the area south of the St-Lô–Périers highway by heavy bombers of the Eighth Air Force. Two infantry divisions, the 9th and 30th, would then make a three-mile-wide breach between Marigny and St-Gilles, immediately west of St-Lô, the two armoured divisions, the 3rd and the 2nd (the latter formerly with V Corps) would pass through, and the veteran 1st Infantry Division, now motorised, would exploit the breach. Joe Collins's massive corps was then further enlarged with the return of the 4th Infantry Division, which was also put into the assault. The British and Canadians had one army apiece in Normandy; with Collins's big corps, the First Army and the Third Army, the Americans effectively had three.

While VII Corps were charging south-west for Coutances, VIII Corps – the 'pressure force' for this attack – would advance down the west coast, weighing down on the enemy forces to its front. When these moves had been completed, the entire First Army, having pivoted at Caumont, would consolidate on a line between Coutances and Caumont, facing east. All this was in conformity with the original Montgomery plan but – if all went well – the troops were then to push on and exploit any advantage to gain ground without waiting to consolidate: and they had the force to do this. Meanwhile, the US troops in the two corps east of the Vire, V Corps and XIX Corps, were to keep the German units on their front fully occupied, XIX Corps by patrolling action and shelling, V Corps by an attack to the south on the second day of Cobra. When First Army had cleared the Germans out of the way, Middleton's VIII Corps would lead Patton's Third Army out of the Cotentin and on to Brittany and the Loire.

Bradley's plan had been modified somewhat by Collins, whose VII Corps had now been increased to six divisions – 'virtually an army' agrees the US Official History,[9] and this was sensible because the entire success of Cobra really depended on Collins. In the final plan, three infantry divisions of this corps, the 4th, 9th and 30th, were to make the initial breakthrough by making rapid follow-up after bombing. Once they had torn a breach in the German line, the 1st Infantry Division and a combat command of the 3rd Armoured Division would drive directly for Coutances and the sea. The rest of VII Corps would head in the same direction but on a wider front, aiming to envelop Coutances and any German troops left in the area.

Collins did not intend that the advance of his corps should impede the southward thrust of Middleton's VIII Corps towards Avranches. If Middleton could storm ahead down the west coast, Collins would not get in his way or let VII Corps units get across his front. To aid this attack, VII Corps would also have the benefit of most of First Army's artillery and a vast quantity of ammunition – 140,000 shells for the initial bombardment – but the crucial element in this breakthrough was the heavy bombing just before the attack.

Bradley's plan, especially after Collins's adjustments, was to strike the enemy a devastating blow with this whole 'army-sized corps' and then pour in troops and armour and keep going until the enemy collapsed; the German front might be tough but by now it had to be thin. Very few reinforcements were reaching the German front lines, what did arrive was immobile and without motor transport and there were only one and a half Panzer divisions – 2 SS and what was left of Panzer Lehr – to provide the basis for counter-attacks. The answer to any attack is a counter-attack and the Germans had no power to make one.

And then, the final element, air power. To ensure that the bomber com-

manders understood the importance of their input to the opening phase, Bradley
went to England on July 19 and went over the plan carefully with the USAAF
commanders for both the Ninth and Eighth Air Forces.

As described, the start line was the 'bomb line', the St-Lô–Périers highway.
To avoid any short bombing, the troops would withdraw to positions half a mile
north of this road and all the bombs were to be dropped *south* of it. This was
still very close but had the advantage of offering a rapid follow-up on to the
defenders' positions before the defenders recovered. The bombs were to fall in an
area 7,000 metres long and some 2,500 metres wide – say four and a half miles
wide and a mile and a half deep.

Bradley made it clear that the US bombers were not to fly in over the ground
troops but across their front, east to west if the attack was in the morning, west
to east if the attack was in the evening, to keep the sun from the bombardiers'
eyes. The air commanders did not like this plan, saying they were being forced
to bomb down the narrow axis of the target and that the 800-metre safety zone
was not enough. For this attack the Eighth Air Force was committing all its
heavy bombers – B-17 Flying Fortresses and B-24 Liberators – and the Ninth
Air Force all its medium bombers and fighter-bombers. All the aircraft would
be dropping light-case bombs to avoid the heavy cratering that could halt a tank
advance. The aim was for some 2,500 bombers to smite an area of six square
miles, dropping 5,000 tons of explosives, the newly invented jellied gasoline –
napalm – and white phosphorus over two-and-a-half hours, blasting a path for
the tanks and infantry.

As a result the US ground commanders did not anticipate much opposition.
Apart from the devastating effect of the bombing, intelligence estimates from
Ultra suggested that there were no more than 17,000 Germans south of the
highway with perhaps 100 battleworthy tanks – about the strength of a single
US division. These came from General Paul Hausser's Seventh Army for the
bulk of the German forces were still in the east, in Eberbach's Panzer Group
West. Following Goodwood, von Kluge, who had now taken over direct responsibility for Army Group B as well as continuing in command of OB-West,
was convinced the breakout would come at Caen and sent any available forces
there.

However, von Kluge had also ordered Hausser to form a reserve ready to
strike against any American thrust from the Cotentin. This reserve was to

contain the only armoured divisions in Seventh Army, Panzer Lehr and 2 SS Panzer. In the event, Hausser only moved two SS tank companies into reserve, suspecting that the end of Goodwood by the British in the east indicated a fresh assault by the Americans in the west.

Hausser had plenty of units in Seventh Army but not enough troops; all his divisions had been written-down in the fighting since D-Day. He urgently needed fresh divisions or reinforcements for although many famous fighting divisions were there, facing Collins's corps – the 243rd Division, the 91st Division, the 6th Parachute Regiment, 17 SS Panzer Grenadier Regiment, Panzer Lehr – they were pale shadows of their former selves; Panzer Lehr, for example now mustered 2,200 troops and forty-five tanks instead of its designed 15,000 troops and 200 tanks. There were only 650 soldiers left of the well-trained 352nd Division that had fought so well at Omaha; only 2 SS Panzer was anywhere near up to strength. Even so, the Ultra estimate of German strength was not accurate; Hausser had some 30,000 troops opposite VII Corps. They had dug-in deep in the *bocage* and turned every deserted French village and farm into a strongpoint. These were German soldiers and they would make a fight of it, whatever came against them.

D-Day for Cobra was set for July 24, H-Hour 1300hrs, but when Air Chief Marshal Trafford Leigh-Mallory, Commander of the Allied Expeditionary Air Force (AEAF) arrived that morning to watch the bombing he decided that the poor weather and low cloud would make accurate bombing impossible and ordered the attack delayed for twenty-four hours. This decision was correct but came too late to stop an accident. Although most of the bombers were contacted and turned back, and others, unable to see the ground decided not to bomb, 300 bombers in the last formation did bomb, their cargo falling on the 30th Infantry Division, killing twenty-five soldiers and wounding 125 more. This bombing also alerted the Germans to the forthcoming attack so, fearing that the enemy would advance to the St-Lô–Périers road and thereby overrun the American start line, General Collins ordered the VII Corps attack to proceed. This attack was under way when he was informed that the twenty-four-hour postponement also applied to the ground attack and he was to halt his troops. The forward elements of VII Corps were already engaged and sustained casualties before the front was stabilised and the waiting began again.

During that twenty-four-hour wait the army and the USAAF commanders quarrelled over the undoubted fact that, in spite of the agreed plan, the aircraft *had* come in to bomb over the heads of their troops and not parallel to them, along the axis of the road, as previously agreed. This argument was unresolved when H-Hour – 1100hrs – came round again on July 25.

Once again the bombers came in over the heads of the waiting divisions and once again the bombs fell short. Nearly 2,000 US bombers, 1,500 heavy bombers from the Eighth Air Force and 350 medium bombers from the Ninth, plus 550 fighter-bombers, deluged the area with bombs and a significant number fell on the US positions. The 'short bombing' on July 25 caused many more casualties than the previous one. Some 600 American troops became casualties, of whom 111 were killed, including Lt General Lesley J. McNair, the provisional commander of the 1st US Army Group.[10] A good description of the bombing comes from Jack Capell, an infantryman of the 4th Infantry Division:[11]

> I could hear a great droning, like a million bees and like a lot of other guys got out of my foxhole to watch the attack. Hundreds of bombers were coming over, a marvellous display of air power, and the first bombs fell well to our front, in and beyond the German line. Then one fell short, in the next field, then another and another, and then one landed in our field, knocking me off my feet and I got back into my foxhole – fast. After that it was just … *indescribable*. The noise was terrible, the earth shook, we just took cover and hung on and it went on for what seemed like hours. When it was over and I crawled out the ground looked like the surface of the moon. We lost around 600 men in that short bombing.

The bombing was spread widely among the assaulting formations but in spite of the inevitable confusion this caused, the American infantry attacked anyway, surging forward over heavily cratered ground – the rains had softened the ground and even light case bombs caused craters. This attack was supported by heavy artillery fire and helped by the fact that by no means all the bombs dropped fell on US troops. The great majority fell on the German positions south of the St-Lô–Périers highway and caused a useful amount of alarm and despondency; more than 1,000 men were killed, three command posts of Panzer Lehr were wrecked and at least one German battlegroup, Kampfgruppe Heinz, on the right flank of Panzer Lehr, effectively ceased to exist.

The first objectives for the attacking force were the towns of Marigny and

St-Gilles, three miles behind the German lines, and the gap between them. While the VII Corps lunged for those positions, the 330th Infantry Regiment from the 83rd Division was diverted west, along the highway to Périers, to block any attempt at a German flanking attack into the advancing US divisions. The 330th advanced for a while but were then halted by shellfire and determined opposition from the 5th Parachute Regiment.

More German opposition was halting the advance of the 9th Division on the right of VII Corps, in front of Marigny. In the centre, the 4th Division had a mixed day but with the assistance of eighteen tanks the leading battalions took the little town of La Chapelle-en-Juger. On the left the 30th Division – though strafed as they advanced by US fighters and fighter-bombers – battered their way towards St-Gilles, their advance contested all the way by German troops and tanks who stopped the Americans at Hebecrevon.

By nightfall on July 25, the total gains were limited; VII Corps had got across the St-Lô–Périers highway and, on average, about a mile south of it but none of the declared objectives for that day had been taken. The US History[12] attributes some of this to the disappointment among the attacking troops at the failure of the bombing to quell the German defences – 'They thought that all the Germans would be killed or wounded; they had looked forward to the prospect of strolling through the bomb target area. The fact that some enemy groups survived and were able to fight seemed to prove that the air bombardment had failed to achieve its purpose.'

In fact, the Americans had done better than they knew. They were indeed encountering opposition but this opposition was the best that Seventh Army could manage. They could do no more and this was soon noticed. Herb Coleman, another 4th Infantry Division soldier comments:[13]

> After Cobra, once we got out of the hedgerow country, it went a lot faster. There would be skirmishes every day, mostly in the late afternoon, and then the Germans would pull out overnight. We had plenty of transport, which they did not, and we would pile into trucks and head after them, until we caught up with them in the next day or so and that went on until we reached Paris three weeks or so later.

The German defence line across the St-Lô–Périers road was tough but very shallow; those defence lines and interlinked fields of fire that had held up the Goodwood offensive were not present south of St-Lô. There was nothing behind the German front line at St-Lô, for the reserves that should have been there, to hold the line or counter-attack the advancing American divisions, were standing behind Caen; so here was a great opportunity. If the US forces pushed on July 26, the German line would snap and the Allies would achieve that long-desired breakthrough – and General 'Lightning Joe' Collins was just the general to keep pushing on.

Such a move had already been planned if the chance arose and it only required General Collins to proceed with the second part of his plan, the commitment of armour and the lorried infantry of the 1st Division. The fighting of July 25 had not provided the ideal conditions for this commitment but Collins had earned that nickname for swift, decisive action and he did not hesitate now. On the afternoon of July 25, while his infantry were still closely engaged across the St-Lô–Périers highway, Collins decided to send in his armour.

General Hausser spent the night of July 25–26 attempting to shore up his defences and find some help. He had been asking for the attachment of 9 Panzer Division for the last two weeks, all without avail, and when reports came in to his headquarters that evening, showing that his defences had already been penetrated in several places, they left him with no option but withdrawal – and that was forbidden by the Führer's orders. Nor was von Kluge being very supportive. The field marshal was keeping his back covered while the Gestapo and SS sought out the July 20 plotters and he did not intend to go against the Führer's orders now. That apart, he feared that any withdrawal at this time could easily turn into a rout. He therefore ordered Hausser to move all his forces forward and offer one strong defence line against the next American attack. This only compounded the problem. Hausser's defences were already inadequate and by forming another single line von Kluge was putting all his eggs in one basket. If the Americans broke that line nothing could stop them rolling forward into Brittany and on to the Loire.

Following Collins's orders on July 25, the front-line divisions spent the rest of that day and night clearing their front to let the armour through. Apart from the casualties caused by the bombing, losses had not been high; the 9th Division had not reached its objectives and had run into stout opposition once clear of the bombing zone, but it had lost only 200 men on July 25 while the 4th and 30th Divisions, although caught by the bombing, had advanced with tank support and got forward of the road. No division had gone very far on July 25; by nightfall most of VII Corps had halted about a mile south of the highway, less than two miles from their start line,[14] and this cautious advance is attributed to the effects of fighting for a month in the *bocage* where caution was highly advisable.[15] Now the *bocage* was being left behind and it was time to move.

On the following day the US advance continued and rapidly picked up speed. German units were overrun, artillery concentrations and fighter-bomber attacks broke up weak German counter-attacks, and by late afternoon Collins could feel that the enemy front was coming apart. His massive corps was now on the move, infantry as well as armour, pressing on for five, then seven, then ten miles, south of the St-Lô–Périers highway, a great advance in the context of the Normandy campaign so far, a mighty deployment of American military muscle.

'This thing has busted wide open,' cried General Hobbs of the 30th Division on the morning of July 27 – a comment echoed by von Kluge that evening – 'As of this moment, the front has burst.' With no reason to hold them back, Hobbs committed his only reserve regiment, the 120th Infantry, which drove south for more than six miles along the river Vire without encountering significant enemy opposition.

The same was true all along the VII Corps front. The 9th Division was barrelling forward opposed only by light shelling and mortaring; all infantry and tank opposition had subsided. Collins pulled the 9th Division into reserve and sent the 4th Division forward to mop-up on the corps front. As they did so, the rest of the corps went forward but suddenly German resistance was beginning to stiffen. The 1st Infantry and Combat Command 'B' of the 3rd Armored Division got up to Marigny before being halted by elements of the 353rd Division and some tanks of 2 SS Panzer. Fortunately, on the left flank, the 2nd Armored Division and Buck Lanham's 22nd Infantry Regiment of the 4th Division had already taken St-Gilles, allowing Combat Command 'A' of the 2nd Armored to pass through, and with the taking of St-Gilles on July 26, the Cobra breakthrough was achieved. It was now necessary to exploit the breach and turn the breakthrough into a breakout.

The next step to that end was to close the gap towards Coutances and cut off the Seventh Army units left in the Cotentin. These were to be crushed between VII Corps coming in from the north-east and Middleton's VIII Corps coming down the coast from the north. This relentless pressure would stop the Germans forming a new defensive line across the base of the peninsula and get Patton's Third Army moving out of the Cotentin, south and west into Brittany. This pressure by Middleton's strong VIII Corps, in reality another 'army' with five divisions – four infantry divisions, an armoured division and nine battalions of artillery[16] – would also 'tie the Germans down and prevent their disengagement before the completion of the VII Corps envelopment'.[17] This envelopment required the taking of Coutances by VII Corps, but the road to Coutances was blocked at Marigny.

This could not be allowed. On July 27, Major General Huebner ordered Combat Command 'B' of the 3rd Armored Division to clear the way, circling Marigny to the west while the 18th Infantry Regiment battered its way directly through the town. Marigny was duly cleared and 1st Infantry Division pressed on to clear the high ground and *bocage* further west while Combat Command 'A' forged on down the road for Coutances. This was a true spearhead advance. The width of attack was scarcely wider than the road; the country on either side of the road still contained Germans, some fleeing towards Coutances, others more than willing to contest the American advance, and their presence slowed Combat Command 'A' considerably. By nightfall they had only made about three miles and got less than halfway to Coutances. As a result they lost two opportunities – the prestige of taking Coutances and the chance to take large numbers of prisoners. In the first three days of their advance on this disintegrating front, 1st Infantry took only 565 prisoners – most of the Germans escaped to fight another day.

Middleton's VIII Corps – the 'pressure force' – had moved south on the morning of July 26 but immediately ran into strong resistance which halted the 8th Division north of Lessay. The attacks of two other divisions of this corps – the ill-fated 83rd and 90th – did no better. The 83rd attacked along the banks of the river Taute and although they had twice the strength of the German defenders, the 83rd 'didn't do a thing' and advanced no more than 200 yards.[18] Their performance improved on the following day when they put a regiment across the Taute. VIII Corps took 1,150 casualties on July 26, many from the mines, and had very little ground to show for it – and fewer than 100 prisoners, which indicates that they were facing good troops – but the 90th Division entered the shattered ruins of Périers after the Germans had pulled out. However, by the evening of July 27, VIII Corps had crossed the Lessay–Périers highway and were beginning to squeeze the remaining German forces in the south of the Cotentin.

On the VII Corps front, German resistance continued to stiffen. It remained stiff when Combat Command 'B' and the 1st Infantry Division took up the advance again next day, July 28. Cambernon fell in the afternoon but the American advance had slowed sufficiently to let the German forces get away, slipping out from the trap forming at the base of the Cotentin as VIII Corps advanced south of the Lessay–Périers highway. The 1st Division and Combat Command 'B' were also obliged to halt two miles from Coutances and wait there while VIII Corps entered the town. As a result, large numbers of German troops got away, the American pursuit being held up by a carpet of mines, anti-tank and anti-personnel, which the German forces had left behind. The Official History[19] sums up the final result at Coutances:

> Aided by the terrain, the weather, the darkness, the absence of Allied night fighters and the extreme caution of American troops who had come to respect the ability of the Germans to fight in the hedgerows, the German troops facing the VIII Corps had neatly slipped out of the trap set by Cobra. American commanders began to suspect an impending withdrawal … and operations in the VII Corps sector confirmed it. Despite precaution, warning and suspicion on the part of the Americans, the Germans gave them the slip.

This judgement by the US Official History, if accurate, seems harsh. Here, as later in the Falaise 'pocket', there was disappointment because the plan had not succeeded one hundred per cent – by trapping all the German forces – a complaint which overlooked and therefore diminished what had been accomplished: the breakout from the Allied bridgehead.

It is also fair to point out – whatever was claimed later – that it was Montgomery's *strategic* plan that had worked and stretched the German line to breaking point, without employing that 'attacking all the time and everywhere' policy advocated by Eisenhower. Carping about the escape of some shattered German units from Coutances should not be allowed to obscure that fact – or this great American success. Besides, many elements of the German forces had been trapped and on July 29 German columns on roads near Roncey were attacked by Allied fighter-bombers. Over 500 German vehicles were destroyed in this fighter-bomber feast, good practice for the slaughter they would inflict on the Germans later, east of Falaise.

Operation Cobra lasted officially for only three days. By the evening of July 27 Bradley could see that he had achieved a breakthrough. Now he had to exploit it by getting all his forces engaged, notably those of XIX Corps and V Corps east of the Vire, who had to start that pivoting movement towards the east from Caumont. Their main task during Cobra was to stay active enough to prevent any movement of enemy forces into the flank of Cobra. Now they could make more positive moves – but which? General Gerow of the much-reduced V Corps only had two divisions, the veteran 2nd Infantry and the newly arrived 5th Infantry. This force – with an abundance of artillery and strong tank support – still outnumbered the Germans to their front but Gerow's front was too wide.

Therefore, several days before Cobra, the British front had been shifted west, giving the Second Army responsibility for Caumont. British artillery therefore supported Gerow's attack south and west to the banks of the Vire on July 26. This attack went slowly and was still continuing on July 27 when Bradley informed General Gerow that XIX Corps was being shifted west of the Vire and that V Corps, strengthened by the 35th Division, would be responsible for the ground between that river and the British; this widened Gerow's front yet again and thinned out his forces.

Bradley had already digested the gains of Cobra. Now he wanted to continue his attack on a wider front, without giving the enemy any time to regroup. For Corlett's XIX Corps this meant an immediate advance south to take the town of Vire and the Forêt de St Séver, seven miles to the west of it. Vire was a major road junction and possessing Vire would give the Americans another hinge for when they turned their forces east. Meanwhile, Patton's Third Army was to become operational on August 1 and turn into Brittany.

Not only XIX Corps were heading for Vire. So was Gerow's V Corps. Bradley seems to have neglected V Corps at this time, for Gerow had been given no specific objectives, merely told to keep Bradley informed of his intentions and progress.[20] Gerow therefore decided on classic pursuit tactics; to follow the enemy on his front closely, wherever he went to prevent him digging-in or establishing any kind of defence line. The German forces opposing V Corps were trying to do just that, attempting to fall back to some defensible position, dig-in there and hold it against any oncoming forces. Under Gerow's pressure they fell back, but slowly.

The terrain astride the Vire was *bocage* country. The Americans fighting there would not get out of the hedgerow area for a while yet or gain ground without further losses. On July 30 alone the Germans inflicted almost 1,000 casualties on V Corps in the fighting around Torigni-sur-Vire. Meanwhile, the British on V Corps' left were coming up fast in their latest attack – Operation Bluecoat – and the US XIX Corps on Gerow's right were advancing south and widening their front. If these advances continued, the British and the US XIX Corps would pinch V Corps out of the line before Vire. Gerow therefore decided that, pending further orders from Bradley, he would halt his forces on the general west-east line formed by the rivers Vire and Souleuvre, seven miles north of Vire.

West of the river, Corlett's XIX Corps were coming down on Vire from the north-west, with currently little in front to oppose it. There was a yawning gap in the middle of Seventh Army to the XIX Corps' front but this happy situation did not last. Von Kluge was at last bringing forces west, most notably 2nd Panzer from Panzer Group West which was tasked to cross the Vire, close the gap and launch a counter-attack on the American forces west of Caumont in conjunction with the II Parachute Corps. This order was later changed to place 2nd Panzer under command of the 84th (LXXXIV) Infantry Corps to shore up the positions of the 352nd Division on the west bank of the Vire. More than that von Kluge could not do; the Canadian II Corps were attacking south of Caen and Caen was still the critical front.

Corlett's XIX Corps were moving on Tessy-sur-Vire but 2nd Panzer got there first and when the troops of General Hobbs's 30th Division moved on Tessy from the Moyon–Troisgros line on July 28 they ran into strong opposition. Fighting continued all that day and on July 29 but no progress was made. On the other hand, the committal of 2nd Panzer to stop XIX Corps at Troisgros, although it had plugged the gap in the Seventh Army line, prevented 2nd Panzer carrying out its second and far more important task, a counter-attack into the flanks of VII Corps.

Fighting continued in this area for the next two days, with the German forces increased by the arrival of yet another armoured division, 116 Panzer, which crossed the Vire on July 30 and began to butt against the lower shoulder of the

XIX Corps advance at Beaucoudrey, west of Tessy, where Combat Command 'A' of the 2nd Armored Division were swinging east to confront them. Hanging on to Beaucoudrey became more immediately important than taking Tessy.

American pressure was increasing in the west and would go on increasing. There was nothing the Germans could do to prevent the build-up of forces on their front and as the pressure continued the German front west of the Vire began to crumble. On August 1 General Hobbs of the 30th Division was finally able to send a force of infantry into Tessy. This attack was not completed; the town still contained defenders and shells continued to fall on the town from German positions further south for some days but in the broader sense this hardly mattered. By containing the German attempted counter-attack on Collins's corps west of the Vire, XIX Corps had given the rest of First Army time to widen their breach south of Coutances.

First Army had broken out of the bridgehead and opened up a gap in the German defences which von Kluge had no means of filling. The way to the south was now wide open and by August 1 American troops were pouring out of the Cotentin, heading at speed for the Loire and Brittany.

13 SPRING AND BLUECOAT JULY 25-AUGUST 6

The dogged courage and determination of the British foot soldier ...
was never more fully displayed than during Bluecoat.

BELFIELD AND ESSAME *The Battle of Normandy*

With the American breakout from the bridgehead at the end of July, the third phase of the Normandy battle had been completed. At this point, before moving on to what followed, it would be as well to summarise the various events of recent weeks, through the build-up to the breakout, sum up the situation in Normandy at the end of July and ventilate some of the still-prevailing myths.

Operation Cobra – or the 'St-Lô breakout' as the American veterans call it – came as a great relief to the Allied commanders and their political leaders in London and Washington. They would now cease carping, at least for a while, and the relief was general, although some of the senior commanders at SHAEF may have regretted that the St-Lô breakout stymied their on-going campaign to get rid of General Montgomery.

The recent discontent had focused on Montgomery and the British Second Army and this feeling would lead to greater discontent in the future when the territorial progress of the American armies, the First and Third, was matched with that achieved by the British Second Army and the Canadian First Army. The popular myth, that the American forces did all the fighting in Normandy while the British and Canadians sat in is largely based on the events after Cobra but has its origins in the fighting of the previous weeks. The progress of the Allied armies certainly varied but for several very good reasons.

Second Army's numerous critics rarely compare like with like, not least in

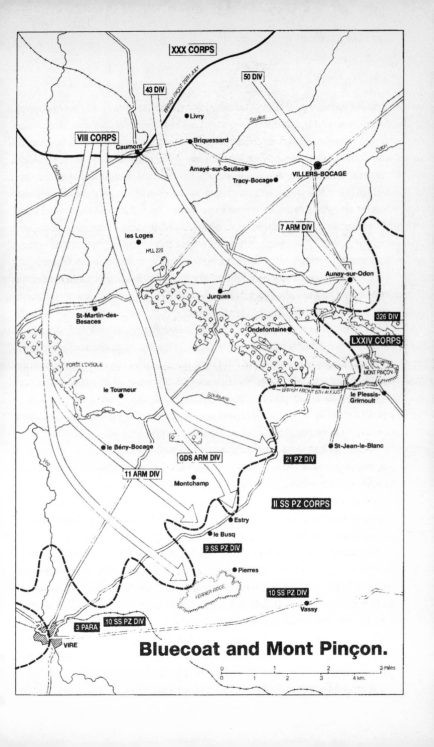

Bluecoat and Mont Pinçon.

terms of enemy opposition. As is clear from the previous chapters, the opposition faced by the Americans at Cherbourg and St-Lô was far less in both quantity and quality than that confronting Second Army at Caen. The numerous American delays in June and July, on which many American historians are surprisingly reticent, were largely due to the weather, which affected both armies, and the terrain – the *bocage* – which was wider and deeper in the west than in the east but by no means exclusive to the First Army front. All the Allied armies had problems with supply at this stage, especially of artillery ammunition and later on with petrol. The British delays were also due to the defences of Caen and the strength and tenacity of the enemy forces in manning those defences.

The American forces certainly made great gains in the south and west at the end of July and in early August, after the St-Lô breakout, and deserve full credit for this – but the breakout came in the First Army sector on July 26 because Monty had always planned that it should, largely because the Americans had both the men and the space to employ them. Nor was there much opposition; as the US History readily admits:[1] 'No German defensive capability was apparent in the Pontaubault–Brécey–Villedieu-les-Poêles sector' – the post-breakout area crossed by the US armies on Cobra. The same cannot be said of the area chosen for Bluecoat and Spring, the operations in which the British and Canadians were now to be engaged.

Selecting and maintaining the aim for a battle or campaign is the prime task of any commander and hindsight suggests that a more nationalistic or chauvinistic leader, eyeing posterity and the subsequent claims made by historians, might have let the Americans take on the Panzers while the British advanced to take the ground – and hog the subsequent credit. That was not Montgomery's plan. That plan was dictated entirely by strategic considerations, particularly over the question of ground and the known abundance of American manpower. Whatever complaints are made against Monty – the man – the plan that worked in Normandy was prepared and executed by Monty – the commanding general – and he deserves full credit for it.

The success of this strategic plan, in diverting German armour to the Second Army sector, is shown by the distribution of German Panzer and infantry forces at midnight on July 24, just before the St-Lô breakout. In the American sector, between the Cotentin and Caumont, were two Panzer divisions, 2 SS Panzer and Panzer Lehr, mustering a total of 150 tanks, plus 17 SS Panzer Grenadier

Division – lorried infantry – and five assorted infantry divisions. All these units, with the exception of 2 SS Panzer, had been well written-down in the last six weeks and were short of transport, both motorised and horse-drawn.

Facing the British Second Army between Caumont and Caen were the seven German Panzer units of Panzer Group West: 12 SS Panzer, 10 SS Panzer, 9 SS Panzer, 1 SS Panzer, 21 Panzer, 2nd Panzer, 116 Panzer and the 7th and 8th Werfer Brigades of II Panzer Corps, and six infantry divisions, together mustering no less than 645 tanks and ninety-two infantry battalions. Many of these units had also been written-down in the previous fighting – seven Panzer Divisions on full establishment should have had over 1,200 tanks – but the discrepancy in numbers is still clear.

Not only were there more German Panzer divisions ranged against the British Second Army, but these were larger and better equipped divisions; an SS Panzer division mustered around 20,000 men – with six battalions of infantry – while a Wehrmacht Panzer division mustered around 12,500 men with four battalions of infantry. Panzer divisions were also fully motorised while Wehrmacht infantry divisions, which had been reduced to a ration strength of around 8,000 men relied on horse-drawn transport; a Panzer division, especially an SS Panzer division, was more formidable than a standard Wehrmacht division in every way – as anyone who fought the SS will attest. Here again, these figures are 'ration-strength' figures and do not reflect the writing-down of German divisions in the battle so far, but again, the discrepancy between the US and British front is clear.

Then there is the question of quality. At the end of July, according to SHAEF, the Allies had captured 78,000 Germans, of which 14,000 had been taken by the British and Canadians. Eisenhower's naval aide, Captain Harry C. Butcher, reports this information in his memoirs,[2] clearly believing that it represents another American first. Captain Butcher was a naval officer with no knowledge of land fighting and his job at SHAEF was chiefly concerned with media relations – Butcher was a PR man. He therefore may not have realised that these figures indicated the varying quality of the German troops on the Normandy front; 64,000 of these gave up and surrendered to the Americans – more than 30,000 at Cherbourg – while only 14,000 gave up and surrendered to the British. The German forces on the British front tended to go on fighting; good troops do not surrender in any quantity.

These facts and figures should be considered when estimates are made of ground gained on the respective Allied fronts and chauvinism does not enter into it. General Bradley, for one, was well aware of the help the British containment of the SS Panzer divisions on the Caumont–Caen sector gave to his own advance from St-Lô, but this broad picture was to change immediately after the breakout. Suddenly, if belatedly, grasping Montgomery's strategy, the Germans hastily switched two of their tank units – 2nd Panzer and 116 Panzer – west, in an attempt to stem the American advance.

By that time it was too late and further transfers of armour were stopped by the need to contain the British thrust south from Caumont – Operation Bluecoat – but the retention of the German Army on the Second Army front was of inestimable benefit to the American forces in the west as Bradley freely admitted:[3] 'Monty's primary task,' he wrote, 'was to attract the German troops to the British front that we might more easily secure Cherbourg and get into position for the breakout. In this diversionary mission, Monty was more than successful.'

One might quibble slightly with the phrase 'diversionary mission' or suggest that 'Dempsey' is more accurate than 'Monty,' but the general point seems clear. The British took on the Panzers until the Americans could make their breakout and since the Panzer divisions were never less than formidable, the sooner this breakout came the better. After Goodwood some swift action was necessary, if only to silence the rising tide of complaints at SHAEF. The British Official History, in a rare moment of acerbity, comments:

> None of the discomfort at home and in America would have arisen if the
> erican attack in the west could have started on the day after Goodwood ended,
> as originally intended. At the time it seemed to the public that the capture of
> St-Lô and the Goodwood attack had done nothing to quicken the slow pace
> of Allied progress.

Apart from the weather, the *bocage* – and the enemy – one reason for the slow progress across the Allied front since D-Day had been the chronic problem of supply. This was because, even at the end of July, they still did not have a large working port. Cherbourg was open but working at nothing like normal capacity and the Allies were still forced to land stores via the remaining Mulberry at Arromanches, through the limited facilities of Port-en-Bessin or Courseulles, or by transshipping men and stores from ship to shore in DUKWs or landing craft, manhandling them ashore over open beaches.

Inevitably, without the facilities of a working port, there were delays. One major factor inhibiting the progress of the armies, and one that would grow as the campaign became more mobile, was a chronic shortage of fuel but even so, the tonnages sent ashore were vast. By the morning of D plus 50 (July 25) no less than 631,000 men, 153,000 vehicles and 689,000 tons of stores, plus 68,000 tons of POL (petrol, oil and lubricants) had been landed in the Second Army sector alone. The number of vehicles included tanks, but the sheer quantity of vehicles in the cramped bridgehead created problems, not least in the rapid deterioration of the few metalled roads and the constant clouds of dust which attracted enemy shellfire.

If troops and stores were on the way in, the wounded were on the way out and casualties were mounting. Up to June 30, Allied casualties had totalled 24,698 British and Canadian and 37,034 Americans. American dead came to 5,113 and British and Canadian dead to 3,356, the larger American figure being accounted for at this stage by the losses on Omaha on June 6. To make up these losses, 38,000 British and Canadian troops and 41,000 US troops were landed in the bridgehead in the first three weeks after D-Day. The casualty figures at the end of the battle will be given later but every army on the Normandy front was having trouble with manpower. At the end of June, the German Seventh Army alone had lost a total of 80,783 men – including nine generals – more than the combined casualty total of the Allied armies.

The British–Canadian and US troop figures would soon diverge for the British were almost out of manpower. Although the US First and British Second each had fifteen divisions in France, there were only six British or Canadian divisions left in Britain to reinforce 21st Army Group. The Americans had nine divisions in Britain waiting to cross the Channel and many more divisions in the USA or already crossing the Atlantic. These new American divisions would be landed directly in France and in time the US forces in Europe would muster sixty-one divisions.

Even at full strength the British and Canadian armies in Europe could not produce more that twenty-two divisions ... and that figure could not be maintained for long as casualties mounted. These factors should be borne in mind before we return to the Caen to Caumont front where the British and Canadian armies were attacking again.

While the US First and Third Armies were forging south out of the Cotentin and past St-Lô towards Brittany and the Loire, the British were engaged in yet another slogging dogfight in the difficult country south of Caumont. Caumont had represented the meeting-point between the British and American forces in the first days of Overlord when the town itself had been in the American sector but, as related, the dividing line between the American and British Armies had shifted west in the last days of July to cover the advance of VIII Corps on Avranches. The American XIX Corps moved west of the Vire, V Corps followed and by the beginning of August, Caumont was in the Second Army sector. After Cobra, this situation presented Montgomery with an opportunity for Second Army. Following Goodwood and Cobra, two strong attacks on the flanks, it appeared likely that the German front in the centre, south of Caumont, would be starved of troops and tanks and ripe for an attack.

There was, however, a problem with terrain. First of all the area south of Caumont was *bocage* – the largest town in the area is Villers-Bocage – and the front is hemmed in on the east by the steep-sided Orne valley, steep enough to have sheer rocky escarpments, and on the west by the bulk of a dominant hill feature, Mont Pinçon. The forces defending this terrain therefore enjoyed a clear advantage in the ground. It was therefore recognised that any advance south of Caumont would be a hard slog, and so it proved.

From the west, the Allied line-up at the start of August was as follows: US Third Army, US First Army, British Second Army and Canadian First Army. The US 12th Army Group became operational under Bradley on August 1 with General Courtney Hodges taking command of the US First Army and Patton arriving in Normandy to take command of the US Third Army. For the moment, however, General Montgomery remained in *operational* command of the Allied forces in Normandy, remaining in post as Ground Force Commander until General Eisenhower took command of the armies some time in the not-too-distant future.

The launching of the Canadian Second and US Third Armies into the Normandy battle will be covered in the next chapter, but the prime task of the British and Canadian Armies now was to fix the German Panzer divisions in position and prevent them switching west to impede the American breakout. It was also necessary to advance south, in order to deny the Germans a hinge, some secure point on which their armies could swing as they fell back – or were pushed back – from the Cotentin and Vire. One way to prevent the Germans finding such a hinge was to maintain pressure towards the south and take the most likely hinge, the German positions around the 365m (1,200ft) high Mont Pinçon, which stood due east of Vire.

This attack, Operation Bluecoat, by three corps of Second Army, would go in as soon as British armoured units could be shifted to the west end of the British line. Meanwhile, to keep up the pressure in the east, the II Canadian Corps, reinforced by the 7th Armoured Division and the Guards Armoured Division, struck south down the Caen to Falaise road on Operation Spring. This attack had been planned on July 21, during the final stages of the Goodwood battle and the Canadian advance began early on the morning of July 25, the day the US Army to the west started Cobra. General Guy Simonds, who was in charge of Operation Spring, was fully aware that this was a 'holding operation', to engage the enemy divisions on his front and no major territorial gains were anticipated. The spearhead of this Canadian attack was the veteran 3rd Canadian Infantry division, advancing on Tilly-la-Campagne, where it was swiftly engaged by units of 1 SS Panzer.

The fight around Tilly went on all day, while on the west of the Caen–Falaise road the 2nd Canadian Infantry Division advanced through Verrières towards Rocquancourt where they were held by fire from the Verrières ridge. Neal Hamilton was a forward observer-signaller of the 4th Royal Canadian Artillery working with the infantry of the 2nd Canadian Division:[4]

You will have to remember that I was a very scared kid and did not keep any books or notes so it is just flashes from that time. I remember one day as we were waiting in our Bren-gun carriers to move forward, we saw an infantry soldier with a heavy load of ammunition crawling up the ditch. He came to a dead horse and did not want to stand up and so he crawled over it and when he was on top it just caved in under him; I'm pretty sure his buddies did not hug him for a while after that. Our first job was burying dead Germans and that was terrible but what they tell you is true, you soon get used to it.

Our Troop had a total of four guns, the battery eight, our regiment 72. My job was observing and passing corrections to the guns a mile or so in the rear. At first I was driver-operator in an armoured car; we had a captain with us who was never sober but he was soon replaced by a great officer, Captain Harvey. We crossed the Orne for the attack on Verrières; the river was wide and a mess, dead cows, horses, bodies, all floating, everything black from the hot summer sun.

Out on the plain there were many burned-out tanks from previous battles and the shelling and firing was still going on; we had to dig in as when those 88s come by you are glad of some shelter, believe me. My crew took casualties, and we changed around many times but all I got was some shrapnel in my legs, and shock. We accompanied the infantry as they advanced, travelling with the CO to get him artillery support when he needed it like at Verrières. We were so under-strength that you could go 30 hours on the radio without a break; the guns were switched to support different battalions so you never got to stop. As we went on we met SS and once we went to help a wounded Jerry when he produced a pistol from his tunic and had to be disposed of. There was a lot of sniping and that did not stop all the way to Falaise.

This Canadian battle spread rapidly to the banks of the Orne and although May-sur-Orne at the northern end of the *Suisse Normande* was taken, lost and retaken several times that day, no real progress was made by the Canadian infantry, although the attack was pressed with great resolution; 1,500 men of the 2nd Canadian Division had been lost by the time the battle ended at dusk. This hold-up for the infantry held up the two tank divisions, who were given no breach to exploit. 7th Armoured – the Desert Rats – and the Guards Armoured came forward to engage the tanks and anti-tank guns of 1 SS Panzer and 9 SS Panzer; a number of German tanks were knocked out, some by British tanks, others by aircraft of 2nd TAF, but the two British armoured divisions lost fifty-six tanks that day and made no ground. Nevertheless, the main aim had been achieved; the crack 1 and 9 SS were retained on the Caen front in the first hours and days of Cobra. The Canadian Official History[5] records that the II Canadian Corps 'struck a stone wall' at Verrières and that, with the exception of the Dieppe raid in August 1942, July 25, 1944 was the Canadian Army's costliest day of operations in the Second World War.

On July 27, Montgomery met Bradley and Dempsey to review the situation and issued new instructions for future developments. The main blow of the campaign had now been delivered by the US First Army and it was clearly imperative for the other elements of 21st Army Group to do whatever they could to help the Americans forward. Even now, six German Panzer divisions were still based on the British-Canadian front east of Noyers – 116 Panzer having gone west to shore up the German line against the Americans south of Tessy-sur-Vire – so Monty decreed that the Second Army must strike a heavy blow west of Noyers, between that town and Caumont, where there were currently no Panzer divisions at all.

Attention now shifts to the thrust of the British Second Army south from Caumont towards Mont Pinçon – Operation Bluecoat – and the move of the US V Corps on their right flank towards Vire. Switching strong armoured forces from one side to the other of the Second Army front took a little time and in that time the US V Corps advanced on Vire. This V Corps attack would be limited by the need to keep in touch with the British on their left but once the Germans had started to move back it was essential to keep them going. In his directive to the V Corps' divisions, General Gerow underlined this point 'We must keep going to remain contact and not give the Boche time to dig-in. See that all understand this'.[6]

The opposing German forces came from the II Parachute Corps. This unit was pulling back to maintain contact with German forces west of the Vire which were coming under pressure from the US XIX Corps. On July 28 V Corps duly followed up the II Parachute Corps withdrawal, taking the St-Jean-des-Baisants ridge, encountering little resistance, and taking very few prisoners from the doughty Parachute Corps. The next objective for V Corps was the Souleuvre–Vire river line, eleven miles to the south and west, a considerable bound forward in itself and especially so for the country was a jumble of low hills and woods with plenty of *bocage* in the intervening valleys.

This bound presented Gerow with a dilemma; if he did not press on, the enemy could dig-in; if he did press on while the British were still forming for Bluecoat he might expose his left flank to enemy attack – and getting tangled up in the *bocage* was just an added complication. Fortunately, the Germans withdrew beyond the river line and on July 29 V Corps were able to form a front between the village of Condé-sur-Vire and the British line near Caumont.

In spite of the steady German withdrawal, the V Corps advance had not been uncontested. The II Parachute Corps left plenty of small parties behind, sowed an abundance of mines and kept the advancing Americans on their toes with a number of those small counter-attacks from company-sized formations backed with tanks and mortars. On July 29, with Second Army attacking on the following day and in the knowledge that the Germans were now in full retreat south of the Cotentin to the west, Gerow ordered all his troops to push on, brushing aside any resistance to get into the town of Vire. This order came just a day late.

By the evening of July 29 the enemy had formed a fresh defence line at Torigni-sur-Vire, a village four miles east of the Vire river. Attempting to take that village and the surrounding hills cost V Corps over 1,000 casualties and halted their advance for the moment. Only for the moment though; on July 31 von Kluge ordered the II Parachute Corps to fall back rather than be outflanked by the bulging front formed by XIX Corps to the west. This enabled V Corps to press on quickly across otherwise ideal defensive country to the Vire–Souleuvre river line, meeting more resistance as they neared the river. Three Allied corps, the British VIII Corps on the left, the US V Corps in the centre and the US XIX Corps on the right, were now converging on Vire, the first two from the north, the latter from the north-west. V Corps in the middle looked like being pinched out unless it could get ahead of the rest and grab the roads.

Gerow ordered the 5th Division to halt on the river line but some battalions were to go across and establish a bridgehead, just in case they could go forward again, as Gerow fully intended to do; 'In short,' he told one of the tank regiment commanders, 'hurry.' This order again came a little late. British armour from VIII Corps had already got ahead, crossed into the V Corps zone and taken two bridges across the Vire. The V Corps infantry followed up the British tanks, but the narrow Norman roads were not big enough for two corps to use at the same time. Some confusion reigned as the British advance moved down from Caumont, with the 11th Armoured Division moving on to high ground east of the river Vire, just within the Second Army boundary.

Meanwhile, west of the Vire, the US XIX Corps were also moving south and exploiting east. There was very little to stop it to begin with and a useful gap XIX Corps might hope to exploit was still open between the 84th (LXXXIV) Infantry Corps and II Parachute Corps, a gap that von Kluge was most anxious to fill, moving 2nd Panzer Division from south of Caumont for that purpose. Another unit moving west was the 58th (LVIII) Panzer Corps, a major unit transferred from Fifteenth Army to Panzer Group West, a corps which von Kluge intended to use in a counter-attack towards Marigny and St-Gilles on the VII Corps front. These plans faltered because the situation on the western end of the line was changing so rapidly that plans were rendered out of date before they could be issued. The fundamental fact, however, was quite clear. If von Kluge was to stabilise his front in the west and conduct an orderly withdrawal to some sound defence line in the east, he must have more troops west of the river Vire.

He therefore had no option but to take troops from the front south of Caen. The 116 Panzer Division, formerly with Fifteenth Army, went across to Seventh Army where, with 2nd Panzer, it was to attack north and west and close the gap at the Vire river by Notre-Dame-de-Cenilly. This move began on July 27 and was followed on July 28 when the 67th (LXVII) Panzer Corps took command of 2nd Panzer and what was left of the 352nd Division and Panzer Lehr. Coming up in support was 2 SS Panzer which deployed east of the village of Percy on July 29 and was poised to thrust north-west against XIX Corps – now making for Vire against opposition estimated by General Corlett as no more than 3,000 battered and ill-equipped enemy soldiers.

This proved an underestimate. While all these German units were short of kit and battle-weary, Combat Command 'A' of the 30th Division ran into 2nd Panzer just west of the Vire on July 27 and met stout opposition. On the morning of July 28, 2nd Panzer was able to put a motorised regiment of panzer grenadiers and about twenty tanks to oppose them while the rest of 2nd Panzer was assembling around Tessy-sur-Vire. With the aid of attached elements from the other German units, the XIX Corps advance was brought to a halt on a narrow front between Troisgots and Moyon.

Fighting in this area went on for the next three days with 116 Panzer adding weight to the defenders' line; Troisgots did not fall until the evening of July 31. On the following day, Combat Command 'A' of the 30th Division led the 29th Division towards Tessy-sur-Vire, which finally fell on August 2. This advance further reduced the German strength in this sector while stopping the Seventh Army constructing a new defensive line across the base of the Cotentin. Further attempts to stem the collapse of the German position in this central sector between Caumont and Vire were ended by the advance of the British VIII Corps from Caumont.

Caumont is the closest Normandy can offer to a hill town. Perched on a high spur, it offers commanding views over the surrounding countryside, most of which, even today, sixty years after the battle, is the worst form of *bocage*. South of Caumont, the small field and high hedgerow pattern, typical of the Norman *bocage*, is reinforced by woods, steep-sided valleys and hills. There are even fewer roads than usual and only one led south; otherwise the narrow lanes south of Caumont link up small villages which the Germans had long since turned into fortresses.

These villages were occupied by the 276th and 326th Infantry Divisions with 21 Panzer in close support; add a great quantity of mines, many laid by the Americans when they were in this sector, throw in a good number of *nebelwerfer* mortars and machine-guns, add a few Tiger tanks and *jagdpanthers*, and the country below Caumont can be imagined as a very formidable obstacle indeed. The ground between Caumont and Mont Pinçon undulates like a green sea in a heavy swell, each undulation a perfect defensive position. The claim in the US Official History[7] that 'only the bombed and inexperienced 326th Infantry Division stood in the way' of the Bluecoat attack would seem to be incorrect.

The Germans had defied eviction from this sector by the US V Corps for the last seven weeks and stiffened their defences considerably in the process. General Dempsey had allocated six divisions of XXX Corps and VIII Corps for this Bluecoat operation; the 43rd (Wessex), 50th (Northumbrian), and 15th (Scottish) Infantry Divisions plus 11th Armoured, 7th Armoured and Guards Armoured. These last two armoured divisions would be in reserve, ready to exploit forward when the chance arose; because of the terrain, the first part of Operation Bluecoat was primarily an infantry operation.

The task of XXX Corps and VIII Corps during Bluecoat was to strike south and overrun the country between the Vire and the Orne with the aim of preventing the Germans using the main feature, the Mont Pinçon ridge, either as a bastion in their next defence line or as the hinge for a withdrawal across the Orne. Standing at the westward end of a long, wooded ridge, Mont Pinçon is ideally suited for that purpose. An examination of the planning for Bluecoat indicates that the Allied armies were finally starting to get the hang of this *bocage* fighting. Most of the artillery concentrations fired would use air-burst shells, since the *bocage* banks and hedges absorbed the effects of ground-bursting ordnance.

The British Official History[8] also comments that the 11th Armoured and 7th Armoured Divisions, 'mindful of their experience of the *bocage* during the Odon battle', had reorganised their two armoured brigades (they also had a brigade of lorried infantry), so as to provide each armoured brigade with an equal number of tank and infantry units.

This was a wise if somewhat belated move. Close tank and infantry co-operation, while always desirable, was doubly so in the close country of the Normandy *bocage*. The tanks had to help the infantry against the enemy strongpoints and machine-gun posts, the infantry had to protect the tanks against anti-tank guns, from well-concealed infantry armed with *panzerfausts* or from snipers who could pick off the tank commanders in their turrets. Operating 'with the lid down' was not possible in the *bocage*; the tank commanders had to stand up in their turrets to see the way forward and were extremely vulnerable to snipers while doing so.

This close infantry co-operation also enabled the tank commanders to be more adventurous and thrusting; many, especially those accustomed to the open deserts of North Africa, had at first found the *bocage* fighting unnerving, and progress in the narrow lanes all but impossible. Once assured that they were not forging forward to become 'Tiger fodder', that their flanks were being protected and that the infantry were in close support to deal with snipers and *panzerfausts*, the tank commanders were willing to push ahead and engage the enemy.

The initial attack would be supported by the usual opening deluge from Bomber Command and the tactical air forces, but the fighter-bombers and rocket-firing 'Tiffies' (RAF Typhoons) would be kept in 'cab-ranks', flying above the advancing troops and on call, ready to deal with any precisely located target. Hosing a leafy area with fire and rockets – and hoping for the best – was no longer seen as best practice since it led to too many 'friendly fire' incidents. The infantry divisions, which had recently taken part in the Odon battles, were pretty tired but by July 29 everyone was in position and at 0600hrs on July 30, Operation Bluecoat began. 'Almost everywhere,' says the Official History 'the troops were met by heavy fire as they began moving forward but their biggest trouble at the outset was with minefields.'

A study of the map on page 291 will be helpful at this point. The basic plan for Bluecoat called for an attack on a narrow front, with XXX Corps swinging south and east to a line between Villers-Bocage and Aunay-sur-Odon, while VIII Corps swung out through Beny-Bocage towards Vire and Tinchebrae. Once there, the general thrust was towards Mont Pinçon where the two attacking corps would link up with XII Corps. XXX Corps duly advanced, the 43rd Division attacking another hill, Point 361, west of Jurques, while 50th Division went for the high ground west of Villers-Bocage. Trouble began at Briquessard, two miles east of Caumont, which was stoutly defended by tanks and infantry and well protected by mines. The 130th Brigade of 43rd Division took Briquessard by noon but XXX Corps made little further progress through the minefields that day, hampered by a stout German defence of every house and hedgerow.

An example of what the troops were up against comes from the experience of the 6th Guards Tank Brigade on the first day of Bluecoat. Having advanced, they were deployed about Point 226, and ordered to hold the hamlet of Les Loges 'at all costs'. At around 1800hrs, the Guards' tanks had just been joined by a company of infantry and were digging-in for the night when heavy and accurate mortar and shellfire fell on their positions from somewhere in their rear. This in itself was alarming; within minutes six Churchill tanks were in flames and enemy fire was coming in from all directions. Then three German tanks, 45-ton *jagdpanthers*, each mounting an 88mm gun, rumbled into the village and began to rake the British position with machine-gun fire and solid shot.

More Churchill tanks went up in flames but the *jagdpanthers* were alone and in the face of stout resistance from the Guards' tanks and infantry they eventually withdrew, two being found later that day with their tracks shot away. There were still plenty of snipers about and mopping-up the Les Loges position took up most of the night. By midnight, a brigade of the 15th (Scottish) Division had come up in support and deployed their anti-tank guns forward of Les Loges to secure the position. It had been a close-run thing and strong German tank and infantry counter-attacks were to become a regular feature of the Bluecoat battle.

Leonard Watson was with the 15th Scottish Reconnaissance Regiment:[9]

One of the many actions we were involved in was Bluecoat, the Caumont breakout. The 15th Scottish had moved secretly to Caumont and we were well briefed for this operation with a bomber force to start the offensive provided the weather was good enough. I remember a Lancaster bomber appearing through a gap in the clouds and a huge cheer going up as we thought our task would be easier. We could plainly see the bombs being dropped in front of us on Villers-Bocage, which was well demolished when we drove through it.

Sergeant Knibbs gave us a nip from his hip flask as we drove down the hill through standing crops and backing out of a field labelled 'Minefield'. At another hedgerow I recall our Sergeant firing at the glass of a German artillery telescope and this hedgerow had been planted to look like the real thing, with deep trenches from which we soon extracted five prisoners; one had a gold watch which we liberated before handing them over to the Seaforth Highlanders.

Shortly after that I was knocked flat on my face by a sniper's bullet which hit the rim of my helmet. I could hardly believe this until I took off the helmet and found part of the bullet still in the rim. Fortunately our helmets were of the type that came lower down than the infantry type but I still had a terrible headache. We were mortared by Moaning Minnies, and soon learned how effective German Spandau fire could be. Our carrier caught fire, another lost a track and the driver was wounded, so we soon learned that a slit trench was essential. Sgt Knibbs was badly wounded on his birthday along with Cpl Chapman, Cpl Frost, Trooper Baker and Trooper Johnson. I still wonder what happened to that Scottish infantry officer we saw that day, being supported by two of his men, his legs shattered by a mine.

Doug Peterson was a Lieutenant in 'B' Squadron of the 15th Scottish Reconnaissance Regiment:[10]

Bluecoat was my baptism of fire and my orders were to carry out a simple recce from Caumont to the village of Bremoy and find out if it was still occupied by the enemy. The day started well enough and we soon experienced the strange silence of No Man's Land and crossed a fairly open piece of ground to reach a small wood. We passed a wrecked Daimler armoured car where first-aid equipment and bloodstains indicated a casualty among the crew but eventually reached high ground where it should be possible to look down on Bremoy. The crest was reached, the leading carrier halted as ordered and then moved forward for some reason, but no more than a length. I was dismounting from my carrier, intending to walk forward when there was a shattering explosion.

The lead carrier rocked to a halt, having run over a mine hidden in the brushwood; the crew suffered shock and ruptured ear-drums and careful inspection revealed another mine and by now we were under intermittent mortaring from somewhere on our right. Observation from the hill failed to reveal any signs of enemy activity in the village but I had to be sure so I took a foot patrol down into the village where the only inhabitant was an elderly woman, chopping wood and clearly as mad as a hatter. We then returned to the carriers and sent the signal, 'Bremoy unoccupied'. This event played no particular part in the campaign but on reflection I was satisfied that I had been tested as had the members of the Troop and we had learned a great deal, something that stood us in good stead in the testing days ahead.

Reg Spittle of the 2nd Northamptonshire Yeomany describes the Bluecoat battle:[11]

> Bluecoat was not like the other offensives, which lasted just a few days; Bluecoat went on for weeks, a real grinding battle with the circumstances changing day by day, hour by hour sometimes. We in the 2nd Yeomanry in our Cromwells were the odd job lads of 11th Armoured, always pushing forward. Only the 3rd RTR had been in the desert and a lot of us were still curious about the battle and had a lot to learn about dying.
>
> We had a good start at Bluecoat for the Germans appeared to be pulling out and we chased them back. Then we got down to the Vire to Caen road and then it got harder. We were on the right flank of 11th Armoured with no infantry support, just our 60 or 70 tanks rolling along. We should have had the Americans on our right flank but there was no sign of them – all we had on our right flank was the Germans.

The British VIII Corps had got along better on July 30, moving astride the road to Beny-Bocage, but when they got there on the following day here too resistance began to stiffen, elements of 21 Panzer and the 352nd Division appearing on their front at St-Martin-des-Besaces. From then until August 3, Operation Bluecoat became a slogging match, most expensive in tanks and lives but successful in strategy. By August 3, 9 SS Panzer and 10 SS Panzer had been brought over from the east in an attempt to stem the grinding forward progress of the two British corps but the Germans were always aggressive in defence and charged a heavy price for any ground given up. These German soldiers did not merely hold a position and defy eviction. Their response to any attack was a counter-attack from infantry and armour; this procedure made the British advance expensive, but did not stop it.

On August 1, the 11th Armoured Division of VIII Corps took Beny-Bocage and Guards Armoured Division battered its way towards Estry. XXX Corps then sent 7th Armoured Division against Aunay-sur-Odon and 50th Division. made ground towards Villers-Bocage. On August 2, 50th Division took Amaye and pressed on up the valley of the river Seulles. VIII Corps were then engaged in a hard battle on the outskirts of Vire where the 2nd Armoured Division fought a stiff engagement against enemy tanks and infantry. Over that ground, against such resolute opposition, progress was inevitably slow but in the context of the strategic objective of Bluecoat, that did not matter.

The British aim was to keep German attention fixed, however reluctantly, on the retention of Mont Pinçon while the Americans flooded out through the side door into Brittany and towards the Loire. Even so, Montgomery decided that this grinding progress called for some changes in command and a desert war veteran, Lt General Sir Brian Horrocks, replaced Bucknall in command of XXX Corps.

The increase in enemy strength as more Panzer divisions arrived on the Bluecoat front was then countered by the commitment of the 53rd and 59th Divisions of XII Corps, which struck south towards Noyers and the Villers-Bocage road, which they crossed on August 4. Further east, the armoured car regiments of the tank divisions were battling through the *Suisse Normande* along the floor of the Orne valley towards Grimbosq and Thury-Harcourt. With three British corps now engaged against a strong German opposition fighting in ideal defensive country, the battle on the Second Army front settled down yet again to a grinding process of attrition.

Montgomery's account of the Bluecoat battle comments:[12] 'The (German) front began to firm up between Aunay-sur-Odon and Vire. Desperate resistance continued between these two places because it was vital for the enemy to hold firm in this sector while his forces to the south-west swung back.'

Montgomery then goes on to make some shrewd guesses about the current German dilemma. It was tacitly assumed on the Allied side that after the St-Lô breakout the Germans would withdraw their forces to somewhere east of the Orne and form a new defence line in the east. This assumption was made by professional soldiers – and no one on the Allied side disputed it – because it made professional sense. If the German forces could regroup behind the Orne, Seventh Army and Panzer Group West would be buttressed by Fifteenth Army and could then conduct an orderly withdrawal to the Seine. As Montgomery comments: 'From a strictly military point of view he (the enemy) was now placed in a situation in which the only logical answer was a staged withdrawal to the Seine.' A glance at the map will reveal the sense of Monty's assessment but the illogical factor here was Adolf Hitler.

The Seventh Army, though supported by Panzer Group West, was in an increasingly untenable position in the first days of August. There were now four Allied armies in Normandy and the superb quality of German troops and tanks would be increasingly negated by the crushing effect of superior numbers, by the loss of the defensive bonus provided by the *bocage* and by Allied air power which would grow even more fearsome once the protection of the *bocage* was removed. By August 7, there were thirty-seven squadrons of the Second Tactical Air Force in France, operating from eleven airfields, and the Ninth US Air Force was equally well placed. The Germans had fought a very good fight in Normandy for the last two months but they could not reasonably expect to fight there much longer.

The wild card in this assessment was Adolf Hitler. Retreat, even *'reculer pour mieux sauter'*– stepping back the better to jump forward – was anathema to Adolf Hitler and this attitude presented the Allied armies with a further opportunity. If Hitler ordered his soldiers to fight on there was every chance that the Allied armies could cut off and destroy the four German divisions in Brittany and – with any luck – most of the German forces in Normandy west of the Seine as well. This fate was almost inevitable for the Seventh Army; with the British and Canadians coming down from the north, the US First Army about to swing round and come in from the west and Patton about to start bustling along the Loire to the south, the Seventh Army divisions were gradually being forced into a pocket.

The German line might have been broken at Caen – the first proposed hinge for the Allied line in Normandy. That hinge had held for a long time but the failure to take Caen until early July was no great loss as long as its retention forced the enemy to commit troops there. The next hinge was at Caumont and that had now been broken. Then came a possible German hinge at Mont Pinçon; if that could be broken, the German forces west of there must fall back or be taken in the flank and rear. The resulting scramble would allow the Americans to press forward with greater speed on a line from Avranches through Mortain towards Argentan and the Seine. What the Germans must not be allowed to do was to hang on to Mont Pinçon and use that as the hinge on which their forces facing the Americans could swing back east in an orderly fashion.

To prevent such a move – at whatever cost – the British forces pressed on across the *bocage* towards the slopes of Mont Pinçon. The advance continued and success came, but slowly. On August 5, tanks of the British 11th Armoured Division were on the high ground north-east of Vire, the 43rd Infantry Division were moving up towards Mont Pinçon and the 7th Armoured Division, which had made a slow start in this battle, entered Aunay-sur-Odon on the afternoon of August 5 and sent tanks towards Thury-Harcourt, deep in the *Suisse*

Normande where the British XII Corps were sweeping up to the Forêt de Grim-bosq. The main delay now was caused by the terrible state of the roads through the *Suisse Normande* which had been cratered by air attacks and had verges thickly mined by the retreating Germans.

Sydney Jary fought at Mont Pinçon as a platoon commander with the 4th Bn The Somerset Light Infantry:[13]

August 6 was Bank Holiday Monday and my first battle in command of 18 Platoon. The battalion 'O' Group was at 1230 hrs and we were to attack this rugged hill from the West with the 5th Wiltshires on our right and the 4th Wiltshires on our left. We were due to attack at 1500 hrs with 'A' Company leading on the right and 'B' Company on the left. We followed 'B' Company. The ground before us descended to a small stream at the foot of Mont Pinçon and then rose steeply through typical *bocage* fields with thick hedgerows to a thickly wooded area. Inspection through binoculars failed to reveal the existence of any Germans.

'B' Company moved off quickly with our Company deployed about 300 yards behind. Their forward platoons had barely crossed the stream when concentrated Spandau fire came from the front and from both flanks. There must have been about 12 machine-guns firing on them at one time and this devastating display of firepower stopped the battalion in its tracks. There was no way forward or to the flanks and no way to retire. Some of the guns engaged 'D' Company over the heads of 'B' and one of my men, Private Morris, was killed.

Powerless and crouching in a hedgerow, I tried to identify the Spandau positions. This proved impossible as they kept up this crushing display of firepower. In my ignorance I expected that they would soon expend all their ammunition but they did not. Nor did they do so in many subsequent battles.

Captain Scammell commanding 'A' Company was killed and Major Thomas commanding 'B' Company was severely wounded and their companies were badly cut up. On our right the 5th Wiltshires did no better and with their CO killed and casualties mounting their attack faltered. As the afternoon turned to evening, shelling and mortaring increased, much of it passing over our heads to isolate us from the reserve battalion. Shortly before dark some tanks arrived, one of which crossed the stream and gave us some brave support but it was not enough to get the attack moving again.

Any movement to our front brought down instant and concentrated Spandau fire; fortunately the enemy did not seem to have any anti-tanks guns so our armoured friends were comparatively safe; the fact remains that about twelve Spandaus had halted a battalion attack without our locating even one of them. As dusk fell a new plan was made. 'C' and 'D' Companies would advance through 'A' and 'B' Companies and using the cover of darkness, infiltrate the enemy position, climb to the top of the hill and consolidate.

Not a shot was fired. By some miracle we passed right through their position without being detected. Our luck had changed. Up the hill we scrambled, through the trees to the rocky gorse-covered summit. German voices could be heard in the mist, calling to each other unawares that we were now the kings of the castle.

On that day, August 6, two infantry brigades of the 43rd Division supported by tanks of the 13th/18th Hussars finally gained a foothold on Mont Pinçon after a hard advance from Ondefontaine and as described, later that day, aided by a squadron of tanks of the 13/18th Hussars which had found a passable uphill track through the woods, the infantry pushed up to the top of the hill. One of those taking part was Patrick Hennessey, a tank commander in the 13th/18th Hussars:[14]

We pressed on south, against heavy opposition and came at last to Mont Pinçon, a hill around 1,200ft high which dominated the surrounding area and gave the Germans a great tactical advantage. Naturally, they wanted to hang on to it and the capture of Mont Pinçon became a priority. The task was given to the 5th Bn The Wiltshire Regiment, with 'A' Squadron, 13th/18th Hussars in support.

On August 6 we fought our way across to the foot of the hill, against heavy machine-gun and mortar fire that took a toll of our infantry. The day was hot and sultry, full of dust and the stench of dead cattle and every movement stirred up more dust which brought down more enemy fire and curses from the infantry who were in their shallow slit trenches, waiting for the order to cross the river and climb the steep scarp. The sappers were working to clear the mines from the bridge under cover of a smokescreen – and a lot of enemy fire. Eventually the bridge was clear and we went across, the 13th/18th tanks followed by the infantry. We were half-way across when the enemy came to life again with machine guns and mortars, catching our infantry in the open.

Within two minutes the leading companies of the 5th Wilts had been practically wiped out. The Commanding Officer of the 5th Wilts came forward to rally them but was quickly killed and the attack petered out, though we were now on the far side of the river, at the base of the hill. It seemed impossibly steep, covered with bushes and scrub and we milled around in our tanks, dealing with pockets of enemy infantry until, at around 1800hrs, we spotted a track that looked as if it might lead up the hill. I reported this over the radio and we were told to press on upwards as quickly as possible. Two tank Troops under Captain Noel Denny went crashing uphill along this narrow path, with a high bank on our right and a steep drop on our left. Sergeant Rattle's tank slithered into a quarry and almost overturned but we kept going.

It was a good hell-for-leather cavalry action and we reached the top and surprised the few Germans we found there, chasing them away and going into all-round defence. We felt pretty lonely up there, just seven or eight tanks with no infantry support as yet but then a mist came down and although we could not see very far we could hear the Germans near by. Fortunately, the infantry then arrived to consolidate the position and we were very glad to see them. They had been in action all day and were absolutely exhausted by the time they reached the top of the hill.

Only seven tanks made it to the top of Mont Pinçon and infantry losses were severe – the 5th Wilts, for example, being reduced to less than 100 men – but by the evening of August 6 Mont Pinçon had been taken; any chance of the Seventh Army using this feature as the hinge of their withdrawal from the west of Normandy had vanished.

George Treloar was a gunner in 'B' Squadron, 13/18th Hussars, during the attack on Mont Pinçon:[15]

I recall firing our machine-guns and the enemy putting up flares to find us but we got to the top on our own and one man from each tank had to get out and act as infantry in the hedgerow and while lying there I remember hearing the Germans talking. Finally the infantry came up, the Wiltshires having lost a company of men that day by the river.

In the morning Lt Aldam tried to shoot at a church spire which he said was a German OP bringing fire on us and killing our infantry but after twelve shots he had not hit it so I asked if I could have a go. I set the crosswires in the corner of the tower of the church, put HE in the breech and fired, the spire came crashing down and a great cheer went up from the boys.

On August 6 10 SS Panzer mounted a strong counter-attack against the British advance between Vire and Mont Pinçon. This attack drove 11th Armoured back a mile or so. Then the division rallied, the ground lost was quickly retaken and on this day, with the taking of Mont Pinçon, the balance finally tilted against the German forces south of Caumont. From then on a general and quickening advance began, south and south-east towards the Vire–Condé-sur-Noireau road, and the Orne valley. Guards Armoured were heavily engaged but moving forward at le Busq and Estry, and 59th Division of XII Corps had crossed the Orne at Grimbosq, south-east of the shattered town of Villers-Bocage. Much of the fighting took place in the *Suisse Normande,* where steep hillsides, woods, flooded streams and small villages and hamlets strengthened the German defensive positions. Even so, the British attack pressed on relentlessly, the line shifting south towards more open country.

The Germans still clung on to the far slopes of Mont Pinçon on the night of August 6 but by the morning of August 7 a strong force of British tanks and infantry had been assembled on the hill. Advancing under cover of the morning fog, they were able to clear the far slope of the hill and advance towards the Vire–Condé road, seven miles to the south. This success did not mean the end of Bluecoat and the fighting continued. The divisions of VIII Corps were engaged by 10 SS Panzer on the Périers ridge, just north of the Vire road and held there, with 9 SS Panzer on their left flank closely engaged with Guards Armoured.

The British armour was fighting well and the two German Panzer thrusts were thrown back on August 7, having gained no ground. The skies now cleared and hundreds of Allied fighter-bombers ranged the skies south of Caumont, striking at any enemy movement on the ground. All was going well, the western end of the German line was in disarray and it looked as if Seventh Army would soon be either ground into dust or put 'into the bag' if this southward thrust from Caumont could cut the German line of retreat towards the Seine. Then, on that day of August 7, when all was going well but before the trap could be closed, the Germans struck back hard, at Mortain.

14 BRITTANY AND FALAISE AUGUST 1-10

*Along the whole front now held by the First Canadian and Second British
Armies it is essential that the enemy be attacked to the greatest degree possible*

DIRECTIVE FROM GENERAL MONTGOMERY Commander, 21st Army Group, July 27 1944.

Before moving on to the German counter-attack at Mortain on August 6 it is
necessary to go back briefly to the end of July and cover the progress of the US
armies after Cobra. In this period – late July and early August – two new armies
took the field and there were some changes in the command structure. On July
23 the Canadian First Army under Lt General H. D. G. (Harry) Crerar became
fully operational. On August 1 the US Third Army under Lt General George
Patton entered the fray and with two US armies in Normandy, the US 12th
Army Group was activated under General Omar Bradley.

Canada had provided a notable contingent to the British Second Army since
the start of the Normandy campaign. The 3rd Canadian Infantry Division had
gone ashore on Juno beach and struck out for Carpiquet on D-Day, after which
this rugged and hard fighting division had taken part in all the battles of I British
Corps. As more Canadian units arrived, the Canadian element expanded, first
to corps level for the Spring offensive and finally, on July 23, to army level under
Crerar. General Crerar had established his headquarters at Amblie in Normandy
on June 18, just before the Great Storm. After that the chronic delay in building up the Allied forces inhibited the formation of the Canadian Army which
Crerar had been awaiting for some time but now this army was ready to take
the field.

Canadian servicemen had been fighting in the European theatre for years, manning convoy escorts of the Royal Canadian Navy in the North Atlantic and providing an entire Group – 6 Group, RCAF – to RAF Bomber Command. Canada had sent many fine units to the British Army in Italy and the 2nd Canadian Division had provided the main landing force for the ill-fated Dieppe raid in August 1942.

Les Wager of the 1st Bn The Queen's Own Rifles of Canada describes his personal motivation:[1]

> Until late in 1944 every Canadian soldier you saw overseas was an unconscripted volunteer. Whatever his personal rationalisation for going to war, that Canuck was there because he chose to be there. As to what made me go to fight in a 'European' War, that is an American idea, not a Canadian one. We never had a revolution, our ties with Britain were facts of heritage and history that we never dreamed of turning our backs on. Hitler was a menace to the world and that heritage and history were his victims, however far from our own peaceful country they lay.

General Crerar had led the Ist Canadian Corps in Italy. Crerar was a calm, competent and experienced commander who enjoyed the support of another Canadian, Lt General Guy Simonds, who was rated, correctly, as one of the best corps commanders in any of the Allied armies. Simonds was to command the II Canadian Corps in Normandy where he displayed considerable talent in the handling of troops and the conduct of battle and Crerar, who was steady rather than brilliant, was lucky to have him.

General George Patton was a rather more problematic character. The oldest of the Allied generals, born in California in 1885, Patton was commissioned in 1909 into the 15th Cavalry Regiment. He served on the Mexican border in Pershing's expedition into Mexico against the bandit Pancho Villa in 1916 and went to France in 1917 as a member of Pershing's staff, transferring on arrival to the newly formed Tank Corps. The Great War ended before he could see much service but Patton had meanwhile become a tank devotee. Although he went back to the cavalry when the US tank units were disbanded in 1920 he returned to armour as soon as those units were reformed in 1940.

Patton entered the Second World War with the Torch operation in North Africa, where, newly promoted to major general – from colonel – under Eisenhower, he took command of the Western Task Force. This force went ashore on November 8, 1942, but within three days the Vichy French had capitulated and Patton spent the next few months as the Military Governor of Morocco, a political appointment and one not to his taste.

George Patton wanted action. His chance came at last in March 1943 when he was given command of the US II Corps which had just been badly mauled by the Germans at the Kasserine Pass. Patton got a firm grip on the II Corps and at their next encounter on March 23, his troops fought the enemy to a standstill. As a result, Eisenhower gave Patton command of the Seventh Army for the invasion of Sicily where Patton led another storming advance – and fell out badly with the British commander in Sicily, Bernard Montgomery.

Things were going well for George Patton in 1943 when suddenly it all went wrong. When visiting a military hospital, Patton elected to slap a shell-shocked young soldier about the face and accuse him of cowardice. For an officer to strike an enlisted man was a court-martial offence in any army and there was no excuse for it, but 'battle fatigue' was not an ailment George Patton recognised. When news of this incident got into the press – and some accounts allege it happened more than once – there was a storm of protest. Patton was threatened with court-martial, obliged to apologise to his troops and only saved from total disgrace by Eisenhower's personal intervention. Eisenhower decided that an Army command was about Patton's limit and when the time came to form up for Overlord, command of the US forces for the initial assault and then of the US 12th Army Group went to Lt General Omar Bradley, who had been one of Patton's corps commanders in Italy.

Patton put his foot in it again in April 1944, making a speech in Britain declaring that after the war the United States and Britain should dominate the world. This speech was widely reported, gave great offence to the Russians and was deeply regretted by Patton's political masters. Once again, Eisenhower had to intervene but he kept Patton around and gave him the Third Army because Patton was known to be a 'thruster', a general who would drive his men on, whatever the cost; none of the Allied armies had too many of these.

As with Montgomery, George Patton's problem lay in his character. Patton was a war-lover, arrogant and tactless, barely controllable by his superiors, hardly in control of himself, the epitome of the 'gung-ho', fighting American general, a latter-day Custer. This was the image Patton loved to portray; he was never seen without his steel helmet and his pearl-handled revolver, always ready for action although, by comparison with his detested rival, Bernard Montgomery, George Patton had not actually seen much action.

This may have been part of the reason for Patton's deep and open dislike of Monty. By September 1944, without counting active service on the North-west Frontier of India and in Palestine, Montgomery had had nine years of front-line service in two world wars, in every rank from second lieutenant to field marshal. All the American generals put together could not match this experience and Patton for one resented it.

Apart from his personal failings, some of those who knew Patton well had no great faith in his military abilities. Bradley was less than enchanted to have Patton commanding the Third Army in 12th Army Group and admitted as much after the war, writing: 'He (Patton) had not been my choice for army commander and I was still wary of the grace with which he would accept the reversal of our roles. I was apprehensive in having George join my command for I feared that too much time would be spent curbing his impetuous habits.' Bradley, ever honest, went on to say that Patton had proved a stalwart support in the field.

Nor was Patton wildly popular with his soldiers. American generals tend to have nicknames but Patton's army nickname, 'Old Blood and Guts' attracted the wry comment from Third Army soldiers, 'Yeah, his guts ... our blood'. On this point Jack Capell of the 4th Infantry Division writes:

> When we became part of Third Army later in the war we heard this rumour that Patton had actually swum across the Saar river to get at the enemy. I never met anyone who saw this feat which was probably the invention of Patton's fertile publicity machine. We in the 4th Division were not admirers of General Patton. He was an accomplished battlefield commander but more reckless with the lives of his troops than other generals we had served with.

Patton's never-abundant stock of modesty and humour was also sorely taxed by the baiting he had to endure from the US Army ETO cartoonist, Sergeant Bill Mauldin, whose drawings in the US Army newspaper, *Stars and Stripes*, drove Patton frantic and all the more so since Mauldin's cartoons were extremely popular with the troops and Patton could not put a stop to them.

Patton did have one gift that all front-line generals require; he was lucky.

Luck is an important asset for any general but was particularly important in Patton's case for Patton took chances. Given the chance he would press on, regardless of cost or the extent of the opposition, with considerable speed and energy. The quiet and retiring Bradley made good use of Patton's energy – a critic might call it recklessness – and to a certain extent the two men complemented each other, Patton supplying the speed, Bradley the weight.

Patton's army had been gradually assembling in the Cotentin during July but Patton's involvement had been carefully concealed to maintain the Fortitude deception as long as possible. As related, the first elements of the Third Army to arrive, Middleton's VIII Corps and the 90th Division, had been attached to the First Army for operations. Now VIII Corps would spearhead the American breakout into Brittany, tasked to take Rennes and the vital ports of St-Malo and Brest, while the rest of Third Army came on behind and headed for the Loire.

This chapter will look at two moves in early August, advances which took place on the extreme flanks of the Allied front in Normandy; the American VIII Corps advance into Brittany and the thrust by Simonds's II Canadian Corps down the road to Falaise – Operation Totalize. Previous Canadian actions with Second Army have been covered in earlier chapters; the only point to be remembered at this time, early August, 1944, is that the components of the Canadian First and British Second Armies were to some extent interchangeable.

For example, II Canadian Corps came under the command of Second Army after the fall of Caen and served with the Second Army during Operations Charnwood, Goodwood and Atlantic – the final taking of Caen. With the establishment of a full Canadian Army, the I (British) Corps under Lt General J. T. Crocker became an integral part of the Canadian First Army and – as the Canadian Official History comments[2] – when headquarters, Canadian First Army, became operational in July 1944, it had no Canadian divisions under its command at all.

About half the troops in the Canadian First Army would always be British and another significant element in the Canadian Army was the 1st Polish Armoured Division, which joined in August. Therefore, when Crerar took over his new army on July 23, his first task was a visit to Crocker on the following day. Their association began badly, with Crocker flatly refusing to carry out the orders Crerar had sent him on July 22.

These orders anticipated the establishment of the Canadian Army and concluded that the 'immediate task' of I Corps was to gain possession of the road
that runs south and east of Caen from Bréville through Le Marais to Le Petit
Homme. The aim of this task was to remove the chronic problem of German
artillery fire falling on the little port of Ouistreham. Crocker was extremely dismissive of this proposal which, he said, would cost him up to 600 casualties
and the operation was, in his opinion, 'not on'.[3] Further discussion failed to
change Crocker's mind and General Crerar was well within his rights when he
asked Montgomery to replace Crocker with some more-biddable corps commander.

Montgomery was not over-endowed with competent corps commanders in
Normandy and reluctant to replace one who – whatever his faults – knew how
to command men in battle. Writing to Alan Brooke on this affair, Monty said:

> He (Crerar) had a row with Crocker the first day and asked me to remove him.
> I have spent two days trying to restore peace, investigating the quarrel and so
> on. As always, there are faults on both sides but the basic cause was Harry; I
> fear he thinks he is a great soldier and was determined to show it the moment
> he took over command at 1200hrs on 23 July. He made his first mistake at
> 1205hrs and his second after lunch. I have had both of them to see me and
> I now hope I can get on with fighting the Germans instead of stopping the
> generals fighting among themselves.

This letter shows an altogether pleasanter, gently humorous side of Montgomery's character. Monty managed to smooth the matter over and it is worth
recording that Crerar and Crocker went on to establish a good working relationship and ended the war together, and as friends. Montgomery clearly had
a quiet word with Crocker, pointing out that Crerar was his army commander
and had to be obeyed. The two men then had another meeting and ironed out
their differences before Montgomery's directive M 515 of July 27, following the
Cobra attack, landed on Crerar's desk. This stated (Point 4):

> Along the whole front now held by First Canadian and Second British Armies,
> the enemy must be attacked to the greatest degree possible with the resources
> available. He must be worried, and shot-up and attacked and raided, whenever
> and wherever possible. The object of such activity will be to improve our own

position, to gain ground, to prevent the enemy from transferring forces across to the western flank to oppose the American advance and generally to write-off German personnel and equipment.

This sounds very like the aims for Goodwood. The immediate task of the Canadian Army was to hold as many German troops as possible on their front while the US V Corps moved on Vire and the British Second Army fought their way south from Caumont in Operation Bluecoat; these actions have been described in the previous chapter. On July 29, Crerar elected to provide this support with an attack down the axis Caen–Falaise road, with the objective of taking Falaise; Operation Totalize.

This thrust south would be made by Lt General Guy Simonds's II Canadian Corps, with the 51st Highland Division and the 33rd British Armoured Brigade from I Corps under command, joined later by the 1st Polish Armoured Division. During Totalize, Crocker's I (British) Corps would attack towards Vimont, to cover the left flank of II Canadian Corps as it made for Falaise. These attacks were to go in as soon as possible and not later than August 8.

The demands of Bluecoat for artillery ammunition then prevented the launching of this attack but it was decided to 'blood' the newly arrived 4th Canadian Armoured Division – in effect to give it some battle experience – by committing it to another attack on the little town of Tilly-la-Campagne, which was held by units of 9 SS Panzer. The fighting around Tilly and St-Martin-de-Fontenay went on until the afternoon of August 5 when the Canadian forces, from the 2nd Canadian Infantry Division as well as from 4th Armoured, were eventually driven back. Meanwhile, General Simonds was proceeding with his plans for the II Canadian Corps attack towards Falaise.

Norman Richardson of the 4th Canadian Field Artillery took part in this attack:[4]

The Army Service Corps brought up ammunition for two days before the attack dropping off cases of 105mm ammunition at each gun position and bringing in more all the time. The barrage started at 0815 hrs and lasted for more than three hours after which we fired on targets called in by FOOs (forward observation officers) who were with the infantry. In all we fired fairly steadily for about six hours.

As we moved to our next position I saw my first dead Canadian soldier. By this time I had seen many dead Germans but the sight of that dead Canadian was a shock. Unfortunately this sight was so frequently repeated afterwards that I have forgotten most of the others though it was always grim; I will never forget the first one though.

This forward position was on a forward slope overlooking Tilly-la-Campagne and it was not a peaceful place. Jerry had no trouble spotting our guns when we fired and shelling by Jerry was frequent as were visits at night by Jerry bombers dropping anti-personnel bombs. One day an infantry platoon that had been in support came through and stopped with us for a chat and a smoke. As they arrived Jerry threw over a few shells and strangely, the infantry said they did not know how we stood this sort of thing and they wanted to get back to the front line where they did not have to take so much shelling. On the other hand we always admired the guts of the infantry who were up where that killing fire – small arms fire – was more prevalent. I guess it is a question of what you get used to.

Simonds knew that an advance towards Falaise would be difficult. Not only was the ground favourable to the defence the enemy had been improving his defences for weeks and had demonstrated just how strong his defence lines were during Operation Goodwood. Simonds therefore told Crerar that for Totalize he would need another infantry division, another armoured division, and total air support from 2nd TAF for about forty-eight hours; hence the addition of troops from I Corps and the newly arrived Poles. With such assets Simonds believed that the attack on Falaise – Operation Totalize – though tough, could still achieve worthwhile results and D-Day for Totalize was therefore fixed for Monday, August 7.

Before following the fortunes of the Canadian Army on Totalize, we must now move to the western end of the Allied line and catch up with the progress of events in Bradley's newly established US 12th Army Group. The situation as August opened was that the German front had crumbled and the US forces were trying to keep the enemy on the run, pushing south towards the Loire, the US First Army forcing the Seventh Army back from the foot on the Cotentin, and allowing Patton's Third Army to push south towards the Loire and debouch into Brittany with VIII Corps.

Bob Sales was in this advance into Brittany with the 29th Infantry:[5]

When St-Lô fell we were given a short rest. Then the 2nd, 8th and 29th Divisions were sent to swing down to the Brittany peninsula. This was slow fighting all the way to Brest and Brest was at the far end of that peninsula and it took us a long time to clear it. Brest was a submarine base but the Americans wanted Brest for its port but Hitler had taken the troops there to fight to the death and it took us a month or so to take Brest.

In the initial plan, it had been thought that the reduction of German forces in Brittany would take several corps or even the entire resources of Third Army. Now it appeared that the German forces in Brittany had been much reduced because many German units had been sent east to join the fighting in Normandy – an excellent example of how the demands of battle can change previously laid plans, although in this case to the Allied advantage.

On the afternoon of August 1, General Wood's 4th US Armored Division of Middleton's VIII Corps, Third Army, began moving on Rennes. The 4th Armored Division made forty miles that afternoon and it soon became evident that a single corps would be sufficient for Brittany. This left the rest of Patton's army free for operations elsewhere. The US Official History states[6]: 'It had long been planned to turn the VIII Corps westward into Brittany as soon as the Americans reached the base of the Cotentin at Avranches'. VIII Corps were to 'precede other units of Third Army which would clear the whole of the Brittany Peninsula'. Now it appeared that VIII Corps could manage this task on its own.

The German forces west of the Vire, reduced to around 16,000 men with a small quantity of tanks, were now in full retreat, broken into scattered groups and in no state to resist a strong push by the VII Corps towards Villedieu-les-Poêles, a town east of Granville. Even so, the American advance was not fast enough for General Collins and he brought forward his two best and favourite divisional commanders, Generals Huebner of the 1st Infantry Division and Barton of the 4th Infantry, to get a grip on the advancing units and keep VII Corps moving.

This achieved the desired result. By August 1, one week after the opening of Cobra, VII Corps were at the base of the Cotentin, having advanced nearly thirty miles since they crossed the St-Lô–Périers road on July 25 – a rapid advance in Normandy terms. VII Corps had now outflanked the left of Seventh Army and had only to turn east and commence rolling towards the Seine while Patton sent his troops west into Brittany and south towards the Loire.

The spearhead of this last move was made by Middleton's VIII Corps on the west coast.

The advance of VIII Corps towards Granville and Avranches had begun on July 28. Two spearheads, each consisting of an armoured and an infantry division, began the move and Coutances, twenty miles north of Granville, fell that day, as already related. The advance to Avranches continued, barely checked by the scattering of mines and whatever opposition could be offered by those German units already in full retreat. The leading US divisions sustained only thirteen casualties, including three killed on July 28. The commanding general, in this case George Patton, was not pleased with the rate of progress.

Pressure was applied to General Middleton, who duly passed on the message to Major General Grow of the 6th Armored Division, now heading for Pontorson and Dol, urging him to *'put on the heat'*. General Wood of the 4th Armored Division was doing just that while heading for Rennes but repeatedly pointing out to his superiors that he was advancing in the wrong direction – west and not east. The 4th Armored Division then made even better speed against slight opposition – the usual factor determining rapid Allied advances in Normandy – and on July 29 Combat Command 'B' of this division advanced ten miles and lost only thirty men. And so, against slight opposition, on July 30, VIII Corps took Avranches.

It was very important to keep up the pressure on the retreating German troops and not let the advance dawdle simply because there was no pressure in front to lean against. If the Germans were allowed to get away or given a breather or allowed to dig-in, there would be plenty of opposition; keeping hard on the Germans' heels was therefore highly advisable and there could be no pause for celebration at Avranches.

Besides, just taking Avranches was not enough. It was also necessary to take the narrow corridor over the Sélune river at Pontaubault, four miles further south, to gain the one highway that would allow Patton's tanks and infantry to get round the corner at the foot of the Cotentin and over the Quesnon river into Brittany. It then transpired that the Germans had been reinforcing the troops in Avranches and the battle for the town might not yet be over. This proved a false alarm; the advancing Germans were driven back with loss and the vital Pontaubault bridge was taken intact on July 29. The way to Brittany was open; all Patton had to do was forge ahead and take the entire province.

This fact was all-too-apparent to the commander of the German troops in Normandy, Field Marshal von Kluge. From his new HQ in Le Mans, von Kluge was now commanding OB-West and Army Group B, attempting to co-ordinate the moves of the Fifteenth Army, Panzer Group West and Seventh Army and find out what was going on elsewhere – with his communications in chaos. He also had to stave-off the demands of Adolf Hitler and the Staff at OKW, who wanted to know where von Kluge had prepared his defensive positions and what his plans were for driving the Allies back. It is hardly surprising that on July 31 Von Kluge described the situation in Normandy as a '*riensensauerei*' – 'a hell of a mess'.

On that day, July 31, von Kluge informed the Führer that it was *impossible* to stem the American advance, that the only static defences he had were the ones the Americans and British had already broken through, and that a with-drawal from Normandy was now inevitable. The German defensive line had been stretched too thin and had been torn open in the west because it only had the necessary defensive depth in the east. Once General Hausser of the Seventh Army had lost Coutances he had lost the Cotentin. The large and mobile US forces in the west could no longer be penned-up and the American armoured divisions, so long limited by the nature of the terrain, were now making at speed for more open country.

The collapse of the German position had also been noted at SHAEF. Having visited Monty's HQ on July 30, Eisenhower wrote next day to Montgomery:[7] 'Your plan continues to develop beautifully. I learn that you have a column in Avranches. This is great news. Bradley must make our position there impreg-nable ... and permit armour to continue thrusting.'

If there is any truth in the allegations that Eisenhower never really under-stood what Montgomery had been trying to do in Normandy since June 7 – which seems more than likely – the coin had finally dropped. This is confirmed by another message, on August 2, in which Eisenhower urges that since 'enemy resistance seems to have disintegrated very materially in the Avranches sector, our mobile columns will want to operate boldly against the enemy'. This they were already doing with bold thrusts by the armoured columns of Middleton's VIII Corps now racing into Brittany.

The advance into Brittany by Middleton was a fast and bold advance ... and largely a waste of time. There were very few Germans in Brittany and they could have been penned-up by small armoured forces, the French Resistance – the FFI – and the Allied air forces. The *sole* object of sending an American army moving west was to take ports, but the two main ports, St-Malo and Brest, were held by garrisons which defied eviction for weeks or months until the ports they defended were in ruins.

St-Malo was totally shattered, never used by the Allies, and had to be totally rebuilt after the war. The defenders of Brest held on until September 18 – the day *after* the British 1st Airborne Division landed at Arnhem in Holland and Allied troops had already overrun Belgium and were hundreds of miles away on the frontiers of Germany. Lorient, the last Breton port of any size, and St-Nazaire both held out until the end of the European war.

The Breton ports were needed after D-Day because there, on the west coast of France, they could take in American transports full of men and material coming directly from the USA. There was, however, an in-built snag with this plan, as General Wood of the US 4th Armored Division had pointed out. These ports lie in the west of Brittany, a large, elongated province reaching far out into the Atlantic, a rural province without good roads in 1944. While the Breton ports were being taken and cleared of obstructions, and this took months, the American armies were moving away to the east and north, to Paris, the Ardennes, Luxembourg and the frontier of Germany.

As a result Brest and St-Malo were never of any real use to the Allies and the Brittany campaign – *at the time it took place* – was a waste of effort. The Americans should have taken Brittany in late June or early July, as soon as possible after D-Day; that would have given them more space in which to expand, a place to absorb their new divisions and access to four ports close to the Normandy battlefield. They could not do any of this, however hard they tried, because German opposition in the *bocage* prevented the US armies getting to Brittany until August.

Now it was too late and this being so, the story of Brittany and its fading place in the Normandy battle can be quickly told. Two armoured divisions of Middleton's VIII Corps, 4th Armored and 6th Armored, were sent west. The 6th Armored rapidly outran its communications, at least with General Middleton. It did manage to communicate with General Patton, who tended to overlook the usual communications channels and deal directly with the divisional commanders when he deemed it necessary, and that is what happened here.

The advance went quickly against slight German opposition, 4th Armored Division reaching the outskirts of Rennes on August 1. The 2,000-strong garrison of Rennes held on for three days before withdrawing on August 4. American columns then pushed south-east towards Angers on the Loire, west towards Brest and along the north coast of Brittany to St-Malo. Having placed a bet with Montgomery that his troops would take Brest within a few days, Patton told General Grow of the 6th Armored Division to ignore all side missions and head directly for that port. Middleton, unaware of this order, told Grow he was not to leave either Dinan or St-Malo in enemy hands. When Grow halted to clear these towns, Patton appeared at his headquarters near Dinan, asked what he was doing there and told him to push on. 'I'll see Middleton', said Patton. 'You go ahead to where I told you to go.'[8]

Grow duly went to Brest but he could not take it. The port and town had been strongly garrisoned and when the investment began on August 7 the defenders greeted the American troops with an abundance of artillery fire and beat back the first US infantry probes with loss. On August 8, Grow sent in a message under a flag of truce, telling the garrison commander of Brest that resistance was pointless and surrender advisable. This appeal was rejected – and the garrison continued to resist the Americans for the next five weeks. The taking of Brest finally cost the US Third Army almost 10,000 casualties and when it fell the port facilities were unusable.

Bob Sales of the 29th Infantry again:[9]

The Germans had these forts in the walls of Brest and we lost a lot of good men getting them out of there. My friend Toad Paget got badly wounded there, he got away from me one night and into a cave and a German dropped a grenade at his feet and tore his stomach right open. We got him on a jeep and took him away and to hospital but we did not think he could live. He did live after many operations and is still living in West Virginia and a good friend.

Finally we made it to the high ground overlooking Brest and one of the biggest air raids I have ever seen was sent over and they bombed Brest and we watched it. You would think nothing could survive that amount of bombing but when we finally got real close to Brest we put up loud-speakers and told them that they had to surrender as we had artillery on the high ground and could fire in point blank and just blow them to pieces. When they came out there was over 30,000 of them down there; you never saw as many prisoners in your whole life and this ended our fighting for a while as we were not close to the front any more as the front had moved all the way up into Belgium.

Nor was Brest the only port to hold out. St-Malo – regarded by OB-West as the best defended fortress on the west coast – was first besieged on August 4 and held out until August 17. Forbidden to surrender, German troops then held out in the outlying positions and on offshore islands, denying the Allies all access to the port until September 2, although pounded by aircraft, artillery and the guns of the British fleet, including the 15-inch guns of the battleship HMS *Warspite*. When the port and city finally fell the city was in ruins and the port was unusable – 'destroyed beyond hope of immediate repair' as the US Official History puts it.[10]

While the fighting at Brest and St-Malo continued, it is time to leave this side-show in Brittany and catch up with the battles now raging in Normandy after the breakthrough at Avranches, beginning with the Canadian advance on Falaise on August 7 – Operation Totalize. By August 6 the British Second Army had reached the southern limit of its advance on the Vire–Condé road and was swinging east, pivoting on the left-hand XII Corps. To the left of XII Corps lay the II Canadian Corps which, as already related, was planning an advance on Falaise.

This was an opportune time for an advance to the south. The Cobra breakout had obliged the enemy to shift divisions west from the Caen front, more German divisions had shifted west to oppose Bluecoat and for the first time since D-Day there was a fair chance of a clear run across the Caen–Falaise plain. On the other hand, the German divisions moving west from the Caen front were Panzer divisions and these were being replaced by fresh, strong infantry divisions, transferred from Fifteenth Army – von Kluge and Hitler having finally realised that Fortitude had been a sham; there would be no Allied landing in the Pas de Calais.

Most of these divisions were intended for Panzer Group West – the 326th and 323rd arrived on July 30 – but the 84th Division, which arrived on August 1 went west to shore-up Seventh Army against the Americans and its place in the east was taken by the 89th Division. The point here is that while the enemy had moved some units out of the way, other units, admittedly smaller and without motor transport, had moved in to replace them. This being so, if the Canadian attack was to take advantage of these changes, it had better go in soon. Nor had all the Panzers gone west; the Canadians would also encounter their old enemies, 12 SS Panzer, which was dug in before Falaise and 1 SS Panzer, active south of Tilly-la-Campagne.

During the first week of August, the Canadian forces waiting to advance had harassed the German forces to their front, maintaining the pressure in order to keep the Germans uncertain about the next Allied move. The general pattern from June 7 until now had been a series of attacks at either end of the bridgehead; this being so, the enemy might anticipate an attack south of Caen in the immediate aftermath of Cobra. Things were different now because Cobra had led to a breakout and been followed up with Bluecoat but the Caen–Falaise line remained an important point on the German line, more so than ever after the loss of Mont Pinçon and one they had to protect. To break this line and advance to the Falaise road was the purpose of Totalize.

Monty issued a new directive to the Allied armies on August 4 in which the tasks of Totalize were listed as follows:

> *Object of the operation.* A. To break through the enemy positions to the south and south-east of Caen, and to gain such ground in the direction of Falaise as will cut off the enemy forces now facing Second Army and render their withdrawing eastward difficult – if not impossible. B. Generally to destroy enemy equipment and personnel as a preliminary to a possible wide exploitation of success.

The broad strategy of all the Allied armies was now to swing their right flanks round, pushing the Germans back and forming a common front north to south, facing east towards the Seine. With all bridges over that river destroyed and kept in ruins by the Allied air forces, the Seine was the barrier against which the German forces in Normandy could be pressed back and destroyed – but the Canadian First Army had first to gain enough space to swing its right flank round, and that meant an advance to Falaise.

General Simonds's plan for II Canadian Corps called for a three-phase advance, with the usual massive air and artillery support. The first aim was to break into the German positions between Fontenay-le-Marmion and La Hogue. This would be done by a strong, surprise, night attack by two infantry divisions and two armoured brigades – with no prior artillery bombardment but a massive bombing on the corps front by 1,020 bombers of RAF Bomber Command.

Then, Phase Two, the 3rd Canadian Division and the 4th Canadian Armoured Division would go in by daylight, with plenty of air and artillery support and breach the second German position between Hautmesnil and St-Sylvain.

In the third or exploitation phase, two armoured divisions, the 4th Canadian and 1st Polish, would exploit the breach and push south to the high ground just north of Falaise – Point 195 (metres). That done, both armoured divisions would extend their front while keeping in contact with the enemy. The role of the other element in the Canadian Army, Crocker's I (British) Corps, was a subsidiary one. This was all it could manage because its main units – 3rd British Infantry Division and 4th Armoured Brigade – had been sent to Second Army for Bluecoat and other units had been transferred to Simonds to support this attack by II Canadian Corps. Crocker's much depleted corps was to hold its front but advance in conformity with II Canadian corps and cover its left flank.

Simonds's plan incorporated one very novel feature, the first-ever use of APCs – armoured personnel carriers, then called *Kangaroos* – which were either tanks without their turrets or Priest self-propelled guns without their armament: 'unfrocked' Priests, in the jargon of the time. Putting the infantry into APCs – and Simonds is credited with the invention of the APC – provided the infantry with both protection and mobility. The only snag was that in these improvised APCs the troops had to dismount by clambering over the top, in full view of the enemy and exposed to fire and not out through doors in the rear as with the modern, twenty-first-century APCs. Before the attack was launched seventy-six Priests had been converted into Kangaroos; they were to prove most useful and very popular with the troops and the use of Kangaroos became a normal feature of Canadian Army operations.

Totalize began at 2330hrs on August 7, after half an hour of bombing in which 3,462 tons of bombs were dropped in the enemy positions by RAF Bomber Command; not one RAF bomb fell on the Canadian positions. The armour and infantry made good progress to begin with, but the dark, then a thick morning mist at dawn on August 8 and an intense smoke-screen put up by the enemy to restrict visibility caused a number of units to go off line.

Their advance continued and although the defenders of May-sur-Orne and Fontenay-le-Marmion put up a good fight – the defenders of May were only quelled after a hosing with fire from Crocodile tanks – these positions were in

Canadian hands by early afternoon on August 8 and the Canadians moved south on the right bank of the river Laize towards Hautmesnil. Meanwhile, the Scots of the 51st Highland Division were pushing down the left of the Falaise road past Hubert-Folie to take Tilly-la-Campagne. Losses were not severe but were higher in the marching units than in those riding in Kangaroos – the three battalions in Kangaroos lost a total of eight men killed, the four battalions on foot lost sixty-eight men killed, mostly by mortar fire; General Simonds's invention was already proving its worth.

The Germans had not been taken by surprise. Some reserves were available to the 89th Infantry Division, the only one on the attack front, including elements of 101 SS Heavy Tank with nineteen Tigers and two flame-throwing Tigers. The 89th also had a quantity of 88mm anti-tank guns from III Flak Corps and Kampfgruppe Waldmuller of the 12 SS Panzer Division which had twenty tanks, half of them Tigers, and was under the close eye of Colonel Kurt Meyer who sent his men and tanks forward as soon as Totalize began.

The two forces collided at St Aignan where Captain Michel Wittman, the commander of the 101 SS Heavy Tank Battalion – the man who had stopped the British tanks at Villers-Bocage in June – was killed by shellfire or by tanks of the 2nd Yeomanry. The first phase of Totalize went well and it could not have come at a better time. With the launching of the German counter-attack at Mortain on August 6, the enemy forces available to support the 89th Division and Meyer's scanty forces north of Falaise were limited and could not be reinforced.

However, the second phase of Simonds's battle did not go so well and began to go seriously awry when the 4th Canadian Armoured Division had difficulty reaching its start line over churned ground, through other units halted ahead and under a steady rain of shells and mortar bombs. Exhortations to the divisional commander, urging him to push on, filled the airwaves from Corps and Army HQ but little could be done ... and then the USAAF bombers came in and twenty-four of them dropped their bombs on the assembling Canadian and Polish formations.

These bombs fell on the 1st Polish Armoured Division and the 3rd Canadian Infantry Division; sixty-five men were killed and about 250 wounded, including Major General R. F. L. Keller of the 3rd Canadian Division who had led this division since D-Day. This 'short bombing' landed some way behind the first-line troops and the advance units for this phase, most of the Poles and the 4th Canadian Armoured Division, crossed the start line more or less on time – H-Hour for phase 2 was 1400hrs on August 8.

Thereafter progress was slow and losses started to mount. The Polish Armoured Division ran into the Tigers of Kampfgruppe Waldmuller south-east of St Aignan and the sum total for the second phase was that neither of the armoured divisions, 4th Canadian nor 1st Polish, made anything like the planned amount of progress. General Simonds ordered them to continue advancing overnight and make up the distance next day. One result of this was the loss of 'Halpenny Force', a composite force made up of the 28th Armoured Regiment – the British Columbia Regiment – and the Algonquin Regiment, a force tasked to capture the village of Bretteville-le-Rabet on August 9.

The Halpenny Force moved forward from Hautmesnil at first light and then lost its way, eventually deciding to head for all it could see in the morning mist, a village on some high ground directly to its front. This high ground was, in fact, the ridge supporting the village of Estrées, two miles south-east of Bretteville-le-Rabat, which the force had missed in the dark. The force was now totally lost, out on its own – and coming up against strong elements of Kampfgruppe Wunsche of 12 SS Panzer. The Kampfgruppe encircled the Halpenny Force near Estrées-la-Campagne and shot it to pieces. In a day-long battle on August 9 the British Columbia Regiment lost forty-seven tanks – almost all it had – and 112 men, while the Algonquin Regiment lost 128 men, including forty-five killed.

This disaster did not prevent some ground being gained. Point 195, just north-west of Falaise, was taken and by midnight – 2359hrs – on August 10, the Argyll and Sutherland Highlanders of Canada were in a commanding position, a mile outside Falaise. This was a spearhead position, well in advance of the rest of II Canadian Corps which fell back from that advanced point, most of the Canadian units lying east of the Caen–Falaise road. The main thrust of II Corps had been blunted by German resistance in the Quesnay woods, two miles north of Falaise.

This position was held by that resourceful officer, Kurt Mayer, who had assembled all the available tanks, 88mm guns and *nebelwerfer* mortars in this position to back up some tough survivors of the 12 SS Panzer Grenadiers who were determined to hold his position to the last man. The fighting for Quesnay woods lasted most of June 10 and the SS inflicted a considerable number of casualties on the Canadians before they fell back.

Les Wager was in the fight at the Quesnay woods:[11]

We were attacking the woods straddling the Falaise road, the Quesnay Woods and there were tanks in there. Nevertheless we put in a brigade attack, Queen's Own – my outfit – on the left of the road, North Shore Regiment on its right, a frontal assault with six tanks off to the left somewhere protecting the exposed flank; the idea was that we should go in that evening fight through to the river overnight so the main armour could cross the river next morning (promises, promises). What we found was one of those little battlegroups of crack troops set up to hold the gap.

We set off at around 1900hrs, Able and Baker Companies leading, Charlie and Dog to follow. Waiting at our start line, watching Able and Baker disappear from view we heard not a sound from the woods from which these positions were masked from us by the high ground of a wheatfield. We set off at 1920 in a familiar, deployed battle order and about a hundred yards into the wheatfield we found ourselves in stubble – and I was thinking – on a beautiful killing-ground. Why hadn't they used it, I wondered?'

Moments later, I had my answer. The stubble was raked by machine-gun fire from God knows how many guns. They were waiting for the second wave – us – which they knew would be coming up and this killing-ground had been kept just for us.

I had never heard so many machine-guns firing at me all at once. They were even using tracer and you could see it smoking through the stubble. I watched one tracer pass between my legs and another go inches to the right of my right ankle, I was thinking that if I had been zig-zagging, one of those would have got me. We had a new Company Commander, a captain on his first action with us – also his last as it turned out. He'd taken off his pips because of a sniper threat from the woods and carried a rifle instead of a Stengun or side-arm. The only one who looked like he might be the Commander was me, moving in my usual place, 5 yards the other side of the radio man, carrying my rifle and a map satchel. When the shooting started and since things were rapidly falling apart under the weight of machine-gun fire, I started waving my arms about trying to get things organised, so guess who Jerry thought was in charge?

We were still moving, running forward and as we reached the top of the slope there were three Tigers at the edge of the woods. They had been creaming 14 Platoon to our left but now they saw the radio man and this jackass of a hero waving the troops on and dropped a set of three shells right on top of us. I was surrounded by dust and smoke and thought maybe now they cannot see me but this was wrong because they were raking the open slope with machine-gun fire. I went running out of the smoke and there was half a man lying there staring at me, we'd come to the regiment together in early '43. Ahead, 14 and 15 Platoons had gone, disappeared. On my right Coy HQ had disappeared and I was thinking – God, where is everyone?

I was still running, zig-zagging now, trying to get out into the standing wheat but my inner voice told me I was not going to get that far and had to find cover right now and I found a mortar crater and dropped into it. A tank shell hit about 3 feet to the left of me, lifting me out of the hole and dumping me back in it and I stayed there, playing dead.

Playing dead is an act one cannot quite excuse of oneself and I got out of there as soon as it got dark and made my way back to Bn HQ and tried to tell the story but I was confused and rambled a lot. When we had collected all those who made it back we headed to the rear to regroup and pick up replacements. The way took us through the artillery area and everytime a gun went off I fell over and I kept falling, tripping. I was obviously suffering from some kind of shell-shock but fortunately no one thought I should be taken off to hospital.

I say 'fortunately' because had that happened I might never have recovered. We had seen some of that, hospitals returning ruined men to us that could no longer last a day in the line. As it was, when the next action came along, I stayed and I survived. The stress caught up with me after the war.

Anyway, let me add a little to round out that action in the woods on August 10; the German unit there was Battlegroup Krause, one of three battlegroups that Kurt Mayer had set up from the remnants of the 12 SS and the 89th Infantry Division, plus elements of the 85th Division that were just beginning to arrive in the area.

I suspect the Americans could never imagine the tier-on-tier of defensive lines we had to penetrate to force the Caen-to-Falaise road against many of the élite of the German forces – and Patton's idiotic remark from the other side of the Gap at Argentan – the one about coming across and driving us back to the sea

for another Dunkirk – gave us about the same feeling about him as the one we
had about the 12 SS we had to deal with on this side.

With the failure to take the Quesnay woods – which cost the leading Canadian
rifle companies almost 200 men – Operation Totalize was over. It had been
brought to a halt by stout opposition from well-trained German troops in good
defensive positions, a little ill-management at the start of Phase Two, and a lot
of bad luck. Even so, the gains were not inconsiderable; II Canadian Corps had
advanced nine miles through that series of German defence lines and were now
within sight of Falaise. On the other hand, the Germans were still in possession of that town and it would take another full-scale attack to evict them. This
attack, Operation Tractable, would not go in until August 14, which allows us
time to leave the Canadians in front of Falaise and turn our attention to events
taking place further west where, since August 6, the German Panzer divisions had
been making a counter-attack at Mortain.

15 THE MORTAIN COUNTER-ATTACK AUGUST 7–12

If you haven't fought the Germans you don't know what fighting is. Even when they are up against it, they will still find something to throw at you.

LT COLONEL PETER YOUNG, DSO MC No. 3 Commando, Normandy, 1944

To explain the next major development in the battle we have to go back to August 7, the day the Germans launched their armoured counter-attack at Mortain. With this attack and its eventual defeat, the battle of Normandy entered its penultimate stage. This being so, it is again necessary to visualise what was happening across the Normandy battlefield in early August when all the Allied armies were engaged in squeezing the German defenders out of position and contributing, in their various ways, to the final outcome of the Normandy campaign.

Starting in the west, the US Third Army had one corps, the VIII, heading into Brittany and the port of Brest. The rest of Third Army were heading south towards the Loire, intending to curve their right flank round between First Army and that river, form a front and head east, north of the Loire, past Laval and Le Mans, heading on a broad front towards the Seine. Progress here in the open country north of the river would be rapid for there was little opposition from the Germans and no established defence lines.

Then came the US First Army, now under Courtney Hodges, completing its move to the base of the Cotentin and pivoting there to head east towards the Seine on a line Avranches–Mortain–Domfront. By early August, the First Army line was virtually perpendicular, north to south, from Carentan through Villedieu-les-Poêles to the main Fougères–Mayenne road, which formed the boundary with Third Army.

Pushing east against fragmented but sometimes stout opposition, the First Army front lined up with that of the British Second Army just east of Vire. This town lay in the First Army zone and the Second Army front ran north-east from Vire to take in Mont Pinçon, Thury-Harcourt and, curving east of Caen, reached the sea east of the Orne at Ouistreham. The country to the east of the Orne, south along the axis of the Caen–Falaise road, was now the territory of the Canadian First Army. All these armies were pressing to the south and east, bearing round to force the Germans back to the Seine. The total effect was to put immense pressure on the forces of Second Army and Eberbach's Fifth Panzer Army – the former Panzer Group West – between the Vire and the Orne.

With the British and Canadians grinding down from the north and two American armies pushing from the west, the German position in Normandy was serious and unsustainable. By any rational military appraisal, only a rapid retreat to some defensive line west of the Seine – or on the Seine, or east of the Seine – could save them from a crushing defeat. By the first days of August the German position in Normandy was crumbling and simple military logic should have compelled the German commanders to accept that fact and pull their forces out of the trap that was closing round them.

This von Kluge and his commanders might well have done but Adolf Hitler thought otherwise. On his maps the greatest threat to the German hold on Normandy now was the American thrust east from the Cotentin and south into Brittany and towards the Loire. If these could be held, thought the Führer, the German position in Normandy could be sustained until his V-weapons landing on London forced the Allies to the conference table. This view was held by no one else at OKW or OB-West but in the aftermath of the July plot no one on the general staff was willing to argue the point. Therefore, on August 2 Hitler ordered von Kluge to muster his tank forces and carry out a major push against the Americans, with the aim of breaking through their lines, separating the two American armies on the line Mortain–Avranches and pressing on across the Cotentin to the Atlantic coast.

The aims of this attack were to cut the American forces in two and bar any further American progress to the east. To do this it would be necessary to collect the Panzer divisions on the British–Canadian front and send them west. This was exactly where General Montgomery now wanted the German armour to go; the further west the German tanks were when the German front collapsed, the more German Panzer units would be caught in the subsequent pocket. Tactics had changed because the nature of the battle had changed – it had been static, now it was fluid – but the main strategy, to write-down the German forces – as ordered for Goodwood and Totalize – remained intact.

On the night of August 2–3 von Kluge received a visit from General Walter Warlimont, Deputy Chief of the Wehrmacht Operations Staff. General Warlimont had come to explain the Führer's plan in detail and the details left von Kluge in despair. At a meeting on August 3, General Eberbach, commanding Panzer Group West, and Sepp Dietrich, commanding the I SS Panzer Corps, added their objections, Dietrich pointing out that if the SS divisions were pulled out from south of Caen, the British and Canadians would attack there and break through. Warlimont pointed out that the SS divisions were not in their proper place south of Caen, where they were being used in a static defensive role and should be sent west to halt the Americans.

Eberbach rebutted this argument by pointing out that while infantry divisions were being brought on to the Caen front, Panzer divisions would still be needed in the rear to support them. None of this made any difference; whatever the generals on the spot thought of Hitler's scheme – and they thought it absurd – the Führer wanted an attack towards Avranches and the generals in the field were obliged to make one.

On August 3, while these meetings with Warlimont were in progress, von Kluge told General Adolf Kuntzen of the 81st (LXXXI) Corps that the Mortain counter-attack would not fundamentally alter the current situation; an Allied victory in Normandy was now inevitable.[1] As far as von Kluge was concerned, the only advantage of counter-attacking towards Avranches was that the attack would probably halt the US advance for a while and give him time to withdraw his forces from Normandy to a new defence line. This hope was predicated on another hope, that OB-West would actually be permitted to organise such a defence line further north, or that OKW already had this matter in hand – which was not the case – or that the Allied air forces would not savage the panzers both during the attack and the subsequent withdrawal.

Nor was von Kluge at all happy with the state of the troops available for this counter-attack. Every unit in Seventh Army was either tired out, or already engaged, or written-down to a skeleton size. The main unit tasked for this Mortain attack was the 67th (LXVII) Panzer Corps, consisting of 2nd Panzer, 2 SS

Panzer, 1 SS Panzer, 116 Panzer, all reinforced with units from other Panzer divisions, plus the remnants of Panzer Lehr – a force which von Kluge knew was neither strong enough or fresh enough for an all-out attack. These divisions could only muster about 120 tanks of various marks, although this was boosted to 190 by the time of the attack. The only fresh troops available to reinforce this Panzer Corps would have to come from Adolf Kutzen's 81st (LXXXI) Corps, the 9 Panzer Division which was currently at Alençon, south of Falaise, and the 708th Infantry Division which was en route from the south of France.

There was also some disagreement on where this force might be directed. Von Kluge wanted 9 Panzer to thrust at St-Hilaire-du-Harcouêt; General Hausser of Seventh Army wanted to send it to Mayenne. Neither course of action was possible for it soon became apparent that these fresh divisions would not arrive in time to take part in the Mortain attack. It should be added that this diversion of tank strength still left 9 SS Panzer, 10 SS Panzer and 12 SS Panzer facing the British and Canadians south of Caen; they too had been written-down but, as related in the previous chapter, were still capable of a formidable resistance.

Lacking enough troops or tanks, von Kluge decided that the plan of attack must be altered. Instead of attacking through the country north of Mortain, between that town and the river Sée, he thought that the attack should head south-west, directly through Mortain. It took some time and not a little pressure from the Seventh Army staff to convince von Kluge that an attack on a northern axis, towards St-Hilaire-du-Harcouêt, between Mortain and the river Sée, would be a much better bet, being both the most direct route to Avranches and one which kept the German forces on higher ground. Final plans were then drawn up to implement this plan but the OB-West Staff were interrupted late on August 6 by a further call from Adolf Hitler.

On the face of it, the Führer's call brought good news. Hitler wanted a report on von Kluge's intentions and preparations but informed the OB-West Army Group B commander that he was releasing no less then sixty Panther tanks, eighty Mark IV tanks and all the armoured cars held in the reserve east of Paris for the Mortain attack – a fairly massive increase to Seventh Army's hitting power. This good news had just been digested when OB-West received another call from Hitler's Chief-of-Staff, Generaloberst Alfred Jodl. The Führer had been mulling over Seventh Army's plans and wanted some changes made. This call came in less than twenty-four hours before the Mortain attack was due to go in and the Führer's changes were radical.

The first change was that the attack was not to be led by General Funck of 67th (LXVII) Panzer Corps but by General Eberbach, commander of the Fifth Panzer Army, who was at present engaged against the British and Canadians. Further exchanges on this point revealed that von Kluge and the Führer were not thinking on the same lines at all. Von Kluge was now on the point of launching an attack – as ordered by the Führer – towards Avranches with the aim of stabilising the German line and cutting the US armies in two. The Führer now wanted a much larger attack commanded by Eberbach and consisting of every Panzer unit in Seventh Army. This was a problem because, clearly, while von Kluge's plans were almost complete, Hitler's plans were just being formulated – thus, chaos loomed.

Von Kluge's reaction to this order is not recorded but it must have brought him close to despair. First of all, this command totally ignored the situation now developing on his southern flank, around the city of Le Mans. Patton's army had taken Laval and were now heading for the big German supply bases at Le Mans and Alençon; delay now in taking some action to halt this advance was not an option. The northern front, where the British were pressing forward relentlessly towards Mont Pinçon, was liable to collapse at any time. Finally, there was the overriding fact that unless the attack towards Avranches was made soon, all surprise would be lost and the outcome disastrous. Von Kluge had been informed by a German intelligence agency that the Allies already suspected he was forming up his troops for a counter-attack – another Allied bonus provided by the Enigma code-breakers of Bletchley Park – and, all in all, he doubted if his troops could hold their lines for much longer *anywhere*. If this fresh attack did not go in soon, it could not be mounted at all.

This being so, he contacted Hitler and made a heartfelt and personal appeal, that the Mortain attack should go ahead, as planned and as soon as possible. Hitler could usually be persuaded by the promise of an attack – his constant complaint was that his field commanders were too cautious and not attacking often enough – but he still felt that the Mortain attack lacked weight. Even so, he permitted von Kluge to proceed but added that after the 67th (LXVII) Corps reached Avranches, Eberbach was to take over from Hausser and swing the attack north-east, into the right flank of the US First Army, thereby – the Führer hoped – disrupting and perhaps even halting the US breakout. This Führer instruction concluded: 'The C-in-C West has a unique opportunity, which will never return, to drive into an extremely exposed enemy area and thereby to change the situation completely.'[2]

Seen in the context of the German position at that time, this final comment – on *'changing the situation completely'* – indicates the full extent of Hitler's dream world. The Mortain attack was seen at OKW as the long-overdue stroke against the invader, one that would divide the First Army from the Third Army at Avranches and split the American forces in two. After that, the German panzers would turn north and east and drive the Americans into the sea. What the Allied air forces and the rest of the US First and Third Armies would do to Eberbach's forces during this attack – and what the British and Canadian Armies would be doing to the enemy lines of communication and those enemy forces on their southern front at Falaise at this time – had not been factored into the Führer's calculations at all.

Von Kluge's field commanders were rather more realistic. General Hausser felt that his forces could get to Avranches – probably. After that, it would be more difficult but if he could hold that place *and* keep the First and Third Armies apart *and* stop the retreat, Hausser believed he would be doing well, as indeed he would. Further ambitions would have to wait on the outcome of the next day's attack. And so, with Avranches as the objective, the Mortain counter-attack went in shortly after midnight on August 6–7. It was made without a prior bombardment and achieved a certain amount of surprise.

The leading element in the Mortain force would be three Panzer divisions, moving in line abreast. On the right wing was 116 Panzer Division, tasked to strike along the north bank of the river Sée and head for Chérence. In the centre was 2nd Panzer, reinforced for this attack by two tank brigades, one each from 1 SS Panzer and 116 Panzer. This unit was to strike along the south bank of the Sée, using the St Barthelémy–Reuffuveille road as its main axis of advance. Finally, on the left, surged 2 SS Panzer, tasked to sweep forward on either side of Mortain, and reinforced for the purpose by all that was left of 17 SS Panzer Grenadier Division, now reduced to brigade strength.

This first wave would be followed by two tank brigades of 1 SS Panzer Division, which were to surge forward through the breach created by the leading divisions and press on to enter Avranches and reach the Atlantic coast. Meanwhile, a strong reconnaissance battalion, all that was left of the once-mighty Panzer Lehr, would cover the south flank, and the 81st (LXXXI) Corps was to remain alert on their southern flank and block any thrust by Patton's Third Army towards the vital supply bases at Alençon. As plans went, it sounded workable.

This force of four reinforced Panzer divisions looked formidable on paper but it actually amounted to fewer than 200 tanks. To give just one example, 1 SS Panzer had forty-three Panthers instead of the sixty-seven it should have had at full establishment and only fifty-five Mark IVs instead of 103. The striking force had also been rapidly assembled, some of the units had been engaged by the tactical air forces when making their way to the assembly area and others had been held up in traffic jams on the narrow Normandy roads. All this caused delay. The attack should have been launched at 2200hrs on August 6 but it was found necessary to put H-Hour back to 2359hrs that day because the exploiting force from 1 SS Panzer had been delayed by air strikes and traffic congestion on the narrow roads and was still six miles from its start line at H-Hour.

Neither had 1 SS Panzer sent the promised armoured battalion to reinforce 2nd Panzer in the first line. Nor had the 116 Panzer Division, and the 67th (LXVII) Corps Commander, General Funck, therefore wanted the commander of 116 Panzer, Generalleutnant Graf von Schwerin, sacked forthwith. Hausser declined to do that but he sanctioned a two-hour delay in order that 1 SS Panzer could catch up. When all were finally ready and in position, the panzers rolled forward.

The available evidence suggests that this attack caught VII Corps by surprise. There was no opening artillery bombardment to alert them and 2 SS Panzer quickly outflanked Mortain, then captured the town and took the high ground towards St-Hilaire-du-Harcouét, 'against no significant American opposition'.[3] By noon on August 7, 2 SS Panzer had taken up positions between Mortain and St-Hilaire and was protecting the southern flank of the attack. The only force in the way was the 2nd Battalion of 120th Infantry from the 30th Infantry Division which occupied Hill 317 (Côte 314) just east of Mortain, a position which overlooked the low country to the east and provided good observation for the American forward observers. From that commanding height the American infantry were able to call down artillery fire on 2 SS Panzer and bring it to a halt.

The key to any advance or defence on this part of the front was the small town of Mortain (pop. in 1944, 1,600). Mortain lies at the southern end of the *Suisse Normande,* and stretches along a ridge just below a steep hill listed on the US military maps as Hill 317. The 1st Infantry Division had entered Mortain on August 3 and occupied Hill 317 but by August 7 the 1st Infantry had moved to Mayenne. Mortain and the hill above it were now held by elements of the 30th Infantry Division.

Like the rest of First Army, the 30th Division was expecting resistance to its advance east, but not a strong counter-attack by armoured formations. The division had been preparing to move east from Mortain on August 7 and attack Barenton on the following day when a warning order arrived from VII Corps, advising that a counter-attack might come in during the next twelve hours. General Hobbs of the 30th Division was therefore instructed to hold his ground and reinforce the troops on Hill 317, the key to the entire Mortain position.

The first German attack came against the positions of 1st Infantry Division near Barenton at around 0430hrs on August 7, when six tanks and an infantry battalion from 2 SS Panzer came surging out of the night. The forward elements of 1st Infantry fell back but the Germans did not follow up; the division had only sporadic contact with the enemy for the rest of the day, and spent it protecting the routes into Mayenne.

The attack against the 30th Division at Mortain was far stronger. The 2 SS Panzer Division came into the town with tanks and infantry soon after midnight on the 6–7 and rapidly overran the positions held by the 2nd Battalion of the 120th Infantry Regiment in the centre of Mortain, isolating the 1st Battalion of the 120th on Hill 317. One of the 2nd Battalion companies held its position on the outskirts of Mortain and is credited with knocking out around forty German vehicles, including tanks, over the next couple of days. Other elements of the 30th Division were also under attack, the headquarters of the 117th Infantry was surrounded by German troops and enemy troops and tanks were already through the town, surging west towards Avranches. In spite of all this activity the 30th Division did not report the German attack to VII Corps headquarters for another three hours, until 0315hrs on August 7.

Fortunately, the 4th Infantry Division, in VII Corps reserve when the action opened, joined the fray early on. Their guns put down heavy artillery concentrations on the German forces along the north bank of the river Sée while the rest of the division stood-to to resist any attack on their position. For a few hours everything depended on Hobbs's 30th Division but more and more American divisions came into the fight as the day wore on and the American position at and around Mortain gradually grew stronger.

Fighting in the 30th Division sector went on for most of the day, a mixture of strong attacks by German tanks and infantry and infiltration of the American position by snipers and fighting patrols. The 30th stood its ground and fought back steadily; 'There were many heroes today, both living and dead,' reported one battalion commander, and by nightfall on August 7 General Hobbs could report proudly that although the division had taken over 600 casualties that day, their positions had been held. Nor was the German attack making much progress elsewhere.

In the centre of the attack, 2nd Panzer got off to a slow start along the river Sée and again surprised the Americans. The right-hand column of tanks therefore made good progress to le Mesnil-Adelée before encountering any resistance but when it ran into artillery fire three miles west of le Mesnil-Adelée the column stopped. The left-hand column of 2nd Panzer had not moved off at midnight, but stayed on its start line until the Panzer battalion promised by 1 SS joined at daylight. The left-hand column then made good progress to the outskirts of Juvigny before it was stopped by American resistance and daylight which, with the arrival overhead of RAF Typhoons, made further progress impossible.

The sum total was that no element of 2nd Panzer reached even its first objective on August 7. In mid-morning that day General Funck sent in 1 SS Panzer in a bid to take Juvigny and get the attack moving again, but while the advance was stalled the tanks were very vulnerable to air attack. Once the morning mist had cleared at around 1100hrs, the *jabos* were soon at work, swooping down to strafe and rocket the panzer columns, causing havoc in the soft-skinned transports and obliging the panzer grenadiers to take to the fields. These German columns were also coming under fire from American artillery on either flank while the north flank of the German attack along the river Sée, which should have been covered by 116 Panzer, was actually wide open. General von Schwerin, the commander of 116 Panzer Division, had failed to advance at all.

By noon on August 7, General Hausser was probably wishing that he had listened to General Funck and sacked the 116 Panzer commander on the previous night. It now transpired that, fearing American attacks would encircle his position if he moved towards Chérence, and convinced that the 84th Division, which was due to cover his rear, would be unable to hold out against increasing American pressure, von Schwerin had kept the attack order from his subordinate commanders. Von Schwerin therefore elected to disobey all his orders and neither send a tank battalion to 2nd Panzer nor take part in the Mortain attack. Such a flagrant breach of orders was virtually unheard of in the German Army – or indeed in any army – and at 1600hrs on August 7, General Schwerin was relieved of his command.

Even so, the damage was done. The 116 Panzer Division finally advanced at 1630 hrs but the Americans were now fully alert, the sky was full of Allied aircraft and the division made no progress. So, instead of a devastating blow by four Panzer divisions, the Mortain attack on August 7 was delivered by just two divisions, neither fully up to strength in either tanks or men. Moreover, the German troops, knowing that the *jabos* would soon be about once the morning fogs had cleared, abandoned all attempts at forward movement by midday and dug-in for protection against air attack.

The US Official History[4] records: 'British Hurricanes and Typhoons firing rockets struck awe into the German formations', and the support promised to the Panzer columns by the Luftwaffe failed to appear. Those German pilots who took off from airfields in the Beauce around Chartres were quickly intercepted by Allied fighters and not a single German aircraft appeared over Normandy to support the Mortain attack. All this was bad enough but the final blow against the success of this operation was delivered at the end of the afternoon by Adolf Hitler.

The Führer had spent the day poring over von Kluge's plan yet again and come to the conclusion that it had a number of flaws. First, von Kluge should have sent 1 SS Panzer against St-Hilaire, not against Mortain. Secondly, he should have waited until the Panzer force was fully assembled before attacking at all. However, the Führer could not see how the second, smashing, follow-up blow with the three Panzer divisions of Eberbach's Fifth Panzer Army – 9 SS, 10 SS and 9 Panzer – could now be resisted. The fact that these divisions were now fully engaged elsewhere, stemming the British or the Canadian Totalize attack south of Caen, did not concern him. The stalling of the first attack was clearly all von Kluge's fault and the Führer decided he had no option but to take personal charge of the Mortain offensive.

His first order was a command to prosecute the attack 'daringly and recklessly to the sea'. He also ordered that, whatever the risk to the German position on the Caen front, three Panzer divisions – 9 SS, 10 SS and either 12 SS or 21 Panzer – were to be withdrawn from Fifth Panzer Army and committed to the Mortain attack in order to 'bring about the collapse of the Normandy front by a thrust into the deep flank and rear of the enemy facing Seventh Army'. This was accompanied by further exhortations calling for 'daring, determination and imagination at all echelons of command'. The attack was scheduled for the evening of August 9.

By the evening of August 8, von Kluge had already decided that such exhortations would not remedy the situation. The Mortain attack had failed and with American pressure mounting on either flank of the thrust, unless the forward elements were withdrawn quickly there was every chance that they would be encircled, cut off and destroyed piecemeal. This view was confirmed by a call from General Eberbach. Eberbach was sure that he would be unable to hold his front at Falaise unless he was quickly reinforced, for the Canadian Totalize attack was now developing. Von Kluge had already diverted the newly arrived 331st Division to the Fifth Panzer Army and was mulling over a decision to send units from Seventh Army east towards Falaise when the order from Hitler regarding the second Mortain attack arrived at his headquarters.

When the Führer's new order was digested, gloom descended across the command centres of Normandy but – unlike General von Schwerin – Günther von Kluge always obeyed orders. He duly telephoned Eberbach and informed him that not only would he not be getting any reinforcements, he would also be losing three of his best divisions. There is a touch of madness about this action for as von Kluge informed Eberbach, 'I foresee that the failure of this attack (at Mortain) can lead to the collapse of the entire Normandy front, but the order is so unequivocal that it must be obeyed.' Eberbach's response is not recorded, but von Kluge then phoned Hausser to tell him that 10 SS and 12 SS would be joining his command the following day and were to be committed to renewing the stalled attack on Avranches on August 9.

Hausser admitted the failure of the attack so far, a fact he attributed to Allied air power, the non-participation of 116 Panzer on the first day and steadily growing American resistance. This is a fair summation and apart from the fact that 116 Panzer were now in the field – if not actually moving much – it was not likely that the situation would improve in the near future. Hausser also doubted if even a reinforced thrust on Avranches could now succeed, but orders were orders for this SS general and he prepared to carry them out.

Carrying out a fresh attack would not be easy. All surprise had been lost and General Collins now had seven divisions – five infantry and two armoured – in position to crush the German salient west of Mortain. The only division still in serious trouble was the 30th and that was still hanging on and fighting back around Mortain, in spite of the fact that two of the division's nine infantry battalions were absent – one in Barenton, one attached to the 2nd Armored Division in Vire – and the division was still absorbing around 800 replacements. General Hobbs was also without any reserve and General Collins sent him a regiment from the 4th Division in order to provide one.

Although the tenacious fighting of the 30th Division on Hill 317 was crucial, the major factor in halting the Mortain attack was air power. Once it got light, the German tanks and guns could not proceed and had to be driven off the roads and into the woods and fields where they were hastily camouflaged. This appears to have limited the subsequent losses but not prevented them. Ten squadrons of 2nd TAF took to the air over Mortain on August 7, and of seventy tanks making the initial penetration that morning less than half were still mobile by the end of the day; by the morning of August 8 only twenty-five German tanks were still in action on the Mortain front. Now these forces had to hold on to the ground they had gained, carry on the struggle for Mortain itself and await the arrival of reinforcements from Eberbach's army. These reinforcements could not move in daylight either, so the attack scheduled for August 9 had to be postponed until August 11.

Eberbach, as directed, took personal command of the divisions sent to Mortain – which were therefore designated Panzergruppe Eberbach – leaving the command of the Fifth Panzer Army south of Caen to Generaloberst Sepp Dietrich, previously commander of I SS Panzer Corps. On arriving at Seventh Army HQ, Eberbach soon decided that he could not attack on August 11 either since his force only had 127 tanks, no spares and very little in the way of petrol and ammunition. Moreover, Allied air power clearly dictated that any attack could only take place during the limited hours of midsummer darkness and before the morning mist lifted – say up to 1000hrs; after that the day belonged to the *jabos*. The snag was that tanks were no good in the dark and needed moonlight to move – and the next full moon was a week away.

Eberbach therefore decided that he could not attack before August 20 – a decision that inevitably attracted the wrath of the Führer. There was also another worry; it appeared that the US XV Corps of Patton's army had stopped heading east and was now heading north-east towards Alençon, and those vital German supply depots. If this was linked – as it must surely be – with the Canadian Totalize push on Falaise, then the Allies were obviously trying to put the German divisions at Mortain into a pocket. Von Kluge therefore suggested to the Führer that rather than continue towards Avranches he should use Eberbach's force to drive back this new thrust from the US XV Corps.

On the following day, August 11, von Kluge went further. He told Jodl at OKW that in his opinion and in the opinion of all his commanders, the Avranches attack must be called off, not least because 9 Panzer, now engaged near Alençon defending the fuel and ammunition dumps, was in trouble and needed support. Although the Canadian attack had been halted by August 12, an Allied pincer movement was clearly developing east of Mortain and the only sensible decision was to pull all the divisions in the Mortain salient back, and as quickly as possible. Von Kluge then put these views on paper and sent them to Hitler, wisely including proposals for subsequent action, namely that Seventh Army, having withdrawn from Mortain, would assemble a strong force in the area of Carrouges – 1 SS, 2nd Panzer and 116 Panzer – and attack the US XV Corps south of Alençon, this attack to go in no later than the early hours of August 14.

Hitler gave this suggestion qualified approval. The Seventh Army could withdraw from Mortain but only to reform and attack XV Corps: that done, they were to try again for Avranches. This was not exactly what von Kluge had hoped for but full agreement was rarely on the cards with Adolf Hitler. On the night of August 11, von Kluge began to extricate his divisions from Mortain and they were never to come back.

The Mortain counter-attack had now lasted six days and achieved virtually nothing. Although it brought a brief halt to the eastward advance of VII Corps, it did so at great cost. The 30th Infantry Division, the main US force engaged at Mortain, lost some 2,000 men in the six days of the offensive and the 4th Infantry

Division lost another 600 but German losses in tanks and men were far higher – when the US troops moved forward from Mortain they passed the burning wreckage of more than 100 German tanks.

Nor had this German thrust restricted American progress elsewhere; XIX Corps had continued to push down from the north and joined up with the 30th Division on August 12 and V Corps had moved south of Vire and was now pushing south and east against diminishing German resistance alongside the British Second Army which was across the *Suisse Normande* and heading south and west towards Falaise. All was now ready for a complete encirclement of the German units remaining in Normandy and the final trap began to close about them at Falaise.

16 ENCIRCLEMENT AUGUST 8-18

Better a solid shoulder at Argentan than a broken neck at Falaise.

GENERAL OMAR BRADLEY *A Soldier's Story*

With the ending of the German attack at Mortain, the last phase of the Normandy campaign begins. This would be the advance by all four Allied armies on Falaise and Argentan and the squeezing of the German forces into the Falaise 'pocket'. With so many units involved, moving in different directions at the same time, it is all too easy to lose track of events, and to clarify the picture it will be necessary to go back a few days and pick up the story on August 8 with a telephone call from Bradley to Montgomery.

During that call, Bradley suggested that, rather than simply push east, the two American armies comprising the US 12th Army Group should also swing north, towards Argentan and Falaise, both of which were in the proposed 21st Army Group zone. To avoid collision with the Canadians coming south on Falaise, Bradley added that the US armies should not enter these towns but stop some distance to the south, on the line of the road between Domfront and Sées. This move would narrow the gap through which the Germans must retreat towards the Seine and the gap could be either closed by the Canadians advancing on Falaise and Argentan, or by shellfire and the tactical air forces.

This telephone conversation took place while the Germans were still battering at Mortain and the Canadians had already pushed up to the outskirts of Falaise with Totalize but the idea was sound. If the British and Canadians continued their advance south and east and the Americans swung up from the south to meet them, the German armies west of the Orne would be caught between two arms of a closing vice. The fact that Bradley rang Montgomery with this suggestion should be noted, in view of what happened later.

On August 11, accepting this advice, Montgomery therefore issued a directive that the Americans would head north and east for Alençon while the British and Canadians would come south to secure Falaise and Argentan. A look at the map on page 350 will be helpful and we can pick up the story from August 11, by which time some moves to implement this plan had already taken place. Montgomery's assessment was that the bulk of the German forces in Normandy were now west of a north–south line from Caen to Le Mans, a line running through Falaise, Argentan and Alençon. The aim now was to take those places and encircle the German forces still remaining to the west.

General Hodges had already begun to move forces up from Barenton to encircle the German troops at Mortain and establish a line between Barenton and Domfront. Patton's Third Army, reinforced by two divisions, one of them armoured, was hooking round to a line through Sées and ready to thrust for Alençon. The task of meeting the Canadians – which was rather more than he had been ordered to do – Patton gave to the US XV Corps of Third Army but Monty's directive of August 11 approved of this move. 'Obviously,' he stated, 'if we can close the gap completely we shall have put the enemy in a most awkward predicament.'

However, according to the August 11 directive, Patton's Third Army were to halt on a line between Sées and Carrouges, twelve miles south of Argentan, which would be taken by the Canadians. This would put the German armies in a trap around Falaise but it would still leave a gap between the two Allied armies, the Canadian First and the US Third. This gap would be covered by both the Allied tactical air forces and the artillery who therefore had a twenty-mile-wide 'free fire' zone; anything that moved in the gap between Falaise and a line just south of Argentan could be attacked at will and destroyed. If that plan failed to catch the enemy at Falaise–Argentan they could be pursued east and caught again somewhere west of the Seine. The situation was fluid, everything depended on the events of the next few days and the actions and reactions of von Kluge and Adolf Hitler but, for the moment, Montgomery's directive of August 11 was the one to follow.

At this time XV Corps of Patton's Third Army was pressing on across Maine against light opposition. The Corps entered Le Mans on August 8 and by August

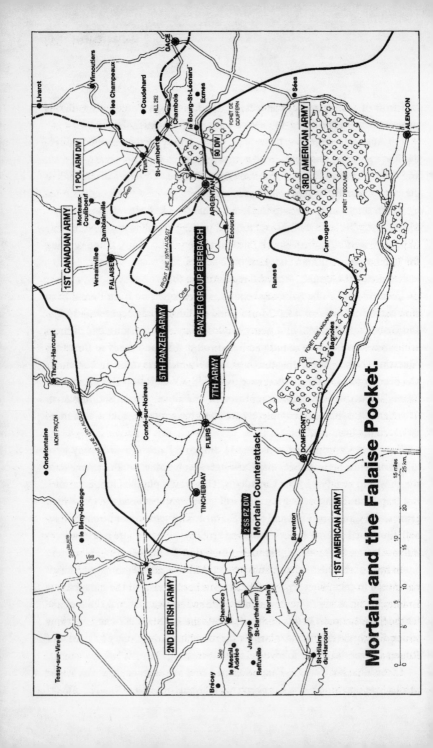

Mortain and the Falaise Pocket.

12 it was heading north for those German supply bases at Alençon, progress now delayed by the stiff resistance put up in front of that town by 9 Panzer. Apart from VIII Corps, which was still rushing west into Brittany, the rest of Patton's army was pushing east to the north of the Loire but – like XV Corps – was now gradually swinging north-east, up towards Chartres and the Seine, west of Paris. The VII Corps of First Army was still held up at Mortain but was gradually regaining the initiative as Eberbach's forces pulled back east. Gerow's V Corps and Corlett's XIX Corps had pushed south and were now beyond Vire, butting hard into the crumbling right flank of Seventh Army, V Corps heading for Tinchebray and XIX Corps heading for Flers.

On the British Second Army front, by August 6 the VIII Corps had reached or crossed the Vire–Condé road with the hard-charging 11th Armoured Division in the lead. On the XXX Corps front the 43rd Division had secured Mont Pinçon but were still being subjected to counter-attacks astride that hill, attacks which aimed to drive them back across the crest. On the left of the 43rd Division, the rest of XXX Corps were pressing on across the Odon and down the Orne valley towards Thury-Harcourt and Condé while XII Corps had reached Thury-Harcourt and were advancing south-east on the road towards Falaise. The Canadian II Corps were also pressing on towards Falaise down the road from Caen, while the rest of the Canadian First Army was expanding to the east across the river Dives.

The word that describes all the Allied tactics at this time, during and after the Mortain counter-attack, is *pressure*. In a wide circle from south, to west, to north, all the Allied armies, American, British and Canadian, were exerting pressure on the German armies, pressure that would squeeze the Seventh Army and most of the Fifth Panzer Army back across the Seine if they were lucky – or into a Allied pocket west of that river if their luck, or their petrol, ran out.

In his account of the Normandy battle,[1] Montgomery states that his original intention – so frequently described in this book – was for the right flank of Bradley's 12th Army Group to make a wide sweep south, then come east and hit the Seine between Rouen and Paris, while the British and Canadian armies struck directly north-east from Caen–Falaise and hit the river somewhere between Rouen and the sea, both forces driving the retreating German before them.

Circumstances, or rather opportunities, had altered this plan. The Allied armies were no longer trying to drive the German forces swiftly out of Normandy. The aim now was to trap the remains of Seventh Army and Fifth Panzer Army west of the Seine and destroy them and it is by the success of that aim that the generals would now be judged. The most important task at the moment was for the Canadians to take Falaise and, said Monty in his directive of 11 August, 'It is vital that this should be done quickly.' Having done that the Canadians could drive on and take Argentan, fourteen miles further south.

The subsequent battle for Falaise and the attempt to close the Falaise 'pocket' has become one of the most contentious parts of the entire Normandy campaign with accusations of 'failure' and the blame for 'slowness' in closing the 'neck' of the Falaise pocket flying about – and eventually settling upon Montgomery and the British and Canadian armies. In part this exercise in recrimination arises because all the Allied armies in Normandy had a share in this final battle around Falaise and their commanders and national historians have since become anxious to claim full credit for their part in the action – and pass the blame for any shortfall on to the rest. An objective review of the evidence would suggest that all the Allied armies – and, above all, both Allied air forces – played a full part in this last battle of the campaign at Falaise and any blame or glory can be equally shared.

Montgomery's insistence on the need for a quick capture of Falaise is worth noting. Many of the subsequent recriminations rest on the allegation that the British and Canadian advance through Falaise was just too 'slow' or 'timid' and that the Americans were not permitted to surge up to Falaise and do the work for them. This allegation will be carefully examined in the pages that follow but no part of this allegation can rest on Montgomery who was urging his commanders to go all out for Falaise.

After the broad picture given above, the progress of events may be picked up in the headquarters of Field Marshal von Kluge, where we can view the developing situation at Mortain–Falaise from the German side. On the night of August 7–8, at the start of the Mortain counter-attack, von Kluge was informed that a force of some 600 British and Canadian tanks were pressing out of Caen and heading south for Falaise – the start of Totalize.

This move could not have come at a worse time for the sorely tried commander of Army Group B. Von Kluge was just about to move three Panzer divisions away from Fifth Panzer Army and use them, as directed by the Führer, for another push towards Avranches. Circumstances now dictated a change in these orders and in the event, only 10 SS Panzer was moved. The orders from 9 SS Panzer and 12 SS Panzer of I SS Panzer Corps were cancelled, the first to contain the British south of Beny-Bocage while 12 SS Panzer remained south of Caen to continue their two-month-long feud with the Canadians.

The defences north of Falaise were then further reinforced by the committal of the newly arrived 85th Division and a Panther tank battalion from 9 Panzer. Having further considered the Canadian offensive, the continued British pressure towards Condé, and Patton's threatening moves against Alençon, von Kluge postponed the second thrust towards Avranches, pending further talks with the Führer. Von Kluge was no fool and he saw no point in pushing his few remaining assets even deeper into the bag.

It had already proved necessary to divert units tasked for the attack on Avranches and deploy them to protect the flanks of the Mortain salient, but von Kluge and Hausser still felt that if the proper arrangements could be made in the shape of reinforcements, fuel, ammunition, supplies and protection for their flanks and rear – a fairly tall order in the current circumstances – this thrust to Avranches could still succeed. This optimistic view was shared by Adolf Hitler and on August 9 he ordered von Kluge to prepare for a renewal of the attack – but added that a quantity of anti-tank and assault guns should be sent to bolster the defences north of Falaise. In short, the Führer wanted his forces to fight a defensive battle north of Falaise against the British and Canadians and an offensive battle against the Americans west of Mortain. This still left the matter of Patton's army in Maine, which apparently did not enter the Führer's calculations at all.

Matters began to go seriously awry on August 10 when von Kluge was informed that the US XV Corps, currently at Le Mans and believed to be driving east, had suddenly changed direction and was now coming north towards Alençon. It took very little time for von Kluge to connect the northern thrust by XV Corps with the southern thrust by Canadian II Corps. Unlike Hitler, he knew that the scanty forces left to his 81st (LXXXI) Corps could not stand for long against a strong American drive and he had to consider whether it might not be better to cancel the thrust on Avranches and send his panzers south to give XV Corps a bloody nose as it came north ... although this too would drive them deeper into what appeared to be an Allied trap. This was a decision that had to be taken by Adolf Hitler, to whom the question was now addressed.

The Führer mulled over the problem again but eventually agreed that in view of the supply dumps, blunting the XV Corps drive towards Alençon took priority – at least for a while. Von Kluge therefore telephoned Eberbach and they agreed that the Avranches move was out of the question at least until the looming possibility of encirclement at Mortain had been eliminated. The Canadian II Corps had by now been stopped by the deep defences north of Falaise and this freed Eberbach's *panzergruppe* for a brief strike south at XV Corps, primarily to protect Seventh Army's vital supply bases at Alençon which contained most of the available German supplies of fuel and ammunition.

Having given Eberbach his orders, von Kluge then phoned Hitler. The consensus of opinion in Normandy, he told the Führer, was that an attack on Avranches was currently impossible. He then added that to attack the US XV Corps with any hope of success he would need at least two fully equipped Panzer divisions. However, if these could be provided, he could attack XV Corps on August 13 and hope to have driven it back by August 16 which still left time – all being well – for Eberbach's promised moonlight strike against Avranches on August 20. This last comment was probably added to divert the Führer's wrath for it was becoming increasingly obvious that a renewal of the Avranches attack was simply not on, however the situation developed elsewhere.

On August 13, a further withdrawal to the east proved necessary in order to stave off British pressure from the north, coming down from Condé to Flers. Von Kluge asked permission to withdraw the Seventh Army to a line astride Flers, running from there north to Falaise and south to Domfront – plugging the gap between the *Suisse Normande* and the high ground running from Mortain through Domfront to Bagnoles – while sending some armoured units to bolster Panzergruppe Eberbach (the former Avranches strike force) at Argentan. 116 Panzer, or what was left of it, had now arrived at Argentan and taken charge of the remnants of 9 Panzer and other German units in the area. Hitler agreed to these steps in order to reinforce what was now described as 'the salient west of Flers'.

Although von Kluge was supposed to be getting reinforcements – 11 Panzer Division was en route from the south of France and might be expected shortly – the units he had were now very short of tanks, men, ammunition, fuel and sleep. Continuous night operations followed by days under aircraft attack were taking their toll. Besides, the only way to support 9 Panzer on the southern flank was to pull 116 Panzer, 1 SS Panzer and 2nd Panzer out of the line at Mortain and let the Americans there push east. Weakening the German line north and west of Falaise was just not on and it was abundantly clear to von Kluge that some hard decisions would have to be made – and made quickly.

The most obvious course of action was to abandon the Mortain position completely and send the forces there against XV Corps, thereby stabilising the left, or southern, flank of Seventh Army while the Fifth Panzer Army and Panzer Group Eberbach fended off the British and Canadians coming in from the north and the Americans arriving from the south and west. Von Kluge had seen the developing trap and decided on his priority – to keep the gap open and his two armies in being even if the Allies pushed them across the Seine; better that than allow the Allies to trap and destroy all the German forces at Falaise.

This conclusion had to be referred to Adolf Hitler for his decision and von Kluge therefore wrapped up the matter in a long report and sent it to Jodl. Hitler's reply came in on the evening of August 11. To von Kluge's immense relief, the Führer was broadly in agreement with his proposals and sanctioned a withdrawal from Mortain. The attack on XV Corps must be made with the existing forces as Hitler had decided to keep the promised 11 Panzer Division in the south of France, possibly in anticipation of the forthcoming Allied invasion – Operation Dragoon – which took place on August 15. This painful decision having been taken, the Germans duly began to withdraw from Mortain on the night of August 11 – and the race to escape the trap at Falaise was on.

In Montgomery's August 11 directive, Second Army were tasked to cross the Orne and the *Suisse Normande* and move on Falaise. Given the importance of the Alençon supply dumps, whose existence was known from the Ultra decrypts, Monty calculated that the Germans would put more effort into defending Alençon – which occupied a strong defensive position between two areas of high ground – than they would into holding Argentan. Argentan therefore became an objective for the Canadians after taking Falaise.

So the final pattern of encirclement emerges; the southern jaw would be the US XV Corps at Alençon, the northern one the Canadians at Argentan; it was therefore vital, said Monty, that the Canadians took Falaise quickly and then moved on Argentan. Meanwhile, to broaden the southern 'jaw', the US First Army would turn north-east, between Domfront and Barenton, and head towards Flers.

Once again, as Montgomery had pointed out, it was all a matter of time, but there was also the problem that the Allied armies attempting to close the Falaise gap were on a series of collision courses. If the Germans were squeezed against some physical barrier – like the river Seine – and could not get across because the Allied air forces and artillery had destroyed the bridges and crossing points and could keep them destroyed, the Germans would be forced either to give in or face annihilation. This had been the case in North Africa in 1943; the German Afrika Korps surrendered when it was forced into a pocket at Tunis and had nowhere to go but into the sea.

The obstacles the retreating Germans faced at Argentan–Falaise were not physical but human – Allied soldiers. If the Allied armies got too close to each other or advanced until their lines met, there was the strong possibility that they would clash. Even if that did not happen, the presence of Allied soldiers and tanks milling about among the German forces would seriously inhibit the actions of the two tactical air forces. The current plan for Allied encirclement would leave a gap of some fifteen miles between Falaise–Argentan, where the two wings of the Allied trap would stop. Through this gap the German Army might be expected to stream east to the Seine and in that zone, spanned by only two escape roads, one to Chambois and Gace in the Canadian sector, the other towards Dreux in the Third Army sector, the Allied air forces, strategic and tactical, could mount a killing spree of awesome proportions. With this in prospect, the battle for the Falaise pocket began – and with it came confusion.

The aims of the northern, Canadian 'jaw' are easy to establish, as are those of First Army. The difficulty lies with the US Third Army – specifically XV Corps – now tasked to head north for Alençon and meet the Canadians somewhere around Argentan. At some point on the way the XV Corps objectives seem to change.

In the three days after August 11, the British XII Corps and Canadian II Corps battered their way across the Orne towards Falaise. By August 14, XII Corps was seven miles from Falaise and the Canadian II Corps six miles. The XV Corps of Third Army had taken Alençon on August 12 and were now moving on Argentan which the US 5th Armored Division had been ordered to take – or so it now appears.

Exactly when this order was given or by whom is not immediately apparent from either the British or US Official Histories. The US History clearly states[2] that the Canadians were to drive south from Falaise and take Argentan and this view is confirmed in the British History.[3] But then, according to the British History, having taken Sées and Alençon on August 12, the US 5th Armored Division were ordered north, to take Argentan.

This order seems to have originated from Patton's HQ on August 8 when he directed General Haslip of XV Corps to proceed to the Carrouges–Sées line, 'and prepare for a further advance northward'. On August 11, states the US History,[4] on the basis of the further advance 'inferentially authorised' – whatever that means – Haslip established *Argentan* as the new XV Corps objective, the 5th Division to head there, the 2nd French Armoured Division of XV Corps to head for Carrouges further south.

However, the Canadians still appeared to have Argentan in their zone. This recipe for confusion might have caused chaos if the Canadians had been able to get through Falaise in time to move on Argentan, but they could not do so in face of the opposition they were currently meeting. Also – as it happened – the American forces were not able to take Argentan either.

As the XV Corps moved north from Alençon to Argentan, German opposition began to mount. On August 13, Patton went even further and ordered Haslip to take the XV Corps *north* of Argentan, but Haslip had not yet taken that town and was unable to do so. A patrol from the French 2nd Armoured Division of XV Corps had entered Argentan on August 12 but was promptly pushed out by a German counter-attack and when the 5th Armored Division attempted to get round Argentan and head for Falaise, all efforts to do so failed. According to the US History,[5] 'German guns, well-sited and skilfully concealed on dominating ground north of Argentan wrought a surprising amount of damage on the French and American formations.'

It transpired that elements of the 1 SS and 2nd Panzer had entered Argentan on August 13 to add their strength to the elements of 116 Panzer which were already there. It seems unlikely that XV Corps could have taken the town but they were now denied any further chance to do so. On the afternoon of August 13, Bradley ordered Patton to break off the XV Corps attack and prepare to move in another direction ... and George Patton was *furious*.

Patton had already proceeded more than fifteen miles beyond the Carrouges–Sées line laid down to separate the American and Canadian armies in

Montgomery's directive of August 11. He then moved up to Argentan which his 5th Armored Division had failed to take but Bradley's decision to call off the Argentan attack infuriated Patton. Patton's remark, or demand, that he should be allowed to push north and 'push the British into the sea for another Dunkirk', ignored the fact that the decision to stop his northward push into the 21st Army Group zone was in line with an Allied directive. It was also a very sensible decision in the circumstances – and issued by his superior officer, General Omar Bradley.

Bradley's memoirs[6] and the British Official History[7] make it abundantly clear that this decision was Bradley's. 'This decision to stop Patton was mine alone', says Bradley, 'Monty had never prohibited and I never proposed that US forces closed the gap from Argentan to Falaise.' At the time, Bradley adds, he considered that the German forces would be 'sluicing back towards the Seine' and that 'nineteen German divisions were stampeding to escape the trap'. This being so, adds Bradley, 'Although Patton might have spun a line across that narrow neck, I doubted his ability to hold it ... the enemy could not only have broken through, he might have trampled Patton's position in the rush. I much preferred a solid shoulder at Argentan to the possibility of a broken neck at Falaise.'

These were sound reasons and given by the one man in a position to know, but the US History tends to dispute them, arguing that Bradley felt he could not let Patton go to Argentan – in the 21st Army sector – without the permission of his superior officer, General Montgomery, who did not give it. The fact that Montgomery was not *asked* to give it is overlooked and overlooks the point already made – that when Bradley had an idea or a suggestion to make to Montgomery, for example the turn north towards Alençon, he never hesitated to make it. Why then, should Bradley not make another suggestion now, if he thought it helpful?

This argument in the US History is a neat but somewhat obvious attempt to switch the responsibility, or blame, for the 'failure' to close the Argentan –Falaise gap from Bradley to Montgomery. This argument ignores several valid points; that the gap had been set up for cogent military reasons – to avoid inter-Allied clashes and leave room for the deployment of air power – and that Bradley left that gap open for some other cogent military reasons, including his doubts as to Patton's ability to hold the gap open against German forces heading east.

As Bradley said later: 'We cannot risk a loose hinge. If the Germans hit us with three divisions there it will make us look foolish and it would be embarrassing for George. George is used to an attack by a single division. He is well enough buttoned-up for that, but he's not used to having three or four German divisions hit him. He doesn't know what that means yet.' Had von Kluge managed to muster more divisions at Alençon, George might have found out.

Why it is necessary to question this decision, taken by Bradley, to halt Patton by advancing reasons Bradley himself never put forward – other than to blame Montgomery for stopping Patton in his tracks – remains a mystery. The US History[8] rambles on about this point for two and a half pages, and eventually concludes that Bradley stopped Patton's advance and he was right to do so. To do otherwise would have meant sticking Patton's neck out against a German thrust from the west and the resistance mounted by Panzergruppe Eberbach astride Argentan to the north.

Nor were Bradley's fears about inter-Allied clashes groundless, as these accounts from Canadian rifleman Les Wager and Tom Robson of 'C' Squadron, 59th Armoured Recce Regt, 59th (Staffordshire) Division make clear. Les Wager:[9]

> Totalize was to go in with heavy bomber support, the first time we had seen American bombers on our front ... and also the last as it turned out. Getting through Caen was a nightmare but we reached our gathering place south of Caen and were on a long slope looking south when the Forts started coming in, fleet after fleet of them, each a solid wedge of planes. We watched and cheered as they went over when suddenly one wedge veered off its southern course and turned west, towards Caen.
>
> A ripple of consternation went along the slope and I saw the yellow smoke of friendly indentification flares start up. We watched in horror as the whole 'wedge', as if one plane, released its bombs and watched them fall like elongated sheets of rain, and the centre of Caen boiled up in a low erupting line of dust and débris. Then another 'wedge' veered off its southern course and then another, three in all I think. Since the main body of our division was running the Caen bottleneck at the time, we had casualties, mainly in Divisional Headquarters, our General for one, and one Company of the Seventh Brigade. We cursed the Americans for this mindless, follow-my-leader, for that was what it appeared to be. We cursed the lack of adequate ground-to-air communication, and most of all we just cursed, from sheer frustration.

And Tom Robson:[10]

We made a night move on the 14/15 August, to the Divisional bridgehead over the Orne in the Grimbosq area. It was obvious that the Germans were pulling out and we were being made ready for a reconnoitring role, to make contact again. We lined up to start shortly after first light, the armoured cars in the lead, the carriers following and the assault troop of infantry bringing up the rear. This was the normal formation on main routes and at the start we entered a house the Germans had recently vacated to find heaps of leaflets they had left for us, describing what the Americans were up to with our wives and womenfolk in England; rather than feel aggrieved we thought these leaflets hilarious and kept them as souvenirs.

We were moving south-east, towards Falaise; it was a blisteringly hot day and absolute hell for me as the Bren-gunner, sitting next to the hot engine plates in the carrier. As we entered the village of St Marc d'Ouilly the villagers came out to welcome us with glasses of cider and Calvados brandy but when we reached the far end of the village we came under a heavy 'stonk' from *nebelwerfers* on the high ground to the left. We dismounted to take cover in a very shallow ditch as the infantry of the 1/6th South Staffordshire Regiment came through to the front.

It was then that the mortaring stopped and the American Thunderbolts appeared. I cannot be sure, but I think there were two of them, though it seemed like more. They flew down from the top of the column, straight down the road, with their cannon blazing, wheeled out above the road and came back in again. We flung out yellow identification panels, put up yellow smoke, but it made no difference. We were laid head to toe in the ditch when they flew away, leaving us in chaos.

The man in front of me never moved and was pronounced dead and that American attack cost us 20 casualties; 13 vehicles also lost. The divisional historian records that during another attack by US fighters that day near Grimbosq we had a further 22 casualties and lost another 4 vehicles. I can recall at the Troop 'O' group next morning someone dryly asking. 'What side will the Americans be fighting on today?'

That was the last operation 'C' Squadron carried out because immediately afterwards the 59th Division was disbanded and the men used as reinforcements to top up other divisions.

Clearly, it paid to be wary of aircraft when moving on Falaise. Both the Allied air forces put in attacks on Allied troops but sticking his neck out – or rather sticking his troops' necks out – was Patton's particular area of expertise. So far in Normandy Patton had been lucky. His forces had met very little opposition and even now, as Patton thrust for Argentan, the US History comments:[11] 'There was no German force to speak of on the right flank', that is in the Third Army zone towards the Seine.

The situation was very different on Patton's left or northern flank where the US First Army and the British had to contend with the Seventh Army and the Panzer units of Fifth Panzer Army were coming east as fast and hard as their tracks would carry them, not to escape at this time but to bolster the defences of Argentan and keep the jaws of the trap apart until their forces further west were able to come up. The Germans were not at this time attempting to escape through the Falaise gap, they were coming back to form a new defence line, and keep the gap open.

Hence Bradley's legitimate concern, but the Third Army advances had been spectacular so far and Patton's always-simmering ego was about to boil over. He was now looking for a fight and the German divisions mustering at Argentan would have given him one, but Bradley rightly thought otherwise. The capture of Falaise on August 16 had already deprived the Germans of the road running south-east towards Trun but they still had the use of the one running north-east, from Argentan to Trun and Vimoutiers, beyond the Argentan–Falaise gap. On the afternoon of August 16, Montgomery directed Bradley to push up to Trun and Chambois from Argentan and at 1800hrs that day, Bradley passed that order on to Patton.

Patton had now divided his forces, without consulting Bradley, and the eventual outcome was that while the 2nd French Armoured Division and the 90th Infantry Division, later reinforced by the 80th Division, were left to butt against the Germans at Argentan Bradley, without telling Montgomery, ordered Patton to take the rest of his army – the balance of XV Corps, XX Corps and the XII Corps – to Dreux and cut the Germans off again, closer to the Seine. Patton set off at some speed through undefended country while Bradley believed that the bulk of the German forces had already escaped from the Falaise pocket. In this he was mistaken; on August 16, violent attacks against the 90th Division at Argentan alerted Bradley to the fact that 'a large proportion of the German forces still remained in the Argentan–Falaise pocket',[12] and these still had to be crushed.

Montgomery had already directed Crerar to send Simonds in again against

Falaise on August 15 – Operation Tractable – with orders to envelop Falaise and the roads leading out of it to the east; Falaise itself was to be taken by the XII Corps of Second Army and as soon as it had been secured the Canadians were to exploit east towards Trun; another look at the map on page 350 will make these moves clear.

Hitler is later reported as saying that August 15,1944, was 'the worst day of his life',[13] and the German situation in Normandy had certainly deteriorated in the last forty-eight hours. Falaise was about to fall, the troops there worn down and exhausted. The 85th Division no longer existed and 12 SS Panzer had only fifteen tanks left. Other units were out of ammunition or out of petrol and were forced to abandon their vehicles and take to the fields and woods when attempting to escape to the east. South-west of Argentan the French were surging forward and were only eleven miles from the British and Canadians north of the gap. Finally, as if Normandy was not a big enough problem in the west, that morning the Allies had landed forces on the Mediterranean coast; Operation Dragoon had begun.

General Bradley also had his problems and not for the first time the source was Patton. Patton was now anxious to head east, as ordered, towards the Seine but on the night of August 16–17 he created a 'Provisional Corps' consisting of the 2nd French Armoured Division, the US 90th Infantry Division and the 80th Division. These were currently tasked to take Argentan which was still in German hands. Patton placed this formation under his chief-of-staff, Major General Hugh J. Gaffay, and ordered him to drive north next day and capture both Chambois and Trun – which, again, were in the 21st Army Group zone and outside Patton's jurisdiction.

This instruction was an extension of Monty's suggestion to Bradley earlier that day, that the Canadian and American forces should meet seven miles north of Argentan, *near* Trun and Chambois,[14] but taking Trun and Chambois was a task for the Canadians – or so it would appear. It appears that army group boundaries were being ignored at this time, certainly by Patton, and these places could in practice fall to whichever army got there first. All the Histories and Bradley's memoirs are vague on this point.[15] Private enterprise in military affairs should usually be encouraged and the situation was extremely fluid – not to say confused – but, as at Argentan, if Patton pushed forces into the 21st Army Group zone, the result might be even further confusion.

Fortunately, Bradley intervened and got a grip of his wayward subordinate: command of all US units on the Argentan front, including Patton's three divisions – 80th, 90th and 2nd French Armoured Divisions – was switched to First Army; and Lt General Gerow of V Corps, which was currently pinched out of the line at Vire, was sent with his headquarters staff to take command. However, when Gerow arrived at the 90th Division HQ he found Major General Gaffey already there and issuing orders for the push on Trun. This caused a certain *frisson* between the two generals and they referred the matter back to Bradley, asking who was in command here. Bradley chose Gerow and on the afternoon of August 17 Gaffey turned his divisions over to V Corps and departed to rejoin Patton.

Gerow postponed the move on Trun and Chambois, electing to wait until the arrival of the V Corps artillery. He also revised Patton's plan, ordering elements of the 2nd French Armoured Division to hold the ground between Écouché and Argentan while the 80th Division passed to the east of Argentan and the 90th Division, supported by French armour, drove on towards Chambois. This advance duly began at 0630hrs on August 18 which, as the Canadian Official History remarks,[16] 'was a *day and a half* after Montgomery had issued the order for the Canadians to close the gap at Trun, and *four and a half days* after Patton had been stopped at the Third Army boundary'. During that time, says the Canadian History, the Canadians had been 'fighting down from the north with painful slowness' and the Germans had been making their way east through the Falaise gap. They were not, however, unimpeded; the tactical air forces and Allied artillery were already taking a fearful toll of the German columns on the roads heading east past Falaise.

Patton's corps duly surged away to the east, heading for Dreux, Chartres and Orléans respectively. None of these places lay in the path of the German retreat from Normandy: only Dreux is close to the Seine, Chartres is on the Beauce plain, south-east of Paris, and Orléans is on the river Loire. It appears that Patton had given up any attempt to head off the German retreat to the Seine and gone off across territory empty of enemy, gaining ground rapidly and capturing a quantity of newspaper headlines. This would be another whirlwind Patton advance – against negligible opposition – but while Patton disappeared towards the east the Canadians were still heavily engaged in the new battle for Falaise – Operation Tractable – which had begun on August 14 and was making good progress.

Operation Tractable began with a slight shift in plan from the previous attempt, Totalize. The Canadians were not to enter Falaise but to envelop it, circling round to take the roads running east from the town while Second Army came in and prised the Germans out, although, in the final event, the centre of Falaise fell to troops of the 2nd Canadian Infantry Division. With Falaise taken, the Canadians were to move rapidly east to Trun, sixteen miles south-east of Falaise and five miles north of Chambois. From Trun and Chambois the road ran to Gacé, one of the German escape routes towards the Seine and this move shifted the Canadians steadily south and east towards the American line. This was the plan on August 14 but the final stages of Tractable were not to work out in detail and its outcome was largely dictated by the events of the next few days – which was only to be expected in the currently fluid situation.

Having tested the German defences astride the Caen–Falaise road at Quesnay during Totalize, General Simonds elected to have the Quesnay area shattered by RAF medium bombers while his force went in over more open country to the east, round the Quesnay woods, over the narrow Laizon river, and so south to Jort and Damblaine, east of Falaise. This attack began at 1130hrs on August 14 with the bombing and strafing of German positions north of Caen, followed at 1200hrs by the advance of the 3rd Canadian Infantry Division and the 4th Canadian Armoured Division, east of the Caen road. All the infantry were now in Kangaroos and this attack was supported by the tanks of the 1st Polish Armoured Division and on the far left by the infantry of the 51st Highland Division, thrusting across the Liazon for St-Pierre-sur-Dives.

This attack went well, but slowly. The Laizon was crossed with help from the bridging tanks of the 79th Armoured Division but the enemy were now active on the Canadian front and brought fire to bear from artillery, mortars and 88mm anti-tank guns. Losses began to mount but the rate of progress picked up in the late afternoon. Then came yet another of those all-too-common short bombings, this time by the RAF.

At 1400hrs, RAF Bomber Command were due to bomb German positions in and south of Quesnay wood. Over 800 bombers took part and although most of the bombing was accurate, about eighty bombers – forty-four of them from the No. 6 Group, RCAF – bombed the yellow smoke markers put out by the forward troops to indicate their positions.

Les Wager of the Queen's Rifles again:[17]

Why it happened has never been adequately explained. The Lancasters flattened the woods and also took out our own artillery and 'B' Echelon (supply) elements. The bombers saw concentrations of troops and vehicles and clearly took them to be German and our identification flares were the same colour as those used by the RAF Pathfinders.

Before it could be stopped the bombing wounded about 400 Canadians, of whom sixty-five were killed – some indication of the great care needed to mark out bomb lines and one which fully justifies Montgomery and Bradley's concerns over 'friendly-fire' incidents in the narrowing gap between the approaching Allied armies. Great care was always taken but such incidents continued to occur.

In spite of this accident, the advance continued into the night, with the 2nd Canadian Division mopping up enemy positions east of the Caen road as it moved towards Falaise from Claire Tizon, six miles north-west of the town. Further pressure on the defenders came from the east, where the 3rd Infantry and 4th Armoured Division plus the Poles, were moving in. That evening the plan was changed and now the Canadians were ordered to clear Falaise. The advance was pressed during the night but at dawn on August 15 the defenders were still clinging on in the ruins of Falaise, although they were now under attack by four divisions, three of them Canadian plus the 53rd Infantry Division of the British XII Corps.

Joe Abbot was in this advance with the 53rd Recce Regiment:[18]

August arrived and we had left behind Point 112, known to the lads as Sausage Hill and advanced towards the river Orne, following a retreating but often stubborn and dangerous enemy. The Orne was crossed on August 12 and we went on to recce the village of Martinville where the infantry advance had been halted by strong resistance from SS troops. We reached the forward infantry and went through them to remarks like 'Sod your luck, mate' which did very little to raise our spirits. Initially we were covered by a morning mist but when that lifted we were exposed to some very disturbing mortar and shell fire on the approaches to a farm.

We decided to send on a section of carriers – three of them – forward through a wheatfield, while Tommy Palmer and I went forward on foot to give covering fire with the Bren if needed. The advancing carrier section became the target for some well-hidden 88s covered by the buildings. Two were hit immediately, the occupants killed or wounded. The third carrier managed to evade the guns and turn back into the wheatfield while my gunner and I were firing away at the enemy entrenched in the hedgerows by the farm, hoping to create some confusion and divert some attention from the remaining carrier. Our Troop officer, Timber Woods, now appeared to the right of our position, turned as if to shout to someone, and was hit by Spandau fire. I scrambled forward with Alec Grant, one of the Troop sergeants, in an effort to help but it was too late to help him. The 88s and mortars were still firing and had set fire to some vehicles on the road behind us and the position was later cleared by a Company attack by the 2nd Monmouths.

We certainly established that the farm was defended but at what cost? The Troop had lost its officer and two of the lads killed, and three wounded and taken prisoner – released later when we overran where they were being held captive – carriers and armoured cars had been 'brewed-up' and it was a much-depleted Troop which rejoined the squadron.

We were immediately sent out on another recce to see if an area on the left flank was inhabited by the enemy. We were creeping forward to a bend in the road with Alec, the sergeant who had helped with Timber, in the lead, when there was a blinding flash and bang. Alec's carrier slewed across the road, Jackie Towle, his gunner was blown clean out and landed in a heap in the road, followed almost simultaneously by Andy Moncur, the driver, with blood covering the left side of his face.

Our first thought was that Alec had been hit by an anti-tank shell but it turned out to be a Treble Teller mine, hidden by the side of the road and triggered by the carrier's track. There was no sign of Alec but the armour plate where he had been standing was curled back like so much paper. Alec was found later by some infantry lads, many yards away, where he had been blown by the force of the explosion.

The Canadian advance into and around Falaise continued during the morning of August 15 and met steady opposition including anti-tank fire which halted the 4th Canadian Armoured Division at Versainville, a mile and a half northeast of Falaise. The infantry of the 1st Bn Canadian Scottish were engaged here by SS troops and the Canadian Official History notes grimly[19] that: 'few prisoners were taken, the enemy, partly at least, preferring to die rather than give in'. The Canadian Scottish casualties that day amounted to 130 men, of whom thirty-seven were killed or later died of wounds. The enemy was still using that successful, counter-attack combination of a couple of tanks supported by infantry and putting up a stiff fight for every metre of ground given, drenching the attackers with machine-gun fire. Even so, the Canadians pressed on and by nightfall on August 15 were within a mile of Falaise.

On the following day, General Simonds ordered the 2nd Canadian Infantry Division to complete the capture of Falaise with the utmost despatch. The 4th Armoured Division was ordered to move on Trun and thereby close the gap between the Canadian First Army and the V Corps of Hodges's US First Army, which was now coming up from the west, while the 1st Polish Armoured Division was to advance on the left flank, cross the river Dives at Jort and keep moving to the south-east, hooking around Trun.

On this day, August 16 reports came in that elements of five Panzer divisions – Panzergruppe Eberbach again – were attacking the tip of the American thrust towards Argentan. It became clear to all that the Germans, sensing the closing pocket, were attempting to force the Americans back and keep the mouth of the trap open. The Allied armies closing the pocket now needed to liaise, those held back giving way to any Allied force that could get ahead, regardless of boundaries – provided the situation was clear.

On August 16, realising that his forces were not able to get forward quickly, General Crerar attempted to do this, writing a personal letter to Patton in an attempt to establish some effective contact between their two headquarters and sort out the question of Army boundaries, only to get a very dusty and unhelpful answer. Crerar sent an officer, Major A. M. Irving, and some signal equipment to Patton's HQ, asking for details of Patton's intentions and inviting Patton to send an American liaison officer to the Canadian First Army HQ for the same purpose.

Irving located but could not find Patton; he did, however, reach the First Army HQ and delivered Crerar's letter which was duly relayed to Third Army HQ. Patton's response is encapsulated in the message sent back by Irving to Canadian First Army; 'Direct liaison not permitted. Liaison on Army Group level only except corps artillery. Awaiting arrival signal equipment before returning.' Irving returned to Crerar's HQ on August 20, with nothing achieved and while such uncooperative attitudes prevailed at the front line, it is hardly surprising that the moves of the Allied armies on Trun and Chambois remained hesitant.

At Falaise, 12 SS Panzer was now down to twelve tanks and had little fuel or ammunition left; even so, they were still fighting. The 85th Infantry Division, facing the Poles astride the Dives, was almost finished as a fighting unit and constant Allied air attacks had obliged the III Flak Corps to turn the muzzles of its 88mm guns against aircraft rather than the swarming tank targets to its front. The 84th (LXXXIV) Corps, facing the British at Condé-sur-Noireau, east of Falaise, were almost out of ammunition and the 1st French Armoured Division of the US XV Corps had come forward to Écouché, south-west of Argentan and was about to link up with the Canadian drive from the north.

Having no choice, Eberbach had put his *Panzergruppe* on the defensive and was attempting to hold the corridor open so that more German troops, if under attack from the air and shelled from either flank, could still escape through Falaise. Falaise, however, was about to fall and when it did the main road east would be cut. On August 16 the 3rd Canadian Division reached the road junction a mile north of the town and the 2nd Canadian Division, coming from the north-west, broke into the town and began to mop up the snipers, machine-gunners and anti-tank positions that still remained to contest their progress. Falaise was in ruins but it was at last in Canadian hands. While the infantry mopped up, General Simonds sent the tanks of the 4th Canadian Armoured Division plunging south-east for Trun, eleven miles away.

It was now necessary to press the Allied attack to the east and south so while Simonds's II Corps headed for Trun, Crerar directed Crocker's I Corps, reinforced with the 7th Armoured Division, to head north-east for Lisieux. This instruction followed a telephone call to Crerar from Montgomery who believed that pressure from the two American armies would oblige those Germans forces who escaped the pocket at Falaise to shift their line of retreat to the north-east, between Trun and Lisieux. If this was indeed their intention, it was increasingly vital to seize the road junction at Trun.

By nightfall on August 16 the Canadian II Corps armour was heading for Trun and Crocker's I Corps, having taken St-Pierre-sur-Dives, was en route for Lisieux. The British Second Army had taken Condé-sur-Noireau and Flers, the US First Army had passed Domfront, Patton had already reached Dreux and the fall of Chartres and Orléans was only a matter of hours; the German position in Normandy was collapsing and on the left flank the 6th Airborne Division and the Commandos were making their bid for the Seine, Operation Paddle. Dixie Dean of the 13 Para mortar platoon, tells their story:[20]

By mid-day on August 17 the battalion was assembled by the cross roads. We did not know what lay ahead but we were fully confident in our ability to beat the Boche no matter where we might meet him. It was a perfect summer day and late afternoon before the order to move arrived, and we went via Troarn to the valley of the river Dives and at a cracking pace to the Dives canal, where the 3rd Brigade had seized a crossing and our task was to clear the enemy from the far bank and capture the high ground beyond, this would be a night attack and we were to give supporting fire from mortars and Vickers MMG as the battalion went in. At 0200hrs on 19 August I gave the order to fire and the full power of the Platoon was directed against the Boche; one thousand rounds of Mark VIII MMG landed on the crest of the far hill and four mortars engaged the enemy with five rounds rapid mortar fire.

We were aware from the sounds of battle that a prolonged engagement then took place but by the following afternoon the 13th Bn were in possession of that hill. We were ordered to move up and rejoin and leaving our platoon sergeants in charge Fred and I set off by jeep for the battalion but nothing prepared us for the news we were about to hear. The battalion had suffered heavy casualties in the assault on the ridge.

'B' Company had made the final charge and borne the brunt of the engagement, our dead were being buried in the churchyard and the German dead lay everywhere, too numerous to count and besides I was too shocked for that. For the first time the bloody business of war was brought home to me on that hillside above Plutot. On the way down I relieved a German officer of his almost-new Luger. He had no further need of it.

While the ground forces were squeezing the enemy, the Allied air forces and artillery were taking a terrible toll of the German forces still in the Falaise pocket. Gunner Bill Hodkinson of 'C' Troop, 4th Royal Horse Artillery, recalls what their guns were doing:[21]

Jerboa Battery of the 4th RHA went into action near the village of Bonnoeil. This was the worst carnage I saw in the Normandy battle and the battery observation post officers worked from dawn to dusk, shooting the guns at everything that moved in the Falaise area around Fresnay le Buffard in the south but at a cost. The battery lost two OP tanks suffering casualties including the 'D' Troop commander. During the 48 hours of action here Jerboa Battery fired 400 rounds per gun, a total of 3,300 rounds. My worst memory of the Normandy battle was the lingering smell of death around Falaise.

Travers Cosgrove was a sapper officer, 53rd Division and adds another strand to this account:[22]

At Falaise our job was to open roads blocked by strafed horse-drawn transport, hit by RAF Typhoons. On the whole the Norman roads were good but at Falaise we had to drive over the dead bodies of horses – and men – to make progress and up into the fields which were semi-*bocage*. If the Germans got away it was sans-transport.

On August 17 alone 2nd TAF and the Ninth Air Force flew a total of 2,535 daylight sorties over the pocket, bombing, rocketing or machine-gunning the enemy below, destroying a vast quantity of German tanks, trucks, guns and troops. Added to this were terrible losses to the German horse-drawn transport and the retreating infantry.

Tony King of the Royal Iniskilling Dragoon Guards – the 'Skins' – recalls the stench of the Falaise pocket:[23]

The infamous Falaise gap lay on the 'Skins' left flank and we got a taste of the massacre which left behind mile after mile of dead bodies and abandoned equipment. It seemed we would never be rid of the stench of decaying human and horse flesh, and the bloated carcases of cattle caught in the bombardments. The extent to which the Wehrmacht still relied on horse-drawn transport for wagons and gun limbers surprised us but of course Germany was suffering from a severe shortage of fuel. On one occasion from a concealed position, we fired HE at a German supply column and scored direct hits on two ammunition wagons which disintegrated in columns of smoke and fire. When we drove over to examine the remains, by some odd quirk of human nature we were more saddened by the dead and dying horses than by the mangled human corpses we found there.

Reg Plumb, the AA gunner from 127 Regt, RA, went through the Argentan –Falaise gap at the end of August and recalls the scene, sixty years later:[24]

Some impressions remain. Tiger tanks in hedgerows, burned or torn by shell fire. Many wrecked vehicles and many more horse-drawn wagons, the kind used extensively by the Germans, the majority of which had been turfed off the roads and were lying overturned in the fields and ditches. Literally scores – hundreds – of horses, cattle, lying dead or burned or torn apart, in the roads or fields. Beside the roads more horses and cows, their legs stuck up in the air, a whole forest of limbs stuck in the air – but the greatest impression of all was the all-pervading stench of bodies – animals and men. You may be assured there was no inclination to linger in the area.

It was a round trip, as I remember, going through Argentan, Trun and Falaise. Our overall impression was one of thankfulness that we had been on the Allied side and clearly identified by the white star on our vehicles.

This was the Falaise pocket after the Allied gunners and air forces had done their eerie work on the retreating Germans. This was a rolling, moving battle, a shifting slaughter as the retreating tide rolled east, under attack all the way. On August 18, the last German resistance was snuffed out at Falaise and the battle shifted east, to Trun and Chambois, where the American units coming up from the south-west, the 80th and 90th Divisions were still being held up by the 116 Panzer Division. This opposition would soon be overcome and with their front in the west collapsing everywhere, the Germans had every reason to worry, but their Führer, Adolf Hitler, had another problem; on August 16, his senior commander in France, Field Marshal Günther von Kluge, had gone missing.

17 CLOSING THE FALAISE POCKET AUGUST 18-23

*During these five days ... the German formations lost their
cohesion and disintegrated into small groups led by men hell-bent
on breaking out from the pocket*

BELFIELD AND ESSAME *The Battle for Normandy*

The events of the Mortain counter-attack had taken their toll of Field Marshal
von Kluge. Ever since his arrival in Normandy he had found himself squeezed
between his loyalty to the Führer and his professional estimates of the situation. The former urged him to obey the Führer at any cost; the latter told him
that Normandy could not be held and that his entire force would be destroyed if
he attempted to do so.

That apart, his strength and resolution had been drained by Hitler's constant
and unrealistic demands; to hold every inch of ground, to counter-attack relentlessly, regardless of the situation and by the Führer's inability or unwillingness
to recognise that a divisional title – 12 SS Panzer, 21 Panzer – now described a
unit that might amount to only a handful of tanks and a few hundred worn-out
men. And so, as matters went from bad to worse, as his forces were eroded and
he was denied permission to fight a sound tactical battle, it dawned on von Kluge
not only that Normandy would fall and fall in the not-too-distant future, but
that Germany was going to lose this war.

Von Kluge took no direct part in the July 20 plot against Hitler but he was
certainly aware of it. Had it succeeded he would have been ready to stop the
fighting in Normandy at once and negotiate with the Allies. When the plot failed
and the round-up of conspirators began, he soldiered on, hoping that his knowl-

edge of the plot would not be revealed by those of his colleagues now being tortured in the Gestapo cellars. His inability to meet the Führer's constantly changing demands kept von Kluge on edge and he had been in serious trouble with OKW since August 8 when the Mortain counter-attack came to a halt.

These problems reached a head a week later, on August 15. On that day, von Kluge set out from Sepp Dietrich's HQ to visit some of Eberbach's units, only to have his staff car strafed by Allied fighters, a common feature of the Normandy battle. Von Kluge and his companions escaped injury but the attack knocked out his wireless transmitters. His party then became tangled up among the retreating German columns, delayed for hours by traffic jams and by the constant need to take cover as the *jabos* swept overhead. As a result, von Kluge did not reach Eberbach's headquarters until midnight, by which time he had been out of touch with his own headquarters – and therefore with OKW – for most of the day. With the Normandy battle in a highly fluid state, this breakdown in communications was bound to cause problems but it did rather more than that.

Von Kluge's absence from his headquarters – coupled with the radio silence – rang alarm bells at the Führer's headquarters. Since the July plot, Hitler had become highly suspicious of all the Wehrmacht generals and was only too willing to believe any rumour of defection. On August 15, the Führer therefore got it into his head that von Kluge's silence could only indicate that he had gone off to negotiate a surrender with the Allied forces in Normandy. Hitler was still brooding over this opinion and consulting his staff about a replacement for the missing field marshal when von Kluge reached Eberbach's command post and came back on the air.

The Führer's suspicions were totally unfounded and misjudged von Kluge. If totally disillusioned with Hitler and resigned to defeat in this war, von Kluge was still willing to fight on – all he asked was the freedom to fight sensibly. Otherwise, the outcome was inevitable: Normandy was already lost and the defeat of Germany would inevitably follow. This opinion he had so far concealed but the root of Hitler's suspicions concerning von Kluge's loyalty was that von Kluge and his forces were no longer meeting the Führer's demands; the fact that his demands were impossible to attempt, let alone execute, eluded Hitler completely.

By mid-August von Kluge was no longer willing to go on attempting the impossible or being forced into actions that only made a bad situation worse.

Therefore, when that order from OKW appeared on his desk on August 16, demanding yet another counter-attack, this time an attempt to destroy the US XV Corps in the Alençon–Carrouges area, adding[1] that 'the 9 SS, 10 SS and 21 Panzer can and must be employed for this purpose' – three units that had been cut to pieces and hardly existed in any viable form – von Kluge phoned Jodl and told him bluntly: 'This order is impossible to execute. To cling to a hope that cannot be fulfilled by any power in the world ... is a disastrous error. This is the situation.'

Having decided to ignore the Führer's order to attack, von Kluge had told his commanders to continue the withdrawal to the Seine. As related, this movement began that night, August 16–17 with the pull-out of Fifth Panzer Army and Seventh Army, which were to move east from the area of Falaise on the axis Trun–Gacé–L'Aigle, with Fifth Panzer Army leading. This retreat was to be commanded by Hausser of Seventh Army while Panzer Group Eberbach stood off the enemy in the Argentan–Gacé area and kept the gap open. Once the Seventh Army were out of the pocket, Panzer Group Eberbach was to disband and Eberbach was to reassume command of the Fifth Panzer Army from Sepp Dietrich.

This move might have saved something from the disaster but when news of von Kluge's actions and a report of his conversation with Jodl reached him, Hitler's reaction was swift. On the evening of August 17, Field Marshal Walter Model appeared at the headquarters of Army Group B and handed von Kluge a letter from the Führer. Von Kluge was to hand over command of OB-West and Army Group B forthwith and present himself to the Führer's headquarters. As he left, the guns and aircraft of the Allies had already begun the final shattering of his retreating forces, grinding his divisions into the dust, increasing still further the number of the dead. The German forces had been encircled; now they were to be destroyed.

The battle for Normandy was then to claim the life of another German commander. On his way back to Germany, perhaps in despair or depressed by his sacking, perhaps in fear of a Gestapo investigation into his knowledge of the July plot, von Kluge committed suicide by taking poison; he was found dead in his seat when his aeroplane landed at Metz and in his pocket was a letter addressed to his once-admired leader, Adolf Hitler:

The attack on Avranches was not only impossible; the attacks ordered were bound to make the all-round position of the Army Group worse. And that is what happened. I do not know whether Field Marshal Model, who has been proved in every sphere, will still master the situation. From my heart, I hope so. Should it not be so, however, and our new, greatly desired weapons, especially of the Air Force, not succeed, then, my Führer, make up your mind to end this war. The German people have borne such suffering it is time to put an end to this frightfulness.

Naturally, the Führer ignored this sensible advice. Nothing changed; the German forces in Normandy were to hold their ground and fight it out where they were; if they did that, then the German terror weapons, the V-1 flying bombs which were falling steadily on London – and would shortly be joined by the even more lethal and quite unstoppable V-2 rockets – would result in Allied pleas for a negotiated peace. The V-1's were certainly taking their toll; by mid-July a total of 3,582 flying bombs had fallen on Britain, killing 3,583 civilians and injuring thousands more; a new evacuation from the capital was taking place, half a million people had left London by the middle of July and another half million would follow by the end of the summer as the bombs continued to fall.

At mid-day on August 17, a flying bomb fell on a bus in Battersea, South London, killing twenty-eight people; a week later another bomb fell on a factory at Southgate, killing another 211 civilians; these were the losses caused by just two of the forty flying bombs that fell on the capital that month but none of this death or destruction would have any effect on the outcome of the battle in Normandy – or force the Allies to negotiate with Hitler. The notion that it would is yet another example of Hitler's growing delusion.

As von Kluge had done on taking up the command in July, Model began by making a rapid tour of his now-crumbling front and assessing the situation. This brought Model face-to-face with the true situation and the plan he came up with was much like the one proposed earlier by von Kluge. Fifth Panzer Army and Seventh Army would form a defence line from the sea at Touques to the town of L'Aigle, twenty miles west of Argentan. Paris would be defended by its garrison and a fresh defence line would be drawn up between the Seine and the Loire. To reinforce the L'Aigle line and form the new one, Model required a considerable number of fresh troops; his request of August 18 called for 'a restriction of enemy air activity, reinforcement by twenty draft battalions, five GHQ engineer battalions, 270 tanks, nine batteries of artillery and 180 light field howitzers and transport of 9,000 tons gross capacity. C-in-C West further asks to be sent the six armoured brigades now being formed in Germany.'

Model might as well have asked for the moon; not only was there no way of sending this equipment to Normandy – even if Hitler had been inclined to do so – the situation in Normandy had gone beyond redemption. Field Marshal Model swiftly got a grip on the situation and at a conference on the morning of August 18, he ordered that the Seventh Army and Panzer Group Eberbach were to be extricated from the pocket as quickly as possible while II SS Panzer Corps (the remnants of 9, 10 and 12 SS Panzer Divisions plus 21 Panzer) held the northern side of the corridor, facing the Canadians and the Poles, and 116 Panzer and 2nd Panzer held the southern side, facing the Americans.

And so we come to the final stage of the Battle of Normandy, the collapse of the German fighting formations and their destruction under the guns, bombs and rockets of the Allied tactical air forces as they gave up any attempt to form another line and fled east to the Seine. What happened to the Seventh Army and Fifth Panzer Army in their flight across the Seine is still regarded as one of the most devastating examples of air power and the sights that met the Allied soldiers on the roads and lanes as they pushed into the sides of the Falaise pocket were truly terrible.

The Canadian History recounts:[2] 'The road, as were all the roads in the area, was lined and in places practically blocked by destroyed German vehicles of every description. Horses and men lay rotting in every ditch ... unburied dead were strewn about by the score.' Eisenhower later recalled: 'Roads, highways and fields were so choked up with destroyed equipment and with dead men and horses that passage through the area was extremely difficult ... it was literally possible to walk for hundreds of yards at a time, stepping on nothing but dead and decaying flesh.'

A detailed picture of the final days of the Normandy battle is hard to describe for at this point confusion steps in, as Ron Ludgater of the 53rd Welsh Division describes:[3]

> My pal Jim Barrance and I were young riflemen from the Rifle Brigade, press-ganged into the Ist Manchesters, a Vickers machine-gun and 4.2in mortar battalion. The 53rd Welsh Division were heavily engaged in the battle for Évrecy and then we moved on towards Falaise, following up the Canadian advance

and four things stay in my memory. First, was the almost complete lack of knowing what was going on and what we and the rest of the Army were doing. Two, when the platoon was parked up on the edge of the wood and then moved forward, we were promptly attacked by American Mustangs. The yellow markers were all laid out forward but they came in at low level and attacked behind the line, destroying one carrier by fire. Three, near Falaise it was quite gruesome to ride up and down over dead bodies of men and horses. Four, mounting some farm horses to round up Germans in the woods. The MPs had erected a POW cage and we were able to round up about 200 Germans and bring them in; they had abandoned their equipment and were quite willing to be taken prisoner and were offering rings and watches in exchange for cigarettes.

My lasting memory of Normandy is that we always seemed to be moving on our own; it was a small platoon world. On some days nothing happened and on others you dug like mad with mortar bombs dropping all around and steel splinters flying everywhere. The worst thing of all was not being kept in the picture, not being told the state of things and the reason for failed attacks. Our advance on Falaise and beyond was mainly due to our armour, artillery and, above all, to the Typhoons.

German units were spilling everywhere as they attempted to escape and reach the Seine, Allied units were surging forward as the scent of victory entered the air or the opposition in front collapsed. As the German forces pulled back, finding a way wherever they could, often by abandoning the roads and taking to the fields and footpaths, disintegration inevitably began in the German units, order and discipline were gradually lost, exhausted men sat down and waited to surrender. The Allied forces acted in accordance with the degree of opposition on their immediate front, attacking the enemy wherever found, pushing on until resisted, keeping up the pressure.

All this activity took place to the ceaseless drone of aircraft engines, the chatter of machine-guns, the crash of bombs and rockets as the *jabos* roaming the Normandy skies came swooping down to rocket and strafe any enemy they could find, rocketing tanks and vehicles and horse-drawn transport on the roads, machine-gunning parties of infantry heading across the fields.

What can be said with some confidence is that there was heavy fighting on both flanks of the corridor between the Allied units and those German units that stayed to fight and keep the neck of the pocket open while other German formations streamed back towards the Seine from the west. The German Army had been defeated and was now in full retreat; it had not, however, been routed. Plenty of German units, large and small, were still willing to fight. This being so, an outline of the situation on August 18 may be helpful as will another study of the map on page 350.

By August 18, the shape of the pocket was much the same as it was on August 12 but the pocket was now much smaller. Shaped rather like a butterfly net, six miles deep and seven miles wide, with its open mouth towards the Seine and its 'bag' curving around in a slight bulge from south of Falaise to the northern outskirts of Argentan, the pocket was gradually being compressed. By August 18 most of the German formations were behind the railway line east of the Falaise–Argentan highway and in the country between there and the river Dives. The British Second Army were pushing against that bulge at Falaise and the 11th Armoured Division had patrols in Argentan by August 19. On the US front, VII Corps were heavily engaged around Ranes while XIX Corps were fighting hard north and west of Domfront and Gerow was pushing the three new V Corps divisions – formerly of Patton's army – up towards Chambois.

East of the Falaise–Argentan road, the 4th Canadian Armoured Division were moving south towards Trun, with the 1st Polish Armoured Division on their left and the 3rd Canadian Infantry Division on their right; their spearheads reached Trun on the 18th and Chambois on the following morning. The overall picture on August 19 is that the 80th and 90th Divisions, now of Gerow's V Corps, were coming north and east towards Bourg-St-Léonard and Exmes, the British were pushing west across the Falaise to Argentan road and the Canadians were starting to extend the pocket now being created around Trun and Chambois, where a scrambling battle was now taking place.

Patton had now veered off towards the Seine. His forces were still forging ahead against light opposition and by August 19 the leading elements of Third Army were only ten miles from Chartres, astride Dreux, and his right flank forces had liberated Orléans on the Loire. Patton's surge to the east took him away from the main fighting but Hodges's First Army, having made a shorter 'hook' around the eastern end of the Mortain salient, was starting to face north and was now forming the southern edge of the pocket, roughly between Argentan and Chambois; this done, the final squeezing of the German forces at the neck of the pocket could begin in earnest. In this battle Hodges's men were meeting plenty of opposition from stubborn German defenders, as were the Canadian forces north of the pocket.

The Canadians were making slow progress towards Trun, making six miles on August 18, partly because they were also encountering heavy opposition, partly because the narrow bridges over the river Dives were neither wide enough or strong enough for tanks. However, once across the river, their rate of progress increased, the opposition slackened and on the afternoon of August 18 Simonds ordered that the 3rd Canadian Infantry Division were to push into Trun and the 4th Armoured Division were to push on to Chambois, a move urged on that afternoon by another order from Montgomery:

> It is absolutely essential that both the Armoured Divisions of the 2nd Canadian Corps i.e. 4 Cdn Armd Div and 1 Pol Armd Div, close the gap between First Cdn Army and Third US Army. I Pol Amd Div must thrust on past Trun to Chambois 4051 at all costs and as quickly as possible.

The Canadian Official History records:[4] 'During the next two days these orders were carried out in the face of frenzied German opposition which slowed progress both north and south of the gap.' Much of that opposition came from the II SS Panzer Corps, which, having escaped from the pocket and reached Vimoutiers, was now sent back in, to help the units still trapped to break out.

II SS Panzer Corps mounted a two-division attack towards Trun and Chambois while from inside the pocket, the II Parachute Corps and the 67th (LXVII) Panzer Corps attempted to break through the Allied lines, head east across the Dives and meet up with them; as always, the Germans were willing to fight and their attacks were truly frenzied. This attack, planned for August 19, finally began on August 20, and the SS Panzers ran straight into the 1st Polish Armoured Division and a bloody and hard-fought final battle over the next two days at Mont Ormel.

The plan required the II SS Panzer Corps, having regrouped at Vimoutiers, to attack west into the Morteaux–Couliboeuf area, north-west of Trun, to stave off the advancing Americans and Canadians and gain time for the units coming from the west. The scene at Trun during the German retreat was a repeat of that seen previously in the Argentan–Falaise gap:[5]

It was a gunner's paradise and everyone took advantage of it. Away on our left was the famous killing ground and all day the roar of Typhoons went on and fresh clouds of smoke obscured the horizon. We could just see one section of the Argentan–Trun road, some 200 yards in all, in which sector was crowded the whole miniature picture of an army in retreat. First a squad of men running, being overtaken by men on bicycles, followed by a limber at a gallop and the whole being overtaken by a Panther crowded with men ... all with the main idea of getting away as fast as they could.

Into this chaos the SS Panzer Corps must return, but Model's order clearly came too late. The flow of German units across the Orne had become a flood and by the afternoon of August 18 OB-West noted that 'Withdrawals in pocket have been continuing. Bulk of forces now on east bank of the Orne'.[6] This being so, the first task of the Allied forces is summed up in the aims of the II Canadian Corps for August 18 – to link up with US forces and hold the line of the river Dives. Stating the aim and preparing the plan was simple but as so often during the Normandy campaign, carrying it out in practice was no easy task.

At this point it becomes clear that the term 'Falaise pocket' is no longer accurate. The arguments about closing the gap at Argentan or advancing on Falaise can be seen as irrelevant, for by the morning of August 19 the pocket had moved some way south-east of Falaise. The widest point now lay between Argentan and Morteaux-Coliboeuf, the narrow neck tightening between Trun and Chambois, the enemy spurting out of the gap on the axis St-Lambert–Coudehard–Vimoutiers. The 4th Canadian Armoured Brigade had crossed the Trun–Vimoutiers road while other Canadian units pushed south from Trun towards Chambois. Meanwhile, the 1st Polish Division had fought its way to Les Champeaux and with other Canadian forces now coming up, the Trun–Chambois gap had narrowed to a few miles and the aerial execution of the enemy continued.

Perfect weather on August 18 provided the Typhoons with a field day for what the pilots described as a 'Bank Holiday Rush' of German tanks and vehicles towards the east. The Allied air forces put up 3,057 sorties that day, claiming 226 tanks destroyed or damaged and a vast quantity – some 3,000 – soft-skinned vehicles stopped and destroyed around the neck of the pocket. Inevitably, with so many aircraft competing for targets, there were more instances of 'friendly fire'. The 51st Highland Division alone recorded no less than forty attacks by Allied aircraft that day, attacks which destroyed 25 of their vehicles and caused fifty-one casualties. The 1st Polish Division had already suffered from Allied air strikes, being attacked on August 8, on August 14 and again on August 18. During these attacks a total of seventy-two Polish soldiers were killed and 191 wounded by the Allied air forces – yet another vindication of Bradley's fears about closing the Falaise–Argentan gap with Allied soldiers rather than aircraft and artillery fire.

While the Canadians and Americans attempted to close the gap in the east the British Second Army was pushing the Germans hard from the west, moving their divisions round south of Falaise to avoid entanglement with the Canadians. The British 53rd Division were now south of Falaise and were five miles further east and pushing on hard by the evening of August 18. On that day the US forces south of the gap – the 80th and 90th Divisions – were brought to a halt before Chambois by an attack from the 116 Panzer Division.

General Simonds had already ordered the divisions of his II Canadian Corps to push south *at all costs* and close the gap with the Americans. From reading the Canadian accounts there comes the feeling that Simonds wanted to get this Falaise pocket battle over, that the enemy were now being hit hard from every side, including the air, and what the Allied armies had to do now was go in and finish the job by closing the gap and taking the ground and pushing on to the Seine.

At 1100hrs on August 19, Simonds ordered his four divisional commanders – 3rd Canadian, 1st Polish Armoured, 4th Canadian Armoured and 4th Infantry – finally to close the gap. No Germans were to escape and the 2nd Canadian Division would take over the 3rd Division's line along the Dives so that the latter division could push on and close all the escape routes. As for the crucial meeting point at Chambois, that was to fall to the 1st Polish Armoured Division, who were ordered to take over the area from Moissy to Chambois as well as Hill 262, in the Canadian sector north-east of Chambois, which was currently reported to be in American hands.

As tended to happen at this time, very little of the plan worked out in detail; the situation was too fluid. The Germans occupying the village of St-Lambert in the middle of the Trun–Chambois gap resisted the Canadian advance, and fighting to hold or take the village, as both sides strove to evict the other, continued throughout August 19. The 4th Canadian Armoured Brigade was engaging the retreating enemy with artillery as the Germans, now abandoning the roads, strove to escape across open fields. It was, a Canadian artillery observer reported: 'An OP (Observation Post) officer's dream ... roads and fields were full of Germans moving eastward seeking a way out of the trap ... the carnage was terrible.'

The Seventh Army breakout towards the north and north-east was led by Panzer Group Eberbach and II Parachute Corps, followed by the 74th (LXXIV) Corps and the 84th (LXXXIV) Corps. This attack was held for a while but eventually a breach was made north of St-Lambert and – according to the German account – some forty to fifty per cent of the German forces trapped west of St-Lambert managed to get through and join hands with the II SS Panzer Corps, although all their tanks, guns and vehicles had to be left behind.

To the east of St-Lambert, at Mont Ormel, a hill near the village of Coude-hard, just north of the Chambois–Vimoutiers highway, the Poles were now heavily engaged with elements of II Panzer Corps which had now re-entered the fray. The 1st Polish Armoured Division had been organised into three battle-groups, each consisting of an armoured regiment and an infantry battalion, all pushing into the gap on a line between St-Lambert in the centre and Coudehard, some distance to the east. The Polish battlegroup on Mont Ormel consisted of around 1,500 men with eighty tanks and for the last twenty-four hours this force had been cut off from support, with German forces deployed across its rear. Strong attacks came in on the Mont Ormel position throughout August 20 and the attacking Panzer troops were then reinforced by those elements of the II Parachute Corps which had managed to get across the Dives.

Attacked on two sides and very short of ammunition, their hilltop an Allied island in a sea of attacking or retreating Germans, the Poles held on. Unable to take the hill, the Germans did succeed in opening a route up the road to Vimoutiers; with this done, the commander of the II Parachute Corps sent a convoy of ambulances, all carrying wounded and marked with the Red Cross, out of the battle area. It is interesting to note that passing these ambulances down the road took some fifteen minutes and while they were on the road not a shot or shell was fired as the column moved through. Only when they had gone did the shelling begin again. While the Poles were thus engaged, a final Allied junction drew near, with the advance of the US 90th Division from the direction of Bourg-St-Léonard. Contact between the two Allied armies was finally established on the evening of August 19, when both the Poles and the Americans claimed to have captured Chambois.

The battle of the 'Gap' was not yet over. It appears that much of the Seventh Army was still inside the pocket and Model was very anxious to extricate it, with or without its heavy equipment. On the evening of August 19, General Hausser of Seventh Army having been wounded – and for a while believed killed – Seventh Army came under the command of Fifth Panzer Army. According to the Army Group B situation report for that day: 'Losses in material were very high because during the last three days enemy fighter-bombers had fired nearly all vehicles and fuel reserves and the artillery had been destroyed by fire concentrations from the enemy's heavy artillery. Gradually the Army lost all its communications and was unable to carry out its command functions ...'

A Canadian account from the South Alberta Regiment confirms this account, stating that the German formations moving against their lines were 'a mass of riflemen' which, 'our tanks were able to mow down'. The US 359th Infantry Regiment, stemming the German troops west of Chambois, records that most of the enemy were 'not attacking, but merely trying to escape'.

The Germans moving through the Polish lines were made of sterner stuff and the battle fought by the Poles trapped north of Chambois on August 20 was a sanguinary affair. The Polish battlegroups were cut off from the rest of the II Canadian Corps, attacked front and rear by Germans retreating from the pocket and by German units coming in from the east and were also short of ammunition and fuel. The same is true of the 4th Canadian Armoured Division which records August 20 as 'very confusing ... Germans attacking from east and west, call made to seal off any German escape routes but units are mixed up and difficult to define any brigade areas.'

Les Wager of the Queens Rifles of Canada provides an eyewitness account of this time:[7]

> Now we were moving in open country again. To the west, on the other side of the valley we saw tanks appearing out of the wheatfields and at the same time out of the valley on this side numbers of Germans started to appear, in full pack and armed, running to escape the tanks. A shell from one of the tanks hit the west of the road about 50 yards away. 'Hit the ditch,' said the Captain and that we did.
>
> From the line of trees I watched more Germans climbing out of the valley,

more tanks coming out on the opposite slope. We held fast in the ditch, waiting for orders. By this time I figured I knew exactly what was going on and that we were about 5 miles out of place. As far as the Germans knew we were either one of theirs or a crack Allied unit that had them surrounded. I took a Bren gunner to the edge of the wood, told him to cover me and went out to wave the Germans in. Seeing me, a number of them started in our direction and when the nearest was about 10 yards away he realised that I was not a German after all. He stopped in terror, face white and, dropping his rifle, began to run back to his comrades, waving his arms and shouting.

We could not have that, of course. I raised my rifle, and fired over his head, as I could not shoot him in the back. Other rifles had come to bear on the Germans in the open and those stricken went down like rags. Then a group of three Germans started across the road, trying to pass behind us, and I put one through the radio man and toppled him into the ditch. Who is to say what bullet did what but none of the three Germans got across the road.

We then stopped a German scout car with a driver and one passenger, who got out with their hands up, having thrown away the key, which we could not find. By now our prisoners outnumbered us and although we could have roughed up the driver and made him find the key it seemed better to stay friendly. By now, from the north, north-west and north-east, the tank attack was beginning but although we were in action that day I don't remember much else.

The wounded were put in the half-track and a Priest mobile gun, a German first-aid man riding with the most severe cases. The remaining troops, including the sergeant and myself, climbed aboard the two leading tanks which had lots of handholds and the 40 or so German prisoners were lined up to walk alongside under the watchful eyes of the riders. And so we set out, in the early evening and we came back to the lines of the British 51st Highland Division, and that's the way the war went for me.

This confused fighting around Trun and Chambois continued on August 21. German infantry were still trying to escape, infiltrating through the Canadian lines in small groups and being caught in the open by machine-guns and artillery, but the main task for II Canadian Corps that day was to re-establish contact with the Poles. During the afternoon contact was made with the Americans coming up from the south and by the end of that day the Trun–Chambois gap had been closed.

The German forces to the east of Trun–Chambois were now pulling back for the Seine; those who remained to the west had little option but surrender. On the night of August 21–22, the term 'Nothing to report' appeared in a 'situation report' – *sitrep* – at Canadian First Army HQ for the first time in a month. There would be some severe fighting and much more skirmishing in the days ahead as the remnants of the enemy retreated to the Seine, but the great battle for Normandy was over.

The Normandy campaign as a whole will be reviewed in the final chapter but what of this last battle – the Falaise pocket? The myth holds that the battle at the Falaise pocket was another missed opportunity and adds that the fault lay – again – with the slowness and timidity of the British and Canadians. The arguments on the last point have gone on almost since the battle ended but if national chauvinism is taken out of the frame the picture is fairly clear.

The decision on how to fight the Falaise battle was agreed by all the commanders involved – Montgomery, Bradley, Dempsey and Crerar – on August 11; and if some aspects had to be altered later – in the light of changing circumstances – no one argued at the time, except Patton. The answer to the main accusation, that the Falaise encounter failed to achieve all it could have done, surely lies in the figures.

German losses in the Falaise pocket were awesome. The popular belief that the Allied victory was incomplete because the bulk of the enemy soldiers were able to escape, albeit at the price of abandoning their equipment, is simply not borne out by the evidence. Army Group B estimated German troop losses ran at between fifty and sixty per cent of their strength during the five days from August 16–21. During that period the German divisions trapped in the pocket lost 20,000 men taken prisoner by the British or Canadian armies and about the same number, 20,000 men, taken by the US First Army; some 9,000 Germans being captured by the First Army on August 21 alone.

Some divisional totals are also interesting, if somewhat puzzling. The 2nd French Armoured Division took 8,800 prisoners and claims to have destroyed more that 100 German tanks and artillery pieces in the Falaise fighting. In four days, the 90th Division, so unfortunate in the early days in Normandy, took over 13,000 prisoners ... and 1,000 horses. These divisional totals are at variance with the Allied totals, some of which are given above, but there can be little doubt that the Germans were surrendering in great numbers, and taking awesome casualties. The US History records[8] that by August 21, 'the strength of the six of seven armoured divisions that had escaped the pocket totalled, as reported at that time, no more than 2,000 men, 62 tanks and 26 artillery pieces'.

Later estimates claim that the total number of Germans escaping across the Seine ranged between 20,000 and 40,000 men; that represents a variation of around fifty per cent and fails to point out that few of these survivors were combat troops and that many who got away were wounded. In the immediate aftermath of the battle the strongest German divisions – with a normal 'ration-strength' of between 15,000 and 22,000 men depending on the formations – could barely muster 3,000 men apiece, and some were down to a few hundred soldiers. All of these soldiers were minus their kit, except for personal weapons; among all the disputes on the outcome of the Falaise battle, what is not disputed is that most of the German soldiers who escaped from the carnage around and east of Falaise had to leave their equipment behind.

Overall German losses for particular units are hard to estimate because their ranks were topped-up during the battle but it is estimated that around 30,000 members of 1 and 12 SS Panzer Division crossed the Dives on August 19–20; these two divisions mustered at full strength some 45,000 troops, so they lost about one-third of their establishment in the final battle alone – and these were crack divisions, filled with highly motivated troops; the losses in other divisions must have been far higher. These figures for the SS are also open to dispute and seem far too high when some individual unit losses are taken into account. It is also recorded[9] that these SS divisions had ceased to exist as a coherent force and had lost all their tanks, *jadgpanthers* and artillery.

On August 21 a strength report on I SS Panzer Corps revealed that 10 SS Panzer had only 300 men, in one *panzergrenadier* battalion, no guns and no tanks. 12 SS Panzer had 300 men, ten tanks and no artillery. I SS Panzer was unable to provide a manpower return at all. The II SS Panzer Corps carried out a similar exercise which revealed that 2 SS Panzer had 450 men, fifteen tanks and six guns. 9 SS Panzer had 460 men, twenty to twenty-five tanks and twenty guns. 116 Panzer had one infantry battalion containing around 550 men, twelve tanks and no guns.[10] These forces were the cream of the German armoured units and they had effectively been smashed; that being so it is hard to see where the larger estimate of 12 SS Panzer soldiers crossing the Seine comes from.

After the battle, the Falaise area was examined by an operational research section of 21st Army Group which discovered – within a limited area – the wreckage of 344 tanks, SP guns and armoured cars, plus 252 towed guns (with their dead horse teams alongside) and almost 2,500 trucks and lorries; all this within one small area. More guns, tanks, vehicles, equipment and men were found on the American front and littered along the roads and lanes leading from Falaise to the Seine. However 'incomplete', the battle of the Falaise pocket was a shattering defeat for the German armies in the West. Those armies had been shattered and the remnants were now fleeing north across the Seine.

The US Official History[11] records the views of an American officer, one who had seen plenty of carnage in two World Wars, on the Meuse–Argonne front in 1918 and St-Lô a few weeks previously, views he recorded immediately after a trip to the pocket. He wrote:

> None of these compared in the effect on the imagination with what I saw yesterday at Trun. I stood in a lane surrounded by 20 or 30 dead horses or parts of horses. I stepped over hundreds of rifles and saw hundreds more stacked along sheds. I walked a mile or more where vehicles had been caught closely packed. I saw probably 300 field guns and tanks. I saw no foxholes or any type of shelter or fortification. The Germans were trying to run and had no place to run. They were probably too tired even to surrender.

No one who saw the carnage around Falaise has any doubts that this was a victory.

18 RETREAT TO THE SEINE   AUGUST 23–SEPTEMBER 1

*The battle front was getting further and further away. The enemy
was still retreating. Our armoured columns were surging forward at such
speed that the Germans were learning the hard way the meaning
of their word, Blitzkrieg*

DOUG PROCTOR 4th Bn The Somerset Light Infantry, *Section Commander*

The crushing of the German forces in the Falaise pocket and beyond by August
20 brought an effective end to German resistance in Normandy but it did not
end the Normandy campaign. The province of Normandy extends to the Seine
and beyond and it is easier to determine the start of the battle – June 7 – than
decide on the precise date it ended. After Falaise the outcome was not in doubt,
but the retreating Germans had now to be pursued and the pressure kept up
until the enemy was finally defeated and their armies ground to dust. This desirable process was brought to a halt by the old problem – supply.

The problem was not simply the difficulty of supplying the front-line units
with fuel and artillery ammunition. Some of the Allied armies in Normandy
were running out of men. There were now four Allied armies in the field but
the British Army could only get smaller as Britain ran out of troops. The breaking up of the British 59th Division – which was already in Normandy – and
some of the tank brigades, in order to supply troops to the other British divisions or brigades was only one indication that British manpower reserves were
exhausted. This was not least because the 'wastage' rate – the number of men
killed and wounded in Normandy – had been far higher than anticipated. As

RETREAT TO THE SEINE 389

with the US forces, the anticipated British losses had been based on casualty figures from the campaign in North Africa. The War Office had calculated that in 'periods of intense activity' – i.e. battle – forty-eight per cent of the casualties would be suffered by the infantry, fifteen per cent by the armoured corps and fourteen per cent by the artillery.

This forecast proved wildly out and extremely optimistic. Taking the Canadian units as an example of the Second Army totals, seventy-six per cent of the casualties were in the infantry, seven per cent were in the tanks units and eight per cent in the artillery. Similar figures applied to the British units. To give some more examples, on August 7, General Guy Simonds reported to Canadian Army HQ that his 2nd Infantry Division was 1,900 men short of establishment – around eighteen per cent. By the end of the month, in spite of reinforcements, the situation was much the same; the nine battalions of the 2nd Infantry Division were now 1,910 men short, all of them 'other ranks'; sergeants, corporals and private soldiers. The percentage losses among the company officers was even higher, ranging up to eighty per cent.[1]

In 1944 a British or Canadian infantry battalion contained thirty-five officers and 786 men – so the 2nd Canadian Infantry Division's nine battalions should have had a total of 7,389 men; the current and chronic shortage of 1,900 men represented a short fall of twenty-six per cent – and since almost all of this shortfall was in the rifle companies, the effect on the battalions' ability to fight was grievous. Richard Harris, a private in the 1st Bn Suffolk Regiment, gives a bleak picture of his thirty-man platoon:[2]

I can only tell you what happened from when we landed on D-Day until August 18 – nearly the end of the Battle of Normandy. On that day I was clobbered by a mortar round and wounded in both legs and my right hand, part of which had to be amputated. A corporal and myself were evacuated that day, the last of the platoon which had landed on D-Day – so our casualty rate in the Normandy battle was 100 per cent.

Losses on this scale soon took effect. An account from the 2nd Bn The Hertfordshire Regiment, which had gone to France on D-Day as a beach group battalion, engaged in beach protection and supply, records:[3]

The whole area of King Beach was extensively mined. In the King Sector we lifted and cleared over 120,000 mines. The battalion then settled down to its

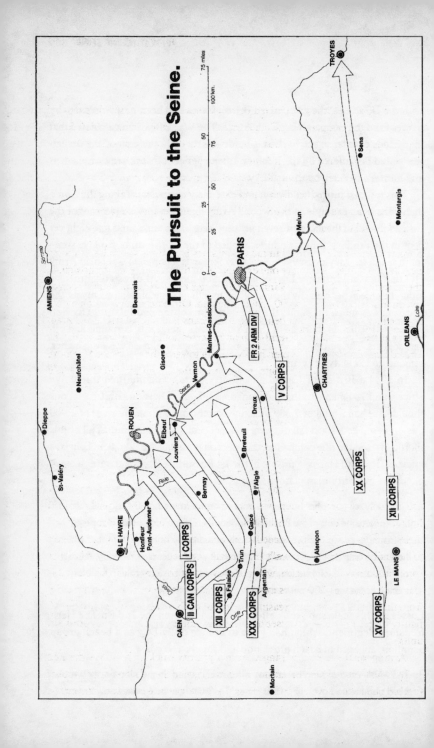

The Pursuit to the Seine.

role of working the beach and moved an average of 1,500 tons per day with 2,000 tons on our best day. On July 15, a letter was received from General Montgomery, informing the Commanding Officer that he would have to use the battalion as infantry reinforcements. We came off the beach and carried out intensive training, hoping that we would be used as a complete battalion but on August 17 the battalion was placed in suspended animation and drafts were duly sent to other units until by 31 August only the Commanding Officer and the Adjutant were left.

Similar stories were recorded in the US infantry battalions which had suffered heavily in the fighting. To give one example from the phases of the campaign, in the advance to St-Lô, the US infantry divisions had lost some 40,000 men of which ninety per cent – 36,000 – were riflemen. Officer casualties in many US regiments exceeded 100 per cent. The Americans had almost unlimited manpower at this time but these terrible infantry losses could not be sustained. The United States' abundance of men finally ran out towards the end of the European War in 1945 when a lack of white troops forced the US military to allow black soldiers to serve in combat units. By the end of the Normandy campaign, General Eisenhower was ordering a comb-out of rear-echelon and administrative units in Britain and transferring fit men from base organisations to infantry units in France.

For the moment, though, plenty of American reinforcements were being shipped in from the USA but the growing number of American units only added further strains to the supply chain. Nor did this strain only affect army units, the air forces were also under pressure; most of the front-line squadrons and fighter groups of the two tactical air forces were now based in Normandy and these forces, air and ground, needed a vast quantity of stores all of which still had to be landed either through totally inadequate port facilities or over open beaches – and autumn was coming on, with the prospect of regular gales. Added to this was the fact that as the armies moved east and north, they moved further away from their ports, thereby increasing the length of their supply lines and the difficulty of getting the most essential supplies, notably fuel, up to the forward units.

Arrangements to do this ranged from a priority trucking service – the Red Ball Express – to taking bombers out of service, rigging the bomb bays with rubber fuel bags and sending them to Normandy as airborne tankers. James Lorenz of the 466th Bomb Group, Eighth Army Air Force, flew one of these aircraft:[4]

> In September 1944, our Bomb Group and the 477th BG were stood down
> from combat to haul gas to Patton's advance area in France. Using war-weary
> B-24s, the gasoline was either in five-gallon jerrycans or in huge rubber tanks
> installed in the bomb bay which could carry 2,500 gallons of gasoline. I flew
> two of these missions and we got no mission credits, though we did lose several
> planes. We also got to see the war close up – and were glad our job was
> flying missions.

The Red Ball Express, so called from the priority signs carried by the trucks and
on road signs, began on August 25, 1944 and lasted officially until November
15, when the restored and repaired railway networks and the opening of more
ports on the Channel coast gradually eased the pressure. The Red Ball Express
operated twenty-four hours a day and was a good example of American ingenuity. Over 6,000 trucks were organised into convoys which carried more than
12,000 tons of stores and fuel each day, from the Channel ports to the advancing
armies.

Such a vast quantity of supplies was needed. In the week of August 20 the
two US armies in France consumed 800,000 gallons of petrol – although around
300,000 gallons was used by the Red Ball trucks in just delivering stores. On a
peak day, August 29 1944, the Red Ball Express succeeded in delivering no less
than 12,244 tons of supplies to the Third Army at Chartres and more than 89,000
tons were delivered to Third Army between August 25 and September 3. Even so,
the Red Ball Express could only be a temporary solution – what the Allies needed
was more ports, nearer the battlefront.

Allied arrangements to mitigate the supply problem displayed considerable
ingenuity and enabled the Allied divisions to keep up the pursuit but with petrol
rationed and supply lines lengthening the pressure on the enemy inevitably slackened, with unfortunate results later on. This became especially clear in September and October, when German units were able to reform, re-equip and hit
back hard, notably at the British 1st Airborne Division at Arnhem and then
at the US divisions fighting in the Hurtgen Forest near Aachen. For the moment,
though, at the end of August 1944, everything looked possible as the Allied
armies ended their efforts at the Falaise pocket and set out to push the enemy
north across the Seine, where all the bridges had already been destroyed

and the Allied air forces attacked any temporary structures put up by the retreating Germans.

Ralph Conte of the 416th Bomb Group, Ninth Army Air Force, was flying A-20 attack bombers at this time:[5]

> We were based at Wethersfield in England and our mission was to hit bridges, enemy encampments, railroad junctions, air fields, marshalling yards and provide support for the ground forces as required. I can recall attacks on Lessay bridge, Belleroy railroad, Vitre bridge and many more. Our formations of 36 or more planes flew at dangerously low levels, in weather which we would not normally fly in, from early dawn to late dusk. We wiped out practically all the bridges over the Loire and the Seine, keeping the Germans from escaping.
>
> Our most memorable mission was the bombing of the last bridge over the Seine which the Germans were using to get their last troops out of the Falaise pocket. We were called on to cut this bridge at Oissel on August 6. This which had been attacked before and damaged but not destroyed; this attack was made at low level and against plenty of flak and eleven of our planes were lost over the target.

The scrambled fighting around the pocket had resulted in some confusion so the next task for the Allied armies was therefore to 'tidy-up' their front and take up the pursuit, 'tidying-up' being a particular requirement in any force commanded by General Montgomery – who was still the Ground Force Commander.

Monty liked a 'tidy' battle, with no loose ends to unravel later and after the pell-mell fighting at Falaise, Trun and Chambois involving three Allied armies, there were many loose ends to tidy-up. The Canadian First and US First Armies, now meeting at Trun–Chambois and facing south and north, had to pull apart and turn east. This would allow the British Second Army which, with the US First Army, had been one of the 'plunger' forces that had squeezed the Germans into the pocket, to take up a central position between the Canadian First and US First Armies for the next phase, the advance to the Seine.

The eventual organisation of the Allied armies for the pursuit up to and over the Seine, had the Canadian First Army moving up the Channel coast, tasked with taking the ports of Le Havre and Dieppe, moving with the British I Corps on the left and the II Canadian Corps on the right. This would enable the Canadians to take Dieppe, where their Second Division had suffered so much during the raid of August 1942 and the 51st Highland Division of Crocker's I (British) Corps to take St-Valéry-sur-Somme, where the original 51st Division, trapped against the sea, had surrendered to Rommel in 1940.

Then came British Second Army, with XII Corps on the left and XXX Corps on the right and the other corps in reserve. The dividing point between the Canadian and British Armies on reaching the Seine would be the city of Rouen. On the right of XXX Corps came XIX Corps of the US First Army and XV Corps of the US Third Army. While other US units had been engaged in the battle at the Falaise pocket, XIX Corps had cut north and moved across to reach Elbeuf and Louviers, south of Rouen, on August 25. This move by the US XIX Corps put them across their British front at Breteuil and about a day ahead of the British forces who got up to Vernon on the Seine on August 26.

Also curving north-east was the US 5th Armored Division from Patton's XV Corps, Third Army, which also ran across the British front before Vernon. There should have been no problem about these moves by XIX and XV Corps, for the aim was to keep up the pressure on the Germans and the British and Canadian divisions had been fully engaged at Falaise and needed to regroup. Inevitably, however, more carping arose, the Americans claiming that the British were 'slow', the British complaining that the Yanks had 'got in the way'.

No one seems to have appreciated that this move had been agreed between Dempsey and Bradley, that the two US corps which had *not* been engaged at Falaise should get their light forces up to the Seine as quickly as possible and destroy the light ferries (*bacs*) which the Germans were using to evacuate their troops and wounded across the river; the heavy ferries and bridges were under constant air attack where they had not previously been destroyed.

XIX Corps crossed the Seine south of Vernon. South of that formation came the US V Corps and VII Corps, heading hard for Paris, moving along on the left flank of the Third Army. The map on page 390 explains this process but, as before, to explain what happened after the victory at Falaise it is necessary to go back and explain what took place before that to the US divisions moving east, south of Falaise.

These divisions, mostly in Patton's army, were making good progress in early August because they were facing comparatively little resistance, so little indeed that on August 17, Bradley had decided that the right flank of Patton's Third Army, moving north of the Loire, could be safely protected by aerial patrols of the Ninth Air Force. Their southern flank thus covered, the 'broad front' advance of Patton's three corps between the Loire and the Seine therefore proceeded apace. While Patton's XV Corps was thrusting for Dreux and Mantes–Gassicourt on the Seine, thirty miles south-east of Paris, on August 19, XIX Corps of First Army moved in to fill the gap between Gacé and Dreux.

That night, while this move was getting under way, the 79th Division of XV Corps, Third Army, entered Mantes and found the enemy gone. There was nothing to oppose a rapid crossing of the Seine at this point and within the next twenty-four hours the 79th Division got across the river and deployed in the country beyond, digging-in there in adequate time to beat off a hastily mounted counter-attack by a fresh German division.

This was the first crossing of the Seine – the move which, in his original plan announced back in May, Montgomery had decreed would be the last act of the Battle of Normandy. Monty had estimated that this act would take place around D plus 90 and it took place on August 20 – D plus 75. Montgomery had therefore beaten his own 'cautious' forecast of the previous spring by two full weeks.

This first crossing of the Seine also marked the point where Allied strategy had to change. This was the last piece in the Montgomery plan for Overlord, his great contribution to carrying out the orders given to Eisenhower, Supreme Commander of the Allied Expeditionary Force to 'enter the continent of Europe and ... undertake operations aimed at the heart of Germany and the destruction of her armed forces'.

The first stage had been now been achieved. The Continent had been entered and crossing the Seine brought the 'invasion phase' of the war against Germany to an effective close. The Allied commanders now had to bring the next moves in the campaign under consideration; what direction their armies should take, what forces should be deployed, what the next bound forward should attempt to achieve ... and also address the looming question of command.

Montgomery had been appointed Land Forces Commander for the 'invasion phase'. Although the duration of that phase had been left vague, with the Allied armies now over the Seine who could now deny that the 'invasion phase' was over? Monty himself had set the time and distance target – the river Seine by D plus 90 – for this phase, so what would happen now? Would Montgomery remain in field command, as he clearly hoped? Or – as almost everyone else hoped – would Eisenhower now take over direct command of the Allied armies and act as his own Field Commander, as well as Allied Supreme Commander?

Monty clearly wished to remain as field commander after the Normandy victory and may have felt that he was entitled to do so. After all, why break up a winning team, or, as the Americans say, 'If it ain't broke, don't fix it.' Whatever the merits of his case, it does not require much hindsight to see that this wish was doomed from the start and that any British claim to field command never stood the slightest chance of success.

Montgomery could have been as able as Alexander the Great and as charming as Charles II and it would have made no difference. This war in Europe was now dominated by the armed forces of the United States of America and from now on the Americans were going to run it their way. Demographics and the US media would see to that.

As the armies moved up to the Seine, pushing the scanty German forces before them, questions on the future command arrangements were frequently asked in the various Army HQs and above all at SHAEF. For the moment they remained unanswered by Eisenhower and the combined chiefs but, even so, certain dispositions and assumptions had to be made. Time was passing, the armies were pushing on and some direction was needed, if only to allow for whatever moves the Supreme Commander wanted when the Normandy campaign came to a close. Such arrangements were also essential to keep the enemy on the run for, whatever happened, the pursuit must be kept up, the enemy forces closely pursued and delay in that pursuit must be avoided.

Therefore, on August 19, the day the 79th Division reached the Seine, Montgomery took the issue in hand and sent out a directive to both army groups calling for the complete destruction of the enemy forces in North-West France. Then to advance northwards, with a view to the eventual destruction of enemy forces in North-East France'. Montgomery was still the Ground Force Commander and fully entitled to issue directives – but this particular directive involved matters of long term strategy.

The August 19 directive called for a push heading generally *north*, through Belgium towards Holland and the lower Rhine. To underline his point, Monty added boundaries for the two army groups, a line running from Argentan to Dreux–Mantes–Amiens–Ghent–Antwerp, with the British and Canadians to the west and the American forces to the east. As Montgomery saw it and stated later, with this plan the Allied armies would move like a great armoured wave, forty divisions strong, marching north in line abreast to the frontiers of Germany.

There they would muster along the Maas and Lower Rhine, cross the river and so debouch on to the North German plain, advancing with their left flank resting on the North Sea to take the Ruhr and surge on to Berlin. American historians tend to refer to Monty's hankering after 'pencil-like thrusts', probably in reference to Market Garden, the Arnhem operation of late September, but it is important to realise that there was nothing 'pencil-like' about the proposal in the August 19 directive – this was a broad front advance by a force of forty divisions – and virtually unstoppable at this time, *provided it could be supplied*.

Events in western Europe from September 1, 1944, after Eisenhower took command of the Allied armies fall outside the borders of this book. The events between the Seine crossing on August 20 and September 1 are only included to round off events at the end of the campaign, but the discussion over the future command and direction of the Allied armies can be said to have begun on August 18 when Montgomery sent a telegram to Alan Brooke:[6]

> Have been thinking about future plans but have not (repeat not) discussed the subject with Ike. My views are as follows. After crossing the Seine 12 and 21 Army groups should keep together as a solid mass of some 40 divisions which would be so strong that it need fear nothing. This force should move northwards, 21 Army Group should be on the western flank, and should clear the Channel coast and the Pas de Calais and Western Flanders and secure Antwerp. The American armies should move on Ardennes, directed on Brussels, Aachen and Cologne. The movement of the American armies would cut the communications of enemy forces on the Channel coast and thus facilitate the task of British Army Group ... Bradley agrees with above conception. Would be glad to know if you agree generally. When I have your reply will discuss matter with Ike.

Montgomery was clearly trying to muster support for this scheme before he put it to the Supreme Commander but in one respect he was wrong. Whatever Bradley had said – or seemed to say – at their meeting on August 17, when future plans were discussed, he did not agree with this project. Bradley had discussed the future with Patton[7] and says that they had decided that: 'The first or American plan called for a thrust to the Reich straight through the middle of France to the Saar and beyond the Saar to the Rhine in the vicinity of

Frankfurt ... both the First and Third American Armies would be required for this effort.'

It might have been better if Bradley had been straight with Montgomery at that first meeting on August 17, but he laid his cards on the table when he saw Monty again on August 19. Monty then learned of this 'first American plan' and heard that Ike supported it – up to a point – and Monty raised no objection to Eisenhower, Bradley and Patton discussing future arrangements without his knowledge. It will be noticed that Bradley and Patton's 'First American plan' seems to have ignored the very existence of the Allied armies from Great Britain and Canada.

Eisenhower – the Supreme Commander – was aware that he had British and Canadians under his command but he wanted to split the Allied forces and send the American half eastwards, towards Nancy and the Saar, while the British and Canadians headed north for Antwerp and the Rhine. Monty knew of this when he issued his own directive, telling Brooke, 'I have so worded my directive that we shall retain the ability to act in any direction.' Here again, it might have been better if Monty had gone to Ike and asked him what his intentions were regarding the British and Canadian forces before issuing the directive. One suspects that Monty still hoped to remain as Ground Force Commander and issued his directive as a prior statement of claim.

On August 22, Monty changed his angle of attack. When the Deputy Chief of the Imperial General Staff, Lt General Sir Archibald Nye, visited his headquarters in France, Montgomery summarised his views on the Allied command structure and future strategy. He was adamant that the direction to go was north, that the two Army groups, US 12th and British 21st, should stay together and that 'Single control and direction of the land operation is vital for success. *This is a whole time job for one man*'. (Author's italics.) He went on to add that the great victory in north-west France had been won by personal command and ended by stating: 'To change the system of command now, after having won a great victory, would be to prolong the war.'

Since none of this ever became Allied policy, it can do no harm to point out that much of what Montgomery stated was quite right and very sensible. To split 12th Army Group and 21st Army Group, when it had just taken their united efforts to defeat the Germans in Normandy, was not sensible; not splitting your force in the presence of the enemy is a basic military tenet. Yes, for the moment the Germans were in disarray but as the British were to find out a few weeks later at Arnhem, and the Americans a month after that in the Hurtgen Forest, the German Army was always a force to be reckoned with.

The best way to the industrial heart of Germany – the Ruhr – was via the north and this would also keep Allied supply lines short, a significant point at this time, when Patton's divisions were already coming to a halt through lack of fuel. On the command point it is at least arguable that combining the jobs of Allied Supreme Commander and Ground Force Commander – Chairman and Managing Director – was a great deal of work for one man.

The underlying objection to this proposal as it stood was that Monty clearly thought that the Ground Force Commander – as at present – should be Bernard Law Montgomery. It is worth adding that when he realised that this was not to be, Montgomery offered to serve under Bradley, maintaining that the idea was sound and the matter of who did the job secondary. As to whether advancing north, rather than north and east, would have shortened the war, how can we tell? It did not happen, so any opinion can only be speculation. The question of whether Eisenhower was a competent field commander will be discussed in the next chapter.

However it was entitled and whatever it contained, Montgomery's directive of August 19 was only a proposal; Eisenhower had not spoken and Montgomery's tacit assumption that he would continue as Ground Force Commander was a pious hope at best. However, lacking other orders at this time, the arrangements to implement this directive duly took place. Canadian First Army would wheel left at Rouen to reach the Channel coast north of the Seine at Le Havre and then advance up the Channel coast, taking or sealing off any German-held ports and overrunning the remaining V-1 sites. Second Army would cross the Seine between Mantes and Louviers and press north to cross the Somme while the US 12th Army Group would consolidate south and south-west of Paris but was not to enter the city until Eisenhower ordered it to do so; wrecking Paris and soaking up infantry in a prolonged street battle was not part of the Allied plan.

The German forces were in no state to resist these moves – provided they were executed quickly. Hitler was still issuing field orders and on August 20 he directed Model to prevent the Allies – in this case the Americans – from pushing south of Paris towards Dijon and hold a bridgehead on the coast south of the

Seine around Touques and Honfleur to collect any forces escaping across the Orne from Lower Normandy. The basic idea was to create a new defensive line from the coast to Burgundy, running down the rivers Seine and Yonne east of Paris, where the relatively unscathed German First Army was deployed, then south to Dijon and east to the Swiss frontier. This line was to bar any progress towards Germany by the Allied armies, including General Devers's 6th Army Group coming up the Rhône valley after Dragoon. As far as the Führer was concerned, if holding this line meant the destruction of Paris, so be it. To bring that battle on, a fresh German division was sent into Paris and two more German divisions were directed to move into the line on the lower Seine.

The Führer's plan was another pipe-dream. Model did not have sufficient forces to create such a line, let alone hold it, and most of the forces he did have – Seventh Army and Fifth Panzer Army – though receiving some reinforcements after they crossed the Seine, were in no state to hold any line without rest and a chance to re-equip. Indeed, it is a misuse of words to call these two forces 'armies'. Sepp Dietrich had only the remnants of the Fifth Panzer Army to hold the entire front from the Channel to where the First Army took over west of Paris, and Seventh Army – especially after General Hausser was wounded on August 20 – was in no state to fight at all. The best German option at the end of August was a fighting retreat until the Allied forces were brought to a halt by their ever-lengthening supply lines but this option looked less plausible as the Allies reached the Seine ... and continued to advance.

21st Army Group advanced on a two-army front, four corps in line, with VIII Corps in Army Group reserve. The advance went well and quickly picked up speed. The 11th Armoured Division entered Touques on August 21, taking L'Aigle on the following day. By August 23, XXX Corps were on the river Risle and met American armoured cars there on August 24. The Canadians crossed the Risle near Bernay on August 25 and on August 26 the 6th Airborne Division and the 1st Commando Brigade, which had been in the line continuously since D-Day, took Pont Audemer and finally came out of the line.

At this time the Second Army was obliged to disband the 59th Division of XII Corps in order to distribute its troops to the other divisions of the army. The 59th Division was the junior division in the British Army and its place in XII Corps was taken by the 15th (Scottish) Division – and so the British advance continued and picked up speed.

The US 12th Army Group began moving on Paris on August 20, XIX Corps and XV Corps from the west, XII and XX Corps coming up from the south. By August 19 there were only about 6,000 German troops in the city and on August 20 the local French resistance, the FFI, rose against them. Sporadic fighting broke out all over the city and Hitler's directive of August 20, to hold the city regardless of the destruction caused, was ignored by the Paris garrison commander, General von Choltitz. Fighting continued until August 22 when General Eisenhower ordered Allied troops into the city and General Le Clerc's French 2nd Armoured Division rumbled in on August 24, followed by the 4th US Division. Before then, however, steps to change the Allied command structure had been put in train.

On August 23, Eisenhower and his Chief-of-Staff, Walter Bedell Smith came to Montgomery's HQ and told him that the forecasted changes in the command set-up would take place on September 1. Eisenhower claimed that the reason for making the change was US public opinion which would not permit General Bradley serving under a British general. The fact that a British general, Montgomery, had been serving under an American general – Eisenhower – for the past nine months was not mentioned. Ike also wanted to head for the Saar as well as Antwerp and the Rhine, but agreed that the Saar attack must wait until the supply situation was easier. On the following day, as was his practice after a meeting with the British commander, Eisenhower wrote Montgomery a letter. The main points of this letter were that he had changed his mind; the Saar push was on again and the two Army groups would be known as the Army Group of the North – Montgomery's 21st Army Group – and the Army Group of the East – Bradley's 12th Army Group.

The fall of Paris on August 25, although a cause of great rejoicing, was a side-show to the main events in this closing act of the Normandy drama. South of the city, the Americans had now crossed the Seine in five places and on August 26 Patton's army advanced another forty miles and entered Troyes. As the American advance continued to the north-east, so the German First Army fell back towards the Marne, while on the British–Canadian front, XXX Corps crossed the Seine against stiff opposition at Vernon and XII Corps crossed at Louviers.

By the evening of August 26 the overall situation was as follows. The German armies were in full retreat but fully capable of turning back for swift and savage strikes at their pursuers. On August 27, for example, Tiger tanks and German infantry appeared before the British bridgehead at Vernon and it cost XXX Corps some 500 casualties to drive them off and advance through the Forêt de Vernon. The II Canadian Corps ran into stiff resistance at Elbeuf where the surviving units of the Fifth Panzer Army were assembling. Fighting along the river line continued until August 29, the German line bolstered by the arrival of a fresh German division from the Pas de Calais and the tenacity of a number of tank and infantry *kampfgruppe* which had been ordered to stay behind and contest the Canadian advance. These actions cost the already reduced Canadian 2nd Infantry Division a further 600 casualties.

Even so, in spite of this dogged opposition, with the Seine behind it and the more open country of the *pays de Caux* and Upper Normandy ahead, the British and Canadian advance speeded up. It continued to speed up and the Second Army now got into that giant stride that would carry 21st Army Group north to Brussels and the river Scheldt west of Antwerp in the next two weeks. On August 29 the Canadians veered west to Le Havre but General Crerar had no intention of letting the capture of that great port – inevitably in ruins – divert him from the pursuit of the Seventh Army forces that had managed to cross the Seine.

So the advance continued. On the right flank of the First Canadian Army, General Dempsey's Second Army began to charge north into Belgium. Their advance began on August 29 behind a screen of armoured cars provided by XXX Corps. German opposition fell away and the 11th Armoured Division advanced twenty miles that day, taking more than 1,000 prisoners, brushing aside any opposition from roving Tiger tanks and scattered pockets of German infantry. On August 30, all the divisions of Second Army were in full cry, heading north through flag-bedecked French villages, through cheering crowds of excited people and under a steady barrage of flowers and fruit. 'The only injury I got in the war' said Ted Smith of the Guards Armoured Division[8], 'was when an apple thrown by a French girl hit me full in the eye somewhere outside Amiens.'

Gisors fell by mid-morning on August 30 and the British armoured cars were in Beauvais in time for tea – there is no record that they stopped for it. Still they pressed on, out of Normandy now and into Picardy, heading for Amiens, the capital of that province across open country ideal for tanks and armoured cars.

At 0600hrs on August 31, the 29th Armoured Brigade were in the centre of Amiens, brought to a halt by cheering crowds who refused to let them past. Two hours later General Eberbach, former commander of the Fifth Panzer Army, who had just arrived to take command in the area, surrendered to men of the 11th Armoured Division.

On the following day I British Corps took Le Havre, the 51st Highland Division marched into St-Valery, and the II Canadian Corps pushed north to Neufchâtel and Dieppe, which fell on September 1. On that day, General Eisenhower, the Allied Supreme Commander, assumed direct command of the Allied armies in Northern France and on that day, General Montgomery was promoted to field marshal, a consolation, perhaps, for some recent disappointments.

And so, on September 1, 1944, the Normandy campaign finally comes to a close. The Canadians were at Dieppe. British soldiers stood among cheering crowds of liberated Frenchmen at Amiens with a German general, the commander of an army that had fought them so hard and for so long, now a prisoner of the British Army. Paris, mercifully undamaged, was a free city after four years of German occupation and the burden of field command had passed to Eisenhower. On balance, and in spite of the great cost in lives, the outcome of the Normandy battle was a good one, far better than many people expected when the Allied troops splashed ashore in Normandy on D-Day. Some, perhaps most, of the credit for that satisfactory outcome might go to Field Marshal Sir Bernard Law Montgomery.

There was time – just a little time – to enjoy this taste of victory before the pursuit began again. The European war would enter another year and this present year would see hard fighting at Walcheren and Arnhem, in the Hurtgen Forest and the Ardennes. The Allied soldiers enjoyed their brief triumph and the plaudits of the crowds that lined the roads as they advanced, but they were old soldiers now. These Allied soldiers, American, British, Canadian, French, Polish, knew that somewhere ahead lay the German Army, still formidable, far from defeated, gathering its strength to fight again. To destroy that army and the regime that sustained it would not be easy and more hard times lay ahead.

EPILOGUE · A VERDICT ON NORMANDY

Critics state that the strategy of World War II was all wrong, that it would have been better to have done this or that. Perhaps ... but the fact remains, we did win the War

GENERAL OMAR BRADLEY *1980*

The Battle of Normandy was a victory – an Allied victory. Since victories usually bring their own rewards it is strange that the verdict on this Allied victory in Normandy, how it was managed and what it achieved, have subsequently been clouded – one might say spoiled – by allegations and accusations that the victory was 'incomplete', that the battle should have been fought in a different way or ended sooner. These claims and accusations focus on the actions of the British and Canadian forces and are largely founded on claims and comments made in the memoirs of the American commanders whose post-war complaints about Montgomery and the British and Canadian forces have subsequently been taken up and embellished by military historians, not all of them American.

It therefore seems essential to stress that the Battle of Normandy was an *Allied* battle and the victory was an *Allied* victory. Attempts by various national historians, not simply to hog the credit, but to dismiss the efforts and sacrifices of their Allies, do them no credit and causes offence to old soldiers such as Frank Rosier of the Normandy Veterans Association:[1]

In 1944 I was Private Frank Rosier, 2nd Bn The Gloucestershire Regiment. We landed in the second wave on D-Day as we were attached to the 50th Division for the landing on Gold. This moan from the Americans that we were slow to progress does annoy us. We had as much *bocage* and a lot more opposition from crack German divisions and we think that the Yanks were pretty slow in taking a month to pivot round us at Caen and get to St-Lô but you don't hear much about that.

Besides, we had to fight differently. We had been fighting all over the place since 1939 and we are a small nation, without the manpower of America; we were putting RAF people and Naval people in as infantry before the end of the Normandy battle. I am sorry if this sounds a bit 'anti-Yank', as I was proud to fight alongside them, but they do try to steal all the glory.

Many British and Canadian veterans will agree with Frank Rosier's comments. It is necessary to add that in twenty years of writing books on the Second World War, all featuring veteran accounts, I have *never* had an American veteran disparaging their Allies or heard a British or Canadian veteran disparage their American comrades. Men who served at the 'sharp end' of war and know what war is really like, do not sink to that level.

The well-honed claims and complaints from historians provide the basis of what we can now fairly call 'the Normandy myth'. To define it yet again, this holds that the plan made by General Montgomery was fundamentally flawed, that the British and Canadians were 'cautious' or 'timid' and 'too slow', did very little fighting at all and sat around in safety, drinking tea until the exasperated Eisenhower and Bradley seized the initiative, revised the plan, smashed their way through the German forces in the west – something they would have done much sooner if Monty had not held them back – and went on to defeat the Germans in Normandy and win the war, largely unassisted, if not actually inhibited, by the British and Canadians.

Those are the claims – and that is the myth. The purpose of this book has been to tell the story of the Normandy battle and in the process examine those claims, or rather that myth, and see if it has any validity in these allegations, always using US official accounts for US actions and British and Canadian official histories for British and Canadian accounts in a – probably futile – attempt to avoid accusations of chauvinism. The story told in these pages and the facts so revealed should have demolished this myth and, I hope, brought the efforts of the various Allies back into balance. The readers can now arrive at their own judgement or do their own research, using the books in the bibliography, to arrive at their own conclusion. That only leaves me to deliver mine.

The aim of this book has been to make a *fair* assessment of the battle, giving due credit to all parties. It is not necessary – and quite wrong – to build up the exploits of one army by decrying the efforts of another, not least because it takes the question out of context, and the context here is an *Allied* battle. A number of historians (no names, no pack-drill, but they know who they are) have been at great pains to analyse and disparage the performance of the British and Canadian forces in Normandy. It would be equally possible, were one so minded, to write a similar critique on the performance of the American forces but that too would take their performance out of context. To get the balance right it seems necessary to compare the performance of all the Allied armies in Normandy. That done, what is a *fair* judgement on the Battle of Normandy?

First of all, the overall impression of this author, gained after three years of researching and writing this book, reading the official accounts and memoirs, listening to the veterans – American, British, Canadian and German – and walking the ground, is that in real terms there is nothing much to chose between the performance of the various Allied armies in Normandy.

Each army was full of gallant soldiers and competent commanders, and every army had a number of less-than-competent commanders and less than heroic soldiers. All of them, from private soldier to army commander, were doing their best in very difficult circumstances, and a careful, critical search fails to reveal any striking difference between their performance in the field. Certainly, they fought in different ways but they faced common difficulties and eventually managed to overcome them; there was no magic formula for victory in Normandy and no Allied army had a monopoly of success or failure.

There are few absolutes in war and this is not an attempt to 'reverse the myth' or present the British Second Army as an army without faults. Every army has faults and if the Second Army has had more attention in this book, that is because it has been less than fairly treated in many other books.

However, it is essential to maintain a balance. Second Army displayed a number of tactical faults, in tank and infantry co-operation, in small unit tactics and in failing to prepare the ground before advancing – the attack on Mont Pinçon and the Canadian attack at Quesnay woods, previously described in this book, are examples of this last fault – and there seems to have been some sluggishness at corps and divisional level. There was a ponderous air about Second Army but it is not enough to point out faults; it is also necessary to find the reasons for them and the reasons why Second Army fought as it did are both logical, sensible and fully understandable in the context of the time.

So is it with all armies in all wars and to single out Second Army as uniquely culpable in this respect during the Normandy campaign is unjust, as the many harsh criticisms of American performance in Normandy – made, please note, in the two volumes of the American Official History – have made very clear.

One fact does stand out from all the sources. The outstanding army in Normandy was the German Army. In terms of kit, training, tactical ability, tenacity and sheer guts, fighting without air cover or naval gunfire support and hampered by interference from Adolf Hitler, the German Army was undoubtedly the best army in the field – and the feat of overcoming it should therefore not be underrated. Progress by the various Allied armies in Normandy was directly related to the number and quality of the German forces which opposed them. Where the Germans elected to defy eviction – as at Caen and in the *bocage* – Allied progress was going to be slow. This was especially the case when the Allies were fighting SS divisions; and for most of the time most of the SS divisions were on the Second Army front.

SS or Wehrmacht, the Germans were also good soldiers; one can despise the cause these soldiers fought for and look forward gladly to their defeat, but no understanding of the difficulties facing the Allies during the Battle of Normandy is possible unless due credit is paid to the superb soldiers of the German Army, fighting a defensive battle in terrain ideal for defence.

That said, there is no need to feel that the Allied victory in Normandy was less than meritorious because these German forces were beaten by superior numbers, air power, naval gunnery and the slow development of the strategic plan, rather than man-to-man in hand-to-hand combat. The Allied soldiers, American, British, Canadian, Polish, beat the Germans in Normandy and that was no mean feat.

John Butler of the British 6th Airborne Division has a point to make here:[2]

Were we in awe of the SS? Never. We – and I include the US airborne in this – considered ourselves to be the *crème de la crème* of fighting men and were quite prepared to take on anything Jerry could throw at us. At the same time we never underrated our opponent. We knew the SS were highly trained and probably better than the average Wehrmacht soldier, but we just knew we were better still. As for the Yanks, it's not that they mean to be malicious, it is just the way they are. On an even playing field I think they were no better and no worse as infantry than their British–Canadian counterparts.

As the battle went on, the Allied soldiers got the measure of their opponents and fought them to a standstill. Some well-led and well-trained Allied units got a grip on the enemy in the early stages of the battle, as witness this letter between a Canadian general and Brigadier 'Jumbo' Leicester of the 4 Commando Brigade after an encounter with the Waffen SS of 12 SS Panzer in mid-June:[3]

> Headquarters, 3rd Canadian Infantry Division,   15 June, 1944
> To Comdr, 4 SS (Commando) Brigade
>
> Dear Brigadier Leicester,
> Just a note to thank you, your staff, and your Commandos for the excellent work you carried out for us, and for your loyal and enthusiastic co-operation during the successful assault.
>   During the last few days I must ask you to congratulate for me Lt Col Hardy and his 46 (Royal Marine) Commandos for their through dealing with the enemy in and along the river line Rots and Rosel; my R de Chauds buried 122 Boche done in by your chaps.
>   Be assured that we all appreciate this and will always deem it an honour to fight alongside and preferably with, the Royal Marines Commandos.
>   Signed: R. F. L. Kellner,
>   Maj. Gen. GOC.
>   3 Can Inf Div.

In time, often a very short time, all the Allied soldiers would have a grip on this battle and time was on the Allied side. The Allies were bound to win this war as soon as an adequate amount of strength was brought to bear on the German forces and eleven months after the Allied landing in Normandy, Adolf Hitler's Germany collapsed. Battle, if a hard school, also produces results but the myths continue to flourish more than sixty years later, most notably the allegation that the victory in Normandy took too long because the British and Canadians under Montgomery were 'too slow'.

Before answering this charge, one must ask, too slow in comparison to what? Who set up a check-time for the Allied advance from the D-Day beaches to the Seine? Without timed phases, how can anyone *know* that an advance was on time, or too slow or very quick? The only two phase lines and time in the original plan was to take Caen on D-Day and reach the Seine by D plus 90 – or September 4. The US 79th Division crossed the Seine at Mantes–Gassicourt on August 20 – D plus 75 – and all the armies had troops across the Seine before the end of the month, days before Monty's deadline. Where is the 'slowness' here?

There certainly were tactical failures, many of which should have been analysed and ironed out in training. Allied troops, American as well as British and Canadian, failed to push on to exploit success and time and again this gave the enemy opportunity to regroup. More use should have been made of night attacks and infiltration, tank and infantry tactics needed revision, and above all some means found of suppressing the enemy infantry's advantage in firepower, especially in belt-fed machine-guns and mortars. It is not much use having the strategy right if the enemy can halt your attacks with superior firepower within minutes of the initial advance.

With consistently heavy casualties in the Allied rifle companies some caution was necessary, not least by the British and Canadian forces who did not have large reinforcements coming ashore every week. The need to avoid throwing men and tanks forward in fruitless attacks for no territorial gain is fully understandable, and why some historians, decades after the battle, feel that more young men should have been sacrificed in a campaign of attrition, is hard to understand and impossible to justify. We were not there; try as we will, we cannot know what the situation on the ground was really like; historians should not set themselves up to dictate the number of the dead.

It is also alleged and need not be denied, that Montgomery did not always push his men forward once the battle stalled and insisted on 'drawing up his administrative tail', before attacking again – an American phrase for ensuring continued logistical support. This is true, but this was Monty's way and one that was well known before he was appointed as Ground Force Commander. Monty liked a 'tidy' battle. If the Combined Chiefs wanted to fight a different kind of battle they should have appointed a different kind of commander. Given the continuing problems of supply, Monty's concern for his logistical back-up was a fully justified one; roaring ahead until you run out of supplies may please the press corps and look good on maps, but it does little to defeat the enemy.

At the very worst, though, this is a matter of judgement. In Monty's judgement, keeping an adequate stock of ammunition and petrol on hand, calling off attacks when the losses were not balanced by the gains, resting and re-organising his forces before another bound was simply common sense. He was, after all, fighting the German Army and all modern battles are largely a matter of supply. A different general might have fought the Normandy battle in a different way but this was Monty's battle – and in the end the way he fought it delivered a victory – and he brought that victory in ahead of time. Allegations that it would have been better to do something else can only be based on speculation – or wishful thinking. No less an authority than Field Marshal Rommel would have appreciated the sense of Montgomery's actions:[4]

> The first essential condition for an army to be able to stand the strain of battle is an adequate stock of weapons, petrol and ammunition. In fact, the battle is fought and decided by the quartermasters before the shooting begins. The bravest soldier can do nothing without guns, the guns nothing without plenty of ammunition, and neither guns or ammunition are of much use in mobile warfare unless there are vehicles available in sufficient quantity to haul them around.

Given the on-going problems of supply, a chronic shortage of artillery ammunition and a steady loss of troops, Montgomery's insistence on ensuring his logistical support before exploiting forward or attacking again is only sensible and should not be used to denigrate his professional ability. His critics usually attempt to shore up their arguments and give them the gloss of impartiality by conceding that Montgomery was an expert in the 'set piece' battle before moving swiftly on to claim that he was virtually useless – that 'slowness' again – in the mobile battle that followed.

Here again, where is the evidence? It was Monty's Eighth Army that marched right across North Africa from Alamein to Tunis in six months, driving the enemy before it. It was Monty's 21st Army Group that stormed from the Seine to Antwerp in four days after the Battle of Normandy, entering that city on September 4. It was Monty who proposed the Market Garden operation leading to Arnhem. Picking holes in these campaigns is easy, but they are hardly the actions of a 'cautious' commander. Montgomery was not a 'one-note' general. He fought his armies according to the situation at the time and – by and large – he fought them well.

Yes, there were Allied commanders – George Patton being the most obvious example – who believed in rapid advances whatever the risk. After the

Normandy battle, Patton stormed away towards the east and took territory, secure in the knowledge that if he got into trouble he would have to be supported. Unfortunately, having neglected the chronic logistical problem, Patton then ran out of fuel – and this impetuosity cost his army heavy casualties. The first attempt by Third Army to cross the Moselle river on September 5 resulted in the 80th Division being cut to pieces; no American soldier remained alive or uncaptured east of the river on September 6, and the survivors had to withdraw. The attack was renewed a week later, by which time the German First Army facing Patton had been reinforced. Although the American attack went ahead for a while, by September 19 the German First Army and Fifth Panzer Army were mounting fierce attacks which continued into October and then into November.

Patton's Lorraine campaign, far from being a mobile advance, rapidly descended into a battle of attrition. By the time it ended, the Lorraine campaign had lasted four months and cost Third Army 97,000 casualties; 42,000 of these were 'battle-fatigue' casualties, men worn out by fatigue, exposure or illness, men pushed beyond their limit – and it will be recalled that Patton did not believe in 'battle-fatigue'. Bradley was certainly wary of Patton's methods before the Third Army became operational and even Eisenhower had had enough of Patton by the time the war ended. Speed over the ground is not everything and high casualties among your own troops is no evidence of competence.

To analyse the other popular claim, or myth, that the victory in Normandy was incomplete it is only necessary to look at the figures and the claims of the Allied Supreme Commander. In his report covering operations since D-Day, Eisenhower stated:

> By August 25, the enemy had lost, in round numbers, 400,000 killed, wounded or captured, of which total 200,000 are prisoners of war. One hundred and thirty-five thousand of these prisoners have been taken since the breakthrough on July 25. 1,300 tanks, 20,000 vehicles, 500 assault guns, 1,500 field guns and heavier artillery have been captured or destroyed, apart from the destruction inflicted upon the Normandy coastal defences.

That hardly sounds like an incomplete victory. The remnants of the German forces that escaped across the Seine were without their equipment and in total chaos; if Normandy was an 'incomplete' victory, the Allies should have had more of them in the Second World War.

By any reasonable standard Normandy was a convincing victory but there was, of course, a cost. Allied casualties in the Battle of Normandy were severe. The Allied total comes to 209,703 casualties of which the US share comes to 125,847, the British and Canadian total to 83,825, the Canadian share of this last total being 18,444.[5] In percentage terms, the Allied losses, British, Canadian and American, at the end of the battle were almost exactly the same; ten per cent of the American, British and Canadian forces committed to the battle for Normandy were killed, wounded or went missing before the battle ended.

Some suggestions for the causes of the high casualty figures among the US divisions have been given in previous chapters, but a recently published and highly praised account of the 29th US Infantry Division in Normandy[6] devotes six pages to the problem and concludes that the replacement system in the US Army had a great deal to do with these heavy infantry losses.

The American replacement system had the merits and defects of simplicity. When a unit needed casualty replacements an equal number of men was sent up from a replacement depot – a 'repple depple'. Each replacement was supposed to have the same Military Occupational Speciality (MOS) as the man he replaced; cooks replaced cooks, drivers replaced drivers. However, since the brunt of the casualties were in the rifle companies, the main call was for Pfcs (Privates, First Class) or riflemen, category MOS 745.

The defect was that these replacement riflemen were sent up in batches, without any attempt to marry them to the division they were joining. Numbers were everything, training, skills and regional or state affiliations nowhere. Men from Maine ended up with Virginians, Texans with soldiers from New York; it may have enabled cut-up divisions to be reinforced quickly for the next fight but these new troops were friendless in their new units.

'Being a replacement is just like being an orphan,' said one 29th Division soldier. 'I have seen men killed or captured when even the squad leader didn't know their names,' said another.[7] Buddies from training camp days were unable to serve together; friendships made on the trip from the USA or at the repple depple were broken when the replacements were sent forward. None of this helped the front-line soldier; the front line is a lonely enough place, a place where friends are vital to survival and morale is as vital to a division as its strength in manpower.

The problem was then compounded because the more casualties a division took, the more replacements it received, so the less efficient it was, the more casualties it took ... thus the situation could only get worse. Nor did this policy only affect the replacements; the 29th Division history recalls that topping-up the division with replacements and keeping it in the line meant that the surviving veterans got no rest. Between D-Day and the fall of St-Lô, the 29th Infantry Division was continually in the line for forty-four consecutive days.

The situation was different in the British Army – and in the German Army. Although there are many accounts of English soldiers being sent to kilted Scottish regiments and gunners to the infantry, as a general rule British reinforcements went where possible to battalions of their own regiment or, were the need desperate, to a battalion in the same brigade. During the Italian campaign some English soldiers mutinied because they were sent to the wrong battalion, but although they were punished for mutiny, their situation aroused the sympathy of Winston Churchill, who pressed for lenient treatment and greater care in the commitment of replacements.

Sydney Jary, commissioned into the Hampshire Regiment, recalls how replacements were handled in the battalion he served with, from the Somerset Light Infantry:[8]

> On arrival they were first given a good hot meal. They were then issued with a new battledress adorned with our battalion and division flashes and a beret with the Somerset Light Infantry badge. They were also allowed to chose their own personal weapon. This may sound like PR but it all helped to make them feel that they were individuals with choices, not simply ingredients in some Kafkaesque meat-grinder. They would then be interviewed by me and introduced to their section commander. I did not tolerate an 'Old Guard' in my platoon or any cold-shouldering the newcomers – every effort was made to make them feel part of the Somerset family.
>
> If we were going back into battle and it was at all possible, they would be LOB – Left Out of Battle – until there was time to fit them in fully and teach them our basic drills. If not, at the least I ran through the routines – that when we came under fire we went to ground and every rifleman fired five rounds in the direction of the enemy and the Bren gunner expended a full magazine; this at least got some fire back, gave the men something to do – and gave me time to think. At any event, it worked; we took losses but we gave as good as we got and bedding-down these new soldiers was a major part of our success.

The question of casualties is interesting. There is a widespread belief among American historians that the reason the US armies took higher casualties than the British and Canadians is that the Americans were doing the fighting while their Allies sat around. How much truth there is in that belief has been covered in this book but the figures show that in terms of troops committed the losses were evenly shared – and the history shows that the Second Army was *constantly* attacking.

Where is the evidence for the widespread allegation that the British did not attack? Recalling the British attacks on Caen and Carpiquet from the morning of D-Day, the terrible battles for Hill 112 and Mont Pinçon, the assaults on the enemy line on the Orne, the Dives and the Odon, plus a continuous series of British and Canadian operations between Caen and Caumont – Perch, Epsom, Goodwood, Charnwood, Jupiter, Tractable, Totalize, Bluecoat, Spring – plus the fact that the bulk of the crack German Panzer and SS units (units larger and better equipped than standard Wehrmacht units) were facing the British and Canadians throughout the battle, why this myth of idleness and caution is still being propagated by American historians is hard to imagine.

The original source of this myth is SHAEF where Tedder, as usual, had a hand in spreading it, frequently alleging that British operations on the east flank were no more than 'company exercises'. Then, on July 21, Eisenhower wrote to Monty comparing Bradley's exploits with Dempsey's slowness, and stating that 'we must go forward shoulder to shoulder, with honours and sacrifices equally shared'. This was after Goodwood but also after the interminable, dragging, three-week-long First Army advance on St-Lô, after the British had just lost 400 tanks and a host of men attacking the lines of German defences south of Caen and when the percentage casualty figures, in relation to the forces ashore, were 9.4 per cent American and 8.3 per cent British and Canadian. One percentage point is a small basis for the extravagant claim that America's allies were not pulling their weight, and this narrow margin would be eroded in subsequent weeks.

There is another problem here. Dismissing the heavy losses in the American divisions as the fault of their Allies is simplistic. Eisenhower might have thought the matter through before relying on newspaper accounts or SHAEF gossip, and another wiser, or more experienced, general might have asked the question: if the British are fighting a superior number of a better-equipped and better-trained foe – which they were – and putting in constant attacks against them – which they were – why are the US divisions suffering heavier casualties – which they also were? Could it be that American training, tactics and replacement procedures are not as good? The question was not asked at the time and is hard to answer now, but in view of the fact that Bradley had to start a retraining programme for US troops already in Normandy – and the comments of the American soldiers themselves – there seems little doubt that their training was inadequate and the 'repple-depple' system unfair to young soldiers. Both factors made a contribution to these high US losses.

As usual, the best arrangements for replacement troops could be found in the German Army. When a replacement went up to the front in the German Army, he went with a batch of comrades from his training regiment, had been destined for that particular division for months, and had already been inculcated with a sense of belonging and unit morale. He knew where he was going and what his job would be when he got there. At his unit he met men – already veterans, men who had been there a week or two – who had followed the same path, done the same training, and were willing to accept him as a comrade.

Where it was applied, this sensible procedure paid off in all the armies; it is noticeable that the two US parachute divisions, the 82nd and the 101st Airborne, both of which had a splendid battlefield record in Normandy, maintained a high morale and effectiveness throughout the battle, probably because their replacements were also trained parachutists, survivors of a tough training process – or willing to become paratroopers when the chance arose. That in itself created the necessary bond. These issues apart, the argument over the Normandy campaign involves matters of strategy.

The original plan, the one drawn up by Montgomery and approved by Eisenhower as the blueprint for the battle, was the plan that the armies in Normandy followed and the one that produced the victory. This is not to say – as Montgomery was foolish enough to claim – that the plan worked out in every detail and went like clockwork. What battle plan, let alone one for a ninety-day military campaign, ever does that?

There were changes, and glitches, and matters went awry, and some aspects could have been handled better; some commanders were incompetent and some were less than forceful. What is new, or different, in any of that? The truth of the matter is that the strategic plan for the Normandy battle went as well as could be expected and delivered the first victory of the Overlord campaign. Carping over who did what, or who deserves the credit for particular parts of the battle, should not be allowed to obscure that basic fact.

For example, when analysing Cobra, the US Official History[9] states that 'the British and Canadian contributions to the development of the breakout are hard to judge'. This is a statement that needs to be considered with some care for it is dismissive of the facts and subject to misinterpretation. The strategy of the breakout was Montgomery's, not a desperate remedy dreamed up by Eisenhower and Bradley after their Allies had failed in the east, and the US breakout was greatly aided by the fact that the crack German units were engaged with the British and Canadians around Caen, as they had been for weeks. The facts speak for themselves; in the west, the Americans had the space and the troops.

As for the popular allegation, that Monty failed to break out in the east, thereby forcing Bradley to break out in the west, again where is the evidence? There is speculation in plenty but Bradley, who was the US commander in Normandy, never – at the time, or in two subsequent books – doubted that the strategy of the battle was for the British to hold the east flank and pull the German armour on to that flank and hold it there, while Bradley and the American forces broke out in the west. If Bradley, the man on the spot, did not know what the strategy was, who did?

The 'development' of the breakout south of St-Lô from July 26 was an entirely American affair and it can be fairly claimed that the British and Canadians had nothing to do with either the push into Brittany or along the Loire; no British general or historian has ever claimed otherwise. If, however, the US Official History is claiming that their Allies made no contribution *whatsoever* to the Cobra breakout, as the sentence seems to suggest, then this claim stands on much shakier ground.

While it is possible to go on picking holes in these allegations over strategy, few of which have any basis in reality, the crux of the argument on the Battle of Normandy lies in an evaluation of the commanders. Here, too, there are few absolutes; anyone who reads a biography in which the subject can do no wrong, or reads an autobiography in which the author makes no mistakes, becomes rightly suspicious. No one is that perfect and even generals make mistakes, and in assessing their performance one must try to be accurate and hope to be fair.

First there is General Dwight D. Eisenhower, the Allied Supreme Commander. Even after sixty years it is impossible to think of anyone else who could have done this job and done it so well. Much of Eisenhower's success was due to his character, his common sense, his clear understanding of human nature and his charm. Ike was astute, quite free from that chauvinism that infected so many of his colleagues, British and American, and determined to reduce the inevitable friction between his subordinates as far as possible. Eisenhower never forgot that he was the *Allied* Supreme Commander and the successful completion of the war in north-west Europe by the Allied armies is due in great measure to the talents and patience of Dwight D. Eisenhower. He deserves all the praise that fell upon him for the way he handled his awesome responsibilities and can be credited as one of the architects of the Allied victory.

Whether he was wrong not to appoint a Ground Force Commander for the entire campaign in north-west Europe and not just for the 'invasion phase' – in practice for the Battle of Normandy – is debatable. Montgomery thought that a Ground Force Commander was necessary and although most people claim, probably correctly, that Monty had himself in mind for this role, it should not be forgotten that Monty also offered to serve under Bradley. Montgomery believed that a Ground Force Commander was essential and if he had to be an American, so be it. As to why he thought such a commander necessary is more difficult to determine but as the battle in north-west Europe went on, there is some evidence that Eisenhower began to feel the strain of fulfilling both appointments.

Writing a personal message to Marshall on January 10, 1945 – during the Ardennes offensive – Ike states:[10]

> Because of the great size of the land forces now engaged on this front it would be more convenient for me if my deputy supreme commander was an experienced ground officer rather than air. In spite of my personal and official admiration for Tedder, he is not in a position to help me by visits and conferences with troop commanders. If I could have a man of fine personality, respected by all and willing to serve as my deputy, and not under independent charter from my superiors, it would be most helpful ... I am afraid it would be impossible to find such a deputy as I describe. The only one I could think of myself would be Alexander, and manifestly he is not available.

Alexander was currently commanding the Allied forces in Italy and Ike was clearly finding Tedder less than fully useful but there is another point here; if

Alexander, and not Tedder had been the Deputy Allied Commander from the start of the Normandy campaign, perhaps much of the bile that swilled around SHAEF – bile which often originated with Tedder – might well have been avoided. Alexander understood Monty, understood ground warfare and could grasp the strategy of the campaign. He also had enough charm and common sense to defuse irritating, inter-Allied situations as they arose. However, as Ike was clearly regretting by January 1945, this was not to be, so Tedder stayed in the post.

Monty was always in favour of neat, tidy arrangements in command and since there were Deputy Allied Commanders for the air and naval forces, it seemed logical that the far more important and far more complicated task of handling ground operations would also require one. That task required the kind of close attention that Eisenhower, who was also the Allied Supreme Commander, would not have time to devote to it. It has to be remembered that Eisenhower did not deny that there should be a Ground Force Commander. He simply claimed that he could fill that post himself, while remaining as Allied Supreme Commander.

Eisenhower felt that he could do the job – or rather both jobs – and since he dealt directly with just three subordinates, the three Army Group commanders, Bradley, Devers and Montgomery, and had the able support of Bedell Smith, he may have been right. After all, even a corporal commands more than three men. If we accept that one man could do both jobs we then have to ask whether this particular man did this one well.

This point is rather less certain. Bradley felt that Eisenhower was an excellent field commander, stating that:[11] 'I need not belittle Montgomery or deny any of his luster to rate Eisenhower his superior as a field commander.' General Bradley's views must command respect but where is the evidence for this opinion?

Bradley states[12] that 'his (Eisenhower's) tactical talents had been demonstrated years before at Leavenworth when he finished at the head of his class in 1926'. This is such a strange statement that one wonders if General Bradley is serious. Can it really be claimed that the tactical ability to command *three* army groups in a major European war, against such an enemy as the German Wehrmacht, in campaigns involving millions of men, bears any relationship whatsoever to peacetime exercises or classroom study, on another continent, eighteen years previously?

Eisenhower never experienced field command, at division, corps or army level. His service had been spent on the staff and his role in the Second World War, from the time he arrived in North Africa in November 1942, was much higher up the command chain, most recently before Normandy as Commander-in-Chief of the Allied Forces in the Mediterranean. In this role he did well but the evidence to support a claim of tactical expertise in the handling of ground forces in the field is lacking.

Bradley states[13] that only himself, Devers and Montgomery can attest to Ike's 'rare astuteness' as a field commander. The snag with that claim is that Montgomery fails to acknowledge this 'rare astuteness' – and again, where is the evidence? The German onslaught in the Ardennes, three months after Eisenhower took over the role of field commander, an onslaught which tore the American front wide open and let the Germans pour through for fifty miles, may have had a number of causes but is hardly a demonstration of Ike's 'astuteness'; and Bradley does not come too well out of the Ardennes débâcle either. It is also worth noting that the Ardennes breakthrough bears a distinct resemblance to the disaster that struck American arms at the Kasserine Pass in North Africa, two years before, when the American line became overstretched and the Germans broke through.

Montgomery, who gets blamed for so much by his American colleagues, cannot be blamed for the Ardennes catastrophe; he had no say in the command set-up at this time or over the tactical deployment of the American divisions in the Ardennes. Perhaps – it is at least possible – that a Ground Force Commander, his eye fully on the strategic situation, with neither an army group to command or higher command responsibilities to distract him, would have noted the thinness of the American front in the Ardennes and taken steps to shore it up.

A fair judgement must surely be that Eisenhower was superb as Allied Supreme Commander but rather less than adequate as a field commander, either because he lacked the experience or the two jobs were too much for one man. The problem with reaching a fair judgement of Eisenhower's talents is complicated by the fact – and in his prime role as Allied Supreme Commander a very relevant fact – that Eisenhower was a thoroughly nice guy, much admired and extremely popular. To criticise Eisenhower in any way is all too often taken as a personal insult – where none is either intended or implied – rather than a query on his professional expertise.

No general is above or beyond criticism. Ike's many excellent and necessary personal attributes tend to conceal the fact that his grasp of matters military was not always sound. He was prone to listen to the siren voices of those who told him what he wanted to hear, notably at SHAEF, where the '*on dit*' held that Montgomery was 'timid', 'cautious' and 'too slow'. When he visited Normandy and came into direct contact with the situation on the ground, Ike quickly grasped the practical difficulties confronting his commanders and gained a fresh realisation of what they were up to, but he lost that grasp quite quickly when he returned to the Byzantine atmosphere of his over-staffed Supreme Headquarters.

Had Ike had a better grasp of strategy and realised that the first task of any commander was, and is, *the selection and, above all, the maintenance of the aim*, he might have had a better understanding of what Montgomery was doing in Normandy – his aim – and respected Montgomery's determination to stick to that aim. Ike would have then been able to keep a grip on Monty's vocal critics at SHAEF whose actions did little to foster Allied unity and nothing to help the troops in the field. If he had sacked Tedder and replaced him with General Alexander – as was suggested later – Ike's problems with Montgomery would have been greatly diminished.

As with Eisenhower, the task of reaching a fair judgement about Montgomery is clouded by a consideration of his personal characteristics, which in Montgomery's case are far less attractive. It is widely agreed and rarely disputed that Bernard Law Montgomery was a vain and boastful man, who was not above altering the facts to fit the case, unwilling to admit to errors or to changing his mind, and far too willing to denigrate his peers and his superiors – although it is noticeable that there are very few such complaints from his subordinates.

General Bradley, an essentially fair-minded man who came to loathe Montgomery in the aftermath of the Ardennes débâcle, could still write in his memoirs:[14]

> During these operations in the lodgement where Montgomery bossed the US
> First Army as part of his 21st Army Group, he exercised his Allied authority with
> wisdom, forbearance and restraint ... I could not have wanted a more tolerant
> or judicious commander.

That happy accord did not last. Monty made many enemies during the war. Some, like Tedder, Morgan and Coningham, had their revenge in Normandy; others, like Patton and Bradley – and Eisenhower – had their say in the post-war years but none of the quite legitimate complaints about Monty's vanity or boastfulness or arrogance should be allowed to obscure the fact that as a general and a field commander, Bernard Montgomery was first-class.

It is impossible to think of anyone else who could have planned, organised and commanded the Allied armies during the Normandy campaign better than Montgomery. Monty's plan, though altered for good reasons from time to time, was largely adhered to and proved successful in defeating the enemy, ahead of time. Most of the other commanders – including Eisenhower but excluding Bradley – were for abandoning the initial strategic plan within days or weeks of the landing, in favour of all-out, ad-hoc assaults along the enemy line, assaults which the Allies had neither the men nor the supplies to sustain.

The root of the problem here, as in so many other areas, was Montgomery's vanity, his careless talk to the media and his later claim that the Normandy battle had gone exactly as planned from start to finish, which was patently untrue. This charge can, however, be discounted. The changes made to the initial plan were necessary changes which recognised the altering situation and did nothing to impede the progress of events. Why Monty did not admit to these changes can again be traced to his vanity, but in the overall context of the Normandy battle, and the subsequent victory, did any of this matter?

Outside the immediate circle of the Allied high command, Monty's personal and social failings are irrelevant. He certainly upset his colleagues but the Normandy campaign was not a popularity contest, the winner judged by his ability to attract favourable headlines in the home papers – although reading the memoirs of some Allied generals can lead you to think that.

It can be said that Monty's personal failings harmed no one more than himself. The sour reactions of his peers – especially his American peers – seem to have been prompted far more by what they read in the papers, second-hand versions of what Monty was alleged to have said, than by what he actually said. It is fair to point out to those who allege that Montgomery was critical of the American commanders that they were also critical of him – and *their* memoirs started the entire argument.

Butcher's *Three Years with Eisenhower* came out in 1946, Eisenhower's *Crusade in Europe* was published in 1948, Bradley's *A Soldier's Story* in 1951; Montgomery's *Memoirs,* rebutting some of their allegations, were not published until 1958. These *Memoirs* gave great and understandable offence to Eisenhower and

Bradley but there is a saying in service circles that if you can't take it, you should not dish it out. Monty was monumentally tactless and should have been firmly 'gripped' by Eisenhower or Brooke in the Normandy battle, sooner rather than later, but in the context of the Normandy campaign these character issues were irrelevant. Constant labouring of the character issue distorts the true picture and overlooks the wider one – that there was a war going on here.

These generals were fighting a war to free a Continent from a monstrous tyranny and engaged in a campaign in which young men under their command were dying every day; later concerns about their subsequent reputations or the constant whining about what they read in the British or American newspapers seems at best petty and at worst disgraceful. They should have had thicker hides or found something better to do with their time.

Claims that the generals were concerned with public opinion at home or the feelings of their troops in the field are usually self-serving. The people at home wanted victory and their menfolk back home in one piece; the troops in the field were far more concerned with what was happening to their immediate front than with anything said in the newspapers – and newspapers are less common in front-line trenches and foxholes than many historians seem to believe. The generals should have known this, and paid less attention to the press and public relations.

Although he missed combat in the First World War and had little experience of troops before 1941, Bradley was a fine general, and a good man, perhaps not untinged by ambition or consideration of his place and reputation in the post-war world, but one who made a sincere effort to get along with Monty and did so until they became equals in command. Then matters began to go awry on both a personal and professional level, but for most of the time in Normandy, as Bradley admits, they got on well. The same can hardly be said of Monty's relations with George Patton.

George Patton was the media-man's dream; the general as sound-bite, the master of headlines. Patton played a part in which he was always the all-American hero, helmeted and pistol-packing, with plenty of strong language – which he fondly and mistakenly believed endeared him to the troops – and master of the unfortunate remark.

Patton's contribution to the overall Normandy battle was not great, for his army was only committed as the German front had collapsed. This was a fortunate time for Patton's notions of war – which largely consisted of pushing hard until something gave way. With little to oppose it, Third Army took a great deal of ground and provided the newspapers with plenty of copy. In a fluid battle, Patton was an excellent general; how he would have managed against German troops fighting in defensive terrain is rather harder to gauge and cannot be commented on fairly in the context of the Normandy campaign.

On the personal, character front, Patton was every bit as detestable as Montgomery, equally vain, equally obstinate and far more chauvinistic. His comment during the Falaise battle, about 'driving the British back into the sea for another Dunkirk', has not been forgotten, but his report to Eisenhower at the end of the Normandy battle, 'Ike, today I spat in the Seine', is more typical of the man, always consciously tough.

Dempsey and Crerar were sound and competent officers with no desire to ingratiate themselves with the public – and careful with the lives of their troops; the Allies could have done with more officers like these, men who simply got on with the job and left their place in history to other voices. At the corps level, the *palme d'or* could be awarded to Collins of the US VII Corps or Simonds of the Canadian II Corps. Collins was a driving general with brains and should have been given an army command, perhaps of the First Army, in place of the undistinguished Hodges. For outstanding divisional commanders, Gale of the British 6th Airborne, or Ridgeway of the 82nd Airborne, or Kellner of the 3rd Canadian Infantry Division all did well and consistently outfought the enemy forces to their front.

Remove chauvinism from the argument and ask the question; can there be a fair, objective and reasoned verdict on the Allied commanders in Normandy? Yes – probably – and it should be a favourable one because most of them, Montgomery and Bradley in particular, were pretty good in their various roles and handled their responsibilities well.

Those who failed, or were perceived to have failed, were sacked and the Americans sacked their commanders in quantity, usually for 'caution', or 'want of dash', which, given the subsequent allegation made against the British and Canadian forces for the same failings, is a rather curious accusation.

General James Gavin, then of the splendid 101st Airborne Division, said later:[15] 'Summarily relieving senior officers, it seems to me, makes others pusillanimous and indeed discourages other potential combat leaders from seeking high command. Summarily relieving those who do not appear to measure up in the first shock of battle is not only a luxury we cannot afford it is very damaging to the Army as a whole.'

The Americans were very eager to sack 'failing' commanders. During the north-west Europe campaign, beginning in Normandy, the Americans sacked two corps commanders, eleven divisional commanders – three from Third Army, the rest from the First Army, and three brigadier generals, all from First Army. General Simpson of the US Ninth Army, a very sound general, sacked no one. Four commanders – MacMahon, Landrum, Brown, Watson, all of First Army – were sacked for 'poor performance in the *bocage*'.

The British were slower – perhaps too slow – to sack, and the performance of 7th Armoured Division and 51st Highland in the early days of the fighting did not show any significant improvement until changes were made at the top, though by that time the Normandy battle was almost over and the rapid advance of Second Army into Belgium was about to begin. But, all in all, with the reservations already expressed, it cannot be said that the Allied commanders did badly in this campaign. On the other hand, they did enjoy a great many advantages over the enemy, not least in artillery, naval gunfire support and air power.

Allied airpower was held to be decisive in the Normandy campaign and from all accounts, official and personal, this seems to be the case. That is not to say that air power came without problems; there are far too many accounts, official and personal of Allied units being bombed or strafed by Allied aircraft. It would be interesting to compute the number of Allied casualties caused by Allied air attacks but most of the veteran accounts mention Allied air attacks on their own forces and the total number of Allied soldiers killed or wounded by the Allied air forces during the Normandy campaign must run into thousands.

Nor is it entirely certain that Allied air attacks were, as claimed, highly effective against German armour; that may be another of the Normandy myths. Writing in the *RUSI Journal*,[16] Dr Remedio Graf von. Thun-Hohenstein claims:

> Available sources about German armour casualties do not support the thesis of the Air Force being the primary cause of their destruction. Of 129 Panther tanks captured in two periods between 6 June 1944 and 7 July 1944 and from 17 December 1944 to 16 January 1945 (i.e. during the Ardennes offensive) only 11 were destroyed by air attack. 52 became casualties to armour piercing

shot, ten by high-explosive shells, seven by hollow charge projectiles, 16 demolished or destroyed by crew, 13 abandoned intact and 18 became casualties by unknown causes. It is quite possible that the crews of the abandoned tanks flew their Panthers when attacked by rocket-firing Typhoons or Thunderbolts and this would add the total to the score of the Allied Air Forces. But interrogation of German tank crews who became POWs under the British, showed that the best way to bear attacks by Allied fighter-bombers for an experienced crew was to stay inside their tanks and wait.

Dr Graf von Thun-Hohenstein states that the most devastating effect of Allied tactical air power was against soft-skinned vehicles which were destroyed in great numbers, as in the Falaise pocket, thus cutting off supplies of fuel and ammunition to the Panzers. 'I think', he concludes, 'that there are some tendencies to exaggerate the role of the Air Force by neglecting or diminishing the decisive role of the ground forces that bore the main brunt of the fighting.'

In the end, that last point is what the Normandy battle came down to; young men, almost two million of them, fighting for ground, struggling to defeat the enemy and end a monstrous tyranny that had held much of Europe in its grip for the past five years. In the end and at great cost – a cost which included the lives of some 12,000 Norman civilians killed in the fighting – the soldiers of the Allied armies in Normandy won this battle and broke that tyranny. These later arguments, over who should be credited with the glory of this victory, seem irrelevant and petty when set against the casualty figures, that long list of the dead and wounded men who paid the price and found little glory in any of it.

The Battle of Normandy was a tough and bloody affair, hard-fought on every front by every army and due credit should be paid to all those who took part in the fighting. They gained the eventual victory and this subsequent haggling for glory by national historians surely demeans their common sacrifice. The glory of the Normandy victory – in so far as there is any – must go to the men who fought there, young men from all the Allied nations, old men now, and to those of their comrades who lie in the earth of that now-peaceful part of France.

NOTES TO THE TEXT

Preface

1. *Crusade in Europe,* p. 242.

Chapter 1

1. R. Conte, letter to author, 2001.

2. Letter to author, 2000.

3. Letter to author, 2001.

4. Letter to author, 1993.

5. US Official History, *Cross-Channel Attack*, p. 183.

6. ibid., p. 187

7. Exercise Thunderclap, April 7, and Final Briefing, May 15, 1944, as recorded in *Master of the Battlefield*, pp. 558-65; 581-9.

8. *A Soldier's Story,* pp. 239-41.

9. *Master of the Battlefield*, pp. 559-60.

10. ibid., p. 13.

11. ibid., p.15.

Chapter 2

1. This unit was then called a Special Service or SS Brigade; the name was then changed, for obvious reasons, to Commando Brigade, and that name will be used here.

2. *1st Suffolks in Normandy* by Eric Lummis.

3. Letter to the author, 2001.

4. Eisenhower was born in Denison, Texas, on October 14, 1890, though his family came from Kansas and returned there two years after his birth.

5. Conversation with the author, 1992.

6. Interview with the author, January 2001.

Chapter 3

1. For German command structure, see US Official History: *The US Army in World War Two; Cross-Channel Attack,* p. 244.

2. Major Hans von Luck, 125 Panzer Grenadier Regt, 21 Panzer Div. – to the author, 1992.

3. Appendix V, Part II.

4. Conversation with the author, 1993.

5. Account supplied to the author, 2001.

6. Interview with Colin Ward on behalf of the author, 2001.

7. Interview with the author, 2001.

8. Tape to the author, 2001.

9. Conversation with the author, 1993.

10. Meyer was tried by a Canadian military court in December 1945, and sentenced to death for multiple murder. The sentence was commuted to life imprisonment and he was released from prison in 1954.

11. The History of 12 SS states that the two Allied units they came to respect in the European campaign were the 2nd US Armored Division and No. 46 (Royal Marine) Commando.

12. Letter from Mrs Gladys Holmes, niece

of Robert Holmes, a Canadian soldier killed in the fight for Rots, containing Bud's account of the battle.

13. Letter to the author, 2001.

14. *Cross-Channel Attack*, p. 336.

15. Taped account sent to the author, 1993.

16. *Cross-Channel Attack*, p. 337.

17. ibid., p. 337.

18. British Official History, *Victory in The West*, p. 217.

19. *Supplying War*, p. 209.

Chapter 4

1. *Normandy to the Baltic*, p. 57.

2. German Parachute formations were under the Luftwaffe for administration but under the Army (Heer) for operations.

3. Taped account to the author, 2001.

4. Interview with the author, 1994.

5. Account sent to the author, 2001.

6. *Ready for Anything*, p. 177.

7. Account sent to the author, 2001.

8. *With the 6th AB Div in Normandy*, p. 99.

9. *Victory in the West*, p. 253.

10. Interview with the author, 1994.

11. *Cross-Channel Attack*, p. 350.

12. ibid., p. 365.

13. It should be remembered that a US regiment is equivalent to a British or Canadian brigade and consists of three battalions; a US Airborne Regiment at this time could muster around 2,000 men, less casualties.

14. Sadly, neither officer survived the war. Lt Colonel Cole won the Medal of Honor for his leadership at Carentan but was killed on the Market Garden operation in Holland a few months later and Major Skopa was killed in the defence of Bastogne.

15. *Cross-Channel Attack*, p. 377.

16. *Victory in the West*, p. 260.

Chapter 5

1. *Memoirs*, p. 237.

2. *RAF Servicing Commandos*, p. 83.

3. *Cross-Channel Attack*, p. 448.

4. *Victory in the West*, p. 265.

5. Letter to the author, 2001.

6. Tape to the author, 1994.

7. Account supplied to the author, 2001.

8. Interview with Colin Ward, 2001.

9. *Cross-Channel Attack*, p. 375.

10. ibid., p. 383.

11. ibid., p. 383.

12. WO file MO3, HH 14.

13. *Cross-Channel Attack*, p. 404.

Chapter 6

1. For a clear explanation of the supply and command set-up between COMZ and SHAEF, see Chapter 12 of *Coalitions, Politicians and Generals; Aspects of Command in Two World Wars*, by Graham and Bidwell.

2. Letter to the author, 2001.

3. Account supplied to the author, 2001.

4. There is controversy over the time anticipated to take Cherbourg, ranging from eight to thirty days, the amount

lengthening after the landings. Chester Wilmot states, (p. 363), that Cossac thought it could be taken by D plus 8. When the Cherbourg garrison was increased in May, Bradley put his estimate up to D plus 15 and it finally fell on D plus 23.

5. *A Soldier's Story,* p. 306.

6. ibid., p. 306.

7. *Victory in the West*, p. 264.

8. Account supplied to the author, 2001.

9. *Victory in the West,* p. 265.

10. *Cross-Channel Attack,* p. 423.

11. *A Soldier's Story,* p. 218.

12. Letter to the author, 2001.

13. Account supplied to the author, 2001.

14. ibid.

15. Letter to the author, 2001.

16. *Cross-Channel Attack,* p. 417.

17. ibid., pp 420–1.

18. ibid., p. 441.

19. *Victory in the West,* p. 294.

20. *Cross-Channel Attack,* p. 443.

Chapter 7

1. *Citizen Soldiers,* p. 50.

2. Another example of how the taking of prisoners is no yardstick when good troops are involved comes from the Japanese advance to Kohima and Imphal during the war in Burma. Some 85,000 Japanese soldiers advanced on India; half of them were killed in the fighting, 20,000 died of disease; the British Army took only 100 Japanese prisoners in the entire campaign and the most senior Japanese officer

captured was a captain. Like the Waffen-SS, these Japanese soldiers did not believe in surrendering.

3. *A Soldier's Story,* pp 325–6.

4. *Victory in the West,* p. 276.

5. ibid., p. 278.

6. Account supplied to the author, 2001.

7. ibid.

8. ibid.

9. ibid.

10. ibid.

11. Ernie Cox, ibid.

12. Account supplied to author, 2001.

13. *Normandy to the Baltic,* p. 65.

14. Letter to the author, 2001

15. *Cross-Channel Attack,* p. 384.

16. *Master of the Battlefield,* p. 738.

17. *With Prejudice,* pp 554–5.

18. See Ambrose, *Citizen Soldiers,* for an example of the latter thinking.

19. Quoted verbatim in Chester Wilmott, *The Struggle for Europe,* p. 370.

20. *Normandy to the Baltic,* p. 68.

21. *Victory in the West,* p. 309

Chapter 8

1. *Crusade in Europe,* p. 289.

2. ibid., p. 290.

3. Letter to the author from Mrs Joan van der Holt, on her uncle, Flt Lt Bernard Yunker.

4. *Victory in the West,* p. 303.

5. ibid., p. 309.

6. ibid., p. 294.

7. *Normandy to the Baltic*, p. 71.

8. Richard Lamb, *Hitler's Generals*, p. 396.

Chapter 9

1. Letter to the author, 2001.

2. *The Victory Campaign*, p. 161.

3. Letter to the author, 2001.

4. *Steel Inferno*, p. 154.

5. *The Victory Campaign*, p. 158.

6. ibid., p. 158.

7. *Normandy to the Baltic*, p. 74.

8. Douglas Proctor, *Section Commander,* pp 4–5.

9. Sydney Jary, *Platoon Commander*, p. 9.

10. *Out of Step*, p. 194.

11. Letter to the author, 2001.

12. Taped account supplied to author, 2001.

13. *Section Commander*, p. 9.

Chapter 10

1. US Official History, *Breakout and Pursuit*, p. 15.

2. ibid., p. 38.

3. Account supplied to the author,1994.

4. Account supplied to the author,1994.

5. *Breakout and Pursuit*, p. 12.

6. ibid., p. 49.

7. ibid., p. 72.

8. ibid., pp 125–7.

9. ibid., p. 125.

10. Account supplied to the author, 1994.

11. *Breakout and Pursuit*, p. 126.

12. ibid, p. 128.

13. ibid, p. 128.

14. ibid., p. 129.

15. ibid., p. 130.

16. ibid., p. 85.

17. Account supplied to the author, 1994.

18. *Breakout and Pursuit*, p. 140.

Chapter 11

1. *Breakout and Pursuit*, p. 175.

2. ibid., p. 174.

3. ibid., p. 177.

4. *Victory in the West,* p. 309.

5. ibid., p. 309.

6. *Breakout and Pursuit*, p.187.

7. *Victory in the West,* pp 330–1.

8. *Breakout and Pursuit*, p. 188.

9. ibid., p. 189

10. *Normandy to the Baltic,* p. 80.

11. *Breakout and Pursuit*, p. 174.

12. *A Soldier's Story*, p. 445.

13. Account supplied to the author, 1994.

14. See *Master of the Battlefield* on Goodwood.

15. *Breakout and Pursuit,* p. 190.

16. *Victory in the West*, p. 320.

17. Account taped by Colin Ward, 2001.

18. Account supplied to the author, 2001.

19. ibid.

20. ibid.

21. *Three Years with Eisenhower,* pp 529–31.

22. *Victory in the West,* p. 354.

23. *Breakout and Pursuit,* p. 188

Chapter 12

1. *Breakout and Pursuit,* p. 197.

2. ibid., p. 188.

3. ibid., p. 198.

4. ibid., p. 201.

5. ibid., p. 201.

6. ibid., p. 201.

7. At the D-Day commemoration in Normandy in June 1994, the author met an elderly American veteran who had landed on June 12, been sent into the line that night, wounded the following day and had no idea what unit he had served with. 'No one told me nothing ... I was in and out in 24 hours ... but I fought in Normandy and I have a right to be here.'

8. *Breakout and Pursuit*, p. 206.

9. ibid., p. 219.

10. General McNair is buried in the US Military Cemetery at St Laurent, close to Omaha beach.

11. Account supplied to the author, 1994.

12. *Breakout and Pursuit,* p. 245.

13. Account supplied to the author, 1994.

14. *Breakout and Pursuit*, p. 245.

15. ibid., pp 245–6.

16. ibid., p. 267.

17. ibid., p. 266.

18. ibid., p. 269.

19. ibid. p. 271.

20. ibid. p. 290.

Chapter 13

1. *Breakout and Pursuit,* p. 331.

2. *Three Years with Eisenhower,* p. 543.

3. *A Soldier's Story,* p. 325.

4. Account supplied to the author, 2001.

5. *The Victory Campaign,* p. 194.

6. *Breakout and Pursuit,* p. 290.

7. ibid., p. 294.

8. *Victory in the West,* p. 391.

9. Account supplied to the author, 2001.

10. ibid.

11. ibid.

12. *Normandy to the Baltic,* p. 92.

13. Account supplied to the author, 2001.

14. ibid.

15. ibid.

Chapter 14

1. Letter to the author, 2001.

2. *The Victory Campaign,* p. 196.

3. ibid., p. 197.

4. Account supplied to the author, 2002.

5. Tape account supplied to the author, 1994.

6. p. 347.

7. *Breakout and Pursuit,* p. 349.

8. ibid., p. 375.

9. Tape account supplied to the author, 1994.

10. *Breakout and Pursuit*, p. 415.

11. Account supplied to the author, 2001.

Chapter 15

1. *Breakout and Pursuit*, p. 457.

2. Army Group B to Fifth Panzer Army, quoted in *Breakout and Pursuit*, p. 460.

3. *Breakout and Pursuit*, p. 462.

4. ibid., p. 464.

Chapter 16

1. *Normandy to the Baltic*, p. 99.

2. *Breakout and Pursuit*, p. 495.

3. *Victory in the West*, p. 427.

4. *Breakout and Pursuit*, p. 501.

5. ibid., p. 505.

6. *A Soldier's Story*, p. 377.

7. *Victory in the West*, p. 429.

8. *Breakout and Pursuit*, pp 507–9.

9. Account supplied to the author, 2001.

10. ibid.

11. *Breakout and Pursuit*, p. 597.

12. ibid., p. 525.

13. *Victory in the West*, p. 431.

14. *Breakout and Pursuit*, p. 527.

15. For a summary, see the footnote on p. 251 in the Canadian Official History, *The Victory Campaign*.

16. *The Victory Campaign*, p. 252.

17. Account sent to the author, 2001.

18. ibid.

19. *The Victory Campaign*, p. 249.

20. Account sent to the author, 2001.

21. ibid.

22. ibid.

23. ibid.

24. ibid.

Chapter 17

1. *Breakout and Pursuit,* p. 517.

2. *The Victory Campaign*, p. 264.

3. Account supplied to the author, 2001.

4. *The Victory Campaign*, p. 252.

5. Belfield and Essame, *The Battle for Normandy*, p. 209.

6. *The Victory Campaign*, p. 256.

7. Account supplied to the author, 2001.

8. *Breakout and Pursuit*, p. 555.

9. *Steel Inferno*, p. 282.

10. *Breakout and Pursuit,* p. 577.

11. ibid., p. 558.

Chapter 18

1. *The Victory Campaign*, p. 284.

2. Letter to the author, 2001.

3. Account supplied by R. Heather, 2001.

4. Account supplied to the author, 1999.

5. Account supplied to the author, 2001.

6. *Victory in the West*, p. 459.

7. *A Soldier's Story,* p. 398.

8. Account supplied to the author, 1996.

Epilogue

1. Account supplied to the author, 2001.

2. ibid.

3. *By Sea and Land, The Royal Marines Commandos*, p. 156.

4. The Rommel Papers, p. 328.

5. *Victory in the West,* p. 493.

6. *Beyond the Beachhead*, pp 222–8.

7. ibid., p. 223.

8. Interview with the author, 2001.

9. *Breakout and Pursuit,* p. 330.

10. National Archives, Department of Defence, Washington, RG, 218, JCS File, Leahy, Folder 16.

11. *A Soldier's Story*, p. 355.

12. ibid., p. 354.

13. ibid., p. 354.

14. ibid., pp 319–20.

15. See article by Major Daniel P. Bolger, *Military Review,* USA, May 1991. This article goes on to criticise the US performance in 'a disturbing number of botched battles, and especially missed chances. The hellish butchery in the Normandy *bocage*, the incomplete Falaise encirclement, the costly confusion before the West Wall, the bloody fumbling about in the Hurtgen Forest, the shocking initial surprise in the Ardennes ... together form a distressing litany that spans the entire length of the campaign.'

16. August 2001, Vol. 146. No. 4.

BIBLIOGRAPHY

What follows is only a small selection of the books consulted.

Ambrose, Stephen, *Citizen Soldiers, The US Army from the Normandy Beaches to the Bulge*, Touchstone Books, New York, 1997.

   The Supreme Commander, The War Years of Dwight D. Eisenhower, Cassell, London, 1971.

Balkowski, Joseph, *Beyond the Beachhead; The 29th Infantry Division in Normandy*, Stackpole Books, Pennsylvania, 1999.

Barnett, Corelli, ed., *Hitler's Generals,* Weidenfeld and Nicolson, 1989.

Battlefield Tour, *Operation Totalize,* BAOR, 1947.

Bauer, Eddy, *The History of World War II,* Orbis, 1983.

Belcham, Major General David, *Victory in Normandy,* Chatto and Windus, 1981.

Belfield, Eversley and H. Essame, *The Battle for Normandy,* Batsford, London, 1965.

Bennett, Ralph, *Ultra in the West: The Normandy Campaign of 1944–45*, Hutchinson, London, 1979.

Bidwell, Brigadier Shelford, *Hitler's Generals,* Salamander Books, 1977.

Blumenson, Martin, *The Duel for France, 1944*, Da Capo Press, USA, 1963.

   The US Army in World War II: Breakout and Pursuit, (US Official History), Department of the Army, Washington DC, 1961.

Bradley, Omar, *A Soldier's Story: Tunis to the Elbe*, Eyre and Spottiswoode, 1951.

Bradley, Omar and Blair, Clay, *A General's Life*, Simon and Schuster, New York, 1983.

Butcher, Captain H.C., *My Three Years with Eisenhower*, Heinemann, 1946.

Carruthers, Bob and Trew, Simon, *The Normandy Battles,* Cassell, 2000.

Carver, Field Marshal Lord, *Out of Step,* Hutchinson, 1989.

Cassidy, G. I., *Warpath: The Story of the Algonquin Regiment,* Ryerson Press, Toronto.

Chandler, A. D. ed., *The Private Papers of Dwight D. Eisenhower,* John Hopkins Press, 1970.

Copp, Terry and Vogel Robert, *Maple Leaf Route, Falaise, 1944,* Ontario, 1983.

D'Este, Carlo, *Decision in Normandy,* Harper Collins, 1983.

De Guingand, Major General Sir Francis, *Generals at War,* Hodder and Stoughton, 1964.

Eisenhower, David, *Eisenhower at War, 1943–1945*, Random House, 1986.

Eisenhower, General Dwight D., *Crusade in Europe,* Heinemann, 1948.

Ellis, Major, L F., *Victory in the West, Vol. 1. The Battle of Normandy,* (British Official History), 1962.

Fraser, David, *And We Shall Shock Them: The British Army in the Second World War*, Hodder and Stoughton, 1983.

Gelb, Norman, *Ike and Monty: Generals at War,* Constable, London, 1994.

Graham, Dominick and Bidwell, Brigadier Shelford, *Coalitions, Politicians and Generals: Some Aspects of Command in Two World Wars,* Brassey's, 1993.

Green, Michael and Gladys, *Patton: Operation Cobra and Beyond*, MBI Publishing, Osceola, Wisconsin, USA, 1998.

Hamilton, Nigel, *Monty: Master of the Battlefield, 1942–1944,* Hamish Hamilton, 1983.

  Monty: The Making of the General, 1887–1942, Hamish Hamilton, 1981.

Harrison, Gordon A., *US Army in World War II: Cross-Channel Attack,* (US Official History), Department of the Army, Washington, 1951.

Hastings, Max, *Overlord: D-Day and the Battle for Normandy,* Guild Publishing, 1984.

Holt, Major Tonie and Valmai, *The Normandy Landing Beaches*, Moorland Publishing, 1989.

How, J. J., *Hill 112 – Cornerstone of the Normandy Campaign*, William Kimber, 1984.

Howard, Sir Michael, MC, *Grand Strategy, Vol IV*, London, 1972.

Howarth, T. E. B., ed., *Monty at Close Quarters,* Arms and Armour Press, 1985.

Jackson, Bill and Bramall, Edwin, *The Chiefs,* Brassey's, 1992.

Jary, Sydney, *18 Platoon,* Sydney Jary Ltd, for RMA Sandhurst, 1987.

Keegan, John, ed., *Churchill's Generals,* Weidenfeld and Nicolson, 1992.

Keegan, John, *Six Armies in Normandy,* Jonathan Cape, 1982.

Kellett J. P. and Davies, J., *A History of the RAF Servicing Commandos,* Airlife Publishing, 1989.

Kemp, Anthony, *D-Day and the Invasion of Normandy,* Abrams Publishing, 1994.

Lewin, Ronald, *Montgomery as Military Commander*, Batsford, 1971.

Luck, Hans von, Colonel, *Panzer Commander,* Praeger, 1989.

McKee, Alexander, *Caen, Anvil of Victory,* Souvenir Press, 1964.

Metelman, Henry, *Through Hell for Hitler,* Spellmount, 1990.

Montgomery, Field Marshal, Viscount of Alamein, *Normandy to the Baltic*, Hutchinson, 1947.

 Memoirs, Odhams, 1958.

Morgan, General Sir Frederick, *Overture to Overlord,* Doubleday and Co., New York, 1950

Neillands, Robin, *The Desert Rats: 7th Armoured Division, 1940–1945,* Weidenfeld and Nicolson,1991.

 The Conquest of the Reich, 1945, Weidenfeld and Nicolson, 1995.

Neillands, Robin and de Normann, Roderick, *D-Day 1944: Voices from Normandy*, Weidenfeld and Nicolson, 1993.

Patton, General George, *War as I Knew It,* Boston, 1947.

Proctor, Corporal Douglas, *Section Commander,* Sydney Jary Ltd, for RMA Sandhurst, 1990.

Reynolds, Michael, *Steel Inferno,* Spellmount, 1997.

Shave, Major J. S. R. MC, '*Go to it*': *The Story of the 3rd Parachute Squadron, R.E.,* (privately published).

Shirer, William L., *The Rise and Fall of the Third Reich,* Secker and Warburg, 1960.

Shulman, Milton, *Defeat in the West,* Masquerade, 1995.

Sixsmith, Major General, E. K. G., *Eisenhower as Military Commander*, Batsford, 1973.

Speidel, Lt General Hans, *We Defended Normandy,* Herbert Jenkins, 1952.

Stacey, Colonel, C.P., Official History of the Canadian Army in the Second World War. (Canadian Official History), Vol. III. *The Victory Campaign; Operations in NW Europe.*

Stewart, Neil J., *Steel my Soldiers' Hearts,* Stewart-Trafford Publishing, Canada, 2000.

Tedder, Marshal of the Royal Air Force, Lord, *With Prejudice,* Cassell, 1966.

Van Creveld, Martin, *Supplying War, Logistics from Wallenstein to Patton,* Cambridge, 1977.

Wilmot, Chester, *The Struggle for Europe,* Collins, 1954.

Winterbotham, F. W., *The Ultra Secret,* Weidenfeld and Nicolson, 1974.

INDEX